David Barnett

The
Over-the-Counter
Securities Markets

Leo M. Loll

Julian G. Buckley

tHE OVER-tHE -COUNTER SECURITIES MARKETS

4tH EdiTioN

PRENTICE-HALL, INC., *Englewood Cliffs, New Jersey 07632*

Library of Congress Cataloging in Publication Data

Loll, Leo M
    The over-the-counter securities markets.

    Includes index.
      1. Over-the-counter markets—United States.
2. National Association of Securities Dealers.
I. Buckley, Julian G., joint author.   II. Title.
HG4910.L6 1980   332.64'3'0973   80-20897
ISBN 0-13-647172-2

Editorial/production supervision and interior design by Margaret Rizzi
Cover design by Saiki Design, Inc.
Manufacturing buyer: Gordon Osbourne

the over-the-counter securities markets
FOURTH EDITION
LEO M. LOLL and JULIAN G. BUCKLEY

Printed in the United States of America

10

Prentice-Hall International, Inc., *London*
Prentice-Hall of Australia Pty. Limited, *Sydney*
Prentice-Hall of Canada, Ltd., *Toronto*
Prentice-Hall of India Private Limited, *New Delhi*
Prentice-Hall of Japan, Inc., *Tokyo*
Prentice-Hall of Southeast Asia Pte. Ltd., *Singapore*
Whitehall Books Limited, *Wellington, New Zealand*

CONTENTS

PREFACE

This book is designed to help anyone who desires to enter the securities business on either a full- or a part-time basis. It should be particularly helpful to anyone wishing to pass the examination required for qualification as a registered representative. This edition has been revised with special emphasis on the *Study Outline for General Securities Registered Representative Examination.* Most of the topics in this outline have been fully discussed and indexed.

Newcomers to the securities industry are from all walks of life. Some are building full-fledged careers in their newly chosen occupation. Others are employed on a part-time basis, generally as mutual fund salespersons. They view their new job as an interesting and productive way to spend their spare time and supplement their family income. In the past, many new salespersons entered the field with little or no knowledge or experience in the securities business. As early as 1956, the National Association of Securities Dealers, Inc. imposed minimum membership requirements for registered representatives of its member firms. These requirements included the passing of a written examination. Since that time, the entrance standards have been raised and the examinations have become progressively more difficult.

This new fourth edition should help the candidate meet these tougher standards. Further, this book should provide a useful tool in solving some of the complex investment problems that confront the securities salesperson daily.

In this edition extensive chapters have been devoted to the new fields covered in the registered representatives examination. These include chapters on annuities, retirement plans, options and direct participations (tax shelters). Chapters on municipal securities, the NASDAQ, money market funds and taxes have been expanded to keep up with the current investment philosophy.

In particular, the chapter on investment company regulation has been written to coincide with the Study Outline. This should enable the student to master the legislative acts, especially the important Investment Company Act of 1940. In the Appendix of the book are summaries of the main provisions of the Securities Act of 1933, the Securities and Exchange Act of 1934, the Investment Company Act of 1940 and its 1970 Amendments, the Investment Advisers Act of 1940 and the Trust Indenture Act of 1939. These summaries should help the student memorize the salient points of each act.

An important feature of this edition is about 260 multiple choice questions. These questions are designed to test the knowledge of the reader on the content of the text. They are not claimed to have any similarity to the questions that will or may be asked on the examinations of the NASD. The correct answers to these questions are given at the end of this book. In addition, at the end of each chapter review questions are asked. The student should read these questions carefully to determine if he or she has covered the important points of the chapter.

We are particularly grateful to George Christopoulous and Carl Bolton of the New York Stock Exchange; Edward L. Norwesh of E. F. Hutton and Co.; Douglas H. Bellemore, Professor Emeritus, New York University; Jeffrey Bavolar of the Huntington Library; Marion Lee of A. G. Becker, Inc.; Roger Ballard of Cyrus J. Lawrence and Company; Frank J. McAuliffe of the NASD; J. Sheafe Satterthwaite; William O. Telenius; Dr. Alfred T. Gregory; and Charles M. Hewitt.

Particular care has been taken in the preparation of the index of this book. Subjects have been broken down in detail and cross-indexed. This should enable the reader to find not only the precise subject of his inquiry but also other references to the subject.

THE CORRECT ANSWERS TO THE TRUE AND FALSE (MULTIPLE CHOICE) QUESTIONS ARE IN THE APPENDIX OF THIS BOOK.

THE
OVER-THE-COUNTER
SECURITIES MARKETS

visions of the Securities Act of 1933, the Securities and Exchange Act of 1934, the Investment Company Act of 1940 and its 1970 Amendments, the investment Advisers Act of 1940 and the Trust Indenture Act of 1939. These summaries should help the student memorize the salient points of each act.

An important feature of this edition is about 260 multiple choice questions. These questions are designed to test the knowledge of the reader on the content of the text. They are not claimed to have any similarity to the questions that will or may be asked on the examinations of the NASD. The correct answers to these questions are given at the end of this book. In addition, at the end of each chapter review questions are asked. The student should read these questions carefully to determine if he or she has covered the important points of the chapter.

We are particularly grateful to George Christopoulous and Carl Bolton of the New York Stock Exchange; Edward L. Norwesh of E. F. Hutton and Co.; Douglas H. Bellemore, Professor Emeritus, New York University; Jeffrey Bavolar of the Huntington Library; Marion Lee of A. G. Becker, Inc.; Roger Ballard of Cyrus J. Lawrence and Company; Frank J. McAuliffe of the NASD; J. Sheafe Satterthwaite; William O. Telenius; Dr. Alfred T. Gregory; and Charles M. Hewitt.

Particular care has been taken in the preparation of the index of this book. Subjects have been broken down in detail and cross-indexed. This should enable the reader to find not only the precise subject of his inquiry but also other references to the subject.

THE CORRECT ANSWERS TO THE TRUE AND FALSE (MULTIPLE CHOICE) QUESTIONS ARE IN THE APPENDIX OF THIS BOOK.

1

Equities:

Common and Preferred Stocks

In the last decade, the prices of common stocks have shown wide fluctuations. They soared in the late 1960s with the cult of growth stocks, then declined sharply in the early 1970s only to rise again to old heights in the middle 1970s, but dropping in the late 1970s. As may be seen from the following figures, the prices of common stocks as measured by the Dow Jones average of 30 stocks moved horizontally over the 1968-1979 period and the broader Standard and Poor's indexes did only somewhat better.

TABLE 1-1

		1968	1972	1976	1979	1983 5/31/83
Dow Jones 30 Industrials (average high and low)		905	962	936	851	1200
Standard and Poor's (average)	400 stocks	107	121	114	118	182
	500 stocks	99	109	102	105	162

It is small wonder that many investors have become disillusioned with stocks and have fled to money-market and municipal bond funds as well as to other short term securities; but pension funds, investment companies, life and fire insurance companies, and individuals still have large holdings of common stocks. Individual investors that buy a common stock should understand its nature.

The common stock of a corporation is authorized in its certificate of incorporation, which is filed with a designated official of a state. This gives the number and type of identical units, called shares. Corporations issue common and sometimes preferred stock. Proprietorships and partnerships do not issue stock. The holder of a share of common stock has a part ownership in the earnings and assets of the corporation. The stock representing ownership in a corporation is called capital stock. Preferred and common shares have no maturity dates and do not have any fixed claim on the assets or the earnings of the corporation. But, despite these considerations, the common stockholder has certain rights and obligations.

RIGHT TO A STOCK CERTIFICATE

A buyer of a share of stock of a company, be it directly from the company on its formation or from another stockholder, is entitled to an engraved stock certificate *evidencing ownership of a specified number of shares of a corporation*. Each stock certificate contains the following information:

1. the name, address, and number of shares of the holder
2. the number and type (common or preferred) of shares authorized
3. the name of the transfer agent and registrar
4. the signatures of the officers of the corporation authorized to sign the stock certificate

A stock certificate is, in short, the physical evidence of ownership in a corporation. Every corporation has a stated amount of authorized shares that it may issue. Frequently a company will obtain permission from its stockholders to authorize more stock than it actually issues. This allows management to use such stock to acquire another company, to issue a stock dividend, or to sell these shares in the market for additional funds.

Most of a company's stock is outstanding and in the hands of the public. But a part of the stock may have been reacquired by the company and held in its vault or treasury. This stock is usually acquired by purchase in the market or by private sale and is called *treasury stock*. Since *this* stock does not vote or receive dividends, it does not affect the voting control, the dividends, or the equity of the existing stockholders. It may be resold at any price, given to officers, or used to acquire new assets or companies. Usually, preemptive rights, explained on pages 6–7, do not apply except in certain states. In most cases treasury stock is carried as a deduction from outstanding stock.

A company's capital stock may be assigned a fixed or a par value. It represents the minimum original investment in cash, property, or service paid into the company.

When stock is issued it may be $100 par, no par, or low par. In the nineteenth century and early in the twentieth, most stocks had $100 par value and were carried on the books of the company at that figure. Because many of these stocks were quoted at substantially less than $100 a share, there was confusion and often the mistaken belief that the stocks were worth $100 or more. Also, under several state laws, no new stocks could be sold for less than par or $100. This made the raising of new common capital difficult by companies whose stocks had fallen below $100 a share.

At present, most states have laws that permit companies to issue either no-par or low-par stock.

No-par stock, as its name indicates, has no face amount. The stock certificate simply reads: no-par shares. However, the directors of the company prior to the issuance of this stock *designate* a stated value at which the shares are carried on the books of the company. This might be an arbitrary value, or it might represent the amount received at the time the stock was issued. Some states set a minimum amount that the corporations may designate as the stated value of their no-par stock.

Low-par stock has a face value of a definite amount, usually $1.00 to $25.00, and is carried on the books of the company at par value. Sometimes a corporation will find a *tax advantage* to itself and to the stockholders in issuing low-par stock rather than a no-par stock. For the corporation, in this case, the state capital stock taxes are often lower; for the individual, the transfer taxes are sometimes lower.

Par value has no relation to the market value or to the intrinsic worth of a stock. For example, the stock of Union Carbide Corporation on March 18, 1980 had a market value of 37 7/8 a share compared with a par value of $1.00 a share. At the close of 1979, it had a book value of $61.06. (For an explanation of book value, see Chapter 17.)

RIGHT TO BUY AND SELL STOCK

If a stockholder desires to buy more stock, it is not necessary to obtain the permission of the company. The buyer simply acquires more shares by purchase in the open market or privately. Conversely, if someone desires to sell shares, the seller cannot demand that the company buy the stock. A stockholder is free, instead, to seek a buyer for the stock either in the markets or by private sale.

After the sale terms have been agreed upon, the mechanics of transfer are simple. The seller signs his name on the back of the stock certificate and delivers it to the buyer or the broker who effected the sale. Thus a stock certificate is made a negotiable instrument by the owner's signing his name on the back exactly as it is on the face. But it should not be sent through the mails *signed* on the back. Rather, a signed *stock power* should be sent in an envelope separate from the unsigned certificate (see page 219). A record is kept of these certificates by a transfer agent.

The transfer agent is appointed by the corporation issuing the securities. The agent may be a bank, but in some cases the company itself may act as its own transfer agent. The transfer agent examines all the documents to be sure that the transfer is in order. In particular, the transfer agent must make sure that it issues new certificates for the same number of shares represented by the old certificates that were canceled. The transfer agent records the transaction in the stock record book and sends both the old and the new certificates to the registrar.

The registrar is responsible for ensuring that the new number of shares equals the old number of shares. In other words, it is the duty of the registrar to double check the actions of the transfer agent and to prevent improper issue of stock or a fraudulent transfer. Usually the registrar is a bank or a trust company.

In November 1971 the New York Stock Exchange ruled that the function of registrar and transfer agent could be performed by the *same* bank for all listed securities. This is also the policy of the American Stock Exchange. Previously the New York Exchange had required separate banks for each function.

For convenience in handling, many stock certificates are in a *street name*, that is, in the name of a broker or in the name of a person other than that of the owner. The term *street name* should not be confused with *nominee name*. Commercial banks often register the stocks that they hold in custody accounts in nominee names. This makes it easier to collect dividends and to effect transfer. For example, a bank might hold for custody accounts thousands of shares of General Motors Corporation stock for hundreds of accounts. All these shares can be registered in *one* nominee name and one check sent by General Motors for each dividend that the bank credits to the respective custody accounts.

So far as the individual is concerned, however, stock certificates should be kept in a *safe place*. If they are lost or stolen, the stockholder has to go to considerable expense and trouble to obtain a new certificate. In some states, a surety bond must be posted. Even worse, there have been cases in which stock certificates have been stolen and sold.

RIGHT TO A DIVIDEND
IF DECLARED BY
THE BOARD OF DIRECTORS

The declaration of a dividend is almost exclusively the right of the directors. In only a few cases have the stockholders forced the directors to declare a dividend (*Dodge* v. *Ford Motor Co., 1919*). The directors might decide, for example, to pay no dividend even if earnings were substantial, if the company needed the money to pay off bank and other debts or to expand plant and equipment. There is nothing on the common stock certificate that says the company is required to pay a specified dividend or any dividend at all. On the other hand, the directors might pay dividends *in excess* of the current earnings, particularly if the corporation is in strong financial condition or if the outlook for earnings is favorable. If, however, a *dividend has been declared by the board of directors of the company*, then and then only do the stockholders have a *right* to collect it from the company.

In a number of circumstances, depending on the laws of the state in which the company is incorporated, a board of directors *cannot* pay a dividend. For example, in some states a dividend may be paid only from earned surplus. In other states, no dividend may be paid when the company is bankrupt.

Forms of Dividends

When the directors declare dividends, the usual form is *cash*. This means that the company or its paying agents sends checks to all the stockholders whose names appear on the books of the company on the date of record. Each stockholder receives a definite amount of money per share owned. In short, a dividend is a pro rata distribution among the stockholders.

Frequently a company will declare a *stock* dividend. The company accomplishes this by reducing its surplus account and increasing its capital account by the amount of the stock dividend. In other words, the surplus is capitalized. Thus the stockholder who has a share in both the capital and surplus *prior* to the stock dividend does not receive any additional interest in the company by the stock dividend; the size of his share of the corporate pie remains the same but the stockholder has more pieces. Usually a stock dividend is paid to satisfy the stockholders and at the same time to conserve cash. A stock dividend is ordinarily not taxable as income if it is *held* by the stockholder. On the other hand, if the stock dividend is sold, it *is* taxable as a capital gain, the cost being determined by a complicated formula (see pages 358–359 for explanation).

Stock splits are in many ways similar to stock dividends, but there are certain important differences. When a stockholder receives more than 25% additional shares, it is usually called a *stock split*. This is a rule of thumb used by the New York Stock Exchange. In this case, the number of shares is simply increased, usually by reducing the par value or the stated value of no-par stock. The surplus account is unaffected. As in the case of stock dividends, it results in no additional ownership in the assets or earnings of the corporation. If, for example, a $10-par stock is split 2-for-1, the corporation usually sends the stockholder a new certificate of one new share of $5 par for each old share held and in addition sends a $5-par stamp to place on each old $10-par certificate. The new stock received by the stockholder as a result of the stock split is as a rule not taxable *unless sold*.

When the management recommends that the company split its stock or declare a stock dividend, the stockholders are usually pleased.

RIGHTS TO INFORMATION

Stockholders have a right to demand information about the company in which they hold stock. Legally, they can inspect the corporate books of the company. (The corporate books are the minutes of the directors' meetings, the list of the stockholders, etc.) A well known source of information is the annual report to the stockholders. The Securities and Exchange Commission requires all companies with over $1,000,000 in assets and 500 stockholders or more to file an annual report. This includes all companies listed on national securities exchanges. Annual reports contain comparative profit-and-loss statements and balance sheets. They often describe the business of the company during the past year, its problems, and its outlook. Other items often discussed include capital expenditures, research projects, employee relations, foreign investments, affiliates, and changes in management. A complete list of the officers and directors is given, along with their affiliation.

A still better source of information is Form 10 K which the companies must file annually with the SEC. This report includes the annual report and much additional information about the company such as details of subsidiaries, foreign earnings, etc. It may be obtained at the SEC offices; sometimes the company will send a copy on request.

In addition, the SEC requires that all companies listed keep their registration statements up to date (see Securities and Exchange Act of 1934). These registration statements are on file and available to the public.

Last, a stockholder is entitled to attend the annual meeting of the stockholders and ask questions of management.

PREEMPTIVE RIGHT

The board of directors of a company might vote to issue additional common shares. A letter would be sent out to the stockholders outlining the plan and the purpose of the new issue. Usually an investment banker would be asked to form a syndicate to guarantee that the new stock would be taken up at the price offered in the rights. The charters of some companies provide that the stockholders have preemptive rights to the new issue.

A preemptive right is simply the inherent right of the stockholder to maintain his proportionate share of the assets, earnings, and control of the corporation; it is a common law right. In other words, the corporation in most, *but not all*, states must first offer a new stock to its own stockholders before offering it to the public. This is to prevent the company from offering stock to the public at a price substantially below its worth, thus lessening the interest of the old stockholders in the corporate pie. When a company offers new stock to its old stockholders, its price to them is usually set below the current market price. A stockholder has a right to subscribe for new shares proportionately for each share held. A certificate is sent to the stockholder stating the number of rights owned, which corresponds to the number of shares held. It will also specify the number of new shares to which the stockholder is entitled to subscribe and the per share price of such subscription. This privilege to subscribe is of short-term nature, usually expiring in 60 days. On the certificate, the stockholder may indicate whether he wishes to sell the rights or to exercise the privilege of subscription. In the latter case, the money for the subscription price must accompany the certificate. The stockholder must take either course. If the stockholder allows the time limit to run out without acting, the rights become worthless. The stockholder might sell part of his stock and replace the shares sold with subscription to the new stock, as the old stock might be selling at a higher price than the when-issued new stock. Another alternative would be to sell short the shares and cover the short position with the new stock. But these procedures are a little too complicated for the average investor.

There is a simple formula for calculating the market value of rights. For example, suppose that a company offers to its shareholders the stock at $46 a share for each four shares held. This would mean that the stockholder would have to have four shares to have four rights. (For each share a stockholder has *one* right.) If the current market price for the stock is 56, the following procedure could be used in calculating the value of the right:

M = the market price of the stock,
S = the subscription price of the stock,
N = the number of rights for one share,

The formula and solution are

$$\frac{M-S}{N+1} = \frac{56-46}{4+1} = \frac{10}{5} = \$2.00$$

Thus, the value of each right is about $2.00.

After the stock sells *ex-rights* but before the rights expire, the formula is $\frac{M-S}{N}$. To repeat, after the rights expire they have *no value*.

Warrants are somewhat similar to rights. As explained, the number of rights to which a stockholder is entitled is based on his present stock holdings. Warrants, on the other hand, when applied to the purchase of stocks, normally refer to the number of new shares that a stockholder may buy. In other words, warrants represent privileges to buy securities at specified prices.

Warrants are customarily issued with bonds to make them more attractive. The buyer of bonds with warrants has a fixed claim as to interest and principal against the company. Also, the buyer may buy stock of the company at a fixed price and participate in the future of the company. Warrants are usually detachable. This means they may be bought and sold apart from the security to which they were originally attached. Some warrants trade over the counter or on the American Stock Exchange. The warrants are good for a number of years, sometimes forever. Tricontinental Corporation warrants, for example, are perpetual and entitle the holder at any time to buy 3.85 shares of the common stock at $5.84 a share. More often, as in the case of Atlas Corporation warrants, the owner can buy stock at a stated price. Atlas Corporation warrants permit the holder to buy one share of common at $31.25.

Warrants are usually protected against dilution through stock splits or dividends. If a stock is split, the exercise price of the warrant is reduced downward proportionately. For example, if a company has outstanding warrants entitling the holder to buy a stock at $6.00 a share and splits its stock 2-for-1, then the exercise price of the warrants is automatically reduced from $6.00 to $3.00, or split 2-for-1. Sometimes the terms of the warrants will specify that the conversion price of the warrants will rise over the years. That is, a fewer number of shares can be bought with the warrants.

Warrants are sometimes issued to junior bondholders in a reorganization to give them some hope of recovery if in the later years the affairs of the company improve. And underwriters of a company, particularly if it is a speculative new concern, will be given warrants in return for selling the issue.

The valuation of warrants is quite simple. The intrinsic value of a warrant is obtained by comparing the exercise price of the warrant with the market price of the stock. If the warrant to purchase the stock is at, say, 25 and the stock is selling at, say, 20, the intrinsic value of the warrant is zero. If the value of the stock is 27, the intrinsic value of the warrant is $2.00. But, unless the company is faced with serious problems, it is almost certain that the speculative value of the warrant would be at least $5.00 and perhaps as high as $7.00.

As the expiration date of a warrant approaches, the price of the warrant will likely decline. For example, if the exercise price of a warrant is five points above the price of the stock, given several years the stock might well rise to a point at which the exercise of the warrant would be profitable, but given one year or less the chances are much less likely.

Although, as a general rule, the buying of warrants is a speculation, considerable money has been made with warrants due to their leverage factor.

VOTING RIGHTS

Stockholders have the right to select the board of directors as well as to vote on any fundamental changes in the corporation such as dissolution, consolidation, or amendments to the charter or bylaws. But this right is largely theoretical. In most cases, management determines the composition of the board of directors and the basic changes to be made, at annual or special meetings. In advance of the meetings, stockholders are sent notices of the meeting, statements setting forth the directors to be elected, other business to be approved, and proxies that they are asked to sign. The *proxy* is a document by which the stockholder authorizes another person (or a proxy committee), usually appointed by the management, to vote his stock. In short, a proxy is a power of attorney granted by a stockholder authorizing another person to vote that stock.

Sometimes state laws or the charters of corporations provide for *cumulative voting* by stockholders for directors. Here the shareholder is able to multiply the number of his shares by the number of directors to be elected and cast the *total* for one director or a selected group of directors. Let us assume a stockholder owns 50 shares of common stock and that there are ten directors to be elected. Under cumulative voting, the stockholder may cumulate his votes by multiplying those 50 shares times the ten directors to be elected, making 500. Then the stockholder may cast the entire 500 votes for only *one* director, or 250 each for two, or 100 each for five, and so forth. The aim of cumulative voting is to permit minority stockholders to be represented on the board of directors. Under the regular, or *statutory*, voting method, the holder of 50 shares can cast only 50 votes for *each* of the ten directors. The holder cannot concentrate on one director. Under statutory voting, the holder of 51% of the stock can elect *all* the directors, but the holder of 49% can elect none. Cumulative voting, required in some states, is supposed to correct this situation.

Usually, all the proxies are tabulated and a single ballot is cast electing the board or approving the proposals. The stockholder has a right to attend the meeting and to vote for or against the directors and proposals. Also, a stockholder can revoke his proxy at any time, provided it is done before the final vote is tabulated.

A proxy is sometimes confused with a *voting trust certificate*. These are usually issued by companies in financial difficulties. For example, the representatives of bank or bond creditors might feel that, in return for additional money advanced or even for money already advanced, they wish to supervise the management of the company. These creditors would persuade the stockholders to surrender to trustees their shares of common stock in return for an identical number of voting trust certificates. A stockholder having 100 shares of common would receive voting trust certificates for 100

shares. These certificates have all the rights of the common stock *except* the
right to vote and hence to control the company. This power is held by the
trustees representing the creditors. On the other hand, voting trust certificates trade freely, receive dividends, and represent a proportionate interest
in the earnings and assets of the corporation. Also, voting trust certificates
usually have a maturity of four to eight years set by state laws. The holders
of the certificates recover their voting rights at maturity.

When a brokerage house customer is buying securities on margin,[1] the
securities that he has pledged as collateral are not registered in his name but
are held in a street name. Thus, the proxy will go to the street name of the
broker who, in theory, can vote the stock. The New York Stock Exchange,
however, has complicated rules for brokers voting street-name stock without the instructions of the customer, particularly if there is a management
contest in the company.

OTHER RIGHTS
(ULTRA VIRES ACTS)

The shareholder has an inherent right to restrain the corporation from
ultra vires acts. These are acts beyond the powers of the corporation as
stated, or implied, in its charter. For example, if a shoe manufacturing company should suddenly start trading in grains, it would seem to be operating
beyond the implied powers of the corporation, unless the charter gave it exceptionally broad powers.

RIGHT TO SHARE IN THE ASSETS
IN THE EVENT OF DISSOLUTION

It cannot be stressed too strongly that a common stockholder's claim
to the assets of a corporation is *residual*. If a company is forced to liquidate
its assets, the secured bondholders usually have first claim, followed by the
unsecured bondholders and general creditors. After these claims are satisfied, the preferred stockholders, if any, are usually paid par or stated value
per share before the common stockholder receives the final distribution. On
page 319 it will be illustrated how the book or liquidating value is determined.

The liabilities of a stockholder are, as a general rule *limited*—that is,
limited to their initial investment. For example, an investor might buy 100
shares of stock in the XYZ Corporation for $50 a share. If the corporation
goes into bankruptcy, the investor has lost his investment, but the creditors,
no matter what the debts of the XYZ Corporation are, cannot look to the in-

[1]For a detailed discussion of margins see pages 199–202.

vestor for additional funds. There are few exceptions to this general rule. For example, the par value or stated value of the stock must be fully paid under the terms of the agreement to purchase new stocks. If not, the creditors might insist on the full payment of the par or stated value.[2] Also, some states permit the stockholders to be assessed for back wages for a limited period if the assets are not sufficient. But, by and large, the general rule holds that common stocks have the limited liability already described.

YIELD ON A COMMON STOCK

Income, or yield, is the return on investment. To a common stockholder, this means the dividends paid. The common stock dividend of a company is relatively easy to determine. The current dividend rates of companies are estimated on the basis of past policies. For example, over the years a company might pay out 50% of its earnings in dividends. Another company might cling to a fixed dollar rate. American Telephone & Telegraph Company for years paid a $9.00 dividend on its old stock even when earnings were less than that amount. Some companies, such as E. I. du Pont de Nemours & Company and General Motors Corporation, traditionally pay out a high proportion of their earnings in dividends. Other companies that need money for expansion, such as Dow Chemical or Aluminum Company of America, pay out a low proportion of earnings.

The current return, sometimes called the *current yield* of a common stock, is figured by dividing the dividends paid in the past year by the current price of the stock. For example, on March 31, 1980 the stock of Continental Group, Inc. sold at 26 a share. In 1979, the company paid $2.40 in dividends. Thus, the return is the 1979 dividends of $2.40 divided by the current price of 26 or 9.23%. The current return changes with the changes in price and in dividends. For example, if in 1980 the company should establish a dividend pattern of $2.50 a share and the price of the stock rises to 30 a share, the new current yield would be 8.33%.

In years past, many stocks sold at very high prices compared with their dividend payments and consequently had a low yield. As mentioned, payment of dividends is the right of the directors. In declaring dividends, directors are guided by the earnings, the assets, and the outlook for the company.

PREFERRED STOCK

Preferred stock, like comon stock, is an equity or share in the earnings and assets of the corporation, but there are many distinguishing characteristics that should be discussed.

[2]All shares listed on the NYSE are fully paid and nonassessable.

First, after the interest and all the operating expenses and bond interest have been paid, the preferred stockholder has priority over the common stockholder for dividends, but the preferred dividend is declared at the option of the board of directors.

The preferred stockholder has no claim against the company for dividends unless declared. He does not have any of the rights of a creditor or bondholder. He cannot throw the company into receivership for not paying preferred dividends. The only right inherent in preferred stock is the right to receive preferred dividends before the common stock dividends are paid. Preferred stock cannot be included when referring to funded debt.

In addition to preference over common for dividends, the corporation charter may state that, *in liquidation*, preferred stock has preference over common. This is, of course, after the bond, trade, and bank creditors have been paid.

Second, the preferred stockholder receives dividends, usually quarterly, at a stated rate ranging from 3.5% to over 12.00% ($3.50 to $12.00 of 100 par). The percentage rate is usually based on $100 par. Although $100 par is the usual par value for preferred stocks, there are a number of preferred stocks of $50 par and some as low as $10. Also, there are no-par preferred stocks. *The stated rate of a preferred stock is fixed as to maximum but not as to minimum.* This means that, no matter how much money the company makes, the straight preferred stockholder usually receives only his stated rate of 3.5% to 12.00%.

The exception to this rule might be the convertible and the participating preferreds (discussed on pages 13–14). But, if the earnings of the company fall, the directors may decide to pass the dividend for one quarter or a longer period.

Third, most but not all preferred stocks have *cumulative* features. These features are described in the charter of the corporation. They usually provide that, if the full dividend is not paid each quarter, it accrues or accumulates to the benefit of the stockholders. Companies might have large accumulations of back dividends, or arrears, as they are called, yet be in no danger of insolvency. The dividend arrears are not carried as a liability on the balance sheet. However, *the company cannot pay dividends on the common stock until all the dividend accumulations are paid* to the preferred stockholders. Thus the holder of a cumulative preferred stock may or may not receive dividends for a quarter or even for years. At a later time, if the affairs of the company should improve, unpaid dividends will be paid, provided the preferred is cumulative.

Fourth, almost all preferred stocks are callable at the option of the corporation at a specified price. The charter states the terms under which a corporation may call its stock. These terms include the call price, the number of days' notice required, and the place of payment. Usually the price is par or several points in excess of par, ranging from as high as $120 a share for the 4 1/2% preferred stock of E. I. du Pont de Nemours Company to $100 a share of the Aluminum Company of America 3 3/4% preferred. In no-par preferred stock, the call price is stated in dollars per share in the charter. There are some preferred stocks that are not callable at the option of the company. Most of these stocks were sold in the early part of the century when the demand for money was very great. Some of the companies had to pay a preferred dividend rate as high as 8% and provide that the stock could not be called. An example of a noncallable stock is Uniroyal, Inc., 8% preferred.

Fifth, in contrast to a bond, a preferred stock does not have any maturity. Once a company has sold a preferred stock, the money received is in a sense permanent money. The corporation never has to pay it back.

Sixth, usually, a preferred stockholder does not have the right to vote for the directors or have a voice in the management of the company. If, however, the company desires to issue senior securities, merge, or make any fundamental change in the corporate structure, the preferred stockholder usually has the right to vote on these issues. Under the rules of the New York Stock Exchange, preferred stockholders have a right to vote after the company has failed to pay six successive quarterly dividends.

Seventh, a preferred stockholder has no preemptive rights. This means that, if the company offers securities to the public, the preferred stockholder cannot insist on the right to participate in the offering of the new securities.

Eighth, some preferreds have sinking fund provisions. Here the company agrees to retire a stated amount of preferred issue each year. Sometimes an annual dollar amount is fixed. In other cases a percentage of the earnings is fixed.

Ninth, sometimes a preferred issue will be protected by a provision that approval must be obtained by the preferred stockholders to issue a new preferred with priority.

CONVERTIBLE PREFERRED STOCK

Convertible preferred stock means that the owner has the right to exchange a preferred stock for a share or shares of common stock of the same company. As in the case of bonds, sometimes the number of shares of common is given. There are times when conversion is determined on the basis of par value. For example, a $100-par preferred might be convertible into common at $50 a share or two shares of common for each share of $100-par preferred. The holder of a convertible preferred stock usually has a stronger claim than does the holder of a common stock to earnings and assets. In addition, if company earnings increase, the convertible preferred will rise in value. An example of a convertible preferred is Kaiser Aluminum & Chemical Company 4 1/8% preferred. This stock is convertible into common stock of the company at $59.43 a share. Because the par value of the 4 1/8% preferred is $100, the conversion terms, or conversion ratio as it is sometimes called, are found by dividing 100 by $59.43, or 1.683. Thus the holder of the 4 1/8% preferred Kaiser Aluminum & Chemical Company may convert to 1.683 shares of common. Often the number of shares of common stock a preferred holder may obtain by conversion declines with the years.

A company might wish to call a preferred stock. Then the preferred stockholder must be given the required number of days' notice. This will enable him to either convert into common or sell the stock. Because the preferred stock is registered in the name of the holder, the company will notify the holder of the call. This is *not* true of coupon convertible bonds (discussed in Chapter 2).

Conversion privileges stated in the preferred stock issue may be perpetual; that is, the conversion ratio never changes. But there might be a limited period, say, 20 years from date of issue at which time the privilege to convert expires. On some occasions the privilege to convert might not be effective for, say, 3 to 5 years.

PARTICIPATING PREFERRED

As its name implies, the holder of a participating preferred has the right to receive a stipulated dividend and then share in the earnings along with the common stockholders. For years the Chicago, Milwaukee and Saint Paul Railroad Company had outstanding a 5% noncumulative, $100 preferred. A holder was entitled to $5.00 a year and to participate up to $1.00 per share with the common. But this stock was exchanged in 1971 for $5.00 nonconvertible, nonparticipating preferred and three fourths of a share of common. There are on the market today very few participating preferred.

ANALYSIS OF A PREFERRED STOCK

In analyzing a preferred stock, it is important to consider the history, growth, and prospects for the company. Also, the analyst should note in particular the earnings per share of preferred as well as the number of times that the company earns its interest *and* its preferred dividend. For example, a company might earn $25.00 or $30.00 a share and yet, due to high interest charges, cover its interest and preferred dividend only, say, 1.5 times. This situation would indicate that the company is vulnerable to a small decline in business as it is operating on a small margin.

TAXES

Under the existing tax law, 85% of the dividends received on preferred stocks held by most corporations may be deducted when they compute their taxable income. Thus, the individual investor is in competition with the corporations for preferred stocks.

REVIEW QUESTIONS

1. Discuss seven important rights of a stockholder. Does the stockholder have any liabilities?
2. Does a stock dividend add to a stockholder's *share* in the company's assets and earnings? Why does the price of the stock of a company usually rise when a stock dividend is declared?
3. What is a preemptive right and why is it important for a stockholder to have it?
4. Explain the difference between statutory voting and cumulative voting. What is a proxy?
5. If a common stock sold at 65 on May 30, 1980, earned $4.10 a share in 1979, and paid dividends of $3.50 in 1979, what is the current yield of the stock on May 30, 1980?
6. Explain the functions and importance to the stockholder of the registrar and the transfer agent. May the function of both be performed by the same bank?
7. Discuss the rights of the preferred stockholder as to liquidation, dividends, call privileges, maturity, and voting. How do these rights compare with those of the bondholder?
8. Describe and distinguish between convertible preferred stock and participating preferred stock.

TRUE AND FALSE QUESTIONS

1. The following are the rights of a common stockholder *except:*

		True	False
a.	to a certificate	___	___
b.	to buy and sell the stock	___	___
c.	to information	___	___
d.	to vote for directors	___	___
e.	to a guaranteed dividend.	___	___

2. The liabilities of a stockholder are:

		True	False
a.	limited to his or her investment	___	___
b.	the same as a general partnership	___	___
c.	possible if stock is not fully paid.	___	___

3. Treasury stock is: *True*   *False*
    a. stock of a corporation authorized by the U.S.
        Treasury   _____   _____
    b. authorized but <u>unissued</u> stock that is held by
        the treasurer of the company   _____   _____
    c. outstanding stock that the company has ac-
        quired by purchase and held by the company.   _____   _____

issued and reacquired

4. Stock dividends might be distinguished from stock splits because:
                                                               True   *False*
    a. stock dividends are distributions of addi-
        tional shares of under 25%; stock splits are
        distributions of over 25%   _____   _____
    b. stock dividends are *not* taxable to the share-
        holder; stock splits are   _____   _____
    c. stock dividends do not require approval of
        shareholders; stock splits do.   _____   _____

5   If stock of an industrial concern has a par value of $20.00 a share, the
    approximate market value would be: *True*   *False*
    a. close to the par value of $20.00 a share   _____   _____
    b. close to the book value of $45.50 because that
        is the liquidating value   _____   _____
    c. impossible to determine.   _____   _____

6. If company's stock is selling at 42 and it offers its stockholders one
    new share at 30 for each 5 held, the value of the right is:
                                                               True   *False*
    a. $6.00   _____   _____
    b. $2.40   _____   _____
    c. $2.00.   _____   _____

7. A proxy is: *True*   *False*
    a. a written power of attorney granted by a
        stockholder to vote his stock   _____   _____
    b. a power of attorney that once given may not
        be revoked   _____   _____
    c. a legal form whereby an absent director of a
        company may delegate his vote on an issue
        before the board.   _____   _____

8. If a common stock in 1979 earned $3.50, paid dividends in that year of
    $2.00, and sold at 50 on March 30, 1980, the yield is: *True*   *False*
    a. 2.00%   _____   _____
    b. 4.00%   _____   _____
    c. 7.00%.   _____   _____

9. The term *street name* refers to: *True*   *False*
    a. the popular name for a stock (e.g., "Bessie"
        for Bethlehem Steel Corp.)   _____   _____
    b. a stock bought by a customer on margin but
        held and registered in the name of his broker   _____   _____
    c. the generic term applied to all stocks listed in
        the New York Stock Exchange (i.e., Wall
        Street).   _____   _____

10. The function of the registrar of a corporation is: *True*   *False*
    a. to accept old stock certificate and issue a new
        one to the new owner   _____   _____
    b. to double check action of the transfer agent   _____   _____
    c. to register with the Securities and Exchange
        Commission all new issues of securities of the
        corporation.   _____   _____

11. A preferred stockholder: *True*   *False*
    a. usually must receive a dividend before any
        payment to the common stockholder   _____   _____
    b. ranks with the bondholder as far as preferred
        dividends are concerned   _____   _____
    c. may ask the company to redeem his stock at
        par value on 30 days' notice.   _____   _____

12. In comparison with a bondholder, a preferred stockholder:
                                                                         True   *False*
    a. in bankruptcy ranks equally   _____   _____
    b   in bankruptcy ranks junior to all bondholders
        and creditors, but usually senior to the
        common stock   _____   _____
    c. might have their securities called by the
        company.   _____   _____

13. Arrears on a cumulative preferred stock means that: *True*   *False*
    a. the company is in danger of bankruptcy   _____   _____
    b. if preferred dividends are not paid, they
        accumulate   _____   _____
    c. no dividends can be paid on the common
        stock until arrears are paid.   _____   _____

14. A cumulative 5% preferred stock selling at 60 has a current yield of:
                                                                         True   *False*
    a. 5.00%   _____   _____
    b. 8.33%   _____   _____
    c. 10.00%.   _____   _____

15.   Convertible preferreds are frequently bought by investors because:

		True	*False*
a.	they participate along with common stock in the earnings	_____	_____
b.	they give somewhat greater security than common stock in the event of trouble and may be converted to common stock if the company prospers.	_____	_____

16.   A $6 industrial preferred stock reported in 1979, earnings per share of $45 and overall coverage of 1.50 times:

		True	*False*
a.	would seem to be a safe investment because the preferred dividend is covered $7\frac{1}{2}$ times	_____	_____
b.	would only be a safe investment if earnings per share have been high during the past two years	_____	_____
c.	would not be a good investment because the overall coverage is only 1.50 times which indicates high interest charges.	_____	_____

2

Bonds

A bond is an engraved certificate indicating that a corporation has borrowed a fixed sum of money and promises to repay it at a future date. Also, for use of this money, the corporation agrees to pay at specified intervals (usually twice a year) interest at a stated rate. When bonds are issued, the maturity date or the date on which the company must pay the principal of the bonds is usually a long time in the future—20 to 30 years. Bonds are usually issued in $1,000 denominations, but denominations range from $50 to $10,000. Bonds in denominations of less than $500 are called *small*, or *baby*, bonds. The interest rate is stated in percentages on the face of the bond. In short, a bond is evidence of debt, and the bondholder is a creditor of the corporation. A stockholder, on the other hand, is a part owner and holds evidence of ownership in his stock certificate.

The company *must* pay the interest and principal on bonds when due and in full. With the exception of income bonds (discussed later), there is no option on the amount or the time of the payments. Failure to pay interest on principal when due almost always means insolvency and often the appointment of new management. Therefore, corporations make every effort to live up to their contracts by paying principal and interest.

The terms of payment are usually in legal tender, at maturity. In the early part of the twentieth century, bonds were payable in gold at maturity. But the gold clause was legislated out in 1933. Sometimes bonds are payable at the option of the holder in dollars, German marks, or Swiss or French francs.

The interest is almost always payable semiannually. Further, the bondholder, as long as he receives his interest, does not have any voice in the management of the corporation.

The obligations of the corporation are set forth in the deed of trust or indenture drawn when the bonds are issued. The trust indenture outlines the duties of the corporation, such as paying interest, maintaining sinking funds, and keeping the property insured and in satisfactory condition. Also, it outlines the rights of the bondholders in the event of default. It also sets forth the duties and qualifications of the institution—that is, the bank or trust company with capital funds not less than $150,000 that must act as trustee for the bondholders. Above all, the trustee must be independent of the issuing corporation. This indenture usually must be drawn in accord with the Trust Indenture Act of 1939 summarized in the appendix. Basically, this act is aimed to protect the bondholder by the appointment of an impartial, solvent, and competent institutional trustee.

When a corporation defaults, the maturity of the bonds is accelerated. The trustee must take immediate action to protect the bondholders and institute proceedings under Chapter XI or Chapter X of the Bankruptcy Act of 1898 as amended. (Chapter XI is a voluntary reorganization by agreement between creditors and the corporation, whereas Chapter X is a more severe court-ordered reorganization.)

Sometimes to issue new bonds the corporation might ask the holders of an existing issue to give up a prior lien on a piece of property and accept a general lien. For this the holders are often given a higher rate of interest. The consenting bondholders have their bonds stamped.

In the event of a merger, bondholders are usually protected so that their claim on assets is not alienated. This is done by an "after acquired" clause in the bond indenture.

However the trustee does not in any way guarantee the bondholder against loss. A weak corporation that fails may cause severe losses to the bondholder, no matter how strong or able the trustee. Therefore, bonds should by no means be considered riskless securities.

Many of the large bond issues are listed on the New York Stock Exchange. A few issues are traded on the American Stock Exchange, but most bond issues, whether listed or not, are traded over the counter—that is, they are traded over the telephone between securities dealers (see Chapter 9).

BOND QUOTATIONS

Railroad, public utility, and industrial bonds are called *corporate* bonds. These are quoted in *percent of face amount, or $1,000*, using fractions of 1/8, 1/4, 3/8, 1/2, 5/8, 3/4, and 7/8. (Sometimes, instead of face amount, the term *par* value is used, as it is the amount that is stated on the face of the bond.) Because face amount for bonds is almost always $1,000, the following table serves to illustrate the relationships between the quotation and the dollar price.

Quotation	Dollar Price
103 1/4	$1032.50
102 1/8	1021.25
105 1/2	1055.00
97 1/2	975.00

An easy way to calculate the dollar price is to extend the round numbers and then take a fraction of $10. For example, a bid of 103 1/4 for a $1,000 bond would be figured $1,030 plus one fourth of $10, or $2.50, making $1,032.50.

In the case of new issues, the dollar price is often stated in decimals rather than in fractions. For example, late in 1959 the Florida Power & Light Company offered to the public 5 1/4% bonds due 1989 at 101.519, or $1,015.19 per bond.

U.S. Treasury certificates, notes, and bonds (discussed on pages 42–45) are, like corporate bonds, quoted in percent of face amount, but the fractions are stated in thirty-seconds. Thus a U.S. Treasury bond quoted at 101.16 would have a dollar price of $1,015. This is calculated by extending the round number 101 to $1,010 and adding 16/32 of $10, or $5. This would amount to $1,015. Treasury bills are sold and quoted at a discount on a yield-to-maturity basis.

It is difficult to understand or even talk about bonds without having a clear understanding of bond yields.

BOND YIELDS

There are three types of yields: nominal yield, current yield, and yield to maturity.

The *nominal yield* is usually the interest rate shown on the face of the bond. It is stated in round percentages: 7%, 8%, and so forth or in fractions of eighths or fourths. For example, a corporation on August 31, 1971 might issue $1,000,000 of 8% bonds due August 31, 1991. This would indicate that the *nominal* yield is 8% or $80 per $1,000 bond. The nominal yield is seldom the same as the current yield or the yield to maturity.

Interest payments are generally made every six months. In this case, the company would pay $40 twice a year. If the interest rate were 7 3/4%, the company would pay $77.50 a year, or about $38.75 twice a year.

The *current yield* is almost always different from the nominal yield. In some cases, bonds sell at a premium—in excess of $1,000 face value—or at a discount—below $1,000 face value. If an 8% bond sells at a premium over face value, the current yield will be less than 8%. For instance, if an investor buys an 8% bond at 105, or $1,050, that person is investing $1,050 but is only getting $80 a year. Simple inspection will show that the current yield is less than 8%. The current yield in this case may be obtained by *dividing the interest rate by the price of the bond as follows:*

$$\text{Current yield} \ = \ \frac{\text{Interest rate}}{\text{Price of bond}} \ = \ \frac{\$80.}{\$1,050} \ = \ 7.619\%$$

It might be mentioned here that this is the same method that is used to calculate the yield on a common stock—namely, the current dividend rate is divided by the current price of the stock.

The yield to maturity is a little more complicated to compute than the current yield, yet it is important for the investor to understand its principle, because the yield to maturity is the yield most generally used when deciding to buy or sell a bond.

The yield to maturity may be figured by the *approximate method* and by the use of *bond yield tables.*

The yield to maturity, calculated by the approximate method, is the average percentage return taking into consideration the eventual gain or loss through payment at par or at $1,000 at maturity. Take our example of an 8% bond selling at $1,050 due August 31, 1991. The investor knows that between August 31, 1971, the date at which the bond is purchased, and August 31, 1991, when the bond matures, he will lose $50.00, or $2.50 a year over the 20-year period because the bond is paid off at maturity at par, or a face amount of $1,000. Therefore, the interest rate should be adjusted to take care of this loss. On an annual basis, the adjusted coupon would be $80.00 less $2.50, or $77.50.

The average price can be obtained by taking the average of the cost of $1,050 and the maturity payment of $1,000, or $1,025. Now we are ready to calculate our yield to maturity. In this case we use the adjusted interest rate and the average price to obtain the yield to maturity by the approximate method as follows:

$$\text{Yield to maturity} = \frac{\text{Adjusted interest}}{\text{Average price}} = \frac{\$77.50}{\$1,025.00} = 7.561\%$$

A more accurate way of calculating the yield to maturity is to use the *bond yield tables.* (But for all practical purposes, the approximate method is surprisingly accurate.) For example, using the bond yield table, the exact yield to maturity on an 8% bond selling at $1,050 due in 20 years is 7.512%. The bond yield tables are particularly useful when it is necessary to calculate the yield to maturity on a bond with a maturity in years, months, and days, not in an even number of years.

The following example shows how the bond yield table is interpolated. The bond yields are arrayed by years and coupon rates. For instance, to arrive at the yield in the preceding example, you should turn to the page in the bond yield book that shows the yield on an 8% bond due in 20 years and find the yield on the dollar price nearest to $1,050 as follows:

Price	8% due in 20 Years
104.60	7.55%
105.00	x
105.13	7.50

We can see that a bond selling at 105.13 yields 7.50% and at 104.60 yields 7.55%. Therefore, we know that the yield on the bond in question selling at 105 is somewhere between 7.50% and 7.55%. We can solve the problem by taking the proportion or the percentage of the difference represented by the difference between 105.13 and 105.00, or 13, as the numerator of the fraction and the difference between 105.13 and 104.60, or 53, as the denominator as follows:

$$\frac{.13}{.53} \ = \ .245 \ \times \ .05 \ = \ .01225\%$$

In this way, we add 7.5000 and .0122 to get a final yield of 7.5122, or about 7.51%.

We add .0122 because the price of 105.13 yields 7.50%. Therefore, the price of 105 is lower and yields 13/53, or .245% of .05, or .01225% *higher*.

In summary, we have the following yields, which are all *different:*

1.	Nominal yield	8.000%
2.	Current yield	7.619
3.	Yield to maturity	
	By approximate method	7.561
	By the bond yield tables	7.512

In the event that the corporation fails to pay interest or principal, or fails to live up to its agreements, the bondholder has certain rights. These rights are set forth in the Deed of Trust or Indenture that is written when the bonds are sold.

The deed of trust or indenture is a written agreement describing the rights of the bondholders, the duties of the corporation, and the duties of the trustees. The corporation agrees, in addition to paying interest and principal, to keep the property insured and in good repair. Also, there are a number of other clauses or covenants to which the company agrees, such as the amount of the bonds to be sold and the amount to be retired by sinking fund.

The trustee, in turn, agrees to see that the rights of the bondholders are protected. That is, the trustee checks on the payment of interest, the principal and all the other covenants of the indenture. If the company fails to live up to its agreement, the trustee must take legal action to protect the bondholders.

A more detailed discussion of the indenture will be found under the Trust Indenture Act of 1939 in Chapter 21 and in the appendix.

THE ISSUANCE OF BONDS

Bonds are issued in three forms: (1) coupon bonds, (2) fully registered bonds, and (3) registered as to principal but not as to interest.

Coupon bonds have interest coupons attached to each bond by the corporation that issues it. They are also called "bearer bonds." For example, a company might issue 8% bonds due in 20 years. This would mean that attached to each bond would be 40 coupons for $40 each. On the due dates for the interest, the owner clips the coupons and presents them to the authorized bank for payment. Also, the principal, when due, is payable to the holder or bearer of the bonds. In other words, the bond owner should take great care of his bonds. If they are lost or stolen, the company is in no way responsible for the payment to the rightful owner. In short, losing a coupon bond is the same as losing a $1,000 bill.

When a new bond issue is sold, the corporation usually issues *temporary certificates*. These are similar to bonds because they promise to pay the stated amount at maturity. But they often have only two or three coupons. This gives the company time to have printed the so-called *definitive* bonds with all the coupons attached. The bondholder must exchange the temporary certificates for the *definitive bonds* as soon as the coupons on the temporary certificates have been paid.

Fully registered bonds, registered in the name of the buyer on the books of the issuer as to principal and interest, are held by investors who are afraid they might lose coupon bonds or do not wish to bother clipping coupons and presenting them to the paying agent. Registered bonds have the name of the owner written on the face of the bond. Also, the company or its authorized agent, usually a bank, has a record of the name and address of the owner. The interest, when due, is paid to the bondholder by check. If the bonds are lost or stolen, the rightful owner usually may obtain a new bond from the company, but care must be taken even of registered bonds. The owner of a registered bond will have to go through a considerable amount of paperwork and perhaps expense before a new bond is issued.

However, there is always the chance that a stolen registered bond, and for that matter a stolen stock certificate, might be sold by a thief who forges the owner's endorsement. Nevertheless, most of the recent new issues of bonds have been sold in registered form—some *only* in registered form. In fact, registered bonds now are much more common than coupon bonds.

Bonds registered as to principal but not as to interest are self-explanatory. The principal is registered in the name of the owner on the books of the company in the same manner as fully registered bonds. At maturity, the company or its agent sends a check for the principal amount to the holder of record. But the bonds are *not* registered as to interest. In other words, these bonds have coupons that might be detached and presented by the owner or bearer. Thus these bonds, like the coupon bonds already discussed, are also sometimes called bearer bonds.

TYPES OF BONDS

Mortgage bonds are perhaps the oldest type of bond. Here the corporation makes the usual promise to pay a stated sum at maturity plus interest. In addition, the corporation states that the bondholder has a specific claim or mortgage on a part or all of its assets. In other words, a mortgage bond is evidence of indebtedness that is secured by a mortgage or other lien on some underlying real property of a corporation. Many first-mortgage bonds were issued to build the railroads in this country. These usually had a first claim on specified miles of railroad before all other creditors. An example of this type of bond is the Kansas City Southern Railway Company first-mortgage 3 1/4% bond due December 1, 1984. This bond is secured by a first lien on all the property now owned and hereinafter acquired by the railroad. The line is the shortest route between Kansas City and Port Arthur, Texas.

In many cases, railroads needed additional funds for expansion and sold more bonds. But the claim of these bonds is junior to that of the first-mortgage bonds. It is a second mortgage or, as it is often called, a general mortgage. A general mortgage is a promise by the railroad to pay a fixed sum backed by a blanket or second-mortgage claim on all the corporation's fixed capital. An example of a general mortgage is the Northern Pacific Railroad Company general lien 3% bonds due in the year 2047. This bond is junior to the Northern Pacific Railroad Company prior lien 4% bond due in 1997.

Sometimes a railroad will issue a bond that has a first mortgage on one part of the railroad line and a general or second mortgage on another part. An investor should always beware of titles, particularly in the case of railroad bonds. It is not always true that a first mortgage is a safe investment. As will be shown, the safety of a bond depends more on earnings and other factors than on its mortgage position.

Public utilities often use mortgage bonds, but their capital structure is usually simple. Industrial concerns, however, seldom use mortgage bonds.

Mortgage bonds may be open end, closed end, or limited open end. An *open-end mortgage* means that a corporation under the mortgage may issue additional bonds. But the open-end mortgage indenture usually provides that the corporation can issue more bonds only if the earnings or additional security obtained by selling the new securities meet certain tests of earnings and asset coverage.

In a *closed-end mortgage*, the company agrees to issue at one time a stated amount of bonds. After these bonds have been issued *no more may be issued* under the mortgage. Additional bonds may be sold, but they rank as junior to the first-mortgage bonds. In other words, the original issue has priority on claims and may not be issued beyond the specified amount of the issue. Closed-end mortgage bonds were issued in large volume by the railroads when they were built; owing to their restrictive nature they are not currently used. An example of a closed-end mortgage bond is the Northern Pacific Railroad Company's prior lien 4% bond due in 1997, of which $130,000,000 were authorized and no more can be issued.

In a *limited open-end mortgage*, the indenture provides that a corporation may issue a stated amount of bonds *over a period of years in series*. For example, the indenture might provide that a corporation could issue up to $100,000,000 of bonds. The corporation might issue at once $25,000,000 of 5% Series A due 1985; sometime later it might sell $50,000,000 of 5% Series B due 1990, and so forth. The term *series* is used to designate bonds with different issue dates, usually different dollar amounts as well as different coupon rates and maturities. But each series is issued under the same indenture and has the same claim to assets.

Refunding bonds are usually a new issue of bonds sold by a company to pay off an old issue, most often to save interest. For example, in 1979 and early 1980 many bonds were issued bearing coupons of from 9% to 15%. Although most of these bonds had call restrictions to the effect that they could not be called for a stated period—usually five years—many will be refunded by issues bearing a lower rate if interest rates generally drop.

On occasion, a company will refund an issue at maturity to extend the payment of its debt. This is usually done by direct exchange. Generally, the issue offered for exchange is more attractive, with a higher coupon rate, sinking fund, and so on.

Debenture bonds are written promises of the corporation to pay principal at its due date and with interest. Although these promises are as binding as are those for mortgage bonds, debenture bonds are not secured by any pledge of property. They are sold on the general credit of the company. In short, debentures have no specific collateral behind them; they are simple promises to pay principal and interest, and their security depends on the assets and earnings of the corporation. The indenture of the debenture bonds should have strong protective covenants particularly to restrain the company from issuing senior debt.

It might also be mentioned here that U.S. government bonds are debentures. Because they are backed by the general credit of the U.S. government, they are considered prime investments.

Debenture bonds are used extensively by industrial concerns, sometimes by utilities, but to a lesser extent by railroads. In many cases, the debentures of the industrials and utilities are better investments than are the mortgage bonds of many of the railroads. For example, General Motors

Corporation, United States Steel Corporation, and American Telephone & Telegraph Company have sold large debenture issues that have high investment standings.

Convertible bonds, as the name implies, may be converted *at the option of the holder* into a specified number of shares of common stock. On rare occasions, a convertible bond is convertible into preferred stock. The terms of conversion are explained in the indenture. Sometimes the indenture might state that a $1,000 bond may be converted into a specific number of shares of common stock. For example, if a convertible bond selling at $1,000 is convertible into 20 shares of common, the stock would have to sell for at least $50 a share to make conversion worthwhile: a stock at $50 a share times 20 shares would equal $1,000. If the stock went to 75, the bond would be worth about $1,500, or 75 times 20 shares. Quite often the indenture of a convertible bond will say that the bond is convertible into common stock at a *price*. For example, a *conversion price* of $50 would mean 20 shares of common, or $1,000 divided by 50 equals 20 shares. In many cases, the conversion terms change with the passage of years. For example, a convertible bond due in 1991 might be convertible into 20 shares until December 1, 1985, into 18 shares until December 1, 1990, and not convertible from December 1, 1990 until maturity on December 1, 2000.

Conversion parity simply means that the value of a convertible bond and the shares into which it may be converted are the same, or on a parity. For example, if a convertible bond is convertible into 20 shares of stock, its *conversion ratio* is 20. If the bond is selling at $1,000 and the common at $50, the conversion value would equal 20 times $50, or $1,000. Thus the exchange value of the bond and the stock are equal, or at parity. The investor would have little trouble in finding the exchange value of the bond, which is referred to as *parity price of the bond*. All that one has to do is multiply the number of shares that the convertible bond permits the investor to buy times the price of the common stock—that is, 20 times $50. However, determining the *parity price of the stock* is a little more difficult. For example, if a convertible bond is selling at $1,500, the *parity price of the stock* is found by dividing the price of the convertible bond by the conversion ratio or the number of shares the convertible bond receives on conversion. In this case, $1,500 divided by 20 equals $75. Thus the common stock would have to sell at 75 to justify the price of $1,500 for the convertible bond.

The conversion price is usually set by the issuer in consultation with investment bankers. Customarily, it is set at 15–20% above the price of the outstanding shares. Consideration is given to the past history of the company, its trend of earnings, and its outlook. Obviously it is easier to sell convertible securities in a bull market than in a bear market. The length of time allowed to convert would also influence the price—a long period, say, 20 years would be more attractive to an investor than a short one, say, 5 years. When the conversion price has been determined, it is easy to calculate the *conversion ratio*. For instance, if the conversion price is $50, the conversion ratio is $1,000 divided by $50, or 20.

Almost always, the holder of a convertible bond is protected against *dilution*. That is, his conversion privilege changes along with any material change in the outstanding common shares. For example, if a company should split its stock 2-for-1, the conversion privilege of the bonds would also change proportionately, converting into twice as many shares as before the 2-for-1 split.

In some cases, a convertible bond is also a mortgage bond or a collateral trust bond, but more often it is a debenture with a claim on the general credit of the corporation. For a number of years, American Telephone & Telegraph Company sold convertible debenture bonds. Convertible bonds are issued frequently by industrial concerns and commercial banks but infrequently by railroad and electric public utilities.

Often a convertible bond is a *subordinated debenture*, which is much the same as an ordinary debenture. *Interest and principal must be paid at the scheduled time.* An important difference is that, in the event of default of principal or interest by the issuer, the claims of the subordinated debenture holders must wait until the claims of the other debenture holders and perhaps of the bank creditors are satisfied.

Some years ago sales finance companies started using *subordinated* debentures. They needed more capital than the banks were willing to extend, but the companies were unwilling to sell stock. Consequently, the banks agreed to allow the sales finance companies to sell more debentures provided they were *subordinated* to the bank debt and the outstanding debentures. These debentures were not convertible into common. A number of industrial companies and commercial banks have issued subordinated debentures, which are junior to the regular debentures or, in the case of commercial banks, to the depositors, but are also convertible into common stock. Among the large companies that have issued convertible subordinated debentures are Aluminum Company of America, Georgia-Pacific Corporation, and Chase Manhattan Bank.

The holder of a convertible bond has in some respects a double advantage. If, for example, the affairs of the company do not prosper, the investor is, as a bondholder, a creditor. Interest must be paid currently and principal must be paid at maturity. Thus the investor has assured income as long as the company is solvent and a bondholder's claim in the event of financial difficulty. On the other hand, if the affairs of the company prosper, the bondholder can convert to stock and benefit by increased principal and income. Perhaps the only disadvantage of a convertible bond to the investor is the provision that allows the company to *call* a convertible bond. This provision is discussed in more detail on pages 36–37.

On occasion, stockholders are given rights to subscribe to new convertible bonds on the grounds that there is a potential dilution of their equity. However, this privilege is becoming increasingly rare. This, of course, relates legally to the preemptive rights discussed previously.

As far as the corporation is concerned, the convertible bond has several advantages. It can sell convertible bonds at a lower coupon rate than it could sell straight debentures or even mortgage bonds. Convertible bonds are eagerly sought by investors seeking a fixed return with appreciation possibilities. Further, on the conversion of its bonds, a corporation has lower interest charges to pay. Also the company can often get a higher price for its stock by selling convertible bonds that in the future will be converted into stock at a higher price than by selling stock through investment bankers. Selling convertible bonds does not necessarily depress the price of outstanding shares as would be in the case of an offering of stock, because there is no immediate dilution of the equity. The convertible bond device enables a corporation to keep its capitalization balanced between debt and equities. As the conversion takes place, the proportion of debt to equity is reduced.

A disadvantage is the possibility that, as convertible bonds are changed to stock, there may be some dilution of the equity of old stockholders. Also some shift of control might take place. The tax bill of the corporation might increase as it reduces its fixed charges, which are a deductible item. Finally, there is always some uncertainty as to the exact status of the capital structure as long as convertible bonds are outstanding.

A number of industrial companies issue subordinated debentures that are *not* convertible into common. These companies include Crane Company and International Harvester Company. Electric public utilities and railroads usually do not issue subordinated debentures.

Income bonds, sometimes called *adjustment* bonds, are often issued by railroads that have been in financial difficulty. The principal of an income bond *must be paid at maturity*. But the interest depends on the earnings of the corporation. If the interest is earned the directors are, as a rule, required to pay it. On the other hand, if it is not earned it usually is not paid. Many indentures of income bonds provide that unpaid interest will accumulate. But this period of accumulation is often limited to a definite percentage—between 8% and 12%—or for a two- or three-year period. Sometimes the interest on income bonds does not accumulate at all. Due to the contingent nature of their interest payments, income bonds as a class are not considered as safe investments as fixed-income securities. They are issued by companies with fluctuating earnings. Earnings that are good during periods of boom become deficits in periods of low business activity. The income bond enables this type of company to defer interest without danger of bankruptcy in bad times. Furthermore, the cumulative nature of the income bond permits the company to make up, in part at least, the back interest.

When the Missouri Pacific Railroad Company was reorganized in 1956, it issued $59,000,000 of 4 3/4% Series A general income bonds due in 2020. The interest on these bonds, if not paid, accumulates up to 13 1/2%.

Guaranteed bonds are guaranteed by others than the corporation issuing the bonds. During the period of expansion in our country, a number of companies, particularly railroads, purchased other concerns not by cash but by guaranteeing or assuming their stocks and bonds. Usually the parent company guaranteed the payment both of the interest and the principal of the bonds. There were exceptions in which the guaranteeing company assumed only the interest payments but did not promise to pay the principal of the bonds at maturity. However, because most of the securities guaranteed were an important part of the railroad system, the principal was usually paid.

Guaranteed stock should be considered under the heading of fixed-income securities rather than as stock, as its title implies. A guaranteed stock is a stock with dividends guaranteed at a fixed rate by a company other than the one issuing the stock. For example, the 5% *preferred* stock of Carolina, Clinchfield and Ohio Railway Company is guaranteed by Seaboard Coast Line Railroad Company and Louisville and Nashville Railroad Company. This guarantee is joint and several. This means that, if one railroad fails to pay its part of the guarantee, the other must pay the entire amount.

There are also a few guaranteed *common* stocks. For years one of the strongest guaranteed common stocks was Pittsburgh, Fort Wayne and Chicago Railway Company $7 stock, guaranteed by the Pennsylvania Railroad Company. Pittsburgh, Fort Wayne controls 503 miles of main line between Pittsburgh and Chicago and is a vital link in the present Penn Central system. However, due to the failure of Penn Central in 1970, the outlook for all its obligations is somewhat clouded.

Collateral trust bonds are mortgage or debenture bonds that are additionally secured by other securities placed with a trustee.

Collateral trust bonds are often issued by companies whose credit needs to be strengthened. The collateral deposited with the trustee is sometimes the stocks and bonds of subsidiary companies. At times, the collateral is marketable securities. The holder of the collateral trust bond of an industrial company, a public utility, or a railroad company has a bondholder's claim against the company, but also in the event of default can force the trustee to sell the collateral and apply the proceeds to satisfy the claim of the bondholders. An example of a collateral trust bond is Delaware Power and Light Company first and collateral trust 4 3/8% of 1994. The collateral deposited with the trustee as additional security consists of shares of Delmarva Power and Light Company as well as notes of subsidiary companies.

A number of railroads have issued collateral trust bonds. The collateral in these cases is often senior securities of the *same* railroad. For instance, the Louisville and Nashville Railroad Company collateral 7 3/8% due 1993 are secured by a larger amount of first and refunding 7% bonds due in 2003. The trustee of the collateral of a railroad bond does not have the same freedom of action as an industrial or public utility trustee. Railroads defaulting on bonds usually must go through complicated legal reorganization. But the collateral behind a railroad bond is usually given consideration in any reorganization plan.

EQUIPMENT TRUST CERTIFICATES

An equipment trust certificate is a *serial* bond as it matures in part at stated intervals, usually every six months. In addition, it is secured by the equipment of the railroad and sometimes of an industrial company. Let us assume that a railroad wishes to buy $10,000,000 worth of diesel locomotives. The order is placed with the manufacturer, usually with the railroad advancing 20% of the cost price in cash. The balance is raised by the investment bankers' selling equipment trust certificates to investors, largely commercial banks, insurance companies, and pension funds. These equipment trust certificates, when sold under the so-called "Philadelphia" plan, are guaranteed by the railroad as to principal and dividends. The dividends are at a fixed rate and must be paid the same as interest. In this case they are called *dividends*, not interest. The trustees, which must include a bank, hold title to the equipment for the benefit of the investors in the certificates. If the dividends or principal are not paid by the railroad, the trustee can sell the equipment for the benefit of the certificate holders. Equipment trust certificates are sometimes sold under the "conditional sale" or "New York" plan. Here the manufacturer delivers the equipment to the railroad under a conditional bill of sale, with possession passing to the railroad. However, the title remains with the seller. A down payment of about 20% is made the same as in the "Philadelphia" plan, plus a number of deferred payments.

Mention should be made of an equipment mortgage. This is simply a chattel mortgage on the equipment. But it is almost never used because of its weak legal power, for example, the possibility that it might not be possible to seize the assets of a public utility.

Equipment trust certificates are excellent investments. First, they are serial maturities—a part of the total issue matures at stated intervals. Thus the railroad is paying off its debt as the equipment wears out. Second, the certificates are, as a rule, paid off *more rapidly* than the equipment depreciates. Third, the courts have recognized the first claim of the certificate holders to the equipment in reorganization. Among the types of companies issuing equipment trust certificates are the airlines, the meat packing industry, and the private car companies.

A *sinking fund bond* is not a distinct type or class of bond. A sinking fund is a provision in the indenture of the bond issue. Under this provision, the corporation agrees to set aside regularly sums sufficient to retire all or part of the debt prior to maturity. At stated intervals, the company or its agent calls by lot the numbers of a certain percentage of the bonds and then retires them from the proceeds of the sinking fund. Because sinking funds reduce the debt regularly over the life of the bonds, they often improve the credit of the company.

Industrial bonds usually have sinking funds that retire a substantial part of the bonds by maturity. Also, the maturity of an industrial bond is usually shorter than that of the bonds issued by the public utilities or railroads. For example, as will be explained in Chapter 17 American Brands, Inc. had a large number of bonds requiring heavy sinking fund payments. Public utility bonds usually have funds requiring the company to retire their bonds at the rate of about 2% a year.

Most of the railroad bonds were issued before the days when institutional investors were requesting sinking funds; consequently, many railroad bonds do not have sinking funds.

FLOATING-RATE NOTES

Floating-rate notes were first introduced by Citibank in 1974. During periods of high interest rates such as in 1974 and 1979, several of these notes were issued by large commercial banks and a few industrials. Chase Manhattan Bank, Mellon National, New York Bank for Savings, and Standard Oil Company of Indiana have issued floating notes.

Floating-rate notes provide that interest payments would be adjusted every six months to align with some money rate such as the rate on Treasury bills, Federal funds, or even long-term corporate bonds. Usually there is a premium over these rates of 1/2% to 1%. For example, Citibank floating-rate notes pay 1.05% over three-month Treasury bills. Thus, if Treasury bills go to 10.00%, the floating rate notes of Citibank would go to 11.05%. Some floating notes have a floor of, say, 7% for a period of years, dropping every interval of years a 1/2%. Also, some floating-rate notes are convertible. For example, in April 1979, Continental Illinois Corporation issued $200 million of floating-rate notes due in 1987; the interest rate for the first six months was set at 10.60%. Thereafter, the rate was to be set at .50% above the market discount rate for six-month Treasury bills; they were subject to a minimum rate of 6% and convertible into 25-year 8 1/2% debenture bonds.

ANALYSIS OF BONDS

In appraising the merits of a bond, the investor should consider safety, income, and maturity.

Safety of a bond is measured most easily by the service ratings. Moody's Investors Service and Standard & Poor's Corporation evaluate and rate almost all of the large bond issues.

The table illustrates how these two leading services group their bonds according to their ratings.

	Moody's	Standard & Poor's
Top quality—maximum safety	Aaa	AAA
Very high grade—high quality	Aa	AA
High grade—investment quality	A	A
Good grade—medium quality	Baa	BBB
Speculative grade	Ba	BB
Small assurance of continued payment of interest	B	B

Thus, an investor buying a bond with an A or better rating can have some, but not complete, assurance that the interest and principal will be paid. If the investor buys a bond with a lesser rating, he must take great care in selecting it.

Rating services also break down their ratings into municipal bonds and corporate bonds, which include industrial, utility, and railroad bonds.

The following are the ratings and comparative yields from Moody's Investor Service on March 24, 1980:

	Aaa	Aa	A	Baa
Industrials	12.42%	12.85%	13.41%	13.74%
Public Utility	13.07	13.95	14.62	15.02
Railroads	------	10.73	11.53	11.76

U.S. government issues on March 24, 1980 were quoted as follows:

Long-10 years or more	12.50%
Intermediate-5 years	13.01
Short- 3 years or less	13.94
91 day Bills	15.01

Another measure of safety is the number of times interest charges are covered. For example, in the income account of Lobuck Corporation (page 334), we show an operating profit of $1,062,000 (item B) and interest charges of $32,000 (item 5). The interest coverage before taxes would be obtained by dividing the operating income of $1,062,000 by the interest of $32,000, or 33.2 times. This an exceptionally high coverage. More often the interest is calculated *after taxes*, as follows:

Item B: Operating profit	$1,062,000
Item 6: Less federal income taxes	454,550
Balance for interest	$607,450
Item 5: Interest on bonds	32,000
Coverage of charges after taxes— $607,450	
divided by $32,000 equals 18.98 times	

To qualify as an investment, fixed charges should be covered approximately as follows:

	Federal Income Taxes	
	Before	After
Industrial bonds	4.65 ×	3.25 ×
Public utilities	2.70	2.20
Railroads	3.75	3.00

It is also important to note the record of interest coverage over a period of at least five years. Has the interest coverage been steady? The analyst should consider the interest coverage in years of poor business as well as the company's outlook.

Still another measure of safety may be obtained from the balance sheet. In an *industrial* bond, it is generally desirable *to have the bonded debt not in excess of the working capital.* There are exceptions to this rule, as in the case of certain chemical, aluminum, and air transport companies that are expanding rapidly.

In an electric public utility it is not desirable to have debt exceed 55% of the capitalization of the company; for an industrial bond the debt capitalization ratio should not exceed 33%. Capitalization is defined as the sum of the bonds, preferred stock, common stock, and surplus or retained earings (see page 319).

Although balance sheet items are important, it is earnings that pay the interest and eventually the principal.

INCOME AND INTEREST RATES

At a given time, the relative yield obtained on a bond usually depends to a great extent on its quality. An Aaa bond will have a lower yield than a Baa bond. On the other hand, a shrewd buyer will on occasion find an Aaa bond with a Baa yield. This may be because there is a poor market for the bond or because it is an odd lot—under $5,000 worth of bonds.

Another determinant of the income of a bond is the money market. When interest rates are high, corporations—even those with high credit standing—must sell bonds with high coupon rates. In 1946, corporations with high credit standing could sell bonds at 2 5/8%; in 1979 the same companies had to offer over a 12% rate, yet their credit, if anything, had improved.

Interest rates are one of the most important factors affecting the price of high-grade bonds. Take a simple case of an investor who buys a 20-year 5% high-grade bond at face amount, or at $1,000. Let us suppose that all other high-grade bonds are selling at about the same yield basis, or 5%. Then, let us suppose that money gets tight and corporations desiring to sell high-grade bonds find they must offer bonds at 6%. That is, all high-grade bonds are selling on a 6% basis. Obviously the investor who bought a 5% bond at face amount will find it is no longer worth $1,000 in the current market. This decline may be calculated by referring to the bond yield table. It would be simply necessary to determine at what price a 20-year 5% would sell to yield 6%. The answer would be $884.44. A very rough calculation is sometimes made by dividing the new yield into the old. That is, 5% divided by 6% equals $833. In short, bond prices and yields move inversely to each other; that is, rising yields mean lower prices, and the converse.

Interest rates rise and fall with the demand and the supply of loanable funds. In 1979 and 1980 there was a heavy demand on the part of large corporations. New issues of bonds were paying over 12% in 1979 and over 14% in 1980. Also, consumers were demanding durable goods such as automobiles, refrigerators, and the like. As a result the bond market was flooded with new issues, and commercial banks were pressed for loans. The outcome was that interest rates rose and outstanding bonds depreciated sharply.

The following table compares bond prices and yields in May 1966 and in March 1980. All three of these bonds in 1980 had the same high grade rating as in 1966, yet their dollar price had depreciated an average of over 50%.

| | May 1966 | | March 1980 | |
	Price	Yield	Price	Yield
Bell Telephone of Penn 3 1/4 1996	98	3.35%	41	11.28%
Union Pacific Railroad 2 1/2 1991	84	3.30%	44	11.61%
Norfolk and Western Ry 4 1996	108	3.62%	49	10.57%

By carefully selecting maturities the investor can acquire some measure of protection against the drastic changes in interest rates. This can be done by the policy of *spaced maturities*. Spaced maturities means buying securities in a block coming due every year, every three years, or every five years. As the securities mature, the proceeds can be reinvested in securities of longer maturity to take advantage of the higher rates.

Another similar way of arranging maturities is to have a certain percentage of securities in Treasury bills or notes and a part in longer-term bonds. Thus, as interest rates rise, the short-term obligations can be invested in the higher-yielding short-term securities and the overall income improved.

CALL PRICE OF REDEEMABLE
BONDS

The call price is the price at which a company might call or pay off its bonds. Many times in the past companies have paid off their bonds before they came due or matured. Companies in the late 1920s sold 5% and 6% bonds. When interest rates declined in the 1930s, these companies were able to call their bonds and sell new ones with coupons as low as 2 1/2%. The call price is usually set at a premium of 4 or 5 points over $1,000, declining as the maturity date approaches.

If the bond is callable at a price near its maturity value, the company might call its bonds and sell lower-coupon bonds. This practice is often referred to as refunding, and it is undertaken to save interest costs. Thus, an investor should choose, if possible, a bond with a high call price and not pay a price materially above the call price.

For instance, American Telephone 4 5/8s of 1994 are currently (1980) callable at 101.99 until January 31, 1983 and at slightly declining prices thereafter. In September 1979 they were selling at 65. They were selling therefore at a deep discount from their par or face value of $1,000.

Because a call price can place a ceiling on appreciation (companies usually call their high-coupon bonds if interest rates go down), an investor might choose to purchase noncallable bonds. An example of a high-grade noncallable bond is the Atchison, Topeka and Santa Fe Railway Company General 4% due 1995 and selling on September 1, 1979 at 65.

If an investor holds a convertible bond, he or she should watch carefully for a possible call. For example, many convertible bonds, as the affairs of the company improve, advance in price. Then the company might decide to call the bonds. The investor should then immediately sell his or her bonds or convert them into stock. An extreme case was that of the convertible bonds of the Interprovincial Pipe Line Company. These bonds, in June 1953, were selling at about $5,080 a bond and were called at $1,041. Thus a bondholder failing to see the public notice would lose $4,039 a bond.

Notices are usually published in the recognized financial papers, such as *The Wall Street Journal*. Sometimes the entire issue is called, and sometimes only part of the issue is called. In the latter case, only the numbers of the bonds drawn for call by lot are published.

MARKETABILITY

Generally speaking, the larger the bond issue outstanding, the greater its marketability. Marketability means that a security may be bought or sold in reasonable quantities at current prices. That is, there is a substantial volume of trades or transactions in a particular security. A large issue of bonds, over $20,000,000, usually has a good market, but there is no general rule. Sometimes the large investors will hold a substantial amount of a large issue and the marketability will be poor. Marketability usually does not apply to the investment merits of a bond. A bond could have a poor credit standing yet trade in substantial volume and have good marketability. Marketability is a desirable quality if the investor does not expect to hold the bond to maturity. Otherwise it can be ignored.

In summary, the investor analyzing a bond should examine its interest coverage over a period of years, its asset position, its call price, and its marketability. As a further check on the merits of a bond, the investor should look at the ratings of the services, such as Moody's and Standard & Poor's. Finally, and possibly most important, the investor should look at the maturity of the bond, bearing in mind the possible effect of an increase in interest rates.

REVIEW QUESTIONS

1. Define a bond. What are the obligations of a company to a bond-holder as compared with its obligations to a stockholder?
2. Distinguish among nominal yield, current yield, and yield to maturity.
3. If you bought a 20-year 4 1/2% bond at 105, what is the *approximate* yield to maturity?
4. Calculate the *exact* yield to maturity on the bond in problem 3, using the following bond yield table for 20 years at 4 1/2%.

Yield	Price
4.05%	106.1
4.10	105.4
4.15	104.7
4.20	104.0

5. Distinguish among open-end, closed-end, and limited open-end mortgages.

6. Describe debenture bonds. Are they necessarily weaker than mortgage bonds? Explain.

7. What are two advantages of convertible bonds to the corporation and two advantages to the investor? What does the term "conversion parity" mean?

8. Why are equipment trust certificates considered good investments?

9. Describe floating-rate notes. Give some examples.

10. In writing a report for a customer on an industrial bond, what characteristics would you mention? Name three.

TRUE AND FALSE QUESTIONS

1. Corporate bonds include: *True*   *False*
    a. bonds issued by all corporations   _____   _____
    b. bonds issued by railroads, public utilities,
        and industrial concerns   _____   _____
    c. bonds of all sorts—a generic term that
        includes bonds of governments, of
        municipalities, etc.   _____   _____

2. The difference between a coupon and a registered bond is that:
                                                                      True   *False*
    a. coupon bonds are payable, principal in-
        terest to bearer; registered bonds must be
        endorsed and transferred on the books of
        the company   _____   _____
    b. registered bonds, if properly entered on the
        books of the company, have prior claim
        over bearer bonds in the event of default by
        the company of principal or interest pay-
        ment   _____   _____
    c. the marketability of registered bonds is
        better than bearer bonds.   _____   _____

3. Because bonds are quoted in percent of par, a customer buying 10 bonds at 105 5/8 would have to pay (not counting commissions and accrued interest):   *True*   *False*
    a. $1,056.25   _____   _____
    b. $10,562.50   _____   _____
    c. $10,563.00.   _____   _____

4. A bond with a 6% coupon selling at 102 with a maturity in 1988 has a current yield of:

		True	False
a.	6%	____	____
b.	$60.00	____	____
c.	5.88%.	____	____

5. By use of the bond yield table below, the yield to maturity of a 6% bond bought August 1, 1971, due on August 1, 1991, and selling at 102, is:

		True	False
a.	5,880	____	____
b.	5.829	____	____
c.	6.000.	____	____

6% Bond Yield Table

Yield	19 1/2	20	20 1/2 Years
5.80	102.32	102.35	102.38
5.85	101.73	101.75	101.78
5.90	101.15	101.17	101.18

6. Bonds that have a specific claim on a part or all of the assets of a corporation are called:

		True	False
a.	debenture bonds	____	____
b.	convertible bonds	____	____
c.	mortgage bonds	____	____
d.	income bonds.	____	____

7. Bonds that have no specific collateral or pledged assets are called:

		True	False
a.	refunding bonds	____	____
b.	sinking fund bonds	____	____
c.	serial bonds	____	____
d.	debenture bonds.	____	____

8. Bonds that are secured by securities placed with a trustee are called:

		True	False
a.	serial bonds	____	____
b.	collateral trust bonds	____	____
c.	convertible bonds	____	____
d.	mortgage bonds.	____	____

9. A 5% bond due in 1988 selling at 115 is convertible into 20 shares of common stock. At what price would the bonds sell to be on a parity basis with the common stock that is selling at 60?

		True	False
a.	125	____	____
b.	120	____	____
c.	115.	____	____

10. Income bonds mean that: *True*   *False*
     a.   the bondholders get paid on a percentage of
          income   _____   _____
     b.   the bondholders get paid only if the interest
          is earned   _____   _____
     c.   the company does not have to pay the
          principal at maturity.   _____   _____

11. A serial and a series bond are: *True*   *False*
     a.   the same   _____   _____
     b.   a serial bond applies to serial maturities, as
          is the case of equipment trust certificates; a
          series bond applies to new issues under the
          same mortgage   _____   _____
     c.   a serial bond applies to maturities, whereas
          a series bond applies to time of issue under
          same mortgage.   _____   _____

12. The Trust Indenture Act of 1939 is designed to: *True*   *False*
     a.   protect the company against fraud   _____   _____
     b.   set forth the rights of bondholders and the
          duties of the trustee   _____   _____
     c.   ensure the bondholders against default of
          principal and interest.   _____   _____

13. In the analysis of industrial bonds, the investor should consider:
                                                        True   *False*
     a.   Moody's rating   _____   _____
     b.   interest coverage   _____   _____
     c.   working capital-to-debt ratio   _____   _____
     d.   debt capitalization ratio   _____   _____
     e.   outlook for the business   _____   _____
     f.   past record of the business   _____   _____
     g.   all of the above.   _____   _____

14. Increases in interest rates can: *True*   *False*
     a.   cause a drop in bond prices   _____   _____
     b.   hurt, in particular, the public utilities that
          need large amounts of new capital   _____   _____
     c.   bring big profits to banks and other lenders
          of money.   _____   _____

3

U.S. Treasury
and Agency Securities

The total debt of the U.S. government as of December 31, 1982 was $1,202 billion. Congress in May 1983, set a temporary limit to the debt of $1,389 billion. But Congress in the past has, after some fussing, always raised the limit.

From the investors' standpoint, the most important part of the debt is the marketable debt of $530.7 billion. This consists of Treasury bills, notes, and bonds. Since 1933, all U.S. government obligations and U.S. government agency obligations have been subject to federal but exempt from state income taxes.

U.S. Treasury bills are usually offered by the U.S. Treasury through the Federal Reserve banks as agents. Offerings are made on a weekly basis. Commercial banks, corporations, and pension funds in particular find bills an excellent investment medium for short-term funds. Bills may have a maturity of from one or two days to *one year.* They are issued at a discount and are paid in cash at maturity at par or may be used in payment at par for new bills. The difference between the discount price and par is considered *income* and taxed as such. For example, when Treasury bills are offered, notices are printed inviting tenders under *competitive* and *noncompetitive* bidding. In the case of competitive bids (amounts usually over $500,000), a price is named in three decimals, for example, 99.231. Noncompetitive bids are for smaller amounts than those specified as competitive and are taken by the Treasury at the *average* price of the accepted bills. The minimum purchase of bills is $10,000. Bills are traded by bank and nonbank dealers who carry large positions in Treasury bills of which $311.8 billion were outstanding as of December 31, 1982. They have a ready market and a narrow spread between the bid and asked prices. Barring chaotic money-market conditions, Treasury bills may be sold at a profit if held a few days. Treasury bills are traded only over the counter and are always at a discount as no coupons are attached. The appreciation of the discount on Treasury bills is taxable as income.

At one time the U.S. Treasury issued tax anticipation bills (TABs). These were bills offered at competitive bidding; they matured one week after a tax date. For example, a tax anticipation bill might mature and pay interest to April 22nd but could be used to pay taxes on April 15 at par. But these TABs have not been issued in years.

U.S. Treasury certificates have not been offered since 1966. None are outstanding at the present time. They have in the past been offered by the U.S. Treasury with and sometimes without coupons with a maturity not exceeding *one year.* The terms are announced by the Treasury usually at prices attractive in the market and tenders are made by the investors. They were quoted in the over-the-counter market in 1/32nds, issued in bearer form in demoninations as low as $1,000. Sometimes the Treasury would offer new securities—a certificate, a note, or a bond—in exchange for the maturing certificates.

U.S. Treasury notes are issued with maturities of not less than one or more than ten years. Coupon rates, prices, and maturities are set by the Treasury in line with monetary conditions. In other words, they are priced to sell in the market, as they must be attractive to investors who are making application for the notes. As of December 31, 1982 notes outstanding amounted to $465.0 billion. These were held largely by commercial banks, the Federal Reserve banks, and private investors. At maturity they are paid off in cash but more often a new security is offered—a new note or even a bond. Using notes affords the Treasury an opportunity to extend the average maturity of government debt. As far as the private investor is concerned, a note usually offers a higher yield than a Treasury bill. It also, however, has a tendency to fluctuate to a considerable degree, sometimes as much as 4 or 5 points. Notes are quoted in 1/32nds and on rare occasions in 1/64ths and are traded only over the counter; they are issued in bearer or registered form with the exception of the 1 1/2% notes, which are in bearer form only.

U.S. Treasury notes are acceptable to secure public deposits, but they are not acceptable in payment of taxes. Interest is payable every six months. Treasury notes are issued in bearer or in coupon form. They may be purchased in the secondary market or subscribed to at Federal Reserve banks. The minimum denomination is $1,000.

U.S. Treasury bonds usually have a maturity of five years or more. Actually, Treasury bonds may be issued with any maturity. Bonds are issued by the Treasury in the same way as are notes and certificates. That is, the Treasury sets the dollar prices, the coupon rates, and the maturities of the bonds so that they will be accepted in the market. If the issues are exceptionally attractive, Federal Reserve banks will allot the offerings, giving preference to requests, particularly of individuals, for smaller amounts. As of the end of 1982, there were $104 billion on U.S. Treasury bonds outstanding.

For years the U.S. Treasury was not allowed to pay more than 4 1/4% on bonds. But, as interest rates rose in the 1970s, this limitation became unrealistic. Congress from time to time raised the amount of bonds that could be sold without limit as to interest rate. As of June 1983 it was $150 billion (there is no limit on the interest the Treasury can pay on bills, certificates, or notes).

A number of Treasury bonds have single or stated maturities. These are sometimes called *term* bonds. An example of a term bond is the 3 1/2s of November 15, 1998. But a number of bonds have optional call dates. For example, the Treasury 4 1/4s of August 15, 1992–1987 could be called at par by the Treasury any time after August 15, 1987 provided it gave four months' notice prior to the date. These are called optional call bonds as contrasted to term bonds.

On June 6, 1983, 9 bond issues were acceptable at face amount when presented for payment of federal estate taxes. (They are sometimes called *"flower bonds"* because of the peculiar designation by some dealers on their quotation sheets.) For example, the 4 1/4% bonds due August 15, 1992–1987, selling on June 6, 1983 at 91 16/32, and yielding 5.44% might be presented at 100 for estate taxes. But, under the Tax Reform Act of 1976, the estate would be liable for capital gains. Further these securities must be owned by the decedent at the time of his death. All Treasury bonds are issued in bearer or registered form, in denominations from $500 to $1,000,000. Interest is payable every six months.

The government always pays its Treasury bills in cash at maturity, or it permits the holder to use the maturing bills for new bills. But, to the holders of maturing certificates, notes, and bonds, the government often offers a new security—a new certificate, note, or bond. Usually the terms of these new securities are attractive to the investor. Thus the old securities often have a rights value. That is, the old issues will sell above par or 100 just prior to maturity, indicating the right of the holder of the old security to subscribe to the new, which often bears a higher rate of interest than the maturing security. But the government must, of course, pay cash to the investors *not* accepting the exchange. (Treasury bonds are issued in registered or bearer form.)

Offerings of certificates, notes, and bonds are made by the U.S. Treasury through the Federal Reserve banks, usually 10 to 20 days before the issue date. An announcement indicates a period when the books will be open for subscription. Subscription by commercial banks and their customers are made without deposit. However, the bank's subscription for its own account is limited to 50% of its capital. Subscribers other than commercial banks are required to post a deposit, usually 10% for small amounts and 2% for large. If the issue is oversubscribed, small subscriptions (usually $200,000 and under) receive full allotment.

NONMARKETABLE ISSUES

The most important of the nonmarketable issues are U.S. savings bonds. They were pushed hard in the World War II and in the postwar periods to finance government deficits in a noninflationary manner.

Series E bonds were first issued in 1935 and were designed principally for savings of individuals. They were issued at a discount of 75% of the face. The yield to maturity was 5.50% in 1972, compounded semiannually. They were redeemable at the option of the holder according to a gradually increasing schedule. The appreciation was taxable as income and had to be reported at maturity if the holder was on a cash basis.

Series EE bonds were issued in January 1980 in denominations from $50 to $10,000. They have a maturity of 11 years and a yield if held to maturity of 7.00%. After 5 years they may be redeemed at gradually increasing prices. If redeemed or held to maturity, the appreciation is taxed as income if the holder was on a cash basis.

Series H bonds originally could be exchanged for maturing Series E. They matured in 10 years, were issued at $1,000, and had a yield in 1972 of 5.50%.

Series HH bonds were issued in January 1980 in denominations from $500 to $10,000 at par. Their maturity is 10 years, and the rate of interest is 7.00%. They may be redeemed at par six months after purchase.

AGENCY SECURITIES OF THE U.S. GOVERNMENT

These are securities issued and sponsored by the U.S. government but not guaranteed by it. However they are generally considered prime securities.

The Federal Land Banks (FLB), organized in 1917, are supervised by the Farm Credit Administration. The FLB, through Federal Land Bank Associations, make loans secured by mortgages to farmers and ranchers. The consolidated FLB bonds are a joint and several obligation of the 12 Federal Land Banks. They are lawful investments for all trust funds including Treasury tax and loan accounts. They are issued in denominations of $1,000 to $500,000. In a sense these bonds are a moral but not a legal obligation of the U.S. government. However, during the Great Depression of the 1930s, these bonds sold several points below comparable U.S. Treasury obligations.

The Federal Home Loan Banks (FHLB) "Freddie Maes," were organized during the Depression (1932). They are operated under the supervision of the Federal Home Loan Bank Board. Membership consists of over 4,000 thrift institutions, mostly savings and loan organizations. Each member must subscribe to capital stock of the regional bank, which in turn makes secured and unsecured loans to the members. The secretary of the Treasury may buy up to $4 billion of the banks' obligations. Consolidated obligations are the joint and several obligations of the Federal Home Loan Banks operating under a federal charter. Obligations are issued in denominations of $10,000 to $1,000,000. Starting in 1974, the FHLB issued consolidated discount notes in denominations of $100,000 and $1,000,000. These notes had maturities of 30 to 270 days at the discretion of the buyer.

The Federal National Mortgage Association (FNMA), "Fannie Mae," is subject to the control of the secretary of Housing and Urban Development. FNMA provides a degree of liquidity for FHA-insured mortgages and for VA-guaranteed mortgages. These mortgages are bought from approved holders such as savings banks, savings and loan associations, and others. Mortgage sellers are required to buy FNMA capital stock. FNMA debentures are issued up to a limit of 25 times the sum of capital and surplus. They are issued in bearer form, only in denominations from $10,000 to $500,000. Beginning 1960, FNMA issued short-term discount notes, tailored to the needs of institutional investors. They were issued in bearer form with denominations from $5,000 to $1,000,000.

The Government National Mortgage Association (GNMA), "Ginnie Mae," is an adjunct of the Department of Housing and Urban Development. Its purpose is to help finance more housing. GNMA securities are fully guaranteed by the U.S. government. Each GNMA certificate represents a proportionate share in a pool of FHA and VA mortgages. GNMA certificate holders receive monthly interest and principal payments as determined by an amortization schedule of the mortgage pool. The phrase "pass through" is used because the underlying mortgage payments are passed through to the certificate holders. GNMA guarantees that the payments will be made regardless of what happens to the underlying mortgages in the pool. The minimum investment is $25,000 with increments of $5,000. The rate is usually 1/2% less than the underlying mortgages, which usually have a maturity of 30 years.

The Federal Intermediate Credit Bank (FICB) consists of 12 banks authorized to make loans and discount paper for credit associations, banks, credit corporations, livestock loan companies, and others. FICB consolidates bonds that are joint and several obligations. The proceeds of these bonds are used to make term loans to farmers for expenses, machinery, and livestock. The maturities of the loans are short. The denominations of the bonds are $5,000 to $500,000 and are issued in bearer form only.

Banks for Cooperatives (COOPs) are operated under the Farm Credit Administration. The banks make loans to farm cooperatives. The consolidated bonds are joint and several obligations of the 13 banks. The bonds are issued in denominations from $5,000 to $500,000 and in bearer form only.

There are many other agencies of the U.S. government that issue bonds and notes. These include the Commodity Credit Corporation, the Export-Import Bank, the Farmers Home Administration, the Merchant Marine Authority, and the Tennessee Valley Authority.

Trading of U.S. government securities is conducted by a relatively few large money-market commercial banks and a few large and small nonbank dealers. These dealers take a position and make and maintain a market in governments. For the most part, they trade *net* in round lots. Round lots for U.S. Treasury bonds is $100,000, and for bills, certificates, and notes it is $1,000,000. Any amount less than these is considered an odd lot.

As will be explained in Chapter 11, *stocks* are traded in dollars per share. Therefore one point is one dollar. But, as was shown in Chapter 2, bonds are quoted in percent of par, which usually is $1,000. Thus a point in a bond is *1%* of $1,000, or $10. Corporate and municipal bonds are quoted in percent of par in fractions (1/8th to 7/8ths).

U.S. Treasury bills are quoted in 1/100ths of a point (1%) and are traded on a yield basis. *U.S. Treasury certificates, notes, and bonds* are quoted in 1/32nds of a point. A point on a $1,000 bond is 1%, or $10.00. For example, if a U.S. Treasury 9 1/4% bond due on May 15, 1989 is quoted at 91.16, it would have a dollar price of $910 plus 16/32 times $10.00, or $910 plus $5.00, which equals $915.00.

The credit of the U.S. government throughout our history has fluctuated to a considerable degree, yet ever since the end of the Civil War in 1865 the obligations of the United States have been considered prime investments. Moody's Investors Service rates them Aaa—top quality with maximum safety. There seems no possibility of any default of principal or interest, as the government can always print money. If, on the other hand, a default *were to* occur, the security holder could not *sue* for recovery because a sovereign government cannot be sued without its consent. A government's credit depends on its willingness and ability to pay. The United States has never defaulted on its debt, and there appears to be no reason to expect any break in this tradition. Also, the United States has vast revenues—$617 billion in the fiscal year ended September 30, 1982—which are substantial compared with interest charges of about $85 billion. Furthermore, during the past eight years, the U.S. debt has not grown as fast as corporate or personal debt. In sum, despite frequent fiscal deficits, it is believed the U.S. debt has ample security of assets and earning power.

THE ROLE OF THE U.S. TREASURY

The basic role of the U.S. Treasury is to manage the debt and fiscal policy of the government. It should manage the debt prudently. That is, it should meet the maturities as they come due—about 34% of the total debt of the government comes due in one year. The Treasury must try to obtain the lowest cost in terms of interest payments and manage the debt in the interest of the economy, avoiding inflation and deflation. The Treasury must also defend the dollar in international markets.

THE ROLE OF THE FEDERAL RESERVE SYSTEM

The basic aim of the Federal Reserve System is to manage credit. That is, the Federal Reserve must make credit available to the banking system. In a broader sense, the Federal Reserve attempts to maintain a growing economy, full employment, and a rising level of consumption, at the same time trying to avoid inflation and overheating of the economy.

For example, in October 1979, the Federal Reserve System made another attempt to restrict inflation and reduce the expansion of the money supply. The major change was that the Federal Reserve decided to begin to restrict the expansion of the growth of money directly rather than indirectly through the rise in interest rates, which had been the policy up to October 1979.

The discount rate was raised to 13% (the discount rate is the rate that member banks pay to the Federal Reserve banks for loans). In addition the Fed placed an 8% reserve requirement on the so-called managed liabilities of the member banks. Thus the member banks had to apply this reserve to their outstanding certificates of deposit, their Federal funds borrowed, their *Eurodollar* borrowings, and their repurchase agreements. The prime rate in March 1980 of commercial banks went to 19%, Treasury bills to 15%, and Federal funds to 20%.

MONEY

Money is anything that is generally accepted as a medium of exchange. It serves as a standard of value, a store of value, and as a standard of deferred payment. It is useful to think of money as anything that has a fixed price in terms of a unit of account and is generally accepted in a given society in payment of goods and services rendered.

Superimposed on the monetary system is the credit system. Credit may arise when an individual or a company sells goods and services in exchange for a buyer's promise to pay at some future date. Credit may also arise when an individual or company lends money to another in exchange for the borrower's promise to repay money at a future date. Credit might be classed as *longterm*—with maturities of five years or more, *intermediate*—with maturities from one to five years, and *shortterm*—with credit running less than one year, as, for example, Treasury bills (discussed on pages 41–42).

THE MONEY MARKET

There is no specific building or marketplace in which the money market is located. It is essentially where the demand and supply for *short-term* funds meet. In the money market are traded high-quality credit investments with short maturities and high liquidity. The money market should be distinguished from the capital market, which is for *long-term* funds.

The *institutions* of the money market are the large commercial banks, such as the Morgan Guaranty Trust Company: the large government bond dealers, such as Salomon Brothers: Federal funds firms, such as Garvin, Guybutler; the Federal Reserve Bank of New York; the City and State of New York pension funds; and investment companies. These institutions trade in short-term funds with one another, often by telephone or by teletype.

In New York City, the core of the money market consists of about 20 bank and nonbank primary dealers that trade a daily volume of as much as $2.5 billion. These dealers perform a number of functions but perhaps the most important is to *make a market* in short-term securities. They stand ready to supply bid and asked prices on over 300 short-term U.S. government and agency issues. They help the Federal Reserve Bank of New York maintain an orderly market in government securities. Finally, the dealers act as advisors not only to the Federal Reserve Bank of New York on market conditions but also to the U.S. Treasury on new issues. The cities, states, commercial banks, pension funds, and even investment companies consult the dealers on market conditions as well as on individual issues.

Short-term instruments traded in the money market include the following:

1. *Federal funds* is the abbreviated term for federal funds or balances at the Federal Reserve Banks. The Federal funds market means the market for excess member-bank balances at the Federal Reserve banks. Every member bank must keep a balance at the Federal Reserve banks at a stated average over the week ended Wednesdays. For example, in April 1983, member banks in New York City were required to keep a weekly balance at the Federal Reserve Bank of New York of 16 1/2% of their demand deposits in addition to the 8% reserve required on their so called managed liabilities discussed on page 47. [1]Member banks in other districts were required to

[1]This 8% reserve was cancelled in June, 1980.

keep lower balances. Time deposits for all member banks ranged from 1% to 6%. In April 1980, Congress gave the Federal Reserve System power to require *all* the 14,000 commercial banks to post reserves, as well as the savings and loan and the savings banks. Previously, only the 5,000 member banks were required to post reserves.

Federal funds give the holder immediate credit at the Federal Reserve Bank and are sometimes called the "cashiest cash." The most important users of Federal funds are the commercial banks. From time to time, a bank might have more reserves at the Federal Reserve banks than is required, whereas at another time it might be short. The banks with a shortage or a surplus telephone or wire a firm acting as a clearinghouse for Federal funds. For a small fee or sometimes for a brokerage commission, these firms will put banks that are short of funds in touch with those that have surplus. The best known of these firms are Garvin, Guybutler and Mabon, Nugent and Company. The bank with the surplus funds is known as the lender or seller, and the bank that is short is the borrower or buyer. Most of the transactions are for 24 hours and are unsecured loans. The normal restrictions on loans do not apply. The normal unit of trade is $1,000,000 but lesser amounts are traded. Thus the buyer or bank that is short of funds gets immediate credit at the Federal Reserve and in exchange gives its check in clearinghouse funds for the amount borrowed plus interest at an annualized rate for one day computed on a 360-day basis.

2. Short-term U.S. government securities, which include Treasury bills, certificates, and short-term notes, are all used for investment of short-term funds. The bank and nonbank dealers carry large inventories of these obligations. Substantial investors in these obligations include the Federal Reserve banks, commercial banks, muncipalities, corporations, corporate and public pension funds, and investment companies. Commercial banks with large demand deposits must keep liquid; the Federal Reserve System eases the credit of the banking system by buying short-term securities and tightens it by selling the same. Municipalities sell obligations at periodic intervals but spend on a day-to-day basis. Therefore, between sales of securities large funds must be kept invested in short-term securities. Corporations with large taxes and dividend payments make a practice of accumulating funds for these payments and look to obtain some income in the process. Pension funds and investment companies sometimes withdraw from the stock market a part of their funds. These are kept in short-term securities pending a more favorable buying opportunity.

In March 1983, the U.S. government had outstanding and due in one year $312 billion of bills, $115 billion of notes, and $1 billion of bonds. There were also U.S. Agency securities due in one year amounting to about $41 billion. As previously noted, one–year obligations of the U.S. government and its agencies are virtually riskless. There were outstanding in March, 1980 no U.S. Treasury certificates or tax anticipation notes.

3. *Repurchase agreements* are designed to smooth out the fluctuations in the money market. Repurchase agreements consist of two simultaneous transactions. One is the purchase of securities by an investor—the Federal Reserve Bank of New York or a corporate investor; the other is the agreement of the dealer or bank to buy back the securities (usually a short-term government security) at a mutually agreed price at an agreed date. This mutual agreement is called a "repo" or "RP." Repos are a means by which dealers in government securities, who are unable to get money from the banks, may get money directly from the Federal Reserve Bank. For example, dealers need loans to carry a new issue of governments. They then sell their governments to the Federal Reserve, which in turn advances the funds to the dealer. The dealer agrees to repurchase the identical securities at the same price at which they were sold to the Fed. The rate charged is usually the same as the rate that the Fed charges nonmember banks. Repos by the Fed are relatively small compared with total holdings of governments. It should be stressed that the Fed cannot be relied on to supply funds to dealers nor can the rate charged be assured because it depends on the Fed's credit policy at that particular time.

Another use of repos is the one made by nonfinancial corporations when they have surplus funds. They can obtain a return on their surplus funds by making advances to dealers, who turn over government securities with an agreement to buy them back. Repurchase prices and maturities are fixed to provide a predetermined yield. As with other money-market instruments, interest is calculated on a 360-day basis, and transactions are settled in Federal funds. The smallest denomination is usually $1,000,000.

4. *Short-term tax-exempt notes*, are issued in large amounts by cities, states, and public agencies, with maturities of a year or less, The notes are general obligations of the issuer and are sold in anticipation of taxes (TANs), in anticipation of a bond sale (BANs), and in anticipation of revenue from the state or federal government (RANs). The demoninations range from $5,000 to $1,000,000.

Short-term notes are also issued by various local housing and urban renewal agencies under programs sponsored by the U.S. Department of Housing. These notes, referred to as project notes (PNs), are guaranteed by the U.S. government.

5. *Bankers' acceptances* (BAs) are a medium by which international and to a lesser extent domestic trade is financed. They are highly liquid, safe, short-term investments. They are irrevocable primary obligations of the accepting bank and a contingent obligation of the drawer and any endorsers. The accepting bank has the customer's promise to pay secured by warehouse receipts and other documents. An example of a foreign trade transaction might be the following:

Importer A in this country wishes to buy $10,000 of coffee from Brazil. He applies to his bank in New York for a commercial letter of credit. This permits the exporter in Brazil, on submission of shipping documents and other references, to draw a draft on A's bank in New York. This draft of bill of exchange is an unconditional order in writing, requiring the bank to pay on demand $10,000. The bank *accepts* this, at which time it becomes a promise to pay by the bank. (Importer A is also bound to pay his bank.) The bankers' acceptance can be sold in the market.

Acceptances might have maturities of up to 270 days and are eligible collateral for bank borrowing at Federal Reserve banks. Their yield is calculated the same way that Treasury bills are, that is, on a 360-day year. They trade in the money market on a yield basis in relation to prevailing market rates.

From investors' point of view, the only disadvantage of bankers' acceptances is the fact that they sell in odd amounts depending on the transaction being financed. At the end of 1982, there were $79.0 billion outstanding.

Bills drawn by one banker on another are known as *bankers' bills;* when a corporation draws a bill on a bank, as discussed, the instrument is known as a *commercial bill.* Bankers' bills and commercial bills become bankers' acceptances if accepted by the bank on which they are drawn. These bills might be compared with bills drawn by a corporation on another corporation, which are called *trade bills.*

6. *Commercial paper* is a firm's promissory note to finance its short-term credit needs. Commercial paper is issued by domestic corporations, banks, and institutions as well as by many foreign companies. It is an unsecured, written, unconditional promise to pay a fixed sum at a designated date. The maturities can run up to 270 days, but the bulk run to about 30 days. Commercial paper is distributed by about 6 dealers or directly by about 70 companies. Commercial paper is usually backed by a line of credit from a bank to assure the payment at maturity in case of a poor market. Sometimes a strong company such as Aetna Life will guarantee the paper of a weaker concern.

Finance paper is sold largely by sales finance companies, such as Commercial Credit Company, sometimes directly to the investor and at other times through dealers. The minimum round lot is $100,000 running up to $1,000,000. The notes are in bearer form with settlement in Federal funds.

Commercial paper offered by dealers is usually bought and sold at a discount calculated on the basis of a 360-day year.

In 1978, and particularly in 1979, there was a boom in commercial paper sales. By the end of 1982 there were $166.9 billion of commerical and finance paper outstanding. It is feared that the proliferation of new issuers may have lowered the credit standards and that some risky paper has been sold.

7. *Brokers' (call) loans* are an important part of the money market. Commercial banks make loans to brokers secured by listed and government securities for the purpose of carrying margin accounts of customers. (The term "call loan" is out of date and refers to the call money desk on the floor of the New York Stock Exchange in the 1920s.) Currently the banks quote to the brokers the rates on new and renewal brokers' loans. As of December 1979, there were $11.6 billion of brokers' loans outstanding. This is considered somewhat high. Should the stock market drop sharply, brokers would be forced to call their customers' margin accounts, accelerating the decline in the market. The margin required by the brokers and by the banks is set by the board of governors of the Federal Reserve System. As of April 1980, the margin required was 50% of the value of the stocks purchased. It could be set as high as 100%. Stocks held in margin accounts must be in street names (see page 200).

8. *Dealers' loans* are made by New York City and large out-of-town banks to underwriters of primary and secondary issues of corporate, municipal, and government issues. The margin required by the banks is usually around 5% on government issues and somewhat higher for municipal and corporate issues. These loans are mostly short term and are designed to enable dealers to distribute the securities that they have underwritten.

9. *Negotiable certificates of deposit* (CDs) are issued by commercial banks in return for a deposit. Thus the banks are able to obtain loanable funds from corporations and institutions that might otherwise invest such funds in money-market instruments, for example, Treasury bills, commercial paper, and so forth. CDs are issued in amounts ranging from $100,000 to $1,000,000, with maturities tailored to the purchaser's needs. Usually they run about one year, although there are some "term" CDs that have maturities beyond one year. Sometimes a bank will issue a variable CD with one-year or shorter maturity. The rate is adjusted every 30 to 90 days.

The issuing bank cannot pay the CDs before they are due. But, because they are *negotiable*, the holder can sell them in a secondary market. Large investment banking houses such as The First Boston Corporation make a market in CDs. On June 1, 1983 member-banks had issued $94.3 billion of CDs. On that date member-bank commercial loans amounted to $210.7 billion. CDs are quoted on a yield basis for a 360-day year. Since 1973 there have been no limits on the interest that banks may pay on CDs.

Eurodollar CDs are time deposits denominated in dollars that are issued by foreign (largely London) and by foreign branches of major

American banks. Eurodollar CDs are negotiable instruments and have active secondary markets in London and New York.

THE FUTURES MARKET

The Chicago Mercantile Exchange (CME), since 1919 has protected businesses and traders from serious losses from advances and declines in all kinds of commodities. In 1972, the CME formed the International Monetary Market Division (IMM) to provide futures trading in interest-rate dominated U.S. Treasury bills, some notes, long-term Treasury bonds, commercial paper, and GNMAs.

Basically a futures contract is a transferable contract agreement to take delivery of a security or a commodity at a future date. Future contracts in securities can be a means whereby an investment banker, a portfolio manager, a commercial banker, a city manager, or a corporate executive can hedge against the volatility of interest rates and the fluctuation of interest sensitive securities. Treasury bills are particularly suitable as a hedge media because of their close correlation to the fluctuation of interest rates generally. (The unit of trading of Treasury bills is $1,000,000. The IMM is regulated by the Commodity Futures Trading Commission.)

There is a simple rule for trading money market futures. If interest rates are expected to go down, Treasury bill futures should be bought; if interest rates are expected to go up, they should be sold. Let us take two examples. If Mr. Jones, a portfolio manager, expects to receive a large sum of money to manage, and fears that the high interest rates then prevailing will go down, he should buy futures in Treasury bills at a specified rate with three months maturity. If interest rates do go down before Mr. Jones's contract expires, his contract will go up in value and can be sold at a profit.

Mr. Smith, an investment banker, plans to take a large participation in a corporate bond syndicate. He fears that interest rates will go up sharply before he can distribute the issue. Therefore, he *sells* Treasury bill futures for future delivery. If interest rates rise before his contract expires, the value of the futures contract will drop. Mr. Smith can then buy in his contract for a lower price then he received when he sold it, thereby making a profit on the difference. It is reported that some underwriters in the disastrous underwriting of $1 billion of IBM bonds in October 1979, mitigated their losses by selling Treasury bill futures.

MONEY-MARKET RATES

A comparison of the different rates in the money market appears on page 55. Perhaps the most important is the Federal funds rate, which is followed closely by students of the money market who believe that it is the most important reflection of current Federal Reserve policy. Two other money-market rates that should be described are the discount and the prime rates.

The *discount rate* is the rate that Federal Reserve banks charge their member banks for temporary short-term loans. The banks are discouraged from borrowing from the Federal Reserve to make loans or investments at a higher rate than they pay the Federal Reserve; neither are they allowed to borrow for a long period for capital purposes. Loans from the Federal Reserve are strictly for temporary purposes, for example, to meet unexpected deposit withdrawals and so forth. The discount rates are set by each of the 12 Federal Reserve banks but are subject to the approval of the board of governors of the Federal Reserve System. The discount rate is watched very carefully by students of the money market as it usually indicates a change in monetary policy of the Federal Reserve.

The Fed, early in 1974, began to tighten credit and raised its discount rate to 8% in April. But, by December of that year, it was generally conceded that the country had slipped into a recession.[2] The Fed eased its pressure and by January 1976 the discount rate had dropped to 5 1/2%. But in 1978–1979, in an attempt to stem the growth in the money supply and inflation, the discount rate was raised gradually to 13% by March 1980.

The prime rate might be defined as the lowest rate that all sound, well-established (creditworthy) companies must pay their banks for loans. The prime rate was first established in 1934. From 1934 to 1971, it was set by tacit agreement among banks. One large bank, usually in New York or Chicago, would set the rate, and other large banks throughout the country usually followed. Between 1934 and 1947 the rate was 1 1/2% but in later years it fluctuated, reaching 8 1/2% in June 1969 and declining irregularly to 5 3/4% in October 1971. In that month, Citibank adopted the so-called *floating* prime rate, basing its prime rate on a spread of half a percentage point above the 90-day commercial paper rate. At present, each bank has its own formula for setting the prime rate. Usually, it is set at 1 to 1 1/4 percentage points above some base rate, on the average three-month rate for Treasury bills, on the rate for CDs, or on the rate for prime short-term commercial paper.

The prime rate during the impending money panic of 1974 went to 12% in July. But, with the subsequent easing of credit, it declined to 6 1/4% by December 1976. In 1977 it rose gradually to 7 3/4% by year end. But, with the general tightening of credit in 1979 and 1980 it rose to 19.50% by March 31, 1980. The following is a tabulation of some of the most important money market rates on March 31, 1980

[2]This recession dated from the first quarter of 1973 through the first quarter of 1975.

Discount rate	13.00
Federal Funds rate	20.00
Brokers' Call Loans	19.50
Prime rate	19.50
Eurodollar rate*	18.99
Bankers' Acceptances*	17.70
Certificates of Deposit* (CDs)	17.63
Commercial Paper (dealer)*	16.81

*3 months.

American Depository Receipts (ADRs) are negotiable receipts stating that a specific number of shares of a foreign corporation are held by a foreign correspondent of a large New York City commercial bank. First introduced in the 1920s by the then Guaranty Trust and several investment bankers, ADRs are transferrable in the same way that stock certificates are. Dividends are paid to registered holders. The holder of the ADRs may also sell the underlying shares in the markets abroad or demand that they be delivered to him or her in the United States. Several hundred foreign companies have issued ADRs, and their total market value is reported to be several millions. Some quoted in *The Wall Street Journal* include Broken Hill Mining (Australia), Philips Gloelamphen (Holland), and Burmah Oil (Great Britain) as well as many South African and Japanese companies. The great advantage of ADRs is that they are more easily transferred than are the underlying foreign securities. Further they are quoted in dollars, and thus the confusion of quotations in foreign currency is avoided.

REAL ESTATE INVESTMENT TRUSTS (REITs)

As its name indicates, a REIT is essentially an investment company specializing in holding and managing various types of real estate. It gives the small investor an opportunity to invest in real estate by purchasing marketable shares in a diversified package of real estate. Further, salespersonnel of REITs represented that the properties would be managed by experts, that large profits would be realized through leverage and finally that protection against inflation would be obtained.

The representations of the salesmen of the REITs were not deliberately fraudulent but were over-enthusiastic.

Many REITs are Massachusetts trusts. The trustees of a REIT hold and manage the properties for the benefit of the certificate holders. They are required to use the care and judgment of a "prudent man." This many did not do as shown by the sad record of many REITs.

The modern history of REITs start with the Real Estate Investment Trust Act of 1960. Under this act, any company that obtains 75% of its income from mortgage interest and rents and has 75% of its assets invested in mortgages and real estate pays no federal income tax if it pays 90% of its earnings to its shareholders.

REIT trustees and managers must not deal directly in the management of the properties—that activity is left to professionals. At its inception each REIT must have at least 100 shareholders. More than 50% of the shares may not be owned by five or fewer individuals. A number of large REITs were sponsored by the major commercial banks, such as Chase Manhattan and Bank of America, by insurance companies, such as Equitable Life and Connecticut General Life and by brokerage houses, such as Sutro and Merrill Lynch.

There are three main classifications of the activities of REITs:

1. *Mortgage investment trusts* (MITs), which specialize in the purchase of long-term mortgages on all types of property. Sometimes the mortgages were sweetened by the provision that the mortgagee would participate in the sales of the stores above a certain level.
2. *Equity ownership of properties*, which yields income from rents including the ownership of apartments, private homes, motels, shopping centers, and so forth.
3. *Short-term real estate construction and development loans*, which were made by a number of REITs. These loans run three to five years and as their name implies cover the construction of a building, after which time the loan is funded on a long-term basis to a pension fund or to an institution.

    Some REITs are engaged primarily in construction loans, some in the purchase of mortgages, and some in the purchase of properties. But, often, a firm will combine two or even three of these activities.

Between 1960 and 1968, only about 20 REITs were formed with total assets of about $200 million. But, starting in 1970, a boom in REITs took place. Commercial banks, life insurance companies, and brokerage firms were very positive on the merits of REITs. The shares were selling like mad, and by 1974 there were about 145 REITs with total assets of $20 billion. But this was the year of "stagflation." There were rising prices and a faltering economy, but, worst of all for the REITs, there were sharply rising short-term money rates. This was a deliberate policy on the part of the Federal Reserve, to try to stem inflation. Now, basically, a REIT makes its money to a large extent on the spread between its cost of money—raised by bonds, bank loans, commercial paper—*and* the interest and rents that it receives on its investments in mortgages and construction loans and in real estate.

Consequently, the mortgage trusts were hit hard. They had floated some long-term debt but had also borrowed heavily on a short-term basis from banks and through sales of commercial paper. Short-term loan rates soared to 12% in some cases, but the REITs were getting only about 9% on their long-term mortgages.

Short-term real estate construction REITs were also in trouble. With inflation, construction costs went up. Contractors had severe cost overruns, and many failed. Even when the REITs held income-bearing properties the recession caused many vacancies and financial distress.

In fact the REIT industry as a whole was in deep trouble. The banks tried to bail themselves out by making swaps of properties and carrying the REIT loans as "nonperforming." But many REITs failed. The worst was the Chase Manhattan Mortgage Company, sponsored by Chase Manhattan Bank. In any event, total assets of REITs dropped from about $20 billion in 1974 to $13 in 1978. For many, a large percentage of their loans had gone into default.

A few sound companies, about 60, have survived, and most of these are still paying dividends. The managements of these REITs feel that they can also survive the present (June 1979) period of high money rates and the 1979–1980 recession. They have liquidated their short-term construction loans and have been more cautious about long-term commitments. The REITs managed by large life insurance companies seem to have fared best. They have been experts in real estate matters for years and did not fall into the traps that many others did. Life insurance company REITs are quoted on the New York Stock Exchange as are several others. Some are quoted on the American Stock Exchange and a few are traded in the over-the-counter market.

On June 5, 1979, 16 REITs with about $2.4 billion of assets had an average market price of 18 3/4 and an average yield of 8.43%.

In 1972, the National Association of Securities Dealers enacted rules requiring that sales of REITs should be made only to persons reasonably expected to be in the 50% tax bracket or with a net worth of at least $50,000. A wise rule!

A qualified REIT is taxed in substantially the same manner as a regulated investment company is. Undistributed earnings in excess of 10% are taxed at regular rates. Net operating losses can be carried over for eight years after they were incurred.

REVIEW QUESTIONS

1. Describe Treasury bills and explain how they may be purchased and how they are traded. What is their tax status?
2. What are the maturities, the dollar quotations, and the methods of offering of U.S. Treasury notes and bonds?
3. What are "flower bonds"?
4. Describe the activities and the security of the obligations of:
   a. Federal Land Banks
   b. Federal Home Loan Banks
   c. Federal National Mortgage Association
   d. Government National Mortgage Association.
5. Compare and contrast the role of the U.S. Treasury and that of the Federal Reserve System.
6. Describe the important institutions and instruments of the money market.
7. What are ADRs?
8. Describe REITs and explain why they got into difficulty.

TRUE AND FALSE QUESTIONS

1. All U.S. government securities are exempt from: *True*   *False*
   a.   federal income taxes   _____   _____
   b.   state taxes   _____   _____
   c.   capital gains taxes   _____   _____
   d.   estate taxes.   _____   _____
2. All of the following U.S. government securities are traded on the over-the-counter securities markets *except:*   *True*   *False*
   a.   U.S. Treasury bills   _____   _____
   b.   U.S. Treasury certificates   _____   _____
   c.   U.S. Treasury notes   _____   _____
   d.   U.S. Treasury bonds.   _____   _____
3. The following are the characteristics of the marketable obligations of the U.S. government: *True*   *False*
   a.   All marketable obligations except Treasury
        bills are quoted in 1/32nd of a point.   _____   _____
   b.   Income is taxed by the federal government
        but is exempt from state taxes.   _____   _____
   c.   There is no right of suit in default.   _____   _____
   d.   Security depends on the wealth of the
        country and willingness to pay.   _____   _____
   e.   All of the above.   _____   _____

4.   The role of the U.S. Treasury includes all of the following *except:*

		True	False
a.	managing the debt of the country	_____	_____
b.	administrating the budget of the United States	_____	_____
c.	defending the dollar	_____	_____
d.	managing the flow of credit in the money market.	_____	_____

5.   The basic duties of the Federal Reserve System include all of the following *except:*

		True	False
a.	controlling credit	_____	_____
b.	disciplining the member banks	_____	_____
c.	lending to member banks	_____	_____
d.	setting the prime rate.	_____	_____

6.   An increase in interest rates can:

		True	False
a.	cause a drop in the bond market	_____	_____
b.	hurt, in particular, the public utility stocks	_____	_____
c.	bring big profits to commercial banks.	_____	_____

7.   Federal funds:

		True	False
a.	are an abbreviated term meaning Federal funds at the Federal Reserve Bank	_____	_____
b.	give the holder immediate credit at the Federal Reserve Banks	_____	_____
c.	transactions are a small part of the money market	_____	_____
d.	rate is the most sensitive indicator of the money-market rates.	_____	_____

8.   Commercial paper is:

		True	False
a.	an unsecured short-term obligation of a corporation	_____	_____
b.	virtually a riskless security, because it is an unconditional promise to pay a corporation	_____	_____
c.	held in large amounts by many banks and money-market funds	_____	_____
d.	often backed by bank lines of credit.	_____	_____

9.   REITs suffered financial setbacks because of:

		True	False
a.	lack of sponsorship by strong financial institutions	_____	_____
b.	unexpected high interest rates in the 1973–1974 period	_____	_____
c.	falling economy	_____	_____
d.	rising construction costs.	_____	_____

4

Municipal Securities

Municipals is a general term applied to the obligations of states, cities, towns, school districts, and statutory authorities. Municipal bonds are sold to raise money to build public buildings, state roads, schools, subways, and streets. (U.S. government securities are not classed as municipals.)

The most important characteristic of a municipal bond is the fact that the interest is exempt from federal income taxes. The exemption from taxation rests on a number of common law cases, the most famous being *McCulloch* v. *Maryland*, 1819. Also, the present income tax laws do *not* require taxpayers to report their income from municipal obligations; they may exclude it from their taxable income. Of course, Congress could change the laws and the Supreme Court of the United States could decide that municipal bonds *are* taxable. In other words, the exemption from federal income taxes is not written on the face of the bond and is not guaranteed. Whenever a municipal bond is issued, a law firm is asked to give a written legal opinion on the legality of the securities. This opinion says, among other things, that the bonds are legally issued and binding obligations of the state, city or local government. Also the legal opinion states: "in the opinion of counsel the interest on these bonds is exempt from all federal income taxes under existing statutes as thus far construed by the courts." A copy of this legal opinion *must* go with every transaction of municipal bonds. Otherwise, the bond is not good delivery. (In recent years, however, the legal opinion has been printed on the back of the bonds.)

Sometimes municipal bonds are called "tax-emempt" securities. This is a misleading title. Municipal securities are not exempt from inheritance taxes, nor are they exempt from state income taxes in many states. Nevertheless, exemption from federal income taxes has a distinct advantage not only to an individual in the high tax brackets but to corporations. An easy way to measure this advantage is *to take the difference between the tax bracket of the individual or corporation and 100 and divide it into the yield on the municipal bond to be purchased.*

Suppose that an individual is in the 30% income tax bracket. We would then subtract 30 from 100, which equals 70 (or the *supplement* of that person's tax bracket). Further, suppose that said individual can buy a 6.50% municipal bond that is exempt from federal income taxes. To measure the advantage, the buyer would divide 6.50% by 70, which equals 9.29%. Thus an investor in the 30% bracket would have to buy a corporate bond with a yield of 9.29% to equal the 6.50% yield on the municipal bond. The following summarizes this calculation:

For individuals in the 30% tax bracket:

Municipal Bond Yield		Supplement of Tax Bracket		Corporate Yield Equivalent
6.50%	÷	70%	=	9.29%

The mathematics can be proved by assuming the individual buys a 9.29% taxable security and applies the 30% tax rate. This would be 30% of 9.29%, or 2.79%. Then 9.29% less 2.79% would equal 6.50%. If the investor is in the 50% bracket and was offered a 6.50% municipal security, the corporate equivalent would be 13.00%. A corporation in the 46% bracket would find a 6.50% municipal bond equivalent to a yield of 12.04%, or 6.50% divided by 54%.

Not all municipal securities are exempt from *state* personal property and *state* income taxes; this depends on the state. Some states tax the securities of other states but not their own; some states tax not only their own but also out-of-state municipals. Pennsylvania, New York, and Virginia, for example, exempt all their own but tax most out-of-state issues. (One exception is the obligations of Puerto Rico.)

Municipal bonds are not riskless securities. During the Depression years of 1930–1941, millions of dollars' worth of bonds of cities, towns, and districts defaulted in their principal and interest, particularly in the states of Michigan, New Jersey, Arkansas, Florida, and Oklahoma. But most of these municipalities paid their bonds at maturity.

Almost all the revenues of municipalities and states are derived from taxes. The largest percentage of the income of states is from taxes on personal and corporate incomes. Cities, towns, and school districts rely more on real estate taxes. The power to tax is a large factor in reducing risk of default. General obligation municipal bonds usually carry a lower interest rate than do corporate bonds owing to this power to tax and to the exemption from federal income taxes.

There are several types of municipal securities. These include general obligation, special tax, special assessment, revenue, and others.

General obligations (or G.O. bonds) are backed by the full faith and credit of the state, city, or town of issue. Municipalities issuing these bonds usually have unlimited taxing power. Further, most general obligations require voter approval.

Some general obligations are limited as to the amount of taxes that can be levied to pay the principal and interest. For example, a general obligation bond might be backed by a full-faith pledge of the municipality, but the taxes that could be levied on real estate might be *limited* to a stated number of dollars per thousand as in the case of some municipalities in Alabama, Ohio, and Texas.

Special tax securities might be issued but with the interest and principal payable from some specific source such as cigarette taxes, excise taxes, or sales taxes.

Special assessment securities are issued by a district to construct a public improvement, such as a sewer or a water system. The interest and principal of these securities are paid by special assessment, that is, by taxes on the residents of the district. Sometimes the credit of the county or municipality is also pledged.

MUNICIPAL REVENUE SECURITIES

Statutory authorities are political subdivisions of the state. As such they issue revenue securities that are exempt from federal income taxes. They issue bonds to finance the construction of turnpikes, bridges, waterworks, airports, college dormitories, or public utilities that are or will be income producing. The main difference between a revenue obligation and a general obligation bond is that in the former the payment of interest and principal usually depends on the income or revenue of an electric public utility or a turnpike being financed. Revenues include those from tolls on turnpikes and bridges, electricity charges by public utilities, and rents from public housing. Sometimes special taxes are set aside to help these projects. Sometimes, however, states or other public bodies guarantee the principal and/or interest of revenue obligations. Because revenue securities are usually issued by authorities or agencies of the state, interest payments are also exempt from federal income taxes.

For the most part revenue securities do not have to be approved by the electorate of the state. They must, however, be approved by state legislatures. Revenue bonds are not subject to debt limitations because they are not obligations of the states or their political subdivisions. They are issued by authorities that in turn have been created by states, cities, counties, and so forth.

Tax anticipation notes are usually issued by cities in anticipation of tax collections. They are short-term obligations either payable at a fixed maturity and guaranteed by the municipality or maturing by numbers as the taxes are collected. In these cases, the security depends on the amount of the taxes collected being equal to the notes.

There are also *bond anticipation notes*, which are issued in anticipation of the flotation of bonds. Finally, there are *revenue anticipation notes*, which are issued in anticipation of the receipt of revenues from the federal and the state governments. It was the excessive overissue of tax, revenue, and bond anticipation notes that brought on the financial crisis in New York City. Because New York could not meet the maturities of billions of dollars of short-term paper and because it could not sell new paper, the Municipal Assistance Corporation, "Big Mack," was formed to bail the city out—at least temporarily.

New housing bonds are issued under the New Housing Act of 1949. They are tax exempt by act of Congress and thus can be said to be the only truly tax-exempt security in existence. They are a general obligation of local housing authorities and are issued to build apartments. The rents are used to pay the operating costs, the interest, and the principal. Further, the bonds are virtually guaranteed by the U.S. government as Congress is supposed to appropriate money to make up any deficit toward the payment of principal and interest. In 1953 Attorney General Brownell gave the opinion that the full faith and credit of the United States had been pledged. Since that time the bonds have been considered prime investments and carry a Aaa rating by Moody's.

Industrial development bonds (IDB) are issued by states and municipalities to finance capital expenditures of private industries. The purpose is to attract private business and to develop the area through increased employment. The municipality or state sells the bonds, which are tax exempt. The proceeds are used to build a new plant, which in turn is leased to the industrial company with good credit standing. Under the terms of the lease, the cash flow was originally used to pay the interest and principal of the bonds. But in 1968 the tax exemption of any new IDBs was taken away *except* for bonds up to $5 million. Also exempt are projects for sewage or solid-waste disposal facilities, air or water pollution facilities, and other purposes connected with public welfare. As an example, a *pollution control bond* was sold in 1976 by the County of Deer Park Lodge, Montana. These were 6 1/2% bonds due 1996 and guaranteed by Anaconda Copper Company.

Moral obligation bonds were brought out during the administration of Governor Rockefeller of New York State in the late 1960s and early 1970s. A bond attorney named John Mitchell proposed that the state issue, without voter approval, bonds for specific purposes (e.g., to develop housing). Agencies were set up and bonds were sold by these agencies. Further, it was implied that, in the event of a shortfall of fixed charges, the state would make up the difference. On the basis of this implied guarantee, the agency bonds received a favorable rating by the services. But the near collapse of the Urban Development Corporation disillusioned many investors.

Tax-free mortgage bonds, which provide cheap money for mortgages or the repair of houses, were first introduced in 1978 in Minneapolis and in Chicago. Here the bonds are sold by towns and cities and the proceeds are turned over to the thrift institutions, mainly savings and loan associations. These institutions in turn lend the funds to home owners who make monthly payments to the institutions. In April 1979 it was estimated that over 1 billion of these bonds had been sold by 33 localities. The bonds seem secure as they are supported by the credit of the municipality plus the payments of principal and interest by the householder who has pledged his or her home. The Department of Housing and Urban Development and the U.S. Treasury do not approve of these loans.

ANALYSIS OF STATE, CITY, TOWN, AND STATUTORY AUTHORITY BONDS

The Market

The usual trading unit for municipal bonds is $10,000. Less than $10,000 is considered an odd lot. In fact an odd-lot municipal bond has a very poor market and is hard to sell or buy. Thus municipal bonds are not suitable for small investors. For one seeking tax protection, however, a tax-exempt mutual fund is suggested.

The issuer's name has some influence on the price of a bond. Clearly, the name of a big, affluent state government with a Aaa rating such as Texas, Ohio, or Illinois is far more attractive compared with a not so rich state or a small city. Also a state may lose its top rating if it comes to the market too often and increases its debt to limits not deemed prudent. This was true of New York and Massachusetts. Then there are the "museum pieces" such as Rochester, N.Y. and Austin, Texas. These are cities with high credit rating that seldom borrow. Cities with bad names that should be avoided include Cleveland, Oh. and perhaps Newark, N.J. and Detroit, Mich.

In default, issues sell flat; that is, interest does not accrue. When a bond is selling flat, the buyer pays only the agreed sales price and commission, if any.

A sinking fund can also help the market of a bond as the credit of the municipality improves as the bonds are retired. Most important of all in determining the marketability of a municipal bond are the ratings by the services (see page 33).

Too often, however, the investor in both corporate and municipal bonds looks only to the bond ratings. The down-grading of a rating by either Moody's Investors Service or Standard & Poor's can cost a municipality millions of dollars due to the decline in the price of its securities. But it should be stressed that the rating services are not infallible.

The maturity date also has an influence on the market price of a municipal or corporate bond. For example, on November 17, 1979 the New York City (certainly a weak credit) 3s due June 1, 1980 were quoted at 96. If these bonds had been due in 20 years, they would be quoted nearer 60.

Call prices sometimes influence the market, particularly in periods of low interest rates. This applies to term revenue bonds. Most serial and regular municipal bonds are not callable and do not have sinking funds. But the balloon maturities of some revenue bonds sometimes may be called or partially called through a sinking fund. (A balloon maturity is a large proportion of a serial issue coming due in the final year.)

Quotations of municipal securities are hard to find. There are a few quotations of revenue bonds in *The Wall Street Journal* and in *The New York Times.* But to get a quotation on most municipal securities the investor must call a broker. Most brokers subscribe to the Blue List Publishing Company (a subsidiary of Standard & Poor's). *The Blue List* records the municipal offerings of the various brokers and dealers, the amount offered, the yield or price, and the name and telephone number of the broker. Serial revenue and most municipal bonds are quoted on a yield basis, to enable traders and investors to make quick comparisons. Because there are thousands of municipalities and many maturities, it would lead to endless confusion to try to appraise each issue on a dollar basis. Term revenue bonds are usually priced in dollars. Municipal and corporate bonds are issued in bearer or registered form. The denomination is $1,000.

State

A state is considered sovereign; thus it cannot be sued by its creditors without its consent. There are exceptions, however. New York State, for example, grants the right to certain suits against the state.

Therefore, the investor should investigate the past record of debt payment—willingness to pay as well as the state's wealth, population, industries—that is, the state's ability to pay. A good measure of wealth is the per capita personal income of the various states. For instance, the per capita income of New York State in 1982 was $12,328, whereas the Mississippi per capita income was only $7,782 compared with a national average of $11,059. The real test is the relationship of per capita debt to income.

City and Town

Sometimes called municipal bonds, these obligations are issued by cities, towns, school districts, and other political subdivisions of the states. The states must approve, and often limit, the issue of bonds by cities and towns, however. Unlike states and the federal government, cities may be sued on default of principal or interest payment. Yet their analysis depends, as in state and federal obligations, on their ability and willingness to pay. Not all cities and towns have as good a record as the federal government. In the 1930s, there were large numbers of defaults of municipal obligations, particularly in the South.

In analyzing the credit of a municipality, the investor should consider the growth of the population and the type and diversification of its industries. Obviously too great a concentration in one industry is not good. It is important for the investor to know the present and past attitude of the municipal administration toward debt. Have they always paid their obligations promptly? What is the trend of the debt? Are there any large maturities on the horizon? Is there any tax limitation on real estate taxes? What are their non tax revenues? Finally, what is the current tax collection record? (about 97% should be collected each year) The type of city government may also be important. A city manager, as in Cincinnati, is often considered good; less favorable is a strong mayor and city council, as in New York.

A check should be made of the overlapping debt. This is debt for which the municipality is responsible but is not listed as direct debt. Chicago has a small direct debt but is responsible for the debt of Cook County. One of the few favorable points about New York City obligations is that the city has no overlapping debt. Inherent hazards are obvious. California municipal securities usually have a higher yield due to possible earthquakes in that area; the same is true for New Jersey and Pennsylvania, on the basis of possible floods.

Several important financial ratios should be considered by the analyst. The first is net debt per capita. The average debt per capita in 1978 was $629, with a high debt of $1,186 per capita reported by New York City compared with $490 for Dallas. The second ratio is the percentage of debt to full value of the property. Here statistics are somewhat unreliable as it is difficult to assess the full value of a city's property. Some have set this standard at not much more than 10%. The third ratio is the percentage of fixed charges (interest and sinking fund payments) to total budget income. This should be not over 25%. An important point, not a ratio, is the fact that the budget itself should be studied to determine if it is balanced without any gimmicks (such as floating debt to pay current expenses).

As we enter the 1980s, the big cities in particular are faced with serious problems of heavy relief costs, continued wage demands from powerful unions, pollution, racial unrest, and population movement to the suburbs. Even more serious is the movement of big industry to the suburbs. Attempts have been made to cut costs, particularly in the operation of schools and hospitals, but political pressure makes such cutbacks almost impossible to effect. In short, big cities face lower revenues and higher costs. These factors account for the high yields on many big-city obligations. Therefore, these securities should be bought only by those in the high tax bracket who can afford to take risks.

MUNICIPAL REVENUE SECURITIES OR STATUTORY AUTHORITY BONDS

To analyze a revenue obligation, it is necessary to look, first, at the nature of the project and, second, at the financial figures. If the project is a turnpike, one should examine the type of traffic—too many trucks wear out the roadway, for example. Large cities should be reasonably close, as long hauls are less profitable. The New York Thruway, serving many cities, has high density and high interest coverage. The Kansas Turnpike has lower traffic density and interest coverage. The West Virginia Turnpike had poor traffic density and was forced to defer interest payments. As of March 31 1980 West Virginia Turnpike bonds were selling at 49.

The indentures of revenue securities have very important covenants, the most important being the rate covenant. This provides that the administrative body of the authority, commission, and so on will set and maintain rates sufficient to allow the body to cover interest charges as well to assure maintenance, insurance, and operating expenses. Before buying a new revenue issue, careful study should be made of the engineering report to see if the project is feasible. The indenture provides for issuance of additional bonds should the entity need to expand. This means that the indenture is a limited open-end obligation.

Study should also be made of the flow of funds under the net revenue pledge. This would include the operation and the maintenance fund, the bond service account, the sinking fund, and the reserve maintenance fund. This last item is particularly important for a turnpike. Most of the time, revenue bonds are issued in series, the first coming due in about five years and every year thereafter until maturity when there is in most cases a balloon maturity.

Above all, the potential investor should examine the coverage of interest and sinking fund requirements. A desired ratio of overall coverage for a turnpike is 1.25 times and at least 2.0 times for interest charges alone.

Most electric public utility revenue securities can be analyzed according to the analysis criteria for privately owned utilities. Consideration should be given to the territory served, the different types of customers, and such financial factors as interest coverage and capitalization. Interest coverage should be about 2.0 times and debt not more than 55% of capitalization. One of the best known electric public utilities is the Los Angeles Department of Water and Power (DEWAPS), which has high interest coverage and is rated Aa by Moodys Investors Service.

BOND INSURANCE

Some municipal bonds are insured by the American Bond Assurance Corporation and some are insured by the Municipal Bond Insurance Association. Yields on insured bonds can be as much as 2.0% cheaper and the bonds get a much higher rating. Over a billion bonds have been insured. But the insurance companies are very selective in choosing their risks. They would not, for example, insure New York City obligations.

PUBLIC INFORMATION

Financial information on municipals for the average investor and even for the professional is difficult to obtain. Moody's *Manual of U.S. Governments and Municipals* gives some information about most large issues. Sometimes, on offering a new issue, the municipality will give out a so-called "official statement," which does provide some information. But for years municipals were exempt from filing registration statements. Therefore, there was no review by the SEC and hence no prospectus given to investors. For the professional, Dun and Bradstreet writes extensive reports on a large number of municipals. There has been a great deal of agitation to force the municipalities to register and to adopt uniform accounting systems so that the investor can make comparisons and evaluate the security. Currently the Municipal Securities Rule Making Board is trying to set up rules and standards for new issues of municipalities. *The Daily Bond Buyer* has current news about municipalities as well as notices about new offerings. It is published five days a week.

UNDERWRITING OF STATE AND MUNICIPAL SECURITIES

Indicators and Services

The Blue List, mentioned earlier, publishes every business day the municipal offerings of the broker-dealers. In particular, it gives the dollar volume of the total municipal offerings advertised for sale.

The Bond Buyer is perhaps the most important publication devoted to municipal securities. Among its features are (1) indices of municipal bond prices, (2) listings of proposed bond issues, (3) the placement ratio for the week (the percentage of new municipal issues sold during the week), (4) municipal news, (5) the 30-day visible supply of new issues, and (6) invitations to bid on new municipal issues.

Other services include Moody's *Bond Survey*, which gives weekly municipal bond yields and municipal market comments. Also *White's Tax Exempt Market Ratings* should be mentioned. This manual is published every few years (the most recent was in 1979). Its ratings are based on the theory that the *market* rates the value of municipal securities. The user of this service is helped to rate an individual municipal security in relation to other securities. The manual is published by Interactive Data Services, a subsidiary of the Chase Manhattan Bank.

Sources of information on proposed sales include *The Wall Street Journal*, newsletters, and direct mail from the municipalities. *Munifacts*, a wire service, gives news on municipals, but the best source is *The Daily Bond Buyer*.

The Official Notice of Sale of a forthcoming issue is usually found in *The Daily Bond Buyer*. This includes (1) the date, place, and the time the bids must be submitted. A good-faith certified check must also be enclosed. Usually this amounts to about 2% of the issue. On rare occasions oral bids are made in auctions. (2) The amount of the bonds and the maturities of both serial and the term issues. (3) A statement of any limitation as to the coupon rate or the price. Many municipalities cannot sell securities at less than face value. (4) The determination of the winning bid. Usually this is on the basis of the lowest net interest cost. (5) A statement as to the liability for any miscellaneous costs. (6) The right of the municipality or state to reject any or all bids. Finally (7) the issuer agrees at its own expense to provide an unqualified legal opinion approving the legality of the issue.

The function of a bond attorney is very important in a municipal security offering. As explained on page 60, the bond attorney gives a legal opinion as to the tax status of the new issue and certifies as to the authority of the issue. The bond attorney examines the constitutionality of the issue to see if it has been properly approved and if it is within the debt limit of the issuer, checking to be sure there are no law suits outstanding against the issuer that might affect the legality of the securities. The bond attorney identifies and monitors the proper issuance procedures of the securities (i.e., competitive bidding might be required). He examines the bonds to be sure that the obligations are properly worded. Finally the bond attorney issues a written legal opinion.

Types of Groups

As in the underwriting of corporate securities, there are two types of underwritings: competitive and negotiated. Numerically there are many more competitive deals, but in dollars the negotiated deals are by far the greater.

Formation of an Underwriting Group

A group of investment bankers might decide to bid on a municipal issue in the same manner as for a corporate issue. There are historical groups and sometimes new groups are formed to bid. The account formation is similar in either case.

An agreement among underwriters is signed giving the manager of the group the authority to run the account, to allot securities to the members, to make sales for group account, and, if necessary, to stabilize the securities.

The account is usually an Eastern, or united, account. Here the liabilities of the members are joint and several. That is, each member is liable for the sale of the entire issue. The other type of account is a Western, or divided, account in which the member's liability is limited to his alloted share of the securities to be sold.

The allocation of the amount of securities to be sold by each member of the syndicate is handled by the manager. Each member in turn tries to obtain presale orders from his customers. The manager may make large group orders to institutional customers who may in turn decide which members of the group are to receive credit for the sales.

The determination of the syndicate bid involves some simple mathematics. Often the coupon, the maturities, and the size of each maturity are set by the issuer. The group decides the spread. Therefore, the syndicate must calculate the price that will be high enough to win the bonds but at the same time will be low enough to sell them to their customers. Usually the offering circular states that awards will be made on the basis of ANIC (average net interest cost). This is the traditional formula and is as follows:

$$\text{ANIC} = \frac{\text{Total interest payable over the life of the bonds} - \begin{array}{c}\text{discount on sale}\\ \text{or}\\ \text{premium on sale}\end{array}}{\text{Amount of bonds sold} \times \text{average life of bonds}}$$

For example, assume that a municipality sells $30,000,000 bonds at 101, the interest to be paid over the years is $20,000,000, and the average life of the bonds is 10 years. The average net interest cost would be calculated as follows:

$$\text{ANIC} = \frac{\$20,000,000 - \$300,000}{\$30,000,000 \times 10} = \frac{\$19,700,000}{\$300,000,000} = 0.0656$$

There are other methods of calculating net interest cost, but the one shown is the traditional method.

As soon as a bid has been accepted, a public offering is made of the securities on the basis of the dollar price as determined by the syndicate. This consists of the price paid to the issuer plus the spread. From this spread must be paid the manager's fee and the expenses of the deal. The residual is distributed to the members of the group. Finally, the securities are delivered

New Issues

$81,202,400
Illinois Housing Development Authority

$65,740,000
Multi-Family Housing Bond Anticipation Notes (Issue 190)
Interest Rate 8.45%   Priced to Yield 7.85%

$11,470,000
Housing Development Bond Anticipation Notes (Issue 191)
Interest Rate 8.45%   Priced to Yield 7.85%

$3,992,400
Construction Loan Notes (Issue 41)
Interest Rate 7.95%   Priced to Yield 7.35%

(Accrued interest, if any, to be added)

Each issue of the Notes is dated November 29, 1979 and due April 15, 1981.

In the opinion of Bond Counsel, interest on the Notes of each issue is exempt from federal income taxes under existing law (except no opinion is expressed as to interest on any Note during the time it is held by a person who is a substantial user of facilities financed by proceeds of that issue of Notes or a related person, within the meaning of Section 103(b)(8) of the Internal Revenue Code of 1954, as amended). Under the Illinois Housing Development Act, in its present form, income from the Notes of each issue is exempt from all taxes of the State of Illinois or its political subdivisions, except for estate, transfer and inheritance taxes.

The Authority has no taxing power. The State of Illinois is not liable on the Notes and the Notes are not a debt of the State of Illinois.

Each issue of the Notes is subject to the approval of legality by Isham, Lincoln & Beale, Chicago, Illinois, Bond Counsel. Certain legal matters are subject to the approval of Willkie Farr & Gallagher, New York, New York, Counsel to the Underwriters.

Smith Barney, Harris Upham & Co.
Incorporated

Continental Bank	**First Chicago**	**Harris Trust and Savings Bank**
Continental Illinois National Bank and Trust Company of Chicago	The First National Bank of Chicago	

The Northern Trust Company   **Salomon Brothers**

Bache Halsey Stuart Shields   Bank of America NT & SA   **Bankers Trust Company**
Incorporated

A. G. Becker   William Blair & Company   Clayton Brown & Associates, Inc.
Warburg Paribas Becker

The Chase Manhattan Bank, N.A.   Chemical Bank   Citibank, N.A.

Ehrlich-Bober & Co., Inc.   The First Boston Corporation   The First National Bank of Boston

Merrill Lynch White Weld Capital Markets Group   Morgan Guaranty Trust Company of New York
Merrill Lynch, Pierce, Fenner & Smith Incorporated

November 9, 1979

along with the legal opinion to the buyers. Accrued interest to the date of delivery is paid by the buyers, as they collect the full half-year coupon on the first interest payment date.

MUNICIPAL SECURITIES REGULATION

For years municipal broker-dealers were exempt from regulation by the SEC. Also new issues of municipal securities did not have to be registered with the SEC. Broker-dealers, however, were always subject to anti-fraud laws.

Under the Securities Reform Act of 1975, the *Municipal Securities Rule Making Board* (MSRB) was established. This is an independent self-regulating organization. The SEC appointed a board of fifteen members— five municipal broker-dealers, five bank municipal dealers, and five representing the public. Under the Securities Reform Act, all municipal broker-dealers must register with the SEC. A municipal broker-dealer already registered under Section 15 of the Exchange Act (1934) need not reregister. If municipal trading is conducted by a separately identifiable department or division of a bank, the department or division, not the bank, is subject to regulation as a municipal dealer. The SEC oversees all the rules and regulations of the MSRB.

The most important rules of the MSRB at present concern:

1. the professional standards, experience, training, and competence of the municipal broker-dealers
2. the prevention of fraudulent and deceptive devices
3. the suitability of recommendations
4. disclosure of the municipal broker-dealers' connection with a new issue
5. the tests to determine the eligibility of applicants for registration
6. periodic examination of broker-dealers by the National Association of Securities Dealers
7. records and books required
8. disciplinary action—prior to the entry of an order of the investigation of a bank dealer, the appropriate banking authorities must be notified (i.e., the Federal Reserve banks, etc.)
9. customers' confirmations
10. quotations and sales reports
11. uniform practices

REVIEW QUESTIONS

1. What is the basis for exemption from federal income taxes of municipal securities?
2. If a client in the 30% tax bracket is offered a 6.30% municipal bond,

should the client buy it, if comparable quality corporate bonds yield 10%? Explain.

3. Describe the most important types of municipal obligations.
4. For what purposes are municipal revenue securities issued? What are their advantages?
5. Describe (a) tax anticipation notes, (b) new housing bonds, and (c) industrial development bonds.
6. Discuss the factors that influence prices of municipal securities.
7. In analyzing the general obligation of a medium-sized city, what economic and political factors should an investor consider? What ratios?
8. What economic and financial factors should be analyzed before investing in a municipal revenue security?
9. What are the functions of a municipal bond attorney?
10. Describe the formation of a municipal underwriting group. What is the traditional manner of determining a syndicate bid? Give the formula.
11. Where are the best sources of information for (a) background financial information concerning municipals and (b) forthcoming issues?
12. What are eight areas for which the Municipal Securities Rule Making Board has issued regulations?

TRUE AND FALSE QUESTIONS

1. Muncipal securities are exempt from federal income taxes because:

		True	False
a.	state laws provide for the tax exemption of all municipals	____	____
b.	tax exemption is stated on the face of the bond	____	____
c.	on the basis of common law and the federal income tax law	____	____

2. An investor in the 40% tax bracket is offered a 6.60% municipal bond. Which of the following yields after taxes would exactly equal the 6.60% municipal yield?

		True	False
a.	10.00%	____	____
b.	10.50%	____	____
c.	11.00%	____	____
d.	11.50%	____	____

3. Municipal revenue securities are usually issued to construct all of the following *except:*

		True	False
a.	turnpikes	____	____
b.	electric public utilities	____	____
c.	bridges	____	____
d.	railroads	____	____

4. The best way to find a quotation on a general obligation municipal
   bond is: *True*   *False*
   a.   *The Blue List*   _____   _____
   b.   *The Wall Street Journal*   _____   _____
   c.   *The New York Times*   _____   _____
   d.   *The Bond Buyer.*   _____   _____

5. The following are important considerations in the selection of a municipal security: *True*   *False*
   a.   growth and nature of the population   _____   _____
   b.   trend of debt   _____   _____
   c.   tax collection rate   _____   _____
   d.   size of the city.   _____   _____

6. Financial ratios used in the analysis of a city obligation include all the
   following *except:*   *True*   *False*
   a.   net debt per capita   _____   _____
   b.   percentage of debt to full value   _____   _____
   c.   percentage of fixed charges to budget income   _____   _____
   d.   ratio of current assets to current liabilities.   _____   _____

7. The functions of a municipal bond attorney are as follows:
                                                               True   *False*
   a.   examination of the constitutionality of the
        issue   _____   _____
   b.   certification that the issue is exempt from
        federal income taxes   _____   _____
   c.   search for possible law suits against the issuer   _____   _____
   d.   issuance of guarantee that the municipality can
        pay the interest and principal on the bonds.   _____   _____

8. Assume a municipality sells $25,000,000 of bonds at 102, with interest
   to be paid over the years of $18,000,000 and an average life of 11 years.
   The following is the ANIC: *True*   *False*
   a.   .06252   _____   _____
   b.   .06301   _____   _____
   c.   .06363   _____   _____
   d.   .06414.   _____   _____

5

INVESTMENT

COMPANIES

An investment company is either a corporation or a trust through which investors pool their funds to obtain diversification and supervision of their investments. Simply put, an investment company is a financial institution engaged in the business of investing in securities.

Not every company that invests in securities is an investment company, however. Many kinds of institutions, financial and otherwise, with a variety of objectives in mind, invest at least a part of the funds they own, or hold, in securities.

Banks buy investments, for example, but their main functions are to make loans, provide checking accounts facilities, and safeguard the deposits of their customers. Operating nonfinancial companies seldom buy the securities of other companies. A holding company does buy securities of other companies, but their main objective is control, not investment.

Insurance companies buy tremendous quantities of securities, but insurance companies are in the business of insurance, not the business of investing. The investment activities of insurance companies are designed to provide, in part, the dollars needed to pay the claims and annuities they are obligated to pay their policyholders and to provide a return to stockholders, if they are stock companies.

The investment company, however, has investing as its sole business activity and its sole reason for existence. Thus, investment companies are among the few types of institutions that spend all their time and effort on investment activities.

An investment company is generally a business corporation holding a charter. A closed-end investment company may issue bonds and preferred stocks. An open-end company might borrow temporarily from banks (see Investment Company Act of 1940, page 399). The typical investment company, however, obtains its investment funds by selling its own stock. The money thus obtained is reinvested by the investment company in a large variety of securities issued by other corporations.

The list of the securities purchased and held by the investment company is called its *investment portfolio.* The prices of investment company shares are related to the market value of the securities in the investment portfolio.

DEVELOPMENT OF INVESTMENT COMPANIES IN THE UNITED STATES

The concept of the investment company originated with King William of Belgium in 1822. In the 1870s several such companies were formed in Scotland, and in 1893 the Boston Personal Property Trust was formed. In the period 1924–1929 several closed-end investment companies were formed, but the crash of 1929 and its aftermath caused Congress to investigate the securities industry. The result was the passage of the Investment Company Act of 1940. This act, along with the Securities Act of 1933, provided the basic framework for the rules and regulations under which investment companies operate today.

DEFINITION AND CLASSIFICATION OF INVESTMENT COMPANIES

The Investment Company Act of 1940, as amended August 10, 1954, classifies and defines the various types of investment companies and establishes the requirements for their regulation. The act divides investment companies into three principal classes: face-amount certificate companies, unit investment trusts, and management companies. The act defines these three types of investment companies as follows:

1. "Face-amount certificate company" is an investment company that engages or proposes to engage in the business of issuing face-amount certificates of the installment type or has been engaged in such business and has any such certificate outstanding.
2. "Unit investment trust" is an investment company that
   a. is organized under a trust indenture, contract of custodianship or agency, or similar instrument,
   b. does not have a board of directors, and
   c. issues only redeemable securities, each of which represents

an undivided interest in a unit of specified securities, but
does not include a voting trust.[1]

3. "Management company" is any investment company other than a
face amount certificate company or a unit investment trust.

Face-amount certificate companies, as their name signifies, have a face
value payable at the end of an installment period. The principal and interest
are guaranteed and are usually backed by a specific asset such as real estate.
There are only about seven relatively small face-amount companies.

Unit investment trusts are more common. Unit investment trusts issue
redeemable shares. They are fixed trusts that issue shares representing units
of a particular portfolio. The tax-exempt or municipal bond funds are unit
investment trusts. They are, in effect, mutual funds that invest in municipal
securities. Units are sold for $1,000 each. But, since 1976, municipal mutual
investment companies have been much more popular (see page 86).

A second type of trust has as its assets shares of a particular investment company. Planholders in such a trust purchase trust shares under a
contractual plan. In fact, most contractual plans are unit investment trusts.

The management companies are by far the most common type in
operation today. There are two basically different types of management
investment companies. One is the closed-end investment company. The
other is known as the open-end investment company or, more popularly, as
the mutual fund. These companies are called management companies because they manage a diversified portfolio of various types of securities in accordance with certain specified investment objectives.

The Investment Company Act of 1940 defines these two types of
management companies as follows:

1. "Open-end company" is a management company that offers for
sale or has outstanding any redeemable security of which it is the
issuer.

2. "Closed-end company" is any management company other than
an open-end company.

Management companies are divided further into *diversified* companies and
nondiversified companies.

Practically all mutual funds and the majority of the closed-end investment companies are registered as diversified companies under the Investment Company Act of 1940. To qualify as a registered diversified company,
an investment company must have 75% more of its total assets invested so
that:

1. not more than 5% of its assets is invested in any one corporation
and

[1]Most contractual plans are unit investment trusts.

2. not more than 10% of the voting securities of any corporation is
    held by the investment company.

Specifically, the Investment Company Act of 1940 indicates that a
diversified company means a management company that meets the
following requirements:

1. All new companies must be registered with the SEC and have a
    minimum net worth of at least $100,000.
2. Investment companies may borrow from banks provided that
    loans are covered by 300% of collateral.
3. At least 75 percentum of the value of its total assets is represented
    by cash and cash items (including receivables). Government
    securities, securities of other investment companies, and other
    securities for the purpose of this calculation (are) limited in
    respect of any one issuer to an amount not greater in value than 5
    percentum of the value of the total assets of such management
    company and to not more than 10 percentum of the outstanding
    voting securities of such issuer.

The foregoing definition divides the assets of diversified investment
companies into two components. One segment, which must amount to at
least 75% of total assets, must be diversified. The other segment, which
may amount to as much as 25% of total assets, need not be diversified. This
25% of the investment company's assets may be invested in a single
security. This enables a diversified investment company to commit substantial portions of its resources to special situations without losing its
diversified status.

The investment portfolio of the average investment company consists
for the most part of common stocks, although, from time to time as investment policies change, short-term government securities, CDs, and commercial paper are held. Some funds hold bonds and even preferred stocks.
Each holder of one or more shares has an undivided interest in the portfolio
of the fund and has voting rights for each full share. Fractional shares are
issued for investors who desire to accumulate shares rather than take cash.

A nondiversified company is a management company other than a
diversified company.

There are a number of differences between closed-end and open-end
investment companies. The most important and clear-cut distinction that
can be made between an open-end investment company and a closed-end
investment company is the fact that the open-end company or mutual fund
does not have a fixed number of shares in the hands of the public, as is the
case with a closed-end company, but rather is continually offering new
shares to the public. Consequently, the number of its shares outstanding is
constantly changing.

Closed-end investment companies obtain their investment funds in the same way as an ordinary business corporation obtains capital to finance its production and distribution. It determines how much money it wants to manage, and it offers securities for sale in that amount to the general public. Usually, the services of an investment banker are employed, and once the issue is sold no more securities are offered to the public, at least for a period of time. Thus a characteristic feature of closed-end investment companies is that they do not continually offer their securities for sale, whereas open-end companies do. Once the total number of authorized shares of a closed-end investment company have been sold, anyone wishing to purchase some of these shares must buy them from someone who owns them and is willing to part with them for the right price. Closed-end investment company shares are not redeemed by the issuer and thus have no redemption price.[2] Their shares are traded in the open market by broker-dealers, are often listed on securities exchanges, and often sell at varying relationships to net asset value. Thus the cost of buying closed-end investment company shares comprises the market price demanded by the owner of the shares plus the brokerage fees involved in their purchase. The amount received by the owner when the shares are sold is the market price of the shares less the required brokerage fees.

Normally, a mutual fund stands ready to redeem any of its shares at the current net asset value per share whenever a shareholder wishes to turn his securities back to the company.

A mutual fund with an effective sales organization, a sales organization that is continually inducing individuals to purchase more of the mutual fund shares than are being turned in for redemption by other shareholders, can continue to increase its assets year after year.

RECENT GROWTH OF INVESTMENT COMPANIES

Since the time of the Investment Company Act of 1940, investment companies have grown and developed at an extraordinary rate.

Open-end companies in the years 1941–1945 had an average value of $575 million, increased to $59,830 million in 1972 and to a peak of $76,841 million at the end of 1982. These figures do not include money market funds which amounted to about $211,000 million at the end of 1982. There are about 1,600 open-end funds.

Closed-end companies rose from $613 million in 1941 to an estimated $3,700 million at the end of 1982. There are about 20 closed-end funds.

---

[2]However, closed-end companies do sometimes purchase their own shares in the market when they can buy them at a discount from their net asset value per share.

Factors Behind the Growth

The extremely rapid advance of assets of investment companies in the past 37 years has been due to a variety of factors. First, public confidence grew in investment company shares as they steadily rose in price. This was caused by the almost uninterrupted rise in the prices of stocks generally. For example, the Dow Jones 30 industrial stock average rose from about 105 in 1941 to a peak of 1045 in 1972. Second, with continued prosperity in the country, people had more savings to invest in investment company shares. Third, the mutual fund industry was expanding and was making intensive efforts to market the investment company shares.

Inflation and the Investor

Everybody knows that we have been experiencing periods of inflation in 1968, 1971, 1973, 1974, and particularly in 1979–1980. The consumer price index in 1967 stood at 100, but by February 1980 it was 236.4 and rising at an annual rate of close to 20%. Unfortunately, stocks as a whole were not a good protection. The Dow Jones 30 industrial average as of March 31, 1980 was 783 compared with 905 at the end of 1967, a decline of 13.5%.

But carefully selected stocks did do as well or better than the consumer price index. These have included stocks of companies in the computer, energy, oil drilling, coal, and gold mining fields.

Somewhat the same is true of the performance of investment companies. In the 11 years ended June 15, 1979, the 500 stock average of Standard & Poor's showed an average annual total return of 3.5% compared with *Forbes* magazine's investment company average total return of only 2.0%. There were, however, 14 domestic diversified open-end funds that reported an average annual total return for the period of 7.6%. But the best performance was shown by the foreign investment companies, particularly the Japan Fund, with an average annual total return of 19.4%; Templeton Fund, with 18.9%; and International Investors Fund, with 13.5%.

The Desire for Diversification

A potential investor has the dual problem of finding the best securities to buy and having the money to buy some of the securities of all the biggest and more profitable companies. If an investor's funds were spread among the best companies in a wide variety of industries, adverse conditions developing in any one company or industry would have only a moderate effect on his overall investment results.

Obviously, few individuals have investment funds large enough to obtain by themselves the extremely wide diversification of holdings suggested. However, more and more people each year are finding that, by combining part of their savings with the extra funds of thousands of other people, through the purchase of investment company shares, it is possible to diversify widely their holdings in the common stocks of American corporations. Because each investment company shareholding represents a proportionate interest in the widely diversified assets held by the investment company, the average person through these shareholdings is able to share the growth, profits, and risks of the American economy with considerably less wear and tear on the nerves.

Most investment companies diversify their portfolios by investing in several industries. Some funds concentrate on companies in the same or related industries such as the Chemical Fund and Drexel Utility Shares. A few funds concentrate on fixed-income securities such as bonds or preferred stocks. The cash position of a fund is of interest not only to the individual stockholder but also as a stock market indicator. A few funds at present (June 1979) have high cash reserves, some as much as 50% of their portfolio. Usually the funds as a whole hold between 5% and 10% of their assets in cash. As of December 1979 investment companies held 10.1% in cash and cash equivalents. As a rule investment companies have held the greatest amounts of cash at the bottom of market swings.

Thus, to many people, one answer to the complex problem of investing in the securities market is to take advantage of the diversification and professional management provided by investment companies. Because risk cannot be avoided, one way to handle an individual investment problem is to pick a solution that offers a chance for attaining objectives while assuming as little risk as possible.

PROFESSIONAL INVESTMENT MANAGEMENT

In choosing a fund the investor should first examine his own investment objectives. Most investors want income and capital gains; several mutual funds offer both growth and income. Other investors might prefer to place their money abroad in foreign stock funds. Investors willing to take risks for big gains might choose an option or hedge fund. Those wishing a temporary home for cash would buy a money-market fund. Investors in a high tax bracket would seek municipal bond funds.

The investment policies of mutual funds are to some exent restricted by the terms of their indentures as well as by the Investment Company Act of 1940. In particular, the fund is restricted as to how much may be invested in one stock.

The quality of the management of an investment company is some-what hard to determine. But some idea of their ability might be gained from looking at their track record. Questions might be asked such as, What has been the growth of the company's book value and dividend payments? What is the composition of the portfolio of securities held? Although managements are permitted to boast of their past record, they can never use their past performance as a guarantee of future performance. In fact, they should be modest in their claims. Nobody can be sure of the course of the market or of business activity. Thus, they should never imply that the fund will guarantee the investor against loss or assure a gain. They should avoid extravagant or misleading claims as to the ability of the management to either increase or preserve the investor's capital. They should not even assure a return on investment.

Professional fund managers often have in-house research staffs who spend their full time managing the portfolio of the investment company. They also depend heavily on institutional research firms that supply detailed reports on companies. They keep in mind the objectives of the fund, namely, growth, income, and so on. They watch the diversification of the fund to avoid overconcentration. Of particular importance is the timing of purchases and sales. Even the best stocks can be selling "too high" at certain times. When the market generally reaches too high a level, cash should be raised by selling stocks. Conversely, when the market is un-reasonably depressed, courageous buying should be done. Managers must also be familiar with tax laws and their effect on the stockholders, par-ticularly when they decide to take capital gains.

Investment companies provide professional investment management to individuals who otherwise would not be able to afford that service. Furthermore, investment companies enable the small-or medium -sized in-vestor to diversify his investment so as to reduce his overall investment risk. They also relieve investors from most of the bothersome details involved in a diversified investment program.

Few people outside the field of investments have the time or background knowledge necessary to select and manage successfully a port-folio of individual corporate securities. Supervising a list of securities ef-fectively enough to arrive anywhere near the predetermined goal is a rigorous, full-time task that generally can only be accomplished by professionals.

Only a small proportion of individuals have investment funds large enough to justify incurring the fees investment counselors charge for han-dling individual investment accounts. For most people with relatively modest savings accumulations, the investment company provides one of the most efficient devices for obtaining professional investment management.

LIQUIDITY AND MARKETABILITY

Investment company shares enjoy a high degree of marketability. This is particularly true of mutual fund shares, because the issuing fund stands ready to redeem the shares at the net asset value per share any time the securities markets are open. The net asset value per share is generally computed once a day and is published daily in financial columns of the newspaper, so it is easy to determine the value of each share. There is no question that the immediate redeemability of mutual fund shares, at liquidating value, in good markets and in bad, has been a feature attracting a great many investors to mutual funds.

Closed-end investment company shares are sold in the open market, often through securities exchanges and, thus, are also readily marketable. The diversification of the closed-end company's portfolio is often a factor enhancing the overall marketability of its shares.

OTHER ADVANTAGES OF INVESTMENT COMPANIES

For the holder of investment company shares, the problem of safe-keeping is simplified. Instead of having several certificates of individual issues, there is only one or at most only a few. These certificates are evidences of interests in the many securities held by the fund or funds. Further, it is possible to invest fixed sums in full or fractional shares rather than to meet the cost of individual securities. By making regular purchases of fund shares every month, mutual funds provide an ideal medium for dollar-cost averaging (see page 101).

If it is necessary for the investor to raise cash, it is easy to liquidate a portion of the fund without having to choose any particular security. Further, the diversification of the fund is maintained. If a needy investor prefers to hold his investment company shares, he can usually raise a bank loan using his shares as collateral. Finally, many investment companies have families of funds and allow shareholders to shift, usually without charge, from one fund to another.

TYPES OF MUTUAL FUNDS: THEIR CHARACTERISTICS AND INVESTMENT POLICIES

There are several hundred different investment companies currently operating in the United States. So it is small wonder the average investor tends to become bewildered and confused when confronted with the task of selecting the one best investment company to meet his specific investment need. It is the responsibility of the trained securities representative to help a customer interested in acquiring investment company shares to place his funds in the securities of a company with a good performance record and with a fundamental investment objective that matches that of the customer.

Every investment company has a fundamental investment policy. This policy must be specifically stated in the company's SEC registration statement and its prospectus and cannot be changed without approval by its shareholders.

While investment objectives, methods, policies, and degrees of risk vary materially from company to company, the following is descriptive of some of the broad classifications of investment companies currently in existence.

Diversified Common Stock Funds

A diversified common stock fund is a fund that has a portfolio consisting primarily of common stocks. The various diversified common stock funds operating in the United States today have a wide variety of investment objectives and policies. For example, some funds concentrate their investments in "blue chip" stocks; others invest largely in the securities of growth companies.

Growth investment companies are companies whose stated objective is to seek long-term growth of capital. They attempt to accomplish this by investing in the securities of companies that plow back a substantial part of earnings for expansion, research, or development purposes. In recent years many "growth stocks," such as Polaroid and even IBM, have been a disappointment. But investors are still looking for growth stocks among the smaller "second-tier" stocks.

The stated investment objective of a diversified common stock fund might well call for both reasonable *growth of capital and reasonable current return* or invested capital. Such a company may reserve the right in its registration statement to take defensive positions in cash, bonds, and other senior securities whenever current conditions indicate such action is warranted. This policy would enable the company to retain maximum flexibility in managing its portfolio by avoiding any restrictions on the proportion of various classes of securities to be held.

Some investment companies have the stated management objective of maximum current income. These are known as income funds. People who must live on the current income they receive from their investments often select this type of investment company, which strives to provide a higher than average investment return.

Income funds attempt to achieve an above-average investment return by investing in securities that are characterized by relatively high dividend payout. Frequently these securities have below-average growth potential and are considered to be of above-average risk.

A specialized investment company invests in securities of companies in a single industry or in allied industries. This type of company is also referred to as an industry investment company.

Specialty funds exist in the bank, chemical, energy, general science, oceanographic, and precious metals area.

Balanced Funds

A balanced fund is an investment company whose stated policy is at all times to have some portion of its invested assets in bonds and preferred stocks as well as in common stocks.

The fund is *balanced* in such proportions of each type of security as seems desirable in light of investment considerations as they exist at any given time. During periods that appear favorable for increased market prices for equities, a higher proportion of the assets will be invested in common stocks and other equity types of securities. At other times, when the bond market appears "right," a higher proportion of bonds, short-term securities, and cash may be held. There is always some relationship of balance between the two classes, however.

Generally, a balanced fund may be expected to follow a more con-servative investment policy than a common stock fund. Because the prices of the securities held in its portfolio are less volatile in a rising market, the balanced fund will not show as much gain as would be expected of a common stock fund. Conversely, in a declining market, the net asset value per share of the balanced fund should decline less than that of a common stock fund.

A balanced fund would be suitable for an investor who is seeking an investment that proves a reasonable conservation of capital with a relatively high quarterly income. Many people in their retirement years would be expected to have an investment objective comparable to that of a balanced fund because there would be expected appreciation during time of inflation with a related increase in current income.

Bond and Preferred Stock Funds

A number of investment companies hold corporate bonds of electric public utilities, of industrials, and of a few railroads. Some of these funds concentrate on high-grade bonds and some buy medium-grade bonds. The main objectives are the security of principal with as much income as possible. There are also some funds that combine bonds with preferred stocks and some funds that hold preferred stocks only. In an attempt to have safety of principal and yet some appreciation possibility several funds specialize in convertible bonds.

Tax-exempt or Mutual Bond Funds

Between 1961 and 1976 a number of tax-exempt mutual bond funds were sold. These funds were classified as *unit* municipal investment trusts. Yields on these trusts ran from 4% to 6%. As explained on page 60, the interest paid on municipal securities is exempt from federal income taxes. By forming a unit investment trust, investors could pool their money, buy municipal securities, and receive tax-exempt income. But this unit trust form was rigid. Once a trust invested all its funds in municipal securities, it could neither buy nor sell issues. These units were offered initially, not continuously. They were redeemable at the bid price by the fund. They were, therefore, not managed, and there was no over-the-counter market for the funds.

The 1976 Tax Reform Act permitted the formation of municipal investment companies that could manage municipal security holdings in the same way as any other investment company would operate. That is, the managers could buy, hold, or sell municipal securities. Consequently, there was a rush to form municipal investment companies. By 1979 there were 37 municipal funds with over $3.3 billion of assets. Essentially, these new funds are diversified open-end investment companies. They hold short-, medium-, and long-term municipal securities. Some are limited as to quality; that is, no security will be bought unless it has a rating by the services of A or better (see page 33).

Usually, there is no load charge, but the management fee is about 0.6%. (The load is the amount charged the customer on the initial purchase of the shares ranging as high as 8 1/2% of the total; see pages 98 and 463.)

Money-Market Funds

By purchasing these funds the small investor obtains high current income, preservation of capital, and liquidity. Money-market funds, as their name implies, invest in money-market instruments such as U.S. Treasury bills, commercial paper, negotiable time certificates of deposit, Eurodollars, and bankers' acceptances. A minimum investment of $1,000 to $10,000 is usually required. Thus, the small investor is able to participate in the purchase of money-market instruments with a relatively small contribution.

Money-market funds almost never charge a sales load for selling the funds. But they do charge an annual expense fee for management. In 1979, about 60 money-market funds charged an annual expense fee ranging from $0.38 to $1.18 per $1,000. The average for 11 large money-market funds in 1979 was $0.64 per $1,000.

One of the advantages of money-market funds is their liquidity. Shares may be redeemed at any time without any fee. Most funds permit withdrawals to be made by check, by mail, or by telephone. Additional payments sometimes may also be made, usually in minimum amounts of say, $500. A second advantage is these funds' high yield. Currently (March 1980), they are yielding over 14.0%. However, if the interest rate should decline due to a slackening of business and lower rates of inflation, money-market funds would be less attractive.

A third advantage is their relative safety. Professional managers invest these large pools of funds in a diversified list of high-grade money-market instruments.

Growth of these funds has been phenomenal particularly in periods of high interest rates in 1978–1979. In June 1976 money-market funds amounted to $2.7 billion, in June 1978 they were $7.0 billion, and by June 1983, they were $169 billion.

However, in March 1980, the Federal Reserve Board ruled that the money market funds must post a reserve equal to 15%[1] of the difference between the level of their funds on March 14, 1980 and the average for a 30 day period following that date. Further, this reserve had to be maintained as long as the level of the funds were above the level of March 14, 1980. This ruling caused a great deal of confusion among the managers of the money-market funds. Several stopped selling their funds entirely. A number of fund managers started new funds popularly called "clone" funds. Although these money market funds were required to maintain the 15% reserve balance, their yield was still attractive even though it was 2 or 3 percentage points below the old funds. Also most indentures provide that the funds cannot sell short, buy puts, or calls.

The minimum initial investment is usually between $1,000 and $5,000, although at least one fund has a minimum of $10,000.

Investors have liquidity in that shares may be redeemed at net asset value taken at 4 P.M. every business day.

Dual-purpose or Leverage Funds

The idea of a dual-purpose fund originated in England and was introduced in this country in 1967, when nine dual-purpose funds were formed. They are closed-end funds, seven of which are listed on the New York Stock Exchange, and two trade in the over-the-counter-market. A dual-purpose fund is divided in two equal parts. The first has, as its announced purpose, income, and its shares are called income shares. The second, has as its

[1]In June 1980, this 15% reserve was eliminated.

announced purpose, *appreciation*, and its shares are called capital shares. Let us analyze these concepts in greater detail.

The income shares are in some respects similar to preferred stock in that a minimum stated rate of dividend payment is reasonably assured. This dividend, like most preferred, is cumulative. In addition, holders of the income shares have a right to all the net dividends and interest paid to the fund on *both* the income and on the capital shares but do not participate in any capital appreciation. Also, the income shares are callable after a period of years at around the issue price.

The capital shares receive no dividend for ten or fifteen years or until the income shares are paid off. But in theory they receive the benefit of the capital appreciation of *both* funds. They are able to realize this appreciation only after the income shares are paid off, usually about ten years after issue.

In summary, the income shareholders receive income from twice their investment whereas the capital shareholders participate in the growth or loss of twice their investment. After retiring all the income shares, the fund may become and open-end investment company. But the dual-purpose funds seem to have been a one-year phenomenon, as none have been formed since 1967. As of June 1979, there were 18 dual purpose funds with total assets of $376 million.

Swap or Tax-Free Exchange Funds

These funds allowed the investor to exchange or swap his or her individual securities, which had appreciated in value, without incurring immediate tax liability on capital gains profits that would have been incurred if the individually held securities had been sold. The capital gains tax is due and payable eventually, of course, whenever the investor sells his fund shares, as the tax cost of the mutual fund shares that the investor acquired is the same as the tax cost of his original holdings. Thus, the swap fund investor did not eliminate the capital gains tax but *postponed* paying it until the swap fund shares are sold. Another advantage to the investor in a swap fund is diversification of holdings.

But in October 1976 Congress passed a law making it impossible to sell any new tax-free exchange funds. There were, however, nine tax-free-exchange, closed-end funds with assets of $443 million as of June 15, 1979.

Index Funds

The philosophy behind index funds is, "If you can't beat them, join them." The record of the money managers of the large institutonal funds in the 1970s was so miserable in comparison with the common stock averages that many trustees and directors, who were ultimately responsible for the funds, became disillusioned. They reasoned that at least the funds should do as well as the stock averages if they invested in the identical stocks that made up the Standard & Poor's 500 stock average or some other average. Computer specialists were put to work and eagerly developed programs. American Telephone & Telegraph Company and New York City have segregated a substantial part of their pension funds for the purchase of the same stocks and in the same proportion as the Standard & Poor's weighted 500 average. Batterymarch of Boston, Massachusetts uses 250 of the Standard & Poor's issues; Wells Fargo Bank of San Francisco, California uses the New York Stock Exchange 1,500 issues. Only a few index funds offer shares to the public.

Other Types of Investment Companies

There are hedge funds that are suitable for the investor who is willing and able to take risks. These funds take positions in speculative issues. There is even an investment company called the Bull-Bear Management Company that allows the investor to take either position in the stock market.

The option boom caused a number of investment companies that write options to be formed (see page 229). Mention should be also made of funds specializing in foreign securities, which have shown large appreciation in the last few years, particularly the funds holding Canadian, Japanese, and certain European stocks. Capitalizing on inflation fears of many investors, several funds specialize in gold and other precious metals. Finally, there is at least one fund specializing in U.S. government securities.

Performance Comparisons of Mutual Funds

Investment objectives are a basis of comparison and include: (1) long-term capital gains and/or (2) income. Some funds have as their objective both capital gains and income. Other objectives might include the participation in some growth industry, such as high technology, to obtain tax-exempt income or speculative capital gains.

Investment policies adopted to obtain long-term capital gains usually are based on purchases of well-selected high-grade common stocks. For income, the policies are to buy investment-grade corporate bonds or preferred stocks. For income, money-market funds are also in great demand.

The quality of management is of greatest importance as discussed on page 81. Investment companies often show charts and figures in their prospectuses to illustrate their past performance. For example, charts often show the performance of an assumed investment in their fund over a ten-year period, say, 1969–1978. But investment companies are prohibited from using past performance as a guarantee of future performance.

Nonstatistical factors include dividend and capital gains reinvestment plans, systematic withdrawal plans, and exchange or conversion privileges.

Dividend and Capital Gains Reinvestment Plans

Many mutual funds have dividend and capital gains reinvestment plans. Under these plans, the mutual fund shareholder does not take (or does not keep) his distributions from the mutual fund in cash but, rather, re-invests all the dividends and capital gains distributions received in new shares of the fund. Mutual funds have found that the various reinvestment plans are popular. In some funds as much as 95% of the capital gains and dividend distributions made to shareholders are reinvested by the share-holders in additional shares of the same fund.

Many mutual fund underwriters offer *automatic dividend reinvest-ment* plans. In an *automatic* plan, the shareholder does not receive a cash dividend. When declaring a dividend, under such a plan, the mutual fund, or its underwriter, simply notifies the shareholder that his dividends have purchased him X number of additional shares. If the investor does not utilize an automatic reinvestment plan, or if the fund of which he is a share-holder does not have such a plan, the shareholder can nevertheless usually reinvest his dividends simply by sending the fund the money either directly or through its representatives and by making his wishes known.

Some funds will permit their shareholders to reinvest their dividends in new shares at net asset value per share—in other words, without requir-ing a sales charge. Other funds, however, require the full customary sales charge on shares purchased by dividend reinvestment. Some mutual funds fix minimun limits on the shareholder accounts for which the dividend rein-vestment privilege is extended without charge. The policies of each in-dividual fund regarding the dividend investment privilege and other matters can be found in its prospectus.

Under some circumstances dividend reinvestment without the imposi-tion of a sales charge can be a valuable privilege for an investor. The exis-tence of this privilege, or the lack of it, should be one of the factors weighed by an investor when he is deciding which mutual fund can best serve his needs.

Most mutual funds give their shareholders an option to receive capital gains distributions in cash or in additional shares of the fund. The reinvest-ment of capital gains distributions is generally required by the fund if dividends are reinvested. All mutual funds permit their shareholders to re-invest capital gains distributions at the net asset value per share, that is, without imposing a sales charge. The capital gains distributed by a mutual fund to an investor are considered a partial return of his capital. It represents the net realized capital gains from the fund's portfolio transac-tions. Thus the option to take additional mutual fund shares instead of cash is important to an investor as its exercise automatically assures that the full amount of his capital remains invested and continues to earn. Nearly all funds encourage their shareholders to reinvest any capital gains distributions they receive. Many companies automatically declare capital gains distributions in shares unless the shareholder specifically requests cash.

Systematic Withdrawal Plans

Some mutual funds provide their shareholders with a service known as a systematic withdrawal plan. Under this plan, a mutual fund shareholder can receive payments from the fund at regular intervals over a period of time. These payments may be in fixed amounts or may be calculated on one of several other bases. Withdrawal plans are designed for investors who wish to supplement their income for current needs, or who wish to meet commitments of a specified goal, such as college education for their children or their own retirement. A shareholder generally must have a certain minimum amount invested in the fund before such a withdrawal plan can be set up. A $10,000 minimum investment is fairly typical. When the minimum amount required is on deposit and the shareholder indicates the amount he periodically wishes to receive, the payments are begun. A rule of thumb for a "prudent" automatic withdrawal rate is 6% a year.

Dividend and capital gains distributions are used to make the payments required under a withdrawal plan insofar as is possible. However, if the scheduled payments are larger than the amounts of dividend and capital gains distributions the investor has coming for that period, some of the invester's shares will be liquidated in order to make the payments. If the investor chooses not to disturb the capital amount, he must either accept a smaller fixed amount or be prepared to accept a variable amount reflecting the level of investment income. The investor should be aware of the extent, if any, to which his shares are being liquidated to meet his payments.

Because, by their very nature, withdrawal plans carry the risk of exhausting invested capital, any discussion of withdrawal plans or any presentation to the public should be handled with care. See Chapter 22 for a discussion regarding the presentation and use of withdrawal plans sales literature.

Exchange or Conversion Privileges

Some mutual fund management organizations manage a group of several mutual funds rather than a single mutual fund. Typically, each fund in the management group has a different portfolio composition and investment objective from every other fund. By managing funds with a variety of investment objectives, the mutual fund management organization is able to offer appropriate investment vehicles to many different people with a wide variety of investment objectives. Thus, a mutual fund saleperson representing a group of funds has a fund that he can recommend to an individual who desires growth or capital appreciation and a different fund sponsored by the same group that he can offer to a person who needs current income.

Sometimes the investment objective of an individual changes. For example, an investor holding shares in a growth fund may find, on retirement, that more current income is needed from the investment than the growth fund is able to provide. Under such circumstances it would be advantageous for the mutual fund shareholder to be able to exchange his growth shares for the income shares of another fund without paying a sales charge for the privilege. Some mutual fund organizations permit such exchanges within their group of funds. This privilege is known as an *exchange*, or *conversion*, *privilege*.

The investor should be given a word of caution at this point. The U.S. Internal Revenue Service considers the exchange or conversion of the shares of one fund for those of another the same as a redemption and a new purchase. In this case, a shareholder who has considerable appreciation in the value of his shares will be liable for a capital gains tax when they are redeemed. The fact that the investor then goes on to exchange them or convert them into new shares has no bearing on the transaction's taxability.

Problem of Comparing Statistical Base of Performance

It is important to examine the record of an investment company over a period of several years—that is, in periods of up markets and down markets. Management performance can best be observed by comparing the fund's book value over the selected period of years. Has it grown steadily or has it fluctuated widely in the past ten years? Also, the analyst should look at the dividend record, the sales charges, and the expenses ratio.

Sources of Information

The *prospectus*, which must be given to every purchaser of investment company shares, is a summary of the registration statement filed with the SEC. The prospectus is used to give the prospective investor complete information about the company. It states the type of investment company, its policies and objectives, its restrictions, and its officers and directors (along with their backgrounds). Financial details include the holdings of the fund, a long-term record of earnings and net assets per share, sales charges (including volume discounts), and a statement of assets and liabilities. In addition, the prospectus gives the investor details about possible exchange features, redemption features, the investment adviser, taxes, brokerage fees, and so on.

The prospectus must state in bold type that the SEC had neither approved nor disapproved the issue. Charts and tables of past performance may be used, but there can be no promises of future performance. Finally, the figures must be certified by an independent auditor.

The *annual report* usually has some current information. It usually has a lengthy address from the president of the fund concerning the activities of the fund in the last year and the current outlook for the fund and the economy. A detailed listing of the current holdings is given as well as the sales and purchases in the last year. Finally, there is an income account for the current year as well as a balance sheet for the year end.

There are several *financial services* that give detailed information about investment companies including Moody's and Standard & Poor's. But perhaps the best known is Arthur Wiesenberger's *Manual of Investment Companies*. These manuals, which are published annually, contain a detailed record of the investment companies' growth in book value over the years, their officers and directors, their sales loads, their expense ratios, and a description of the types of fund—their objectives and policies.

How Mutual Funds are Organized, Managed, and Sold

The typical mutual fund organization consists of four entities: the fund itself, the management company, the principal underwriter, and the custodian.

The open-end mutual fund is sometimes a trust but more often a corporation, with a minimum net worth of $100,000. It may not issue senior securities but may borrow from a bank with 300% collateral coverage. The fund owns the investment portfolio and sells shares to the public. A mutual fund operating as a common law trust will not have officers, directors, or an advisory board. The investment management function of such a fund is handled by the trustees under the terms of the trust agreement.

The corporate open-end mutual fund sometimes has trustees and sometimes officers and directors. The directors or trustees appoint, and can dismiss, the officers and must ensure that they conform to the objectives and policies of the fund under the Investment Company Act of 1940, not more than 60% of the board may be affiliated with the fund. The directors must approve and are ultimately liable for all investment decisions.

Operations of the Management Group

Some mutual funds have their own research departments. Some make contracts for investment advice with investment counsels. Most funds, however, make contracts with management groups for investment management and for the distribution of their securities. Many of the directors and officers of the management group and of the fund are identical. Sometimes the management group will also employ an investment adviser.

But, before any management group can act, a contract must be approved by a majority of the board of the fund, including a majority of the independent directors and a majority of the shareholders or both. All the details of this contract must be set forth in the prospectus of the fund. Also the stockholders must approve any changes in the objectives and in the policies of the fund. Stockholders of mutual funds also have all the other rights of stockholders as outlined on pages 2–10.

Costs of Operating a Mutual Fund

All business firms have operating and other expenses. Mutual funds are no exception. Because mutual funds are usually corporations, most of them must pay incorporation fees, filing fees, taxes, and various other levies when they are originally formed. During the course of the funds operation, it incurs and must pay executive salaries, directors' fees, costs of holding stockholders' meetings and preparing financial reports, accounting fees, secretarial salaries, bills for postage, stationery costs, and printing expenses. In addition, there are costs involved in collecting income, paying dividends and capital gains distributions, providing custodian services, and paying federal, state, and local taxes. All these expenses must be paid either directly or indirectly by the fund.

A major item of expense for most mutual funds is the payment made to management companies for the investment advice the fund receives. These fees, paid annually to the mutual fund's investment adviser (management company), are known as management fees. The amount of this fee will vary from one fund to another, but typically it is about 1/2 of 1% of the fund's assets. This fee is often subject to sliding-scale reductions as assets increase. The staff of a management company usually consists of economists, industry specialists, and investment analysts as well as the administrative and clerical personnel. Obviously, the services of such a professional staff cannot be obtained without incurring substantial expense. During the years 1966–1970 in particular, there were a number of complaints on the part of the SEC and even suits against the investment companies on the grounds that their management fees were too high.

According to the *Investment Company Amendments Act of 1970*, the fairness of management fees should be tested in the federal courts. That is, the act permitted the fund shareholders or the SEC to file lawsuits to force the funds to reduce management charges. Furthermore, the courts were empowered to reduce the charges if they found that the fund, its management, or its directors had violated their *fiduciary duty* involving personal misconduct in respect of any registered investment company. The suit may be brought against the investment company, its officers, its directors, its principal underwriter, or its depositor. But the award of damages shall be limited to the actual damages resulting from the breach of fiduciary duty and shall in no event exceed the amount of compensation received from such investment company or security holders by such recipient. This section of the act has resulted in a large number of suits against investment company management and directors, causing many problems and constituting a source of anxiety to the entire industry.

Just as with any other corporate operation, the more income the mutual fund takes to cover the expenses of operation, the less there is left to distribute to the shareholders. All management fees, operating expenses, and other costs must be paid out of the mutual fund's gross income before the net income available for payments to shareholders can be determined. Once the expenses have been provided for, dividends can be distributed to the investment company shareholders. Of course, the operating expenses of mutual funds vary from company to company. Some have higher expenses than others. However, operating expenses of investment companies are usually less than 1% per annum of the average net assets of the reporting company. This is the expense ratio.

Operating expenses of investment companies may also be calculated as a percentage of the companies' annual earnings. Some mutual funds have such large annual expenses that, after they are paid, little is left out of their income for distribution to the shareholders. In selecting a mutual fund, an investor should give substantial thought and consideration to this aspect of the mutual fund's operation. The factor of cost should not be considered alone, however, as the ultimate test of a mutual fund is how well it accomplishes its shareholders' investment objective.

MUTUAL FUND CUSTODIANS

Every mutual fund retains a national bank, trust company, or other qualified institution to act as its custodian. The name of the custodian and the functions it is to perform for the mutual fund will be specifically stated in the fund's prospectus.

The institution functioning as the mutual fund's custodian will hold the cash and the securities of the fund and will, in addition, perform a variety of essential clerical-type services for the fund and its shareholders.

Services performed by the custodian may include functioning:

1. as the transfer agent of the fund
2. as a registrar of the fund shares
3. as dividend disbursing agent of the fund

The custodian also receives investor payments and invests those payments in shares of the fund. It keeps custody of the fund shares of individual owners when requested to do so, or when legally required to do so. The custodian also keeps a variety of necessary books and records.

The custodian, acting as transfer agent, issues new shares, cancels the redeemed shares, and distributes dividends and capital gains. It also performs many clerical functions such as the issuance of periodic reports and proxy statements. The registrar checks the operations of the transfer agent to prevent overissue of certificates. The custodian performs *no* management, supervisory, or investment functions, nor does it take part in the sale or distribution of fund shares. The activities of the custodian cannot in any way provide protection against a decline in the net asset value per share of mutual fund securities.

Function of Underwriters (Sponsor or Distributor)

In most cases the management group acts as the principal underwriter. Under its contract with the fund, the underwriter buys the shares at net asset value. It then makes contracts to distribute these shares to dealers in the states in which the shares may be sold. Under the terms of the contracts, dealers continually offer the fund's shares to the public.

Dealers charge their customers a commission on these shares out of which they compensate their sales representatives who deal with the public. The principal underwriter retains the smaller part of the total selling commission. The dealer and his representatives receive the major portion of the commission. The mutual fund itself always receives the full net asset value per share for its shares when they are issued, and all selling commissions are paid by the incoming shareholder.

Most mutual fund shares are distributed as noted, that is, from mutual fund—to underwriter—to dealer—to investor. However, there are other ways in which the shares of open-end investment companies are distributed. For example, some mutual fund shares are sold directly to the public by the underwriter without utilizing the services of dealers.

Under another distribution method, the fund sells its shares directly to investors by advertising. Shares sold in this way may involve a reduced sales charge, or there may be no sales charge at all, in which case they are called "no-load" funds.

The so-called *no-load funds* are offered to the public for subscription at net asset value, without the payment of commissions to underwriters, dealers, or sales representatives. This type of mutual fund is often associated with a firm engaged in the business of rendering investment advice to private clients on a fee basis, thus providing a parallel source of income that enables the advisory firm to supervise the associated mutual fund as though the latter were merely an additional individual client.

In recent years the popularity of no-load (no sales load) funds has increased. Between 1973 and 1978, about 105 funds were formed. Of these 55 were no-load funds with assets of $2,489 million compared with 50 load funds with assets of $3,455 million. It is estimated that in 1978 there were about 144 no-load funds with total assets of about $11,670 million. In addition there were about 60 money-market funds and about 40 municipal bond market funds. None of the money-market funds charged a sales load and only about 42% of the municipal bond funds charged a load (see page 86).

Mutual funds shares are sometimes distributed by the underwriter to a "plan company," which in turn sells these shares to individual investors. Plan companies are usually connected with the contractual plan method of distributing mutual funds. The prospectus of the fund, or of the plan company, will describe the method of distribution.

However, no matter what method of distributing new shares is used, the fee structure as between the mutual fund and its investment adviser is based, in common practice, on a percentage of the net assets of the fund, rather than on a percentage of the fund's income.

Thus, an individual investor wishing to buy mutual fund shares ordinarily would buy them from the issuing company or a dealer and underwriter, not from a present shareholder. The offering price of these new shares would be the same as the net asset value per share of the shares currently outstanding, plus a sales charge. This sales charge on each purchase of mutual fund shares ranges from 1% up to 9% of net asset value per share. The sales charge involved in the acquisition of the shares of any specific mutual fund must be stated in the fund's prospectus as a percentage of the public offering price. It is important to remember that the sales charge is a charge of the selling organization, not of the fund itself.

BUYING MUTUAL FUNDS

Both individuals and institutions purchase the shares of investment companies. Although there are a number of different types of institutions that have found the services of investment companies useful for their investment purposes, the majority of investment company shareholders are individuals.

Individuals buying investment company shares are classified as either regular account holders or as accumulation plan holders.

Regular Account Holders

Regular account holders are those individuals who have made "lump-sum" investments but have not indicated any intention of making periodic investments of additional sums of money. Regular account holders should be made aware of the fact that most mutual fund underwriters reduce their sales charges when quantity purchases of from $5,000 to $25,000 are made. The details for any given fund will appear in the *prospectus.*

The purchase need not be a single lump-sum purchase to qualify for the reduced sales charge if the investor signs a *letter of intent* signifying his intent to purchase the required dollar amount within a period not to exceed 13 months.

To qualify for a reduced sales charge on a lump-sum purchase, or through use of the letter of intent, the purchaser must be:

1. an individual, or
2. an individual, his or her spouse, and children under the age of 21, or
3. a trustee or other fiduciary of a single trust estate or single fiduciary account or a pension or a profit sharing plan qualified under Section 401 of the Internal Revenue Code.

This means that investment clubs or other groups of individuals cannot band together for the purpose of obtaining reduced sales charges on purchases of investment company shares.

The following is a typical schedule of sales charges of a mutual open-end fund starting at a maximum of 7.25%.

TABLE 5-1

Amount of Purchase Plus Confirmed Value of Shares Owned	Sales Charge	% of Net Amount Invested	Regular Dealer Discount as % of Offering Price
Less than $9,999	7.25%	7.8%	6.50%
$10,000 up to $24,999	6.75	7.2	6.00
$25,000 up to $49,999	6.25	6.7	5.00
$50,000 up to $99,999	5.00	5.3	4.00
$100,000 up to $249,999	3.50	3.6	2.75
$250,000 up to $499,999	2.50	2.6	2.00
$500,000 up to $999,999	2.00	2.0	1.50
$1,000,000 or more	1.50	1.5	1.00

LETTERS OF INTENTION OR INTENT

Investors buying investment company shares may take advantage of a device known as a *letter of intention* or *intent.* A letter of intention is an arrangement among the investment company share underwriter, the dealer, and the purchaser. This arrangement permits the purchaser to pay a reduced sales charge on the shares he buys, if certain conditions are met. In the letter, the customer states his intention of purchasing (over a period of 13 months or less) a minimum of $25,000 worth of investment company shares. If the purchaser carries out this intention, the reduced sales charge applies on his entire purchase. There is no penalty if the customer does not make the purchases indicated in his letter of intention. To protect a customer's interest, the salesperson should put the purchaser on notice that a letter of intention is available whenever there is any indication that the total amount of his purchases would make him eligible for a discount, were a *letter* in effect. SEC Rule 22d-1 indicates that letters of intention may not be backdated.

A member who induces the purchase, or makes the sale, of investment company shares by implying a rate of return based in whole or in part on distribution of realized securities profits or who, without full explanation and disclosure, uses any impending dividend or distribution as an inducement for the purchase of such shares may be making representations contrary to the Rules of Fair Practice.

BREAKPOINT SALES

Dealers selling open-end investment company shares generally reduce their sales charge for customers who buy more than a specified number of shares. The quantity at which this sales charge reduction is granted is known as the *breakpoint*.

The sale of open-end investment company shares by dealers in dollar amounts just below the point at which the sales charge is reduced on quantity transactions (as was shown in the preceding table), to share in the higher sales charges applicable on sales below the breakpoint, may subject the dealer to disciplinary action under the Rules of Fair Practice.

Right of Accumulation

Most shareholders of open-end mutual funds have the right of accumulation. This means that consideration is given by the fund to the total shares *already owned* and additional shares acquired. If the value of the shares already owned is large enough to qualify under the breakpoint schedule, the distributor permits each new cash purchase to be charged the reduced fees.

Computation of the Net Asset Value

Let us assume that an investor places an order to buy 1,000 shares of an open-end no-load mutual fund. The investor will pay the *net asset value* (NAV). The net asset value is calculated as follows:

$$NAV = \frac{\text{Securities market value} + \text{cash and other assets} - \text{total liabilities}}{\text{Number of shares outstanding}}$$

$$\$9.55 = \frac{\$940,000 + \$66,000 - \$51,000}{100,000}$$

Also, if an investor decides to redeem his or her shares, that investor will receive the same value upon liquidation.

On days that the New York Stock Exchange is open for business, mutual funds normally compute their net asset value at the close of business, which is at 4:00 P.M.

Typically, the net asset value (NAV) per share is therefore determined on the basis of security prices at the close of business on the New York Stock Exchange. For example, if the liquidating or net asset value of a mutual fund is, say, $9.55 a share, this is the amount that will be paid by the investor if the fund is a no-load fund. Also, it is the value that the holder of the fund will receive on presenting his shares for redemption.

Assuming a sales load of 8%, the asked price the buyer must pay is $10.38. This asked price might be determined by subtracting the percentage of the load, in this case 8%, or .08, from 1.00 and dividing the result into the net asset value of $9.55 as follows:

$$\frac{\$9.55}{1.00-.08} = \frac{\$9.55}{.92} = \$10.38 \text{ offering price.}$$

The sales charge as shown in the prospectus of the fund must be stated as a percentage of the public offering price. The sales charge may be determined in the following way from the bid and asked quotations appearing in the newspaper. The bid is the net asset value per share of the fund and the asked is net asset value per share plus the load or sales charge, as follows:

$$\begin{array}{ccc} \$10.38 & - \quad \$9.55 \quad = & \$.83 \\ \text{(asked price)} & \text{(bid price)} & \text{(sales charge)} \end{array}$$

$$\frac{\text{Sales charge}}{\text{Asked price}} = \text{Sales charge as a percentage of asked price}$$

$$\frac{\$.83}{\$10.38} = 8.00\% \text{ (rounded)}$$

It is important to note that the bid and asked prices are determined at the *end of the day*. These prices apply to all purchases and redemptions made on that day; hence the term *forward pricing*.

To compute its net asset value per share, the mutual fund has to be able to determine the value of each of the different securities in which it has invested its shareholders' money. Ordinarily, in the computation, each mutual fund portfolio security is valued at its latest reported sale price. If no sale of a particular security has taken place since the last time the fund computed its net asset value per share, the average of the latest bid-and-asked prices are used as the value of the security in the portfolio. When no market quotations at all are available, securities are valued at their "fair market value."

In the case of *letter stock*, sometimes called unregistered or restricted stock, which we will discuss on page 375, the directors of the fund are responsible for assigning a fair value. In April 1970 the SEC ruled that mutual funds must disclose their method of valuing letter stock in their shareholders' reports, their sales literature, and their registration statements. In the valuation, the SEC does not allow a fixed percentage of market value. Each evaluation must be tailor-made by the directors. The directors in making their evaluation usually consider the company's earnings, its financial condition, its unfilled orders, its nearness to registration, and so forth.

After the value of each portfolio security is determined, these values are totaled. Added to this aggregate value of the portfolio securities is the dollar amount of the mutual fund's cash and accounts receivable. Next, all the mutual fund's liabilities and accrued expenses must be subtracted to arrive at the total net asset value of the fund. Reduced to its simplest terms, the fund totals the value of everything it owns (except buildings, supplies, and equipment, etc., which normally would never be converted into cash in the normal operation of its business), it subtracts the amount of everything it owes, and the remainder is the amount the mutual fund is worth. Using this "total of worth," it is a simple matter to arrive at the mutual fund's net asset value per share. It is computed by dividing this "total of worth" by the number of shares the fund has outstanding.

DOLLAR-COST AVERAGING

Dollar-cost averaging means investing equal sums of money at regular intervals regardless of price levels. Dollar-cost averaging, of course, does not protect the investor against loss in the value of his securities in declining markets. It does, however, enable the investor in a declining market to purchase more shares of a particular security with a given amount of money as the average price of each share is declining.

Dollar-cost averaging assumes a continuous flow of funds. Let us assume that each year $1,000 is invested in the stock of XYZ Corporation at the then market price. The following would be the result:

TABLE 5-2

Year	I Amount	II Price Per Share	III Number of Shares	IV Cum. Total Owned	V Total Investment Cumulative
1	$1,000	75	13.3	13.3	$1,000
2	1,000	80	12.5	25.8	2,000
3	1,000	60	16.7	42.5	3,000
4	1,000	90	11.1	53.6	4,000
5	1,000	51	19.6	73.2	5,000
6	1,000	80	12.5	85.7	6,000

From the table it may be noted that the investor acquired 85.7 shares. The *average cost* is therefore $70.01 a share ($6,000 ÷ 85.7 = $70.01). The *average price* is the sum of the market prices per share for each transaction, that is 75 + 80 + 60 + . . . = 436. This figure divided by 6 equals $72.67, or the average price. Thus, the average cost is here and is always lower than the average price because during the period more shares will be bought at less than the average price.

Dollar-cost averaging is a good way to obtain a position in a stock. But this stock over the years should fluctuate, enabling the investor to buy more shares at low prices. However, the price of the stock should have an upward trend over the years. To avoid the hazard of selecting a poor stock, dollar-cost averaging of a good mutual fund is suggested.

For years the SEC has prohibited the use of the phrase "dollar averaging" or "averaging the dollar" in referring to any plan of continuous investment in the shares of an investment company, at stated intervals, regardless of the price level of the shares. However, the phrases "dollar-cost averaging" or "cost averaging" may be used when referring to such plans.

When discussing or portraying any Periodic Payment Plan referred to in Section 27 (a) of the Investment Company Act of 1940 (or when discussing the merits of dollar-cost averaging), the sales literature must make the following points clear:

1. That the investor will incur a loss under such a plan if he discontinues the plan when the market value of his accumulated shares is less than his cost.
2. That the investor is putting his funds primarily in securities subject to market fluctuations and that the method of investing being used involves continuous investment in such shares at regular intervals regardless of the price levels and trends.
3. That the investor before committing himself to such a plan must take into account his financial ability to continue the plan through periods of low price levels.
4. That such plans do not protect against loss in value in declining markets.

It might also be added that the investor should avoid the stock of a company that is showing a long term decline in earnings and in financial position.

Discussions of the advantages of voluntary or noncontractual plans for the periodic purchase of investment company shares must include an explanation that such plans cannot assure profits nor protect against losses.

HOW INVESTORS SELL THEIR MUTUAL FUND SHARES

Mutual fund investors can sell the shares they hold in mutual funds at any time they wish. Ordinarily, a shareholder wishing to dispose of his shares would sell them back to the issuing fund through the same securities dealer or underwriter through which he purchased them in the first place. Because a great proportion of mutual fund shares are purchased through a particular sales representative of a dealer or an underwriter that has a sales agreement with an issuing mutual fund, it is only natural that the same firm should be contacted by the investor when the investor wishes to convert his shares back into cash. This process of converting mutual fund shares into cash by selling them back to the issuing company is known as *redemption.*

It is not mandatory that a mutual fund shareholder go through the same channels to sell the shares as he did to buy them. If he wishes to do so, an investor can take his shares directly to the issuing company or send them to the company through the mail, and the company will repurchase the shares directly from the shareholder. Mutual funds also will generally redeem shares in the possession of their shareholders upon presentation of these shares in proper order at the custodial bank of the mutual fund.

The shares of no-load mutual funds are generally sent through the mail for redemption. Because no sales representatives are employed by such funds, and because their shares are originally sold directly to the investing public through the mail, that is how they are redeemed.

Briefly stated then, a mutual fund shareholder may redeem his shares by depositing his stock certificate, properly endorsed, at the office of the issuing mutual fund, its distributor, or its custodian. The stock certificate should be accompanied by an irrevocable offer to sell the shares back to the issuing mutual fund at the net asset value per share.

The specific redemption procedures and provisions for any mutual fund will be found outlined in detail in the fund's prospectus.

Redemption Price is the Net Asset Value Per Share

When a mutual fund shareholder turns his shares back to the company for redemption, the amount he receives is determined by dividing the total number of shares the company has outstanding into the total net assets of the company at that time. This redemption price is called the net asset value per share.

Most mutual funds will redeem their shares without charge at any time on written request. Shares must be surrendered and endorsed. Often, the signature must be guaranteed by a member firm or a bank. Also, most open-end companies' distributors will redeem these shares at net asset value. Some, however, might make a small charge; for example, 1/2 of 1% of the proceeds. For example, Mr. Jones wishes to redeem 1,000 shares of PDQ mutual fund with a bid price of $9.55 and an asked price of $10.38. Because we have already explained that the bid price is the same as the net asset value, Mr. Jones should expect to receive $9.55 a share. But in this case Mr. Jones might be charged by the dealer a fee of 1/2 of 1%. Therefore Mr. Jones would receive $9,502.25 calculated as follows:

Cash received by Mr. Jones = (1,000 shares × \$9.55) − (\$9,550 × .005)
                                    = \$9,550 − \$47.75
                                    = \$9,502.25

Redemption Proceeds Paid in Few Days

Usually the mutual fund will pay the investor for his shares in cash within one to five days after the shares are duly presented for redemption. Legally, the mutual funds can take somewhat longer in redeeming their shares.

Under the provisions of the *Investment Company Act of 1940*, mutual fund redeemable shares must ordinarily be redeemed within *seven* days after they are tendered (that is, offered for redemption). However, under the act's provisions, the board of directors of the issuing mutual fund may suspend this right of redemption and postpone payment of the redemption price during any period:

1. when trading on the New York Stock Exchange is restricted or when the NYSE is closed for other than weekends and holidays
2. when the Securities and Exchange Commission has by order permitted the mutual fund to suspend the redemption right for the protection of shareholders
3. when an emergency exists that makes disposal of the fund's portfolio securities or the valuation of its net assets not reasonably practicable

Only once since the passage of the Investment Company Act of 1940 has the New York Stock Exchange closed its door due to an emergency. This was on the day of the assassination of President John F. Kennedy, Friday, November 22, 1963.

The sales representative should always stress to the prospective investor that redemption value may be less or more than the cost to the investor.

Redemption in "Kind"

It is legally mandatory that mutual funds redeem their shares when called upon to do so by their shareholders. Frequently, however, mutual funds reserve the right under unusual circumstances to make redemption payments in something other than cash.

When so stated in its prospectus, and when faced with an emergency, the board of directors of a mutual fund can make redemption payments to the fund's shareholders in securities, or in other assets of the fund. However, this *payment in kind*, as it is frequently called, seldom takes place. Almost 100% of the time, mutual fund shareholders sending shares in for redemption receive cash in payment from the fund.

INVESTMENT COMPANY EARNINGS AND DISTRIBUTIONS

Investment companies have two main sources of earnings—investment income and income realized by taking capital gains. Investment income consists of the dividend and interest payments investment companies receive from the corporations whose securities they hold in their portfolio. Capital gains are the profit investment companies make by selling a security for more than it originally cost to acquire. Payments to investment company shareholders generally are made from funds obtained from one or both of these two sources. Investment companies are required by law to indicate to their shareholders the sources of each distribution they make. Dividends and capital gains can never be added together when calculating the yield on a mutual fund. Only the dividend income portion of distributions may be used to calculate yield.

Most investment companies pay all of their income, after expenses, to their shareholders. By paying out all net income, investment companies are able to avoid federal income taxes.

Internal revenue authorities, under certain conditions, regard investment companies simply as conduits or pipelines between their shareholders and the corporations whose securities the investment companies hold. Whenever investment companies function simply as a type of passageway through which dividends and interest payments flow on their way from the corporation to the investor, they see no logical basis for taxing the investment company. However, individual investors receiving the income from the investment company must report it as personal income and pay the regular tax rates on that income. Whenever the investment company appears to function as a haven designed to protect investors from taxation, however, it is a different matter, and the internal revenue authorities view the investment company's tax liability differently.

Not all investment income distributed to mutual fund shareholders is qualified for the dividend exclusion provision of the federal income tax law. Part of the interest income which is distributed does qualify. Interest income would be found in the distributions of a balanced fund, for example. The dividend and interest exclusion under federal law is currently (1980) $200 per shareholder. If a shareholder of an investment company receives $220 of qualified income, he will pay taxes at ordinary income rates only on the $20. If a husband and wife both own shares and the husband receives $250 of qualified income dividends and the wife only $80, the husband would report $50 and the wife would report no dividends for taxable income. The husband could not use the additional $120 of the dividend exclusion that the wife could not use.

For an investment company to qualify for the special tax treatment permitted under the federal Internal Revenue Code, it must qualify as a "regulated" investment company. To qualify as a regulated investment company under *Subchapter M of the Internal Revenue Code*, the more important requirements are that

1. it must be a domestic corporation
2. it must be registered at all times during the taxable year under the Investment Company Act of 1940 either as a management company or as a unit investment trust
3. at least 90% of its gross income must be from dividends and interest from securities
4. it must distribute as taxable dividends not less than 90% of its net income for any taxable year.[3]

The effect of this regulation is to permit investment income to flow through the conduit of the fund shareholder who pays taxes at his individual rate without the necessity of the investment company's paying the higher corporate income taxes.

Investment companies, regulated or not, must make provision for and pay federal income taxes on any net income or capital gains they secure during the year that they do not pay out to their shareholders. In other words, if a regulated investment company, after paying out 90% of its income to qualify as a regulated investment company, retains the remaining 10% of its investment income, it would be taxed on this 10%. Furthermore, it would be taxed (at capital gains rates) on any capital gains it had realized during the year but had not distributed to its shareholders.

Every year, funds must report to their stockholders (IRS form 1099) the amounts distributed from earnings and interest as well as separately the amount from capital gains. Stockholders in turn must report these amounts on their federal and state tax returns.

Special Capital Gains Tax Feature

Under certain conditions, the Federal Revenue Act permits investors to pay taxes on some types of income at a rate lower than the rate required on regular income. For example, any profit received by an investor from the sale of a capital item such as securities is taxed as a long-term gain, if the investor has held it over one year. This tax is known as a *capital gains* tax (see page 360).

Investment company shareholders can regard a capital gains distribution from the investment company as a long-term capital gain even if the

[3]There are a number of additional minor technical requirements which must be met to qualify as a regulated investment company. Actually almost all the open-end and a majority of the closed-end investment companies are registered as regulated investment companies.

shareholder has only held the shares for one or two days. This is an exception to the standard rule, which indicates that a capital item must be held by the investor for longer than one year for any profit from its sale to be eligible for the lower tax rate applicable to long-term capital gains.

Investment company shareholders taking dividends in additional shares of stock (in lieu of cash) in most instances do not relieve themselves of the necessity of paying income taxes on such dividends.

Capital gains distributions, when available, normally are declared annually and are considered a return of capital that should be reinvested in order to keep the original investment intact. The reinvestment of capital gains distributions from an investment company (as distinguished from taking them in cash) does not enable the investor to avoid the capital gains tax.

Difference Between Open-End and Closed-End Investment Companies

Closed-end investment companies' shares are usually offered to the public at one time with the support of a large number of underwriters. Only on rare occasions are additional shares offered either to the public or to the companies' own shareholders.

Open-end investment companies' shares are *continuously* offered by broker-dealers. The important difference between an open-end and a closed-end investment company is the fact that the closed-end investment companys' shares are just like any other stock—*they cannot be redeemed by the holder*. They may be bought and sold in the market. Their price, however, depends on the value of their underlying securities and the demand and supply for that stock in the market.

Premiums and Discounts

The shares of closed-end investment companies almost always sell at a price that is different from the net asset value per share. But an open-end investment company's shares sell at their liquidating value. On rare occasions a closed-end investment company's shares will sell above their liquidating value. In this case they are said to be selling at a *premium*. This usually occurs in a bull market for an investment company with a good investment record. When a closed-end investment company's shares are selling below their net asset value, they are said to be selling at a *discount*. Discounts and premiums develop because the shares are traded in the open market and the prices at which they trade are due to the forces of demand and supply. Neither open- nor closed-end investment companies are good medium for short-term investors:—open-end because of the load and closed-end because the price of the stock does not move in unison with valuation of the underlying shares.

INVESTMENT COMPANY SHARE
QUOTATIONS

It is generally a simple matter to find the current redemption price and the current offering price of most mutual fund shares. These prices can be found by checking the bid-and-asked quotations of mutual fund shares printed in the daily newspapers. The net asset value per share and the *bid* price for mutual fund shares in the newspapers are one and the same. The net asset value per share, plus the sales charge, is the same as the *asked* price in the newspapers. The *public offering price* is the same as the asked price. It is computed, as provided in the fund prospectus, by determining the net asset value per share and adding the sales charge.

Finding the current market price of most closed-end investment company shares is also simply a matter of looking in the daily newspaper. Because many closed-end investment company shares are listed on securities exchanges, the daily stock market quotations will generally reveal the day's prices of these shares. The day's last trading price is the approximate price an individual would expect to pay for these shares if he planned to buy them the next day or, if he planned to sell the shares, the approximate price he would expect to receive for them. Quotations on closed-end investment company shares not listed on securities exchanges generally can be found in the over-the-counter quotation lists carried in many newspapers.

The sales charge of a particular mutual fund's shares can easily be determined from the newspaper bid-and-asked quotations. The actual dollar amount of the sales charge per share can be found by subtracting the bid price per share from the asked price per share. The actual dollar amount of the sales charge divided by the asked price per share will show the percentage sales charge.

To illustrate, Fictitious Mutual Fund Company shares are quoted in the newspapers as "bid $18.40, asked $20.00."

$20.00 − $18.40 = $1.60   (the actual dollar amount of sales charge)
$1.60 ÷ $20.00 = 8.00% (the percentage sales charge)

MUTUAL FUND ACCOUNTS
AND SERVICES

The minimum dollar or share amounts required by open-end investment companies vary considerably. Some do not have any minimum requirement, some have very low requirements of 10 or 15 shares, and some have fairly high minimums up to $2,500. In particular, municipal bond funds and the money-market funds have high requirements, running up to $10,000.

Most funds provide facilities for, and welcome, the reinvestment of dividends and capital gains. The investor should be aware that the spending of capital gains is a potential reduction of principal. Long-term capital gains are taxable as long-term capital gains regardless of the length of time a shareholder has held his shares. Short-term profits are taxable to the investor as income. Long- and short-term gains must be reported by investors whether taken in cash or reinvested by the fund. Most funds will reinvest dividends and capital gains at *net asset value*. Dividends are usually paid quarterly, although some are paid more frequently, sometimes monthly. Capital gains are usually paid once a year.

Accumulation Plan Holders

Accumulation plan holders are those investors who make formal arrangements to purchase mutual fund shares on a continuing basis. The money used to buy these shares often comes from the investor's current income. Purchases of additional shares are generally made every month or every quarter.

The term *accumulation plan holder* refers only to those investors who purchase the shares of open-end investment companies.

LEVEL CHARGE OR VOLUNTARY ACCUMULATION PLANS

Many funds permit investors to start voluntary plans requiring only an initial minimum purchase of a stated amount as an indication of the investor's wish to invest at intervals—sometimes monthly but at least a minimum stated annual amount. In actual fact, however, investors seldom adhere strictly to a schedule.

Voluntary accumulation plans are just what the name suggests. The person with this type of account does not make any *binding* commitment as to the total amount or the timing of his payments. The investor may increase his payments or may stop them without penalty. At the inception of the voluntary plan, a commercial bank is appointed to act as administrator of the plan to act as depository of the monies and the fund shares. The investor sends his money for the fund shares to the bank. The bank usually makes a small charge for this service. The bank custodian also reinvests the dividends and capital gains. Other advantages are dollar-cost averaging, professional management of the fund, diversification of portfolio, convenience, use of the breakpoint, and withdrawal privileges.

However, in recent years the greatest interest in accumulation plans has been exhibited for the popular Keogh and IRA plans (see pages 127–132). Investors who wish to purchase fund shares in connection with the Self-Employed Individual Tax Retirement Act of 1962 (Keogh Act) or to establish an Individual Retirement Account (IRA) must request forms from the fund. These forms are generally accepted by the Internal Revenue Service. Briefly under the Keogh plan an investor may contribute up to the lesser of 15% of his income or $7,500 a year. An investor who has no pension plan may contribute under IRA up to the lesser of 15% of his salary or $1,500. A married investor whose spouse is not employed may contribute up to $1,750. Investment fund shares made pursuant to these contributions and the accumulations thereon during the life of the plan receive deferred treatment on federal income taxes. A bank is appointed to act as custodian for these plans. The charges made seem reasonable. For example, one well-known bank charges $5 for acceptance of each plan and $5 a year thereafter. Also, a small charge is usually made for withdrawal. Both the Keogh and the IRA plans have penalties for excess contributions and for insufficient distributions after the age of 70 1/2 (see pages 127–132).

Contractual Plans. Contractual accumulation plans involve a definite commitment on the part of the investor. Under this type of plan the investor commits himself to a specific time schedule of periodic investments as well as to a total intended investment amount.

An investment company contractual plan holder can terminate his plan at any time, although in doing so the individual may incur a penalty. The penalty depends in part on the length of time that the investor has participated in the plan. These plans are also often referred to as penalty, or prepaid charge, or front-end load plans.

Plan companies and some underwriters and distributors offer contractual plans under which an investor makes investments of a fixed dollar amount at regular intervals, usually monthly, for a fixed number of years, usually ten years. Essentially, it is a dollar-cost averaging plan. Details are given in the plan prospectus. But a typical contractual accumulation plan might call for a $10,000 total investment accumulated through equal monthly or quarterly payments over a ten-year period. In recent years fund managers have not been pushing these so-called contractual periodic payment plans but have been concentrating more on the Keogh and IRA plans.

Under the Investment Company Act of 1940, a summary of which is on page 457, sales charges on contractual plans were limited to 9% of total investment. Also, the act permitted a deduction for sales charges of up to 50% of the first year's payment. This concentration of the sales charge in the first year sometimes resulted in a serious loss to the investor, particularly if he was unable to continue his payments.

Under the 9% load limit, the investor would pay a high amount during the beginning years and a lower amount later. For example, consider a ten-year, $10,000 plan requiring payments of $1,000 a year. The maximum load would be $900 (or 9% of $10,000). However, of the first year's payment of $1,000, 50% (or $500), could go to the sales representative, the underwriter, and so on, in the form of a sales load. However, the remaining sales load due of $400 ($900 less $500 = $400) would be spread over nine years at $44.44 a year ($400 ÷ 9). Thus an investor who makes all the payments pays no more than 9%. But the SEC complained bitterly to Congress and recommended that the contractual plans be eliminated as far as the front-end load was concerned. Attention should be called to the fact that the term *contractual* is a misnomer as far as the investor is concerned. The investor is not compelled to complete his payments; the investor is not sued if he ceases to meet his installments. But the investor may well lose money if he stops his payments shortly after the first year, as a large part of the first year's payments have gone to pay the load. Hence we hear the term front-end load, prepaid charge, and the improperly used penalty plan.

Under the *Investment Company Amendment Act of 1970*, a summary of which is on page 460, sales charges may be imposed under one of two alternative methods. Under the "spread load," the sales charge is limited to 20% in the first year. But deductions over the first four years must not average more than 16%, that is, 16 times 4 years equals 64% of the total sales load. In the remaining five years, the sales charges must not be over 36% of the total load. Assuming a 9% sales load, which is the maximum sales charge that any accumulation plan can charge, we would have the following:

TABLE 5-3

Ten-Year Accumulation Program

($1,000 × 10 = $10,000)	
9% sales charge	$900
First year, pay 20%	200
Second to fourth years, pay 44%	440
Fifth to tenth years, pay 36%	260
	$900

Under both plans the bank custodian must, within 60 days, send the investor notice of the type of plan and the amount of the charges. Furthermore, the bank must advise the customer that the plan may be canceled within 45 days of the notification. The plan holder will then receive the value of his shares as of that date plus a full refund of the sales charges. In addition, the bank custodian charges a small fee for bookkeeping, mailings, and the like. This might be in the neighborhood of $1.00 a month or a small fraction of the value of the fund.

Under the second plan, as much as 50% of the first year's payment may be deducted as a sales charge, with the remaining 50% deducted in equal amounts over the remaining years of the contract. But the plan holder must be advised, if he misses a certain specified number of payments within

15 to 18 months, that he has the right to cancel the plan. The investor is then entitled to receive the current value of his securities plus a refund of all the sales charges paid that are in excess of 15% of all the payments made to the date of cancellation.

Dividends from net investment income and distributions from other sources are automatically used to purchase additional fund shares under contractual accumulation plans. These payments are taxable to the shareholder despite the fact that they are reinvested. Also within 12 months the plan may be canceled by pleading illness or unemployment with refund of the sales charge.

The use of the contractual plan method of selling mutual fund shares is illegal in some states. Securities representatives should check the statutes of the state in which they operate to determine what restrictions, if any, are imposed on the distribution of mutual fund shares through contractual plans.

A number of funds have declining-term group life-plan-completion insurance available to purchasers of contractual or voluntary plans. Under these group insurance plans, the contractual plan holder pays a premium for the assurance of completion of his program in the event of death. This coverage is much like that taken out by homeowners to assure the payment of the mortgage in case of premature death.

In the event of death prior to completion of the plan, insurance proceeds equal to the unpaid cash balance due on the plan are paid by the insurance company to the custodian and, after the usual deductions, are applied to the purchase of fund shares. No part of the proceeds of the insurance are paid directly to the estate or to the beneficiary of the plan holder, as this function is performed by the custodian at the direction of the new owners of the shares.

REVIEW QUESTIONS

1. Define an investment company and explain the important advantages to investors of holding stocks of investment companies.
2. Describe and distinguish among a management company, an open-end company, a closed-end company, and a diversified company.
3. What are two reasons for the substantial growth of investment companies in recent years? Give detailed reasons.
4. In what way are investment companies a hedge against inflation?
5. Explain how mutual funds are organized, managed, and sold.
6. What does the term *load* mean? What is a no-load fund?
7. Describe regular account holders and accumulation plan holders.
8. Differentiate between level charge and contractual plans.

9. Describe how a holder of mutual fund shares may redeem them. How is the redemption price calculated?
10. Where can an investor in a mutual fund find the redemption and offering prices for his or her shares?
11. Explain the investment policies of a diversified common stock fund, a specialized fund, a balanced fund, and an income fund.
12. Explain in detail a regulated investment company and show how the fact that it is a "regulated" company affects the tax position of the holder.
13. What are the costs of operating a mutual fund? About what percentage are these costs of the fund's assets? About what percentage are these costs of the fund's annual income?
14. Why are mutual funds poor vehicles for short-term investments?
15. Explain two methods by which sales charges on contractual plans may be calculated.
16. Describe briefly money-market funds, municipal bond funds, and index funds. Explain the respective reasons for their growth in recent years.

TRUE AND FALSE QUESTIONS

1. An investment company might be defined as: *True*   *False*
    a. any corporation that invests in securities   _____   _____
    b. a corporation or trust through which investors pool their funds to obtain diversification   _____   _____
    c. a corporation that buys securities to obtain control of a company or companies.   _____   _____
2. An open-end investment company may: *True*   *False*
    a. raise capital by selling bonds, preferred stock, or common stock   _____   _____
    b. is permitted to borrow from banks up to 33% of net assets   _____   _____
    c. sell only common stock.   _____   _____
3. Diversified investment companies: *True*   *False*
    a. cannot invest more than 5% of assets in any one corporation   _____   _____
    b. cannot have more than 5% of voting securities in any one corporation   _____   _____
    c. are the most common type of investment companies.   _____   _____
4. An open-end investment company: *True*   *False*
    a. may issue any amount of debt securities, the same as an open-end mortgage   _____   _____

b. will usually continuously offer for sale its   *True*   *False*
common shares and redeem them at book
value (net asset value)   _____   _____

c. usually requires the buyer to pay book value
plus the commission charged by the New
York Stock Exchange   _____   _____

d. has constantly changing number of shares.   _____   _____

5. Investment companies (open-end and closed-end) usually afford the
investor: *True*   *False*

a. a means of obtaining a diversified interest in
the leading securities of the country   _____   _____

b. some protection in the event of price inflation   _____   _____

c. assurance his fund will be managed to
provide appreciation over the years   _____   _____

d. assurance of being able to redeem his fund
shares on demand at net asset value   _____   _____

e. all of the above.   _____   _____

6. The term *load*:   *True*   *False*

a. is the sales charge made by *all* investment
companies and is divided between the principal underwriter and the dealers   _____   _____

b. is the amount added to the net asset value and
must be stated in the fund's prospectus as a
percentage of the offering price   _____   _____

c. is the fee charged the stockholder of an
investment company for management of the
funds.   _____   _____

7. An open-end mutual fund has a bid price (net asset value) of $9.30 per
share and a load of 7%; the asked price is: *True*   *False*

a. $10.00   _____   _____

b. $9.95   _____   _____

c. $9.90.   _____   _____

8. Regular account holders are: *True*   *False*

a. customers who have agreed to make regular
purchases of investment companies   _____   _____

b. customers who have made *lump-sum* investments but have not agreed to making periodic
investments   _____   _____

c. customers with certain exceptions who may
get a lower sales charge if they sign a *letter of
intent* to purchase a required amount within a
stated period not to exceed 13 months.   _____   _____

9. Contractual plans have certain peculiar characteristics, which include:

		True	False
a.	maximum sales charge of 9% of the amount invested	____	____
b.	right of the investment company to sue the customer if he defaults on his contracts to make the required payments	____	____
c.	privileges to sell them in all states.	____	____

10. Net asset value is usually:

		True	False
a.	calculated by adding the capital stock account, the surplus, and the undivided profits, and dividing by the number of shares at the end of each business day	____	____
b.	calculated by appraising the value of the portfolio once each business day and adding the cash balance, deducting the liabilities, and dividing by the number of shares	____	____
c.	different from the cost of the investment company to the buyer.	____	____

11. As far as redemption of mutual fund shares is concerned:

		True	False
a.	the shareholder usually receives the net asset value of his shares within five days after the shares are presented	____	____
b.	the Investment Company Act of 1940 provides shares must ordinarily be redeemed within seven days	____	____
c.	the directors of a mutual fund may, under certain circumstances, suspend or postpone redemption of their shares.	____	____

12. Diversified common stock funds usually hold:

		True	False
a.	blue chip stocks	____	____
b.	growth stocks	____	____
c.	no bonds or preferred stocks	____	____
d.	stocks with reasonable growth and reasonable current returns.	____	____

13. In a balanced fund:

		True	False
a.	the stated policy is at all times to have a portion of assets in fixed income securities	____	____
b.	greater long-term appreciation is *assured* because in periods of market decline, the assets will be conserved by the fixed-income		

		True	False
	securities and the assets will be increased by shifting the stocks in recovery periods	_____	_____
c.	somewhat larger income is provided than in growth funds due to the presence of fixed-income securities	_____	_____
d.	somewhat greater stability of asset value is provided in a declining market.	_____	_____

14. A specialized fund:

		True	False
a.	usually invests in the securities of a single or allied industry	_____	_____
b.	sometimes seeks its objective by investing in a specific geographical area	_____	_____
c.	has had a poor performance record and should be avoided	_____	_____
d.	usually as as its objective long-term growth.	_____	_____

15. A *regulated investment company:*

		True	False
a.	is a term applied to all investment companies that are regulated by the Securities and Exchange Commission	_____	_____
b.	must pay out 90% income and capital gains to qualify	_____	_____
c.	pays no taxes on the remaining 10% held.	_____	_____

16. The custodian of a mutual fund is usually a commercial bank that:

		True	False
a.	performs management, supervisory, and investment functions	_____	_____
b.	provides protection against decline in the assets of the fund	_____	_____
c.	should be well known to help the sales of the fund shares	_____	_____
d.	performs routine tasks such as acting as transfer agent or registrar, dividend paying agent, or receiver of payments for shares.	_____	_____

17 An investment company shareholder acquired stock on January 3, 1979. On January 10, 1979 the company declared $1.00 a share of long-term capital gains. The shareholder should declare this distribution as:

		True	False
a.	a short-term capital gain as the stock was held for only a week	_____	_____
b.	a long-term capital gain as it is a long term to the company.	_____	_____

18. Mutual funds are not used as vehicles for short-term trading because:

		True	False
a.	the initial sales charge on most funds is high and can run up to 9% of the offering price	____	____
b.	the fluctuations over short periods of time are usually small	____	____
c.	the National Association of Securities Dealers *forbids* brokers to recommend trading of mutual funds.	____	____

19. Closed-end investment companies:

		True	False
a.	almost never issue additional stock	____	____
b.	do not redeem their stock on demand	____	____
c.	seldom sell at book value	____	____
d.	are usually traded on the New York Stock Exchange.	____	____

20. The following are the net asset values and the asked prices of investment companies; they are all probably open-end companies *except:*

	Net Asset Value	Asked Price	True	False
a.	$21.35	$19.14	____	____
b.	9.20	10.00	____	____
c.	10.10	13.20	____	____
d.	11.30	11.30	____	____
e.	4.70	5.00	____	____

21. A holder of a tax-exempt unit investment trust:

		True	False
a.	does not have to pay federal income taxes on interest collected by the fund	____	____
b.	does not have to pay capital gains taxes on the profits realized by the fund	____	____
c.	can take advantage of continuous offerings of the investment units.	____	____

6
Individual Retirement Plans

Fixed Annuity Contracts

Almost all life insurance companies issue fixed annuity policies that guarantee fixed payments to the annuitants, usually for life. The rate of payment is sometimes fixed at a dollar amount each month, for example, at $300 a month. Sometimes the rate is increased. For example, in 1978 Home Life contracts guaranteed not less than 7% interest in the first year and 4% thereafter. In addition, the annuitant participates in higher yield through a dividend declared at the beginning of each year. This rate changes from year to year.

Annuities are bought either by paying a lump sum or by making installment payments (called deferred annuities) during the investor's productive years. Interest on these installments is paid by the insurance company and accumulates tax free until payments are made to the annuitant. If the individual dies before the annuity payments start, his or her beneficiary receives the aggregate premiums paid. Sometimes there are no sales charges. On occasion, companies impose an expense charge similar to the load charge in a mutual fund. But these charges decline as the total amount paid increases.

The cost of a fixed annuity depends on the age and sex of the individual. Insurance companies have mortality tables that show the life expectancy of men and women at every age (women have longer life expectancy than men). Based on these tables, an assumed rate of interest and the estimated expense (e.g., sales commissions), the annuity payments are set.

The investment risk is assumed by the insurance company. Payments for fixed annuities are sometimes commingled with the general funds for investment by the insurance company. But life insurance companies are carefully regulated in most states as to investments, types of insurance written and so on. The bulk of the investments are in bonds and mortgages—relatively few stocks. The annuitant relinquishes control of the principal upon commencement of the annuity payments. However, the annuitant usually gets reports and sometimes the privilege of voting at annual meetings. Some contracts provide that, at any time before annuity payments start, the amounts paid into the fund may be withdrawn.

Annuity payments might continue for the life of the annuitant only and thereafter have no value. This type of annuity is suggested for individuals in good health with no dependents. Another plan might provide for lower payments for the annuitant's life *and* his spouse. This plan is suggested for a man with a young wife. Still another plan might be an annuity with years *certain*, say, 20 years. This means that payments would run for 20 years regardless of the lifetime of the annuitant. If he or she died prior to the certain years, their heirs would receive the balance of the payments. But, if the annuitant lives longer than the years certain, the payments of the insurance company continue.

Variable Annuity Contracts

Variable annuity contracts are self-describing. In return for payments either in lump sum or in installments made by the participant or contract owner, the insurance company agrees to make payments in variable amounts. Usually, a life insurance company forms a separate subsidiary to hold the investments and make payments on the variable annuities. For example, Teachers Insurance and Annuity Association (TIAA) formed the College Retirement Equities Fund (CREF). A large part of the funds of the variable annuity companies are invested in common stocks, largely institutional "blue chips." Therefore, the dollar payments fluctuate with the general stock market. (There is no guaranteed rate of interest or rate of return as in the fixed annuities.) Good management of the stock account can cushion a decline in a poor stock market by increasing the proportion of cash (money-market instruments) but cannot avoid a decline in a severe depression when almost all stocks go down.

The annuitant relinquishes control of the principal paid into the company but retains certain voting rights such as changes in investment policy, the election of managers, and so on. These rights are described in the annuity contract. The risk of investment of a variable annuity is assumed by the annuitant.

Separate Account

A separate account as the name implies, is an account that is separate and apart from the general investment account of an insurance company. The separate account, sometimes designated by a letter, collects the installment payments from the participants (either individuals or groups) who are making payments for a variable annuity to be transferred to annuity units at some future date. During this accumulation period, the separate account invests the proceeds in securities, largely in equities. In other words, a separate account is similar to a diversified common stock investment company. Investments can be made indirectly if separate accounts are organized as a unit investment trust. For example, the Aetna Variable Annuity Life Insurance Company is a subsidiary of the Aetna Life and Casualty Company.

Tax Treatment of Separate Accounts

There are two types of variable annuities—qualified and nonqualified. A qualified annuity is one that has met certain requirements of the Internal Revenue Service. The most important of these is that the qualified variable annuity would not in any way discriminate among employees. This means that all should be treated alike. The officers, for example, would not be favored over the regular employees. Both the investment income and realized capital gains of a qualified separate account are reinvested without federal income or capital gains taxes. But the company reserves the right to make a deduction for taxes should they be imposed in the future.

Sometimes an insurance company might set up a separate account for a *nonqualified* variable annuity. A nonqualified variable annuity might be bought just for officers of a corporation. The organizational setup is the same as for a qualified annuity; investment income is not taxed, but realized capital gains *are*.

It is most important to remember that nontax-qualified variable *annuity contracts* are securities and must be registered under the Securities Act of 1933. Nontax qualified *separate accounts* must be registered as investment companies under the Investment Company Act of 1940. Certain tax-qualified separate accounts are exempt from registration as securities under the Investment Company Amendments Act of 1970. Further, the sales literature is subject to regulation by the NASD and the SEC.

Firms selling interests in separate accounts must be registered as broker-dealers under the Securities Exchange Act of 1934. Separate accounts have their own managers and directors. These include a number of officers from the insurance company and sometimes outside individuals who are experts in the field of finance. Some managements have been more skillful than others. But the regulations of the NASD forbid sales representatives of all securities, including variable annuities, to state or imply that diversification or professional management represents a guarantee of a gain or the avoidance of a loss. Sometimes outside investment advisors are hired to advise the management and make recommendations.

The prospectus of a variable annuity offering lists the officers and directors of the Special Fund as well as their affiliations with the insurance company, their principal occupations, and other connections.

Voting

Generally, each contract owner is entitled to a vote by the proportion of the value of his or her account to the total fund. The contract owners may vote on the board of managers, the public auditors, and the investment advisor and may approve changes in the investment policy. Votes are usually cast by signing proxy statements approving the policies of the management.

Type of Securities Held

The securities in the separate account of a variable annuity are largely high-grade common stocks, which pay dividends, as well as cash—short-term money-market instruments, which pay interest. These payments accrue to the participants as do the realized capital gains and are not subject to federal income or capital gains taxes, provided the variable annuity is *qualified* by the Internal Revenue Service. Unrealized appreciation is not taxed.

Investment Restrictions of the Separate Account

The investment restrictions in variable annuity contracts are similar in many ways to those found in the prospectuses of investment companies. There are limits as to the total investment in one company—usually 5%—and there are prohibitions against trading in commodities and restrictions on short selling. Restrictions are also placed on selling call options, buying real estate, and underwriting securities.

Investment Objectives

The most important investment objective set forth in the prospectus of a variable annuity is to provide a retirement income. Many individuals earn good money during their productive years—from the ages of 30 to 65. They want to cushion the sharp decline in income on retirement. Holders of variable annuities are also concerned about inflation. They are hoping in some way the income from variable annuities will in part protect them against inflation. (To date, as of 1979, this has been a bitter disappointment.) Further, they are fearful that, should a depression or even a recession strike, the income from their variable annuities will fall sharply. For most investors the most important investment objectives are the accumulation and the preservation of principal and income.

At the start or even during the accumulation period, some contract owners may elect to have their net annuity purchase payments accumulated in one or more funds. Further, some variable annuity funds permit contract owners to shift among funds during the accumulation period. However, these shifts are contingent on compliance with certain regulations set forth in the prospectuses.

For example, a contract holder might select a fund that is fully invested in common stocks, another largely in diversified debt securities, and a third in short-term money-market instruments. Investment policies are detailed in each prospectus.

Methods of Purchasing Variable Annuities

Variable annuities are purchased in the same way that fixed annuities are. There are lump-sum payments when a large sum is paid to the variable annuity insurance company and payments start next month. There are lump-sum payments with a variable amount starting at some later date, say, when the annuitant reaches 65. Finally and most common there are the periodic payment, or a deferred variable, annuities. The annuitant in this case pays a stated sum every month for a period of years until he or she reaches retirement age of, say, 65 in return for an annuity at that time. Most variable annuity contracts have minimum and maximum purchase payments. For instance, Aetna requires contributions of at least $50 a month ($600 per year). [The Internal Revenue Service at times imposes a maximum that may be allowed as a deduction.] For example, self-employed individuals under the Keogh (HR-10) plan (see page 127) are allowed to establish for themselves or their employees pension and profit sharing trusts or annuity plans (see page 132). In these plans the limits are $7500.

The contract owner's interest is increased by accumulation of net investment income and capital gains in the separate account. Reinvestment without federal taxes is made of all income and capital gains.

Sales Charges

Details of sales charges are set forth in the prospectus of each variable annuity. Level sales charges are made on (1) single payments for a deferred annuity, (2) single payments for an immediate annuity, and (3) periodic payments for a deferred annuity. (Level sales charges are a fixed percentage of the purchase payments.)

For *single-purchase* variable annuity contracts, the percentage deduction typically ranges from around 3% to about 5%, declining as the amount purchased increases to as little as 1/2% for amounts of around $500,000. There is usually a small annual deduction for administrative (bookkeeping) and collection charges.

For *deferred variable* annuities, deductions are made from payments for (1) investment management, (2) premium taxes when levied by states or municipalities ranging from .50% to 2.50% of the annuity considerations, (3) minimum death benefit charges, (4) brokerage fees, (5) redemption fees, and (6) waiver of premiums. For installment purchase contracts the percentage deductions from premium payments vary from company to company. Some charge as much as 9% of the premium; others charge as little as 4%. In all cases these deductions drop sharply as the amounts paid to the companies increase. Further, firms selling variable annuity contracts offer breakpoint sales and/or rights of accumulation as in open-end mutual funds (see page 99).

Dollar-Cost Averaging

Periodic payments into the separate account to buy accumulation units enables the contract holder to dollar-cost average his account. Because the separate fund is largely stock oriented, it will fluctuate with the stock market. Therefore, as the contract owner makes regular monthly payments, he is bound to catch some of the lows in the market when more units can be purchased (see page 101).

Rights

The contract owner has the right to change his beneficiary or make assignment of all other rights conferred by the contract or allowed of the insurance company such as withdrawal of cash value prior to death. The contract owner usually does not have the right to borrow or pledge his or her contract for a loan.

Death Benefits

In most cases the contract for a variable annuity provides that, if the annuitant dies before the deferred maturity date, the insurance company will pay the cash value of the accumulation units to the beneficiary. The maturity date may be any time prior to the annuitant's 70 1/2 birthday.

Valuation of a Variable Annuity Contract

The value of a variable annuity contract is expressed in terms of units —units that have been paid in by the holder of the contract. Whereas the value of a fixed annuity is expressed in term of dollars, each variable annuity unit has a value derived from the value of the investment portfolio held in the separate account. This portfolio is appraised at the close of the New York Stock Exchange on each business day. But the accumulation units are simply an accounting measure used to determine a contract owner's interest in the separate account during the accumulation period of the deferred annuity contract.

Periodically the investor buys more units at the last closing price adding to the units already held. In each case, a deduction is made for sales charges. Thus, the total value of each investor's units is the number of units times the current market value of each unit.

Rights of Withdrawal and Refund Sales Changes

During the accumulation period of *front-end* load contracts (under the 1970 Investment Company Amendments Act), the investor, regardless of the plan followed for front-end loads, is entitled to a full refund of the value of his account if that investor cancels his plan within 45 days. But, under the 1970 act, a 50% front-end load certificate may be sold, provided the plan sponsors agree to refund 85% of the sales load and provided the notice is given the sponsor within 18 months. Another alternative for front-end load funds permits the fund to spread the load so that no more than 20% may be deducted in any one year or an average of 16% a year during a four-year period.

Some contracts provide that the contract may become paid up automatically if (1) after a stated number of days (usually 31) the contract owner fails to remit to the company the required contribution or (2) as a written notice the contract owner advises the company to change to a paid-up status.

The termination value of the contract will usually be the unit value of all participant individual accounts thereunder less sometimes a small fee (e.g., 2%). If the value of the accumulated units is larger than the cost, the difference is taxable as current income.

Insurance Rider

A minimum death benefit guarantee may be added to the individual account. This guarantee usually provides that, should the contract owner die before the annuity payments commence, the company will pay the beneficiary the greater of (1) the value of the participant's individual account or (2) 100% of the purchase payments. A premium of 1% of each purchase payment is usually charged.

Risks Assumed of the Insurance Company

The insurance company assumes two risks: an annuity *mortality* risk and an *expense* risk. The annuity mortality risk is the company's promise to continue making payments determined in accordance with the annuity tables. The retiree at this time has several choices. He may take full payments for his life with no further payments on his death. Or the retiree may choose to have lower payments made to himself and/or to his spouse. These same options are open to the fixed annuity policy holders. Thus if the retiree lives to be 95 years of age, the company that has written the policy on a mortality table that indicated that the retiree should live only to the age of 76 loses money. The mortality risk, assumed by the insurance company, arises from its obligation to continue to make fixed or variable annuity payments determined in accordance with the annuity tables and other provisions of the contract, no matter how long the annuitant lives. This assures the annuitant that neither his own longevity nor an improvement in life expectancy generally will have any adverse effect on his payments. To compensate the company for assuming this mortality risk, some companies charge a small mortality risk premium.

The expense risk is self-explanatory. The company specifies the charges to the contract owner for expenses in the contract. The company assumes the risk that the deductions provided in the contract for sales and administration expenses may be insufficient to cover the actual cost of such items. If so, the loss may fall on the company. The deductions are designed only to cover the company's anticipated costs. These expense charges are fixed at the start of the contract and do not change.

Thus the annuitant receives a stated number of annuity units. These are a fixed number and do not change.

Group Variable Annuity Contract

These are plans designed for and adopted by employers for their employees, usually when 20 or more participants are involved. A single master group contract is issued. If the plan is for all employees without discrimination, it is a nontax qualified plan. If it is for certain employees only, it is a nonqualified plan. Qualified plans are set up by universities, schools, firms, and the like for *all* employees. Usually, both the employer and employee make contributions. Minimum purchase payments are specified in the contract. The employees are often given the option of contributing to fixed or variable annuities or to a combination of both. On reaching retirement age, each participant receives annuity units with payment options in the same manner as would an individual contract holder.

Annuity Units

When a contract holder reaches retirement age or the time at which he or she wishes to start receiving payments, the number of *accumulation units* held by the participant is exchanged for a promise to pay each month the current value of a fixed number of *annuity units*. (The investor pays into the company for *accumulation* units, but for *annuity* units the investor receives money. Also, the accumulation units over the years increase in number with payments, but the annuity units are fixed as there are no more payments.)

The process of conversion is somewhat more complicated. For example, one large variable annuity fund calculates, first, the value of the accumulation units at, say, $50,000 on April 1. Then by the annuity tables the "annuity factor" is calculated. This is the cost of buying an annuity that will pay $1.00 a month considering the sex and life expectancy of the annuitant. Let us say this is $160 for a male aged 65. In this case an assumed interest rate (AIR) is taken at 4%. Here the annuity company believes that 4% is a reasonable advance earnings assumption to be used in annuity calculations. But no statement should be made that the assumed interest rate (AIR) represents a guarantee of a gain in value of an annuity unit or even of income.

The next step is to see how much income a month the $50,000 of accumulation units will buy for a retiree at the age of 65. This is accomplished by dividing $50,000 by $160 (his annuity factor), or $312.50. To determine how many annuity units will be used each month, the $312.50 would have to be divided by the current value of the annuity units, which, let us say, is $24.55 on April 1. This would be $12.729. *Thus the annuitant would receive 12.729 units every month for as long as he lives.* Looking at it another way, the annuitant would receive $312.50 a month, or 12.729 × $24.55. Now, unfortunately, because this is a variable annuity, the payments are subject to an annual revaluation. The new monthly income would be determined by multiplying the 12.729 monthly units by the *new* annuity value.

Valuation of Annuity Units

The annuity units are appraised each year. The combined earnings from securities held and capital gains and losses are calculated to determine the amount by which the variable annuity unit differs from an assumed rate. For example, if the value of the unit rises from $24.55 to $26.20, the monthly payment would rise from $312.50 to $333.50, that is, $26.20 × 12.729. *In summary, it is the combination of both dividends and changes in capital value that determine the amount by which variable income varies from an assumed rate of income.* It should be stressed that all forms of lifetime annuity payments, whether fixed or variable, include two parts: (1) a partial return of principal and (2) investment earnings.

Payout (Settlement) Options

When the contract holder has completed the payments for his accumulation units, selection must be made of the methods of payments from the new annuity units. These options include the following:

A life annuity pays the highest rate to the annuitant, but all payments cease on death.

A joint and survivor annuity pays for the life of the annuitant and for the life of his surviving spouse.

A life annuity with period certain pays for a specific number of years, say, 20 but also continues payments if the annuitant lives beyond that period. For example if a person with a life annuity of 20 years certain lives for only 12 of those 20 years, his heir would receive payments for the remaining 8 years. But, if the annuitant lives beyond the 20 years certain, he would receive regular payments as long as he lives.

The unit refund life annuity stipulates that a fixed number of units is paid each year to the annuitant for a stated period. At the death of the annuitant, the balance of the units is paid to the annuitant's heir.

The installments for a designated period stipulates, just as it says, that the annuitant may contract to receive payments for a stated period—say, 10, 15, or 20 years. At the end of the period, payments cease. If the annuitant is still alive at the end of the period, there would be no more payments. If the annuitant dies before the end of the period, payments would continue to his heir.

The installments for a designated amount stipulates that a fixed amount will be paid out each year until the amount is exhausted. If the annuitant dies before the amount is depleted, payments will continue to be paid to his heirs until the stated amount is exhausted.

Taxes on Variable Annuities Units

The contract owners as we have seen have not been taxed on the income and capital gains realized on their accumulation units. But the income on the annuity units is fully taxable as income.

Broker-Dealers' Role

Some life insurance companies are joining with broker-dealer firms to sell and manage separate accounts. For example, the Bankers Security Life Insurance Society has separate accounts for five Oppenheimer funds that are managed by the Oppenheimer Management Corporation. Deductions not exceeding 8.5% are made from each purchase for sales and administrative charges and the minimum death benefit. There is also a management fee of 1% of the net asset value.

Self-Employed Pension Plans (Keogh Plans — HR-10)

Under the Keogh Act of 1962 (named after Congressman Eugene J. Keogh), self-employed persons can purchase for themselves and their employees funds intended for retirement income. Contributions are deductible from current taxable income for federal income tax purposes. Every self-employed person must be engaged in business for himself or as a partner owning more than a 10% interest in the capital or profits of a partnership (generally a person who is subject to the self-employment tax provisions of the Social Security Administration). Self-employed individuals include architects, entertainers, dentists, doctors, electricians, independent contractors, lawyers, sale proprietors, and so forth. These people can over the years contribute to an annuity (fixed or variable), a trust, a pension or profit sharing plan, an investment company with a qualified bank custodian, a savings account, or a savings and loan account.

The maximum annual contribution allowed under present laws is the lesser of 15% of earned income or $7,500. Voluntary contributions may be made up to the lesser of $2,500 or 10% of his or her self-employed earned income. These contributions are available only when there are employees in the plan who are permitted to make voluntary contributions. These contributions cannot be a deduction from income for tax purposes, but the income earned by those contributions is *not* taxable until the benefits under the plan are distributed. The fixed percentage applicable each year is specified in the executed pension plan document. The minimum contribution (sometimes called Mini Keogh) applies to individuals who have a small earned income from self-employment. These individuals can contribute the *lesser* of 100% of earnings or $750. Earned income includes all the net earnings from trade or business or personal services; also, a person who works for a salary and in addition receives consulting fees, royalties, and the like might consider this extra income as self-employed income. This is often true for a college professor.

Tax benefits are important. For federal income tax purposes, a self-employed person may deduct 100% of all contributions subject to the maximum amounts mentioned. Further, the income accruals and the capital gains on the retirement funds are not subject to federal income or capital gains taxes. But this does not mean that the income and capital gains taxes can be forgotten. They are merely postponed. Contributions, however, may *not* be withdrawn until the individual is 59 1/2 years old. There are severe penalties for premature withdrawal amounting to 10% of the amount withdrawn. But, when the plan holder reaches 70 1/2 years of age, withdrawls *must* start. The trustee or custodian for the plan works out a systematic withdrawal plan based on the plan holder's life expectancy. These withdrawal payments must be reported and taxed as income. However, the total tax paid by the individual should be less, owing to the typically lower tax bracket of a retired person.

Also, funds may be withdrawn in a lump sum. A special provision of the Keogh plan reduces the tax impact if lump-sum distribution is taken. The contributor can also elect to receive his funds through an annuity contract. The payments received are taxed as annuity income.

In the event of death of the plan holder prior to the completion of the plan or retirement, the payments to his or her heirs depends on the type of plan adopted. For example, one insurance company guarantees the cash value of the annuity set up under the plan or the sum of all the purchase payments made.

Contributions do not have to be made every year and they may even be stopped entirely. In this event, the fund continues to grow by accumulated interest or dividends. However, if the individual has contracted for a specific plan such as for a deferred annuity, regular payments might be required (interruption of payments was discussed earlier). Excess contributions are subject to a 6% cumulative penalty tax.

Keogh plans may also be set up for *employees*. Employees may be included at any time within the first three years of employment and must be included after three years of service. A year of service is any 12-month period in which an employee has worked 1,000 hours or more. Further, the owner-employer must not in any way favor or discriminate against any of his employees. The amount contributed by the employer must at least equal the fixed percentage deposited for his or her personal benefit. For example, if the owner earned $75,000, his maximum contribution would be $7,500, or 10%. Therefore the percentage rate required of other employees would be 10%.

For each taxable year, the employer may make contributions not to exceed the lesser of $7,500 or 15% of the participant's compensation. No more than the first $100,000 of a participant's compensation may be taken into account for this purpose.

Whereas the pension plan also covers persons other than owner-employers, the plan may provide for additional voluntary contributions of all participants. In this event, an owner-employer may also make a voluntary contribution of his own behalf at the same rate for all participants but not to exceed 10% of his earned income of $2,500 annually, whichever is less. Thus the owner-employer may deduct 100% of the amount contributed on his behalf from earned income when computing federal income taxes. All contributions paid into the plan of the employer on behalf of employees may be deducted by the employer as a business expense. Further, the interest and dividends accruing in the account will not be taxed until retirement of the individual participants. Some savings banks and savings and loan organizations charge a small fee for setting up Keogh accounts; some do not.

As in the case of individual Keogh accounts, participants have the right to designate a change of name of the beneficiary who would be entitled to benefits in the event of death. The employee has fully vested rights to all contributions made for his or her benefit. Distribution is made upon termination, by retirement, or otherwise.

In summary, the Keogh plan has several advantages because (1) it provides immediate tax savings via the deduction of contributions from taxable income, (2) it allows the earnings on the accumulating fund to be exempt from income taxes until distributed, (3) it provides for a retirement income when tax rates for the individual will likely be lower, and (4) it is flexible in that unless a specific plan has been set up payments may be irregular.

Individual Retirement Account (IRA)

Under the Employee Retirement Income Security Act of 1974 (ERISA), an individual who is not an active participant in a retirement plan sponsored by his employer and who has wages, salary, or self-employment income is eligible to establish an individual retirement account or annuity. Passive earnings such as interest and dividends do not count. The participant must not for any part of the year be an active participant in any qualified pension, profit sharing, or a similar plan. He or she must be less than 70 1/2 years old at all times during the tax year the contribution is made. Thus the purpose of the IRA plans is to enable individuals *not covered by qualified pension plans* or Keogh plans (HR-10) to build retirement income. An important feature of IRA plans is that they include individuals working for a salary not covered of private pension plans, whereas Keogh covers many self-employed. The IRA is intended largely to supplement Social Security benefits.

Contributions

Contributions must be made to an individual retirement account at a savings bank, a savings and loan association, or a savings account at a commercial bank. Also, contributions may be made to an annuity account of a life insurance company.

Each year a participant may contribute up to 15% of his or her gross compensation income and/or 15% of earned income as a self-employed person, but no more than $1,500, whichever is the lesser. However, if the spouse does not work and has no personal service income (PSI), the deduction could run as high as $1,750 provided his PSI income was at least $11,667 (15% × $11,667 = $1,750). However, the couple must split their total contributions so that half, or $875, goes to an IRA account in husband's name and half, or $875, goes to wife's name.

The maximum a husband and wife can contribute is $3,000, provided the husband and wife each earn at least $10,000.

Tax Status

Yearly deposits or contributions are federal income tax deductible. The tax deduction for IRA deposits is in addition to all other deductions to which the individual is entitled, such as the standard deduction. But any excess contribution is *not* tax deductible on federal income tax return and a

6% nondeductible excise tax on such excess will be imposed. The excise tax will be applied each year to the excess that is permitted to remain in any individual's pension plan.

The interest earned on the savings account and the earnings and capital gains on the annuity or investment account during the accumulation period are tax deferred until the earnings are paid out.

Prohibited Transactions

The IRA plan holder is not permitted to borrow money (or pledge it as security) on his or her plan. The consequence is to disqualify the plan, so that the entire value of the plan will be taxable as ordinary income.

Until the plan holder reaches the age of 59 1/2, no *withdrawal* can be made without paying a 10% penalty tax on the amount withdrawn. Withdrawals may be made without penalty starting after age 59 1/2 or before that age in the case of disability or death.

Death Benefits

In the event of the death of the plan holder before retirement, most institutions pay the IRA deposits to the named beneficiary or to his estate. The amount paid is included in the deceased's gross estate for tax purposes.

If the participant dies after payments have started and while there is still a balance in his account, this balance under certain circumstances may be tax free. To qualify for this favored estate tax treatment, the named beneficiary must be someone other than the participant's estate (the husband or wife, for example). Then, the beneficiary must agree to withdraw the IRA balance in substantially equal installment periodic payments over a span of at least 36 months or his or her life expectancy, whichever is less.

Payout Period

Withdrawals *must* begin in the year the plan holder reaches 70 1/2, they may begin at age 59 1/2. Withdrawals are generally made in periodic (monthly) payments based on the life expectancy or joint expectancies of husband and wife. If the periodic payments fall short of what is required to withdraw, a penalty tax of 50% on the difference is imposed.

Periodic withdrawals (monthly, quarterly, etc.) are taxed as regular income, but the burden becomes less severe as the participant's income on retirement is usually lower. On some occasions, the participant might elect to take a lump-sum payment. This might present a problem. The entire amount might be taxed as income, in which case the only recourse to the taxpayer might be to average his income as allowed by the IRS.

Tax-Free Rollovers

At times an individual might receive a lump sum, for example, when he terminates his pension plan. This amount might be immediately subject to federal income taxes that can be postponed by "rolling over" the funds into a safe haven of an IRA account. To do this the rollover must be made no later than 60 days after the funds are received. The amount is not considered a contribution, so it is not subject to the limitations discussed earlier.

Another use of the rollover technique is to change from one type of individual retirement program to another (e.g., from annuity or retirement bond to a custody account). The funds must be transferred into a new individual retirement program within 60 days after receiving them. Such transfers can be done only once every three years

Simplified Employee Pensions (SEPs)

This plan is tailored for small businesses, partnerships, unincorporated businesses, and so forth that have no formal pension plan. It is like the IRA plans. It does not require compliance with the complicated regulations of corporate pension plans. As in an ordinary IRA, the maximum yearly contribution to a SEP is 15% of income. But the dollar limit on this 15% is $7,500 versus $1,500 in IRA. The employer can set contributions at his discretion so as to turn the SEP into a kind of profit sharing plan.

Employees are permitted to direct their own investments, which includes mutual funds and corporate and government securities. Thus the employer has no fiduciary responsibility. Finally, employees retain ownership of the funds even after resigning from the firm (see IRS Form 5305—SEP).

REVIEW QUESTIONS

1. What are the different types of fixed annuities?
2. Describe the different variable annuity contracts.
3. What is a separate account?
4. Explain the difference between a qualified and a nonqualified variable annuity.
5. Describe the various methods of buying a variable annuity.
6. What are the two risks an insurance company assumes in writing a variable annuity contract. Illustrate by example.
7. What are annuity units? Explain how fluctuations in the stock market affect the value of the unit and the money payments to the beneficiary.
8. Describe the various settlement options of a paid-up annuity.
9. Discuss the Keogh and IRA plans giving for each their maximum pay-

ments, their tax treatment, their withdrawal privileges, and their advantages. What are SEP plans?

10. What is a tax-free rollover?

TRUE AND FALSE QUESTIONS

		True	False
1.	Fixed annuity contracts:		
a.	pay a fixed rate and no more	_____	_____
b.	sometimes provide a higher return through dividend increases	_____	_____
c.	can be bought in two ways	_____	_____
d.	always have a deduction for a sales charge.	_____	_____
2.	Fixed annuity payments might be:	*True*	*False*
a.	for the lifetime of the annuitant only	_____	_____
b.	for the lifetime of the annuitant and his or her spouse	_____	_____
c.	for the lifetime of the annuitant with a lump-sum payment at his or her death	_____	_____
d.	for a definite number of years certain.	_____	_____
3.	Variable annuities:	*True*	*False*
a.	have proven to be a good hedge against inflation	_____	_____
b.	are usually invested in "blue chip" common stocks	_____	_____
c.	give the holders no voting rights as to the changes in investment policies	_____	_____
d.	fluctuate to the same degree as does the stock market	_____	_____
4.	A *separate account* of a variable annuity is:	*True*	*False*
a.	an account separate and apart from the general investment account of an insurance company	_____	_____
b.	set up to hold the installment payments of the variable annuity participants	_____	_____
c.	exempt from federal income and capital gains taxes only if a qualified account	_____	_____
d.	never used for a nonqualified variable annuity.	_____	_____
5.	The investment objectives of a variable annuity are:	*True*	*False*
a.	to provide retirement income	_____	_____
b.	to protect the holder against inflation	_____	_____
c.	to guarantee a fixed income	_____	_____

		True	False
d.	to guarantee the investor the principal of his or her investment.		

6. Sale charges might be made:

		True	False
a.	on a single-payment deferred annuity		
b.	on a single-payment immediate annuity		
c.	on a periodic payment for a deferred annuity		
d.	at lower rates as the amount purchased increases.		

7. The risks an insurance company takes in writing a variable annuity contract include in particular:

		True	False
a.	the mortality risk		
b.	the interest rate risk		
c.	the expense risk		
d.	the stock market risk.		

8. Under the Keogh plan a taxpayer can:

		True	False
a.	deduct as an expense the greater of $7,500 or 15% of his income each year		
b.	deduct as an expense the lesser of $7,500 or 15% of his income each year		
c.	avoid forever paying a tax on the amount set aside under the Keogh plan		
d.	must start withdrawals of his account when he reaches 70 1/2 years.		

9. The advantages of the Keogh plans include:

		True	False
a.	permanent savings of taxes on payments		
b.	allows earnings on investments to accumulate without taxes		
c.	provides a retirement income when taxes will be lower for retiree		
d.	flexibility—the taxpayer can make irregular contributions.		

10. An IRA account enables an individual

		True	False
a.	if not a participant in an employer-sponsored plan to set aside the lesser of 15% or $1,500 of his or her earnings		
b.	under certain conditions to set aside as much as $1,750		
c.	to consider the contribution as a tax deduction		
d.	to borrow on the IRA plan up to the amount paid in.		

7

Direct Participation Programs

LIMITED PARTNERSHIPS

A limited partnership is a form of ownership, an undivided interest in an entity that operates in a business. It consists of general and limited partners. The general partners manage the business and have *unlimited liability*. Limited partners supply the bulk of the capital but usually have limited liability. Limited partnerships are a means whereby investors obtain tax shelters, cash flow, and hopefully capital appreciation.

It is very important to determine if the business organization is truly a limited partnership, not just an association taxed as a corporation. Treasury regulations at present state that a purported partnership will be treated generally as a partnership unless it has more corporate than noncorporate characteristics. Corporate characteristics are as follows: (1) Continuous life. A limited partnership does not have continuous life. The death or retirement of a general partner dissolves the partnership. (2) Free transferability of shares. This is not true of a partnership. (3) Limited liability. This is true of the limited partners but not of the general partners. (4) Centralized management. The management of a limited partnership is vested in the general partners. Currently (1980) the Internal Revenue Service and the tax court have ruled that the limited partnership should be taxed as a partnership. But there is no certainty that this ruling might not be changed.

The General Partner

The general partner should be a person of highest integrity, experience, and skill and possess substantial means. The success of the enterprise depends to a large extent on the general partner. Often a general partner is a corporation or a corporate affiliate.

Revenue Procedure 72-13 prescribes four requirements for a general partner: (1) Limited partners must not own directly or indirectly, individually, or in the aggregate more than 20% of the *corporate* general partner or its affiliate. (2) It is important that the general partner have *substantial* net worth. If the general partner has little wealth and is merely a "figure head," the chances of the partnership's being taxed as a corporation are increased. (3) Limited partners must have neither the option nor the obligation to purchase any kind of security or interest from the general partner. (4) The organization operating as a partnership must be in accordance with state laws relating to limited partnerships. The limited partnership must file with the appropriate authorities a certificate of articles stating the business, the capital contribution of each, the terms of withdrawal of partners, and so forth.

Sources of Revenue to the General Partner

The general partner or partners usually receive 30–40% of the operating profits of the firm. In addition, they might collect acquisition fees, underwriting commissions, brokerage fees, fees in the liquidation of the properties, and even fees per head of cattle sold.

All the connections of the general partners should be checked to see if there is any *conflict of interest*. For example, the general partner or the corporate general partner might own other companies that might be in competition with the firm he or it manages. Funds might be diverted from the partnership; cash flow might be held back.

Limited Partners

Limited partners are basically the investors. They do not and must not make management decisions under pain of being held as general partners and liable for the debts of the firm. *As a general rule, limited partners are not liable for the debts of the firm and can only lose their investments in the firm.* But there are times when even a limited partner might be liable for debts of the firm. For example, should a general partner withdraw or die, the limited partners might be held as co-owners and therefore liable. Furthermore, in certain states in which the company might do business, the partnership laws are not clear. In these states it is possible for limited partners to be held responsible for the debts of the firm. But limited partners are entitled to information. Usually, by a simple majority they may dissolve the firm or discharge the general partner. In some cases, they must approve the sale of the principal assets of the firm. Limited partners put up the bulk of the money and receive about 60–70% of the profits.

The Advantages and Disadvantages of a Limited Partnership

As stated at the outset, a limited partnership consists of one or more general partners (one might be a corporation) and several limited partners.

There are several advantages to a limited partnership:

1. *Tax deductions:* A limited partnership must file a federal income tax return but pays no tax. The depreciation, depletion, and net income or net loss on a pro rata basis flow through to the partners who in turn report to the federal government their pro rata share.
2. *Diversification of financial risk:* This is obtained by the accumulation of a fairly large amount of funds that are invested in various types of projects.
3. *Professional management:* Few limited partners have the expertise to invest wisely in such activities as oil drilling, cattle breeding, or real estate.
4. *Limited liability:* See page 136.

There are, on the other hand, a few disadvantages:

1. *Loss of a part or all of the investment.* Even to a rich individual in the 50% tax bracket, the failure of the firm would mean a loss of half of his investment. Further, there is always the danger that the creditors will succeed in holding the limited partners liable for the debts of the firm as general partners.
2. *Difficulty in liquidating partnership interest* in need to raise cash should arise.
3. *Lack of control* over general partner.
4. *Changes in the Internal Revenue Code* might hold the partnership an association taxable as a corporation.
5. *Recapture of profits* through tax preference (see page 143).
6. *Possible assessment* for additional funds as in the case of oil limited partnerships.
7. *Rising operating costs* in a declining economy.

Investor Suitability

The sponsor or broker must have reasonable grounds to believe, after making inquiry, that the prospective investor in a limited partnership is a person able to bear the economic risk of a long-term illiquid investment. Furthermore, the potential investor should be in a high enough tax bracket to be able to take full advantage of possible tax deductions. The prospectuses of most limited partnerships require that the sponsor (or broker) certify to the aforementioned facts. In addition, many states have suitability standards. The suitability standards vary according to the risk of the type of business (see pages 143 and 148).

Leverage or Trading on Equity

When a firm uses borrowed as well as equity capital, it is said to be leveraged or to be trading on its equity. It maximizes its profits, but it also maximizes its losses. Nonrecourse loans are used for leverage. (Nonrecourse loans are loans a real estate firm obtains but for which the investors in the program are not liable.)

But nonrecourse loans may *not* be used in oil, gas, or cattle limited partnerships. Any asset owned by the limited real estate partnership may be used as collateral. Recourse loans are the responsibility of the general partners and are considered part of the general partners' basis. That is the partners' liability for personal borrowing enables them to obtain full benefit of the deductions available from tax sheltered investments.

Under the Tax Reform Act of 1976, investors in oil, gas, and cattle partnerships are permitted to deduct *only* to the extent of their cash investment and borrowings upon which they are personally *at risk*. This law excludes nonrecourse loans for all but real estate partnerships.

Evaluating a Limited Partnership

Before becoming a limited partner, the investor should determine the objective and economic viability of the partnership. Furthermore, the investor should determine if his or her objectives are in accord with those of the limited partnership. For example, one investor might be interested in oil drilling, another in shopping centers, and still another in cattle. Above all, the prospective investor should check the ability, integrity, experience, and financial strength of the general partners.

The investor should look, first, at the investment aspect of the limited partnership (is the project sound and will it bring economic gain?); second, at the tax consequences; and, third, at the reputation of the organization that is marketing the program.

A more detailed discussion of three individual types of limited partnership follows.

REAL ESTATE LIMITED PARTNERSHIPS

Real estate limited partnerships have the usual objectives: tax-sheltered deductions, cash flow, and capital appreciation. There are several types of programs.

1. *Raw land*. This is a speculative form of investment. No deductions may be made for depreciation. Real estate taxes reduce profit if land is held for a long period of time. Best chance of a good profit is when land is acquired in a developing area.

2. *Development programs*. These include the construction of residences, apartments, and commercial buildings. Investors hope for profits through the sale of completed buildings.

3. *Income-producing properties.* These include all types of existing and improved real estate such as apartment houses, shopping centers, industrial plants, office buildings, and even theaters and lodges. Shopping centers may be hurt by the gasoline shortage, plants and office buildings by a business depression.

4. *Low-income housing.* This activity is sponsored by the Department of Urban Development (HUD). To encourage the construction of low-cost housing, large depreciation charges, as well as tax abatements, are permitted to the builder. Liberal financing is also available from HUD, which, if it approves the project, will guarantee the mortgage.

Working Components

1. *The partnership manager,* usually a general partner, selects the particular properties, arranges the financing, and sometimes hires the superintendents. The general partner has overall responsibility for the day-to-day operation, which includes attracting tenants, making leases, paying expenses, and keeping accurate accounts for the investors. The general partner is usually paid 5–10% of the gross revenue. Also the general partner should be alert to buying new properties and to selling the old—particularly if it is in a declining neighborhood.

2. *The builder or developer* might be the corporate general partner or a third party. It is important that a financially strong and reliable builder be obtained. The failure of the builder might cause suppliers to sue not only the builder but also the partnership for materials used in construction of the building. Even if this does not happen, failure of a contractor can cause costly delays. But, for some one who is interested in the tax side of real estate investment, a property under construction is suggested.

Advantages of a Real Estate Limited Partnership

1. *A fixed supply of real estate* and almost insatiable demand have made real estate one of the best inflation hedges (to date 1980).

2. *Write-offs* for tax purposes are relatively predictable. The useful life of depreciable real estate buildings has been determined by the IRS in categories ranging from apartments—40 years—to warehouses—60 years. An average for 13 of these categories is 45 years. *Often a real estate partnership will generate a positive cash flow* for the limited partners while enabling them to show a loss for tax purposes. Cash flow (see page 140) is simply the amount of cash that flows through to the owners. It is the gross income less operating expenses, interest, and taxes—that is, all cash charges

against the gross. The following example shows the cash flow and the effect of depreciation on net income:

TABLE 7-1

XYZ
Real Estate Partnership

Gross receipts	$10,000
Less: vacancy reserve	1,000
Effective gross income	$ 9,000
Management fee	900
Operating expenses	4,555
Interest on mortgage	1,945
Cash flow	$ 1,600
Allowance for depreciation	$ 2,000
Taxable income (loss)	(400)

This illustration shows cash flow of $1,600 that could be paid to the partners. But, after taking the depreciation of $2,000 (assuming it is allowed by the IRS), there would be a loss for tax purposes of $400.

Component parts of a building are the air conditioning equipment, the elevators, the roof, the carpets, furniture, and so forth. Obviously these items wear out more quickly than the building itself does. Therefore, component parts are usually depreciated over a 10- to 15-year period.

Depreciation

There are several ways of calculating depreciation charges that have been approved by the Internal Revenue Service. The table following shows the depreciation charges of a $50,000 property. This property might be classed as a new or used house or a commercial or industrial property. Column I illustrates *straight-line* depreciation charges. These are calculated by taking the value of the property less the salvage value and dividing it by the number of years of useful life. Taking the value of $50,000 divided by 25 years of useful life, we would arrive at $2,000 a year, or 4% of the value $50,000. These charges of $2,000 a year are made in each of the 25 years of useful life.

For *new residential houses only*, the 200% or double-declining-balance accounting method may be used. Here the straight-line depreciation rate of 4%, or $2,000 a year, is *doubled* in the first year to 8%, or $4,000, as in column II. The new fixed rate of 8% is applied to the declining balance in

TABLE 7-2

Calculation of Depreciation Charges on Property Worth $50,000, 25 Years of Life

Year	I Straight Line		II 200% Double Declining Balance		III 150% Declining Balance		IV 125% Declining Balance		V Sum of the Years' Digits	
	4%	Balance	8%	Balance	6%	Balance	5%	Balance		Balance
1	$2,000	$48,000	$4,000	$46,000	$3,000	$47,000	$2,500	$47,500	$3,846	$46,154
2	2,000	46,000	3,680	42,320	2,820	44,180	2,375	45,125	3,692	42,462
3	2,000	44,000	3,385	38,935	2,650	41,530	2,256	42,869	3,538	38,924
4	2,000	42,000	3,114	35,821	2,491	39,039	2,143	40,726	3,384	35,540
5	2,000	40,000	2,865	32,956	2,342	36,697	2,036	38,690	3,230	32,310
	etc.		etc.		etc.		etc.		etc.	

subsequent years. For example, in the first year $4,000 is depreciated, leaving a balance of $46,000. In the second year $3,680, or 8% of $46,000, is depreciated. Deducting $3,680 from $46,000 we have a new declining balance of $42,320 against which we apply the 8% rate to get a new depreciation charge of $3,385, and so on.

For all new properties other than residential, such as office buildings and shopping centers as well as industrial properties, a 150% declining balance might be used. This is illustrated in column III. Here the rate applied to the declining balance is 150% of the straight-line rate of 4% or 6%. This amounts to $3,000. Thus the first-year amount charged to depreciation is $3,000 and the depreciated property is $47,000; applying the 6% rate to this amount, the amount charged is $2,820 for a new depreciation value in that year of $44,180; and so on.

For used residential housing with useful life of at least 20 years the 125% declining balance is used, starting with the straight-line depreciation of 4%, or $2,000; 125% of these respective amounts would be 5%, or $2,500. Then we apply the 5% fixed amount to the declining balance in the same way as illustrated for the 200% and 150% declining balance.

Also for new residential housing the sum-of-the-years'-digits method of depreciation may be used. This method is illustrated in column V. Here all the digits are added up $1 + 2 + 3 + 4 + \ldots$, making a total for 25 years of 325. This is taken as the denominator of a fraction while the years starting at 25 is taken as the numerator and applied to the total value of the property.

$$(e.g., 25/325 \times \$50,000 = \$3,846)$$

The next year the numerator is dropped to 24, but the denominator is the same,

$$(e.g., 24/325 \times \$50,000 = \$3,692)$$

and so on.

However the impression should not be given that owner-occupied houses can charge against their taxable income depreciation in any form, such as the depreciation allowed on residential properties that are owned as investments by the limited partnerships.

Depreciation Recapture

When properties except low cost housing are sold by limited partnerships, the excess depreciation (the excess of accelerated depreciation over straight-line depreciation) on depreciable real property is fully recaptured and taxed as ordinary income. But, if depreciable real property is sold within 12 months, then all depreciation, including straight-line, will be recaptured as ordinary income.

Minimum Tax on Tax Preferences

There is a 15% minimum tax on certain items of tax preference that includes among other items the *excess* of accelerated depreciation on real property and certain leased property over the equivalent straight-line methods but *does not* include capital gains in excess of the greater of $10,000 ($5,000 in the case of married taxpayers' filing a separate return or in the case of trusts and certain corporations) or one half of the taxpayer's federal income taxes for the taxable year less certain credits. The new alternative minimum tax (December 1978) is applicable only to individuals and is in lieu of regular federal income taxes and adds on minimum tax *if it results in a greater tax liability* than the sum of those taxes. The alternative minimum tax is imposed on a taxpayer's income increased by that portion of net capital gain that otherwise would be excluded from taxable income and certain excess itemized deductions and reduced by $20,000. The result would be taxed 10% up to $40,000, 20% on the next $40,000, and 25% on any amount in excess of $80,000. This alternate tax will not be imposed on the partnership, but each partner includes it in the computation of his own alternate tax liability.

Maximum Tax on Personal Service Income

The amount of personal service income for which the partner might be eligible for a 50% limitation on the maximum tax is reduced by all the items of tax preference.

Suitability

Most real estate partnerships establish suitability standards. Net worth requirements are in the neighborhood of $75,000 to $100,000, and taxable income is subject to a federal income tax rate of 50% or more. Also, many states have suitability standards. In most cases the investor must sign a statement in the limited partnership agreement that he or she meets the suitability standards.

Special Considerations for Real Estate Limited Partnerships

In a real estate partnership, the risks are less than in some other partnerships such as oil or cattle, but they are real and should be recognized: (1) Miscalculation of the potential of the properties held is the most serious mistake. It is hard for the limited partner to appraise properties unless he is knowledgeable in real estate; therefore, the limited partner must rely on the expertise of the general partner. (2) Lack of diversification can occur. For example, a partnership might have large holdings of rent-controlled apartments that possess little prospect for income growth. (3) Properties in declining neighborhood might result in large vacancies. (4) Inflation often raises the value of real estate but at the same time increases costs of fuel, supplies, and labor and hence reduces profits. (5) Competition can be an unexpected problem. For example, a real estate partnership might own a large shopping center that is suddenly faced with competition from the opening of a new shopping center in the neighborhood. (6) Abuse of leverage may result in serious difficulties. Most real estate limited partnerships are set up so that their investments will be leveraged. That is, the partnership finances acquisition of properties by borrowing about 65% of the value. This enhances the partnership's profits but also increases it exposure to larger losses if the properties thus acquired do not come up to expectation.

But, as mentioned, nonrecourse loans are permitted to real estate limited partners. Thus, limited partners may invest in real estate programs without assuming personal liability on borrowings obtained to finance the program. In some programs with conventional financing, there appears what is called a "wrap-around" mortgage. A wrap-around mortgage encompasses the underlying mortgage. It is an all-inclusive loan that includes a first mortgage and a junior mortgage. The lender pays interest on the first mortgage and advances junior money in return for a higher rate on the combined (wrap-around) amount including the first and second claims to the property. Wrap-around mortgages may be used to inflate the value of the property. Also, by advancing a small amount of cash, it is possible for the lender to earn a large percentage of the amount advanced (i.e., on the second mortgage). Sometimes a lender will insist on mortgage points. A mortgage point is 1% of the loan and consists of prepaid extra interest.

(7) Uncontrollable factors such as an economic depression or a local disaster can seriously restrict profits or even cause losses. (8) Mismanagement or even fraud on the part of the general partner, while a somewhat remote possibility, must always be considered. (9) Lack of liquidity, as in all limited partnerships, should be considered. (10) There is always the possibility of conflict of interest on the part of the general partner. There might be competition with the limited partnership from the corporate general partner in the purchase, sale, or lease of properties; there might be competition with the limited partnership from the corporate general partner; and disputes might arise between the general and limited partners over sales commission.

But, of all the tax shelters, real estate is the most popular. People understand real estate better than oil, cattle, or equipment leasing. Real estate is the best tax shelter; some types permit a 200% declining balance, and invested capital can include nonrecourse loans. Finally, the real estate lobby in Washington, D.C. is very strong. Even rising interest rates should not affect most real estate tax shelters because mortgage rates are usually fixed.

All of the risks noted here should be weighed against tax deductions, cash flow, and capital gains from appreciation of real estate values (see suitability requirements, page 143).

OIL AND GAS LIMITED PARTNERSHIPS

During the 1970s a number of oil and gas drilling partnerships were formed. Some of these were well financed and raised as much as $10–$20 million; the minimum individual limited partnerships investment ranged between $2,500 and $10,000. Some blue sky laws required the general partners to subscribe as much as 15% of the capital, but the bulk of the capital was subscribed by the limited partners. Some of the limited partnerships were registered with the SEC.

Most Common Types of Programs

The three most common types of programs are exploratory, development, and balanced. The investment objectives of these programs are, first, to drill and discover profitable oil and gas reserves and, second, to offer to wealthy individuals holding partnership interests the advantage of tax deductions from intangible and development costs and later income depletion charges.

An exploratory, or new field, wildcat is well located on a structural feature that previously had not produced oil or gas. These wells are generally at least 2 miles from the nearest productive area. Industry statistics indicate only about 1 in 9 "wildcat wells" drilled to explore for a new field is successful and only 1 in 40 or 50 is a significant commercial success. Of greater importance is the degree of risk assumed by the operator and his intention to test structure not previously proven. Major oil companies have spent billions in the Baltimore Channel off the New Jersey coast and have obtained to date (1979) only a whiff of gas and no oil.

Development wells are drilled within a proven area of an oil or gas reserve to the depth of a stratigraphic zone known to be productive. If the well is completed for production, it is classified as an oil or gas development well. If a well is not completed for production and is abandoned, it is classified as a dry development hole. About 80% of all development wells are successful. Thus, development wells are more predictable but have lower potential return.

A balanced program splits the drilling between development and exploratory wells. This program is for investors who do not want to assume the risk of exploratory drilling.

Perhaps the safest way to invest is to buy an interest in already producing properties. However, although this property might yield a satisfactory return, the tax benefits might be small as there would be little intangible drilling expense.

Working Components of an Oil Deal

Oil operators might be exploration geologists, petroleum engineers, or production geologists. They explore for oil sometimes as individuals and sometimes as company employees. They make stratigraphic tests—drilling efforts geologically directed to obtain information pertaining to a specific geologic condition that might lead to an oil discovery. In short, oil operators locate prospects, acquire leases, and eventually drill wells.

But usually the oil operators form limited partnerships designating themselves as general partners or program managers. As general partners they are jointly and severally liable for the debts of the limited partnerships. The general partner or manager must first raise the capital for the limited partnership by selling units (a minimum usually of $5,000). In the prospectus is stated in general terms the proposed activities—exploratory or development drilling and the indicated areas of states (Oklahoma, Louisiana, Texas, etc.). But specific areas or leases are not usually mentioned. The selection of these areas is left to the skill of the manager and his staff. As in all limited partnerships great reliance is placed in the general partner and on his integrity and expertise.

Advantage of an Oil and Gas Limited Partnership

The most obvious advantage is the crying need for oil and gas in this country and worldwide as well as its steadily increasing price. A potential investor should consider first the soundness of the partnership. Is there a good chance of finding oil? About 80–85% of the funds of the limited partnership should go to operations of which drilling should be at least 75% and acreage acquisition costs about 5%. Usually the general partner gets 4% of the offering and the broker 8%. Organization and offering costs should not exceed 15%.

Tax Incentives

The federal government offers several tax incentives to find oil. The most important of these are deductions for *intangible drilling and development costs* and *depletion* allowances. Investors should be aware that tax rules are under continuing review by the IRS and regulations and interpretations may be changed from time to time.

Intangible Drilling and Development Costs

Intangible drilling and development costs include labor, fuel, repairs, supplies, tool rental, truck hire, and so forth. These costs are allocated between the general and limited partners so that each is allowed to deduct his distributive share from his income subject to tax. Intangible drilling costs usually represent over 65% of the cost of a productive well. If the project is abandoned as a dry hole, the cost may be deducted in the year of abandonment. In many cases, the deductions allocated to the limited partner might be between 50% and 70% of his investment.

But the investment to be counted must be his funds "at risk." Nonrecourse loans may *not* be counted. Intangible drilling and development costs are included as an item of *tax preference* in the event of sale or presentment of his partnership interest (see page 143).

Personal service income is eligible for the 50% maximum tax. But oil and gas tax preference reduce dollar for dollar the individual's earned income otherwise eligible for this 50% maximum tax on personal service income.

Depletion and Depreciation

There are two kinds of depletion—*cost* depletion and *percentage* depletion. *Cost depletion* allows the deduction of capitalized costs, such as lease acquisition costs, exploratory charges, and legal fees, of a producing property over its life by annual deductions computed on the basis of the actual oil and gas produced each year in relation to estimated recoverable oil and gas. *Percentage* depletion is a statutory allowance equal to a percentage of gross income from the depletable property but not over 50% of the taxable income from the property before depletion. For small producers, it is 22% through 1980 and at a declining rate to 15% in 1984.

Depreciation may be taken for such items as pipe, casings, pump units, tanks, batteries, storage facilities, and lease acquisition costs—all representing capital expenditures. The cost of these items is amortized over their useful life as an expense. In addition the investment tax credit is available with respect to eligible items of equipment.

Borrowing and Interest

The cost of drilling partnerships paid from borrowing and charged to the participant is currently deductible if the adjusted tax basis of his interest is sufficient. Nonrecourse loans do not qualify as debt. However, the Tax Reform Act of 1976 limits the amount of allowable deduction for investment interest to $10,000. But, if a taxpayer and his family own 50% of a partnership or of a corporation, interest deductions of up to $15,000 are allowed.

Rising interest rates should not seriously hurt oil and gas partnerships, as most of the major costs are incurred in the first year and operating costs thereafter are small.

Sale of Partnership Interest (Presentment) and Recapture

The sale of a limited partnership interest is difficult. Some limited partnerships provide for repurchase, but most do not. A limited partnership interest is definitely an illiquid investment. But, if a sale or presentment is consummated, the gain or loss of the interest, if held over a year, will in general be treated as a long-term capital gain or loss. But there are circumstances in which a part or all of the gain might be taxed as income. Intangible drilling, development, and depreciation on lease equipment deductions claimed by the partnership are subject to *recapture*. But the amount of the recapture is reduced by the amount of intangible drilling and development costs that would have been deducted had such costs been capitalized and deducted through cost-based depletion. Further, ordinary income will be realized to the extent of any unrealized receivables or substantially appreciated inventory.

Risk Considerations

There are a number of risks to the investor in an oil and gas limited partnership, many of which are obvious: (1) The drilling venture might find only dry holes and fail. (2) It might find oil and gas but not in sufficient quantity to make the investment worthwhile. (3) Legislation or IRS rules might eliminate deductions or hold the limited partnerships taxable as a corporation. (4) General partners might withdraw, forcing the limited partners to become co-owners and, hence, be liable for the firm's debts. (5) There is no assurance that the limited liability will be preserved in all jurisdictions. (6) Assessments of partners that are usually limited to 10-15% of the original investment might be difficult to meet, in which event his or her interest would be diluted. (7) Conflict of interest or outright fraud on the part of the general partner might cause serious or total losses as in the case of the Home-Stake Producing Company in 1975. (8) Inability to liquidate partnership interest on short notice might bring financial embarrassment. (9) Government price controls might have an adverse effect.

Suitability Standards

Because oil and gas limited partnerships are considered very risky, suitability standards are high. Net worth requirements are in the neighborhood of $200,000 (exclusive of home) and taxable income must be at least in the 50% bracket.

CATTLE LIMITED PARTNERSHIPS

Limited cattle partnerships are engaged mainly in two programs: (1) feeding and (2) breeding.

Feeding programs include the purchase, fattening, and sale of slaughter cattle to beef processors. Usually all feeder cattle is selected and purchased in the open market by the general partner program manager. The number of head to be purchased will be determined according to the size of the subscription received.

Stocker or feeder cattle might be bought. Stocker cattle are generally lighter-weight cattle of 300–450 pounds. If stocker cattle are purchased, they may be backgrounded, that is, placed under pasture contracts for up to 12 months prior to their admittance to a feedlot. The general manager then selects the feedlot operator. The feedlot consists of pens for cattle and a mill for processing feed. Just after weaning, the animals are fed under controlled conditions to a marketable weight for ultimate slaughter. The feeding of cattle in a feedlot is a short-term enterprise as recently weaned calves weighing 250–550 pounds are fed to the average slaughter weight of 1,100 pounds in less than one year.

The feedlot operator sorts, brands, vaccinates, and feeds the cattle. Feedlots are located in California, Colorado, Kansas, Nebraska, New Mexico, Oklahoma, and Texas. In short, feeding programs convert feeder cattle into mature beef cattle as efficiently as possible.

Special Considerations for Feeding Programs

In periods of inflation such as in 1979, beef prices soar. A 5¢-a-pound rise or fall in cattle prices can create a $50 additional profit or loss in a 1,000-pound steer. Thus, the price of beef can rise or drop quickly due to over-or underproduction or a change in demand. But, with a high level of business activity and large relief and Social Security payments, the demand for beef seems to be insatiable. Operating expenses, especially the cost of feed, could increase rapidly. The general partner is usually permitted to hedge against price changes, although it might be costly as minimum commissions must be paid. Conflicts of interest are possible in feeding programs. For example, the general partner might have an interest in the feedlot he selects for the partnership. This feedlot might feed the cattle at higher prices than is true in other feedlots. Other areas of possible conflict of interest include the source of feeders and feed. For example, the general partner might take a kickback in rereturn for large purchases of cattle or feed. As has been constantly stated in this chapter, the most important ingredient for success in any type of limited partnership is the integrity, experience, and skill of the general partner; in the case of a cattle partnership, this includes the feedlot operator as well. The feedlot operator often guarantees the partnership against death or loss due to disease, epidemic, accident, weather, theft, and predators usually in excess of 4%. Insurance on cattle is sometimes difficult to obtain, and expensive; thus it reduces profits.

Breeding Programs

These programs include the acquisition, development and sale of purebred and commercial cattle. Sometimes, at the start, a partnership will have an option to buy from a cattle company, such as the Granada Land and Cattle Company, in the open market or from an affiliate. The program manager selects the original stock and supervises its growth and sale. The partnership will initially incur breeding reorientation expenses (the same as in feeding cattle), namely, for feeding and care.

The general partner will usually hire one or more herd managers to perform the day-to-day functions required for the herd and make marketing decisions. In particular, the general partner will try to develop the herd through retention of superior progeny and controlled breeding practices, that is, by developing a better strain of cattle. One of the more successful new breeds is Brangus cattle. Brangus is a blend of the popular Angus and the Brahman breeds, the latter having an exceptional ability to survive hot climates and vicious insects.

Purebred Breeding Operations

Certain breeds, strains, or crosses of cattle prove more efficient in achieving weight gains and providing higher-quality carcasses for beef processing. Purebred cattle-breeding operations are directed at development and improvement of a more efficient cattle strain.

Commercial breeding animals are maintained primarily for production of progeny to be sold for feeding and slaughter. Some commercial breeders also act as seed-stock producers. Breeding programs require more time than feeding does.

There are a number of *risks* in cattle programs. Cattle might get sick from any number of diseases; there might be a prolonged drought; feed and other operating costs might rise; beef prices might drop sharply; severe storms might kill many cattle; the calving rate might be unusually low; there might be uncertain results from cross-breeding; and the general partner might not be able to get the best price for beef. Finally, the IRS will audit the investors' tax return and may not allow some of the deductions claimed.

The General Partners Compensation

The general partner of a limited cattle partnership usually receives 15–20% of the partnership income. Also he might receive a flat fee of about $4.00 a head as the cattle are purchased. If the general partner is also the promoter of the firm, he might receive a percentage of the initial offering as well as a percentage in the final liquidation.

The Limited Partners' Benefits

Costs for cattle *feeding* are allowed as a deduction for the taxable year in which such feed, seed, fertilizer, and so on are actually consumed. In addition, interest is deductible only for the period to which interest cost is related. The animals are generally sold the following year and the investor recovers his expenses plus, it is hoped, a profit from the fattened cattle.

The purchase price of *breeding* animals is not deductible as such but is subject to depreciation and is deductible over the useful life of the animals. Depreciation may not be taken with respect to partnership herd progeny as the partnership has no "cost basis" for such animals. Similarly, no depreciation is allowable with respect to *feeder* cattle, which are purchased by partnership for resale.

The IRS recognizes a useful life range from 5.5 to 8.5 years for breeding cattle. Partnership operations will result in ordinary gains and losses or capital gains and losses, which will be allocably includable by the limited partners in their individual returns. Sales from cattle-feeding operations will result in *ordinary income*, a loss to the limited partners. But sales from cattle-breeding operations will result in capital gains or losses or ordinary income depending upon the nature of the animals sold. Generally, sales of cattle owned for breeding purposes, if held for 24 months or more and not held primarily for sale to customers, will qualify for capital gains treatment.

In breeding programs there should be sales of some cattle culled from the herd to generate income.

CONDOMINIUMS AND COOPERATIVES

A *condominium* consists of a unit in a building usually with ownership privileges in common areas. (The common areas include parking lots, grounds, swimming pools, tennis courts, etc.) Sometimes, however, these common areas are reserved for the developer. The units might be apartments, houses in a resort area, commercial buildings occupied by professional people, or even buildings used by stores.

Initially, the developer constructs the property largely with the aid of a construction loan from a bank, pension fund, or insurance company. During construction, the sales force of the developer sells the units to individuals who form an association of unit owners. A master lease describing the property is drawn up. The lease gives precise details of the individual units. Each unit is described in a unit deed. Usually the owner receives a fee simple title. The purchase of the units is usually financed by a mortgage and/or from savings. Each unit owner is responsible for the pro rata share of the management, taxes, and maintenance costs of the building in addition to the mortgage interest and amortization payments on his particular unit.

The down payment is usually higher than for a primary residence. Usually the building is managed by a professional. It is most important to obtain an experienced manager. A poorly run building is not only an annoyance; as word gets around, the value of the property depreciates. The manager submits budgets to the unit owners, collects rents, sees to clearing of the halls and to the security of the building, and so on.

The unit owners' association has bylaws spelling out their rights and obligations. A board of managers representing the unit owners is elected. Each unit holder must abide by the regulations, which should be studied in advance by the prospective purchaser. There are the usual rules about excessive noise. Often there are rules about pets or operating a business from the unit (i.e., piano lessons), and some purchasers may be required to buy a "furnishing package" to maintain uniformity among the units.

Subletting is often done by the unit owners. This might be done by direct negotiations, through a local broker, or by a rental pool. A rental pool is a procedure whereby all the tenants wishing to sublet their units advise the building manager. He arranges all the subleases and collects the rents, which are distributed pro rata among the subletting tenants. Furthermore, the manager agrees to promote and maintain the units when held open for rent.

Thus risks of condominium purchase include:

1. the purchase of a condominium that is poorly constructed with inferior material;
2. the decline of the neighborhood in which the condominium is located;
3. a general economic decline forces many unit holders to default on payments and move out;
4. competition;
5. a poor rental manager;
6. a local disaster, which has occurred particularly in the South, where floods and hurricanes have seriously damaged property;
7. possible tax problems. This is true particularly of vacation homes on a limited basis (say, 30 days). This rental income might be con-

sidered by the IRS as hobby income (hobby income losses are generally deductible only against hobby income). Another possible tax problem would be a rumored new law disallowing householding unit owners from deducting interest and real estate taxes from taxable income. Many states have adopted "blue sky" laws to regulate the sale of condominiums.

The laws of California, Michigan, and New York are considered to be some of the most strict in this country. In 1973, the SEC ruled that condominiums should be considered as real estate investments or the same as securities. Therefore, condominiums are subject to the Securities Act of 1933. Thus a prospectus must be issued to give details of the offering; the offerors are subject to penalties for misstatement of a material fact.

Cooperative buildings are in many respects similar to the condominiums except insofar as their structure is concerned. The property of a cooperative is owned by a corporation subject to a mortgage. The shareholders of this corporation are the same as the tenants—holding shares in proportion to the size of their apartment or space in the buildings. A formal lease is executed between the tenants and the corporations for the space. Each tenant pays his share of the pro-rated real estate taxes, mortgage interest, and management expenses—the same as in the case of the condominiums. The officers and directors of the cooperation are elected by the shareholders and make the regulations approved by the shareholders. As with condominiums, the owner shareholders of the cooperative may take deductions for their pro rata share of the interest taxes and depreciation.

Some authorities have claimed that the condominium form of ownership is more flexible than the cooperative. For example, the owner of a condominium unit has an easier time finding a buyer should he wish to sell. The owner can set his own terms for refinancing his own debt, whereas the owner of a cooperative must offer the terms based on the overall mortgage of the building. Also in a condominium the liabilities for maintenance expenses are several, and the owner is responsible for any of his share of the expenses. In the tragic 1930s cooperative tenants moved out in droves, leaving the remaining tenants responsible for the maintenance charges of the entire building. Also it has been claimed that it is more difficult to sublet a cooperative apartment and even rearrange it than in the case of a condominium unit.

REVIEW QUESTIONS

1. U.S. Treasury regulations state that a partnership will be treated as a partnership unless it has more corporate than noncorporate characteristics. Describe these characteristics.

2. Why is it important for a partnership to be treated by the U.S. Treasury as a partnership?

3. What qualifications should the prospective investor seek in a general partner?

4. Under what circumstances might a limited partner be liable for the debts of the firm?

5. Discuss the advantages and disadvantages of a limited partnership.

6. What is meant by investor suitability as far as limited partnerships are concerned?

7. How should a potential investor evaluate a limited partnership?

8. Describe the three most important types of real estate programs.

9. What are the working components of a real estate limited partnership?

10. Illustrate by simple figures how the term cash flow is calculated and how a loss for tax purposes may result.

11. Describe the three methods of depreciation. In what type of property might one use each method to obtain the maximum possible deductions.

12. Explain the following terms: (a) depreciation recapture, (b) minimum tax on tax preference, (c) minimum tax on personal service, and (d) nonrecourse loans.

13. What are the risks of a real estate limited partnership?

14. Describe the three most common types of oil and gas drilling programs.

15. What are the working components of an oil drilling deal?

16. In an oil and gas drilling limited partnership, explain (a) the most important tax incentives, (b) recapture, (c) the risks

17. Describe the feeding and breeding operations of a limited cattle partnership.

18. In a limited cattle partnership, explain (a) the role of the general partner, (b) the risks, (c) the tax advantages.

TRUE AND FALSE QUESTIONS

1. A limited partner of a limited partnership has: *True*   *False*
   a. unlimited liability   _____   _____
   b. liability only to the extent of his investment under most circumstances   _____   _____
   c. liability under certain circumstances   _____   _____
   d. no liability under any circumstances.   _____   _____

2. A general partner of a limited partnership: *True*   *False*
   a. may be a corporation   _____   _____
   b. should have a substantial amount of capital   _____   _____

	True	False
c. manages the firms	___	___
d. cannot be dismissed by the limited partners.	___	___

3. The advantages of a limited partnership include all of the following
except

	True	False
a. tax deductions	___	___
b. limited liability in most circumstances	___	___
c. suitability for small investors	___	___
d. professional management.	___	___

4. The Tax Reform Act of 1976 provides that:

	True	False
a. investors in all limited partnerships may deduct as expense only to the extent of their capital at risk	___	___
b. investors in limited real estate partnerships may include nonrecourse loans in their capital base	___	___
c. investors in cattle and oil and gas partnerships may not include nonrecourse loans in their capital base	___	___
d. investors in all partnerships may include nonrecourse loans in their capital base	___	___

5. Cash flow is:

	True	False
a. gross income less operating expenses, interest, taxes, and other expenses	___	___
b. dividends paid to the stockholders	___	___
c. net income	___	___
d. net income plus depreciation and depletion.	___	___

6. Rapid depreciation can be used as follows:

	True	False
a. for new residential houses, up to 200% double declining balance	___	___
b. for all new properties other than residential, 150% declining balance	___	___
c. for used residential housing, 175% declining balance	___	___
d. for new residential housing, the sum of the years' digits.	___	___

7. When real estate properties are sold by a limited partnership:

	True	False
a. the excess of cost is treated simply as a capital gain	___	___
b. the excess of accelerated depreciation over straight line is fully recaptured and taxed as ordinary income	___	___

		True	*False*
c.	the excess of cost is treated as income	____	____
d.	the capital gains taxes are paid by the limited partnership.	____	____

8. The tax incentives of an oil and gas drilling partnership are as follows:

		True	*False*
a.	The intangible drilling and other costs enable the limited partner to recover 50–70% of his investment in the first year.	____	____
b.	The IRS permits oil and gas drilling limited partnerships to use nonrecourse loans in counting capital against which deductions may be made.	____	____
c.	Depletion deductions may be taken up to 100% of taxable income.	____	____
d.	Unlimited deductions may be taken for interest.	____	____

9. The investor in an oil and gas limited partnership must face the following risks:

		True	*False*
a.	inability to meet assessments, which would mean forfeiture of his entire investment	____	____
b.	the partnership's finding oil and gas but not in sufficient quantity	____	____
c.	withdrawal of a limited partner	____	____
d.	removal of government price controls.	____	____

10. In cattle limited partnerships, the tax benefits are as follows:

		True	*False*
a.	Costs for cattle feeding (seed, feed, and fertilizer actually consumed) are allowed for the taxable year.	____	____
b.	For feeding animals sold in the following year, the investor recovers his expenses plus a profit.	____	____
c.	The purchase price of breeding animals is deductible as an expense.	____	____
d.	Depreciation of progeny may be taken at a cost fixed by the general partner.	____	____

8

NEW ISSUE MARKET

Generally, whenever a new security is issued and marketed, the issuing corporation seeks the advice and help of an investment banking firm. Investment bankers are not really bankers at all. The fact that the word *banker* appears in the name is partially responsible for many of the false impressions that exist regarding the functions performed by investment bankers. Investment bankers are not permitted to accept deposits from anyone. They may not provide checking account or savings account facilities for their customers, nor may they carry out other activities normally construed to be banking activities.

An investment banker is simply a business firm that specializes in helping other business firms (generally corporations) obtain the money they need on the most advantageous terms possible.

Business firms of all types must have adequate capital to operate successfully, and generally, the more successful the business is, the more money it needs. In operating a business, money is needed to meet payrolls, to purchase and carry inventories, to finance accounts receivable, and to finance new plant and equipment expenditures.

Business firms often find it is necessary to employ larger amounts of money in their business to enlarge their facilities to the size needed to meet the growing demands of an expanding population.

When inflation occurs, the amount of money needed by a business firm increases. Additional money is needed by a corporation even if it conducts the same unit volume of business as it did before the inflation began, because of increased costs.

Investment bankers, with their specialized knowledge of finance, are often able to help these companies secure the money they need.

NEW ISSUE MARKET

Investment banking firms underwrite securities by two main methods: by negotiated deals and or by competitive bidding.

The Negotiated Deal

As the term implies, the issuer and the underwriter negotiate all the terms of the sale of a new issue, whereas under competitive bidding the final price and interest cost are determined by the buyers of the issue.

Industrial companies almost always use the negotiated deal. There are a number of reasons for an industrial corporation to want to raise long-term capital: (1) to build new plant, (2) to repay bank loans or refund debt, (3) and to provide money for acquisitions.

The officers of the company might approach the buying or corporate finance department of a leading underwriter. Before doing so, they should check carefully the reputation of the firm, its expertise in the particular line of business of the issuer, its ability to distribute securities, its capital, and its organization. On initial approach the needs of the company are outlined, and audited figures are submitted. The investment banking firm then makes a preliminary study of the firm: its reputation in the trade, its products, its plants, its balance sheets, its earnings trend, and its outlook. Especially important, particularly in recent years, has been labor relations and research expenditures and their effectiveness. In particular, the underwriter must determine if the company is ready for a public offering and will it be successful.

If the underwriting firm is reasonably satisfied, it sends to the issuer a letter of intent outlining in general terms the proposed financing. The underwriter and the issuer each have legal counsel who go over the documents and file a registration statement with the Securities and Exchange Commission. This is a detailed document outlining the business of the company, the purpose of the issue, and the amount and type of the securities (the exact price and spread are left to the final registration amendment, which is issued just before the sale date). Also all important facts about the company such as its products and its markets as well as any problems such as law suits are detailed.

One of the main advantages of a negotiated deal is the advice the managing underwriter gives to the issuer. This advice includes the best type of security to issue under the prevailing market conditions, the best method of offering these securities, the proper timing, and approximately the rate that the corporation should pay for its money.

The Syndicate Manager

The syndicate manager takes over the deal from the corporate finance department to form a group to sell the securities. In selecting members of this group the syndicate manager must bear in mind several considerations: (1) the ability of the house to distribute securities, (2) its capital, (3) its reputation, (4) its knowledge of the particular type of issue, (5) the issuer's wishes (the president of the corporation might have a nephew in a broker-age house), and (6) its willingness to assume risk.

As soon as the manager has made the selections, invitations are sent out to the prospective group members asking them to participate in the underwriting. The accepting members then sign an agreement *among* underwriters that sets the fee for the manager; authorizes the manager to negotiate with the issuer on behalf of the underwriters the price of the issue to the buyers, the spread or compensation to the investment bankers for their assumption of risk in distributing the issue. Also, the manager is authorized to make sales for group account, stabilize the issue, determine the underwriters' retention, and the management of the "pot." These terms will be explained later.

During the next week or so, the SEC reviews the registration state-ment. Deficiency letters might be sent out asking the issuer to clarify or ex-pand parts of the registration statement. If the SEC finds a serious misstate-ment of a material fact, it might issue a "stop order," which would abort the registration.

During this waiting period, sometimes 20 days or longer, the members of the group do their "homework." That is, they sound out the market by calling up their customers to determine their interest in the issue. Also, dur-ing this time, the manager arranges *due diligence* meetings. These are meet-ings of the potential investors, the underwriters, and the officers of the is-suer. The purpose is to give the issuer a chance to explain to the potential in-vestors and underwriters the activities of the company and the purpose of the issue and to answer any questions about the company. Due diligence meetings are particularly important for a company that is not too well known. Further, due diligence meetings partially protect the underwriter from future laws suits by showing that due diligence was taken in investi-gating and explaining the issue.

In short, the purpose of due diligence meetings is to give the under-writer a chance to use due diligence in getting to know the company, its of-ficers, and the quality of the offering. This avoids separate members of the underwriting group having to make independent examination for them-selves. The underwriter must also help the issuer qualify the issue to be sold in various states. This means filing under the "blue sky" provisions of each state.

The members of the underwriting group continue their efforts to ob-tain an indication of interest on the part of the big buyers—the life and fire insurance companies, the trust companies, the pension funds, and wealthy individuals. They send to the prospective customers a preliminary pro-spectus, or "red herring," which states in red ink "A registration statement has been filed———but not yet become effective. The information herein is subject to correction—it is under no circumstances a prospectus." If the in-stitution indicates interest, the underwriter will put a ring around the amount. This does not bind the buyer to take up the issue. It is not a sale as it remains subject to the release of the registration statement by the SEC.

The underwriting agreement is made between the manager and the issuer. It describes the issue, and the terms of the offering, payment, and delivery provisions, and it contains covenants and a market out. A *market out* permits the cancellation of the deal in the event of unusual circumstances such as a panic, war, or national disaster.

Before the price is determined, one or two preliminary pricing meetings of the underwriters are held at the office of the managing underwriter. The members of the group are asked about the indication of interest. Comparison sheets are passed out giving statistics on comparable issues. The prevailing market conditions, including the backlog of issues and outlook for interest rates, are reviewed.

During the next to last meeting, the managing underwriter asks the members of the group for their ideas on the price and the spread. Then, in the final meeting, the managing underwriter in consultation with the majors—the largest underwriters—sets the price. When the price is announced, sometimes a member or members will drop out, but this does not usually happen in a negotiated deal. The issue must be priced to sell and at the same time satisfy the issuer that a fair price is being paid. This is a *firm* commitment of a *primary offering.* The terms of the offering are then communicated to the company for final acceptance. A pricing amendment is filed with the SEC and a final prospectus printed that must be distributed to all the buyers.

After the price has been set, the managing underwriter is very busy. Each member of the underwriting group is allotted the stated amount of stock or bonds that he has agreed to sell in the agreement among underwriters. Most negotiated deals carry several liability (Western account). In other words, the underwriter is liable for his or her agreed amount of securities and no more. The managing underwriter allots to each underwriter part of his agreed allotment amount, called *retention* for distribution; and the rest is retained for the "pot." The underwriting firm immediately tries to sell its retention. The underwriting manager manages the pot, which consists of securities that have been withheld from each member's allotment. The manager might use the pot to make sales for group account. Instead of allowing a number of the underwriters to call a large insurance company such as the New York Life Insurance Company, for example, the underwriting manager might make sales directly to New York Life and would indicate the houses to be given proportionate credit for the sales. Also the manager used the "pot" to equalize the sales of the underwriters. For example, one house might quickly sell its retention and ask for more securities from the pot, whereas another house might have a surplus of retention and want to give back some securities to the pot. The underwriters are also liable for their share of the securities in the pot. This means that the participating firms which can sell, do sell the issue. As a result, in one underwriting a particular firm might sell its allotment of securities whereas another firm might not do so. In the next deal, this order might be reversed.

It is always the hope of the managing underwriter that the issue will sell out and go to a small, not a large, premium; if the issue goes to a premium that is too large, the issuer will be dissatisfied. If the issue becomes "sticky," the manager under the terms of the prospectus is permitted to stabilize the market. A bid is placed in the market on the exchange to purchase the securities at a specific price at a below P.O.P. (price of purchase). The manager is usually limited as to the amount (10–15%) of the issue. Sometimes a manager might overallot an issue. This could cause embarassment to the manager if the issue turns out to be "hot" and moves up sharply in price. To overcome this problem, the "green shoe" doctrine may be used. Here the company agrees to sell to the underwriter 10% more stock at the offering price to cover the overallotment. It is called the "green shoe" approach, because it was first used in an offering by that concern.

Selling Group

Sometimes, particularly if the issue is a large one, the syndicate manager will form a selling group. This means that a large number of registered broker-dealers will be offered a chance to sell the issue at a fixed commission at the offering price.

A typical high-grade bond issue might have the following spread. (A spread is the difference between the price offered to the public and the price paid to the issuer.)

$1.00 management fee
3.60 selling commission to broker-dealer
0.80 underwriter's compensation
0.60 miscellaneous expense
0.25 net to underwriters
$6.25

For common stocks and low-grade corporate bonds, the spread would be obviously higher, possibly 10–15%. When the issue is announced a "tombstone" advertisement (see page 71) is usually placed in the newspapers. This advertisement simply gives the name of the company, the amount of the securities being offered and their price, and a statement that a prospectus may be obtained from the underwriters that are listed. The order in which the firms are listed, called "pecking order," is very important. Their rankings depend on the firms' age and prestige, their distribution ability, their corporate clients, and their capital; usually at the top of the group are the majors, then the balcony group, then the submajors.

Finally the managing underwriter hopes to close the deal in a period of time, usually 30 days, collect the payments from the group, and pay the company. The underwriters have made a firm commitment to pay the company. If the issue does not go well and the group is unable to sell the securities at the price set in the prospectus, the syndicate manager may decide, on consultation with the majors, to cut the price of the issue to sell it to the big institutions. Or the manager may simply dissolve the syndicate and let the price of the securities seek their own level. At all events, it is usually the case that underwriters take their losses rather than tie up capital carrying securities for any long period in the hope of avoiding a loss.

Other Methods of Underwriting

Sometimes a managing underwriter and his or her group will give a company a standby commitment. There are times when a company might give its stockholders, who have preemptive rights, rights to subscribe to new stock or sometimes convertible bonds at a fixed price. The underwriter will guarantee that the rights will be exercised at the price indicated. Some years ago General Motors and Citibank made large rights offerings that were guaranteed for a fee.

An all-or-none offering is self-explanatory. Here the issuer advises the managing underwriter that if they can't get a stated amount of money, they won't take any, as their projected capital expenditure such as a plant requires a stated amount. Sometimes a minimum or a maximum might be accepted of the issuer (mini–max). For example, the issuer might be guaranteed a minimum of $6.0 million but be willing to accept $10.0 million if the underwriters can sell it. Best efforts means what it says—that the underwriter will sell all the securities the market will take at a specified price over a period of time. Here the investment banker acts as *agent* and does not commit his firm to buy any of the securities being distributed.

Competitive Bidding

Another major type of underwriting activity is *competitive bidding*. Competitive bidding underwritings are those that are awarded entirely on the basis of prices (or, in some instances, underwriting compensation) stated in sealed bids submitted at a specific time on a specified date. Competitive bidding in the corporate field is restricted to the sale of the securities of public utility companies of municipalities and railroad companies, except for a few isolated instances. The steps followed in the sale of securities through competitive bidding is similar in many respects to the procedure used in the negotiated underwritings. The major difference between the two procedures is the manner in which the price of the issue is determined.

NASD REVIEW OF CORPORATE FINANCING

1. Members must not participate in an underwriting when the terms or conditions relating thereto are unfair or unreasonable.
2. The NASD cannot assist the issuer in the distribution of its securities in any way whatsoever.
3. The managing underwriter has the responsibility of filing with the NASD the appropriate documents. These include the registration statement, prospectus, legal opinion, and so forth.
4. The Committee on Corporate Financing, appointed by the NASD, reviews all filings. As a result of this review, it makes determinations as to the fairness and reasonableness of the terms and conditions of the offering. If the committee should find the arrangements, terms, and conditions unfair and unreasonable, the managing underwriter is notified. If the managing underwriter does not modify the conditions, terms, and so forth, the committee will advise the members of the group that they must not participate in the distribution.

NASD SELLING GROUP RESTRICTIONS

Selling group and selling syndicate agreements among members of the NASD must state the public offering price, or how it is determined, as well as to whom and under what conditions concessions may be allowed.

No NASD member firm may join with any nonmember broker-dealer in any syndicate or group in the distribution of an issue of securities to the public. This is true even though the nonmember broker-dealer is registered with the Securities and Exchange Commission. Furthermore, a member who is participating in the distribution of an issue of securities (other than exempted securities) as an underwriter or in a selling group may not allow a selling concession to a bank or trust company.

Other NASD rules and regulations governing the sale and distribution of securities under both *primary* and *secondary* conditions are discussed in Chapter 23 under the Rules of Fair Practice. *(For a discussion of underwriting of municipal securities, see Chapter 4; of private placements, see page 375; of Regulation A offerings, see page 376).*

REVIEW QUESTIONS

1. Describe the main functions of an investment banker.
2. Explain the activities of the buying or corporate finance department in a negotiated deal.

3. What factors should a syndicate manager consider in selecting a firm to participate with him in an underwriting.
4. Name the different types of underwriting commitments. Which is the most commonly used?
5. Describe the activities of the syndicate manager during the period of distribution of an issue.
6. What is meant by the term *"managing the pot"*?
7. Discuss when and how a new issue should be stabilized.
8. When is a competitive deal used? What is the major difference between a negotiated and a competitive deal?

TRUE AND FALSE QUESTIONS

1. The primary function of an investment banker is:

		True	*False*
a.	to help business firms obtain capital	_____	_____
b.	to ensure the buyers of corporate securities of a profit	_____	_____
c.	to guarantee the payment of principal and interest on the bonds sold	_____	_____
d.	to hold the deposits of the business firms.	_____	_____

2. A primary distribution is:

		True	*False*
a.	the selling of an old issue by a large underwriter	_____	_____
b.	the selling of any security that has never before been issued	_____	_____
c.	the selling of a new issue of a small corporation by its own employees.	_____	_____

3. The negotiated deal form of underwriting is most often used by:

		True	*False*
a.	electric public utilities	_____	_____
b.	industrial companies	_____	_____
c.	railroads	_____	_____
d.	municipalities.	_____	_____

4. The main advantages to an issuer of a negoitated deal over any other form is:

		True	*False*
a.	the underwriting spread or cost is lower	_____	_____
b.	the underwriters give to the issuer valuable advice as to markets, timing of the issue, and its type	_____	_____
c.	the deal can be worked out more quickly	_____	_____
d.	a larger volume of securities can be sold.	_____	_____

5. Due diligence meetings are held primarily: *True*   *False*
    a. to give the issuer a chance to explain to the   _____   _____
        investors and to the underwriters the activities
        of the company   _____   _____
    b. to help protect the underwriter against possible
        law suits by showing that they had investigated
        the issuing company thoroughly   _____   _____
    c. to promote a new company   _____   _____
    d. to test and investigate the integrity of the
        management.   _____   _____

6. The stabilization of a new issue: *True*   *False*
    a. is not permitted under any circumstances   _____   _____
    b. is permitted provided the conditions are set
        forth in the prospectus   _____   _____
    c. may be done at the discretion of the managing
        underwriter   _____   _____
    d. may be done with the approval of the issuer.   _____   _____

7. The NASD's Committee on Corporate Financing reviews all financing
    participated in by NASD dealers and: *True*   *False*
    a. insists that the terms be fair and reasonable   _____   _____
    b. approves the investment soundness of the issue   _____   _____
    c. can forbid the manager and the members of the
        group from participating in the financing   _____   _____
    d. can fine the issuer.   _____   _____

9

THE
OVER THE COUNTER
SECURITIES MARKET

The over-the-counter securities market handles most of the securities transactions that take place in the United States. In fact, its operations are so extensive that the easiest way to describe it is to indicate what it does not do in the way of securities transactions. The over-the-counter market does not handle the purchase or sale of securities that actually occur on securities exchanges.[1] Everything else in the way of securities transactions, it does handle. Securities not traded on a securities exchange are said to be traded over the counter.

TYPES OF SECURITIES TRADED OVER THE COUNTER

Many different types of securities are traded over the counter:

1. bank stocks
2. insurance company stocks
3. U.S. government securities
4. municipal bonds
5. open-end investment company shares (mutual funds)
6. railroad equipment trust certificates
7. most corporate bonds

[1] Exceptions are securities traded in the Third Market.

8. stocks of a very large number of industrial and utility corporations, including nearly all new issues
9. securities of many foreign corporations

The over-the-counter market is not located in any one central place. Rather, it consists of thousands of securities houses located in hundreds of different cities and towns all over the United States. These securities houses are called broker-dealers, and they are engaged in buying and selling securities usually for their own account and risk. They also buy and sell securities for the account and risk of others and may charge a commission for their services. To transact their business, they communicate their buy and sell orders back and forth through a nationwide network of telephones and teletypes.

Many dealers engage in over-the-counter activities only rather than activities in both markets, and some deal only in particular types of securities, such as government bonds. As will be discussed in greater detail later in this chapter, the over-the-counter market is a *negotiated* market rather than an *auction* market. Prices are arrived at by dealers negotiating with other dealers to arrive at the best price. An exchange market is an auction market in which brokers bid or offer at successively higher or lower prices until a common price is reached and the transaction is completed.

Historically the over-the-counter market has been the proving ground for an unseasoned company to prepare itself for eventual listing on an organized exchange. However, some never qualify and some that do qualify choose to remain on the over-the-counter market for historical or management preference. For example, such companies as Pinkerton's, Inc. and McCormick & Company could easily meet the standards of the Big Board, but for several reasons they prefer to remain in the over-the-counter market. One advantage accruing to the over-the-counter market is the dealer support they receive in the form of merchandising, sponsorship, and stimulation of interest.

For years the exact size of the over-the-counter market has been a mystery. It is estimated, however, that approximately 30,000 government and corporate issues are being traded over-the-counter and that the worth of these issues totals $125 billion. In 1979, there were 2,670 securities quoted by the National Association of Securities Dealers Automated Quotations Systems, NASDAQ (see pages 177-80).

Institutional investors interested in buying or selling large blocks of listed securities (listed or otherwise) do a substantial portion of their business in the over-the-counter market because (1) U.S. government and municipal bonds trade almost entirely in the over-the-counter market. (2) Distribution of new issues is an important part of the over-the-counter market. *Primary distributions* are offerings of securities that have never been issued before; this distribution is accomplished by an investment banker. *Secondary distributions* are issues of securities that have already been subject to primary distribution. (3) Buying and selling can take place there without unduly affecting the price. (4) Large block distributions can usually take place more efficiently in the over-the-counter market.

THE THIRD MARKET

Over-the-counter market transactions by broker-dealer firms in securities *listed* on the New York Stock Exchange and other national exchanges are called "third market" transactions. In 1972, third market activity was equal to 8.5% of NYSE dollar volume. But largely due to the elimination of fixed commission, third market activity dropped in 1978 to about 2.6% of the NYSE share volume.

THE FOURTH MARKET

The fourth market consists of purchases and sales between large institutions, such as insurance companies, pension funds, and trust departments of commercial banks. For instance, Metropolitan Life Insurance Company might exchange a block of bonds of, say, $5 million for a block of bonds of a different company held by New York Life Insurance Company. The broker is bypassed and no commission is paid.

ROLE OF THE MARKET MAKER

The phrase *to make a market* means that the dealer creates and maintains a market in a security. A dealer is said to *maintain* a market in a security when that dealer is known to be willing at all times to buy or sell that security, usually for the firm's own account and risk, at prices quoted in amounts at least equivalent to the security's trading unit (usually 100 shares of stock)

FIRM OR SUBJECT MARKETS

In over-the-counter dealings, markets are quoted either as *firm* or *subject*. A *subject market* is a quotation in which the prices are subject to confirmation. *Firm* market prices are those at which a security can actually be bought or sold. Firm market is sometimes referred to as *actual market*.

Firm bids or *firm offers* are prices at which a dealer is committed to buy or sell a specified amount of securities, whether for a brief moment only or for a given period of time. *Offered firm* means that the seller has made an offering that is good for the period of time specified by the seller or until rejected.

In addition to the terms *firm* and *subject*, the term *work-out* market is sometimes used in connection with the over-the-counter market. A *work-out* market represents an indication of prices at which it is believed a security can be bought or sold within a reasonable length of time.

One thing important to remember is that, unless a dealer specifies to the contrary, the prices he quotes for a particular security are firm at the moment for amounts equivalent to the usual trading units for such a security. Examples of each type of quotation are as follows:

Firm Market	Subject Market
"the market is 65-70"	"it is quoted 65-70"
"it is 65-70"	"last I saw was 65-70"
"we can trade it 65-70"	"it is 65-70 subject"

SIZE OF MARKET

When making a firm market to buy a security at a specified price, it is required that a dealer be prepared to complete the transaction.

Any dealer supplying a quotation as an actual market or claiming to have a firm market in a security is expected to be ready and obligated to buy or sell at the prices quoted in amounts equivalent to what is commonly understood to be the trading unit or *size* in that security. The size is the actual number of shares or bonds represented in a bid or offering that comprises a given quotation. Unless the number of shares of a security named in a firm bid or firm offer is specified, it is understood to be the usual trading unit or size of the security. Unless a smaller or larger amount is specified when the firm market quotation is supplied, the usual size of the market is 100 shares of a stock or 5 bonds.

BID OR OFFERING WANTED

Sometimes securities are offered for sale or sought for purchase by a dealer, but the dealer receives no bids or offers. In such cases, the terms *bid wanted* or *offering wanted* are used. The term *bid wanted*, or BW, means a security is being offered for sale and prospective buyers are requested to submit a bit for that security. The term *offering wanted*, or OW, means that the security referred to is being sought for purchase and anyone wishing to sell that security is requested to submit an offering. Dealers often use these terms when they advertise in the National Quotation Bureau "sheets."

THE BROKER-DEALER: TYPES OF CUSTOMERS, SECURITY POSITION, EXECUTION OF TRANSACTIONS

The broker-dealer acting as a market maker might have several types of customers. Some dealers are wholesalers and trade only with other dealers; some concentrate on trades with the large institutions (i.e., pension funds, insurance companies, and so forth). Many small retail security firms buy from wholesalers and sell to the small investor. Sometimes the wholesale market is referred to as the *inside market*. Finally, some dealers are both wholesalers and retailers. In the wholesale market, the spread between the bid and the offered price is usually smaller.

Sometimes a broker-dealer might take a long position by acquiring a security in the hope that its price will rise. A broker-dealer may also sell a security short in the hope that the price will fall. A detailed discussion of short selling is in Chapter 10. But most dealers try to keep the volume of buying and selling in their issues in *balance*. If, for example, the position in a particular stock becomes too large, the broker-dealer may sell some shares short. Also, the broker-dealer's position in a stock may depend in part on the view of the firm concerning the outlook for the market, the economy, and so forth. But the broker-dealer, like the stock exchange specialist, should maintain a sufficient position in his or her stocks to meet customers' demands on either side of the market.

THE EXECUTION OF OTC TRANSACTIONS

As on the national stock exchanges (see pages 193-4), the most common types of orders are market and limit orders. The *market order* should be executed immediately at the best possible price. A *limit order* sets the price at which the security must be bought or sold. A limit order may be for one day or it may be GTC (good 'til canceled). An all-or-none order is sometimes used for bonds. Here all the bonds must be sold or none. However, the order is not canceled if it is not filled immediately. A fill or kill order is automatically "killed" or canceled it it is not filled at once. A discretionary order permits the broker to use his or her discretion in executing the order. At all times, it is up to the broker to do the best possible for the customer.

TYPES OF TRANSACTIONS
BY BROKER-DEALERS

A great many dealer firms act as brokers or agents as well as dealers. The terms *broker* and *agent* mean the same thing; that is, a person or firm executing orders for the account and risk of others. A broker-dealer registered with the Securities and Exchange Commission and engaged in the investment banking and securities business may buy and sell securities for his own account or risk or, as agent, purchase and sell securities for the account and risk of others. As an agent, the broker-dealer may receive a commission for his services of buying or selling securities for the account and risk of his customers. However, whether or not a person or a firm charges for services, the broker-dealer acts as *agent* when executing orders for the account and risk of others.

A broker-dealer can handle purchase orders from a customer in any of three ways:

1. If the broker-dealer makes a market in a particular stock a customer wants to buy, he can sell the customer the stock out of his own inventory, *or*
2. When the broker-dealer gets the order, if he doesn't make a market in that particular stock, he can act as the customer's agent and buy it for the customer from some other dealer who does make a market in that stock or from someone who owns the security and wishes to sell it, *or*
3. When the broker-dealer gets the order, he can purchase the security for his or her own account from a dealer who does make a market in that security, or from someone who owns the security, and resell it to his customer.

Whenever the firm acts as an agent, it must disclose to its customer any commission charged in connection with the purchase or sale of the securities. The actual commission charged must be set forth in dollars and cents on the confirmation to the customer when a broker-dealer is acting as an agent.

Sometimes it happens that a broker acts for both the buyer and the seller in the purchase and sale of securities. When this occurs, the broker must disclose the total commission to the parties on both sides of the transaction.

In an agency transaction, the commission charged the customer by the broker-dealer must not be unfair and should not exceed the amount that, were the broker-dealer to act as principal, would be in accord with the 5% markup policy.

As noted, under association rules it is required that, in agency transactions, commissions or service charges shall be fair. However, an NASD member who is acting as an agent for his customers may, within reasonable limits and using care to avoid discrimination, vary the commission charged to each, depending on the circumstances relating to each transaction.

DELIVERY INSTRUCTIONS

These are discussed under the Uniform Practice Code on page 211.

CONFIRMATION OF TRADE

A security trade over the counter is consummated by the statement, "we buy" or "we sell" and by the response, "we confirm."

When a customer gives an order to purchase any security accompanied by full payment, the transaction is not completed until the broker-dealer delivers the security to the customer or to the customer's account.

Under all conditions, purchase and sale transactions must be confirmed to the customer *in writing*, and the confirmation must contain certain specific information.

When acting as agent for two principals, a broker must disclose on the confirmation the source and amount of any commissions received or to be received.

THE DEALER MARKUP

Perhaps the most important part of the NASD Rules of Fair Practice is Section 4 dealing with fair prices and commissions. Of this section the key statement is, "It shall be deemed conduct inconsistent with just and equitable principles of trade for a member to enter into any transaction with a customer in any security at any price not reasonably related to the current market price of a security or to charge a commission which is not reasonable."

When a *dealer* sells securities to his customers, the dealer does not charge a commission. Commissions are charged only when an agency or brokerage relationship exists. Acting as a *principal*, a dealer makes his money from the markup on his merchandise. This *markup* is the difference between the amount the dealer pays for the securities when they are purchased and the amount that is received when he sells them to his customers. For example, suppose the dealer buys 100 shares of General Chaos Corporation stock for $50 per share. The purchase price is $5,000. Later the dealer sells this stock to a customer for $51.50 per share. The customer pays the dealer $5,150 for the stock. The difference between what the dealer paid for the stock, $5,000, and what was received for the stock when he sold it, $5,150, is the markup. In this case, the markup is $150, or 3% of what the dealer had to pay to acquire the stock in the first place.

Out of the $150 markup, the dealer must cover his costs of doing business. If any money is left after expenses are covered, the dealer has made a profit. If the markup does not cover expenses, the dealer has had a loss.

If a customer is a seller and the broker-dealer firm buys as principal, the difference between the price paid to the customer and the sale price by the broker dealer to the market maker is called a *markdown*.

When a dealer makes a market (or *takes a position*, as it is sometimes called) in a security, the dealer is taking a risk—a risk that the stock he owns will drop in price before he can sell it to someone.

In the example just given, the dealer invested $5,000 of his capital in General Chaos Corporation stock, marked the stock up 3% and offered it for sale at $5,150. However, assume that before the dealer found an interested customer, some bad news concerning the corporation developed and caused interest in the stock to lag. Under these conditions, the following might occur: The dealer offered the stock for $51.50 a share at first, and later $50 a share, but found that no one was interested in the stock at either of those prices. Faced with this situation, the dealer can do one of two things—sell the stock for less than $50 per share, in which case part of the original capital investment would be lost *or* hold the stock, hoping that some day investor interest in that stock will be renewed so that the stock can be sold at a price that will permit recovery of the original investment.

If the dealer chooses the second course of action and continues to hold the stock, the dealer is taking the risk of a further drop in price. Furthermore, by continuing to hold the stock, instead of selling it, the dealer is tying up part of the money needed to run the business. If this happens too often, the dealer may be forced to go out of business altogether due to a lack of working capital.

As noted, if the dealer chooses the first course of action and sells the stock at a loss, the dealer will lose part of his capital investment. However, by selling, even though at a loss, the dealer regains the use of the remaining capital. With this money, the dealer can purchase other securities that he might be able to mark up successfully and sell at a profit.

Although a great deal depends on the individual circumstances surrounding each case, many dealers, when faced with the dilemma presented here, feel it is best to take their loss and use the remaining capital elsewhere.

Dealers cannot afford to make many mistakes in selecting the securities that they buy and mark up for resale. If they are wrong too often, they will be unable to continue in business.

For a dealer to continue successfully in business, that dealer must be able to sell securities from his inventory at a markup high enough to cover his operating expenses, as well as any losses that occur on the stocks held in his inventory.

This is not as easy to accomplish as it sounds. Almost always there is more than one dealer making a market in any given security being traded over the counter. Very often there are several different dealers competing with one another. The dealers with the highest markups and prices for any given security will have a hard time selling any of these securities. Obviously, no one likes to pay a price higher than necessary for anything he buys.

THE 5% MARKUP POLICY

Apart from the dealer competition, however, there is a second factor that in part determines how much the dealer markup will be; this is the 5% markup policy adopted by the NASD. The association's 5% markup policy was adopted as a *general guide* to its members for their use in determining the prices that might be charged customers, which would be reasonably related to current market prices. The policy is based on Section 4, Article III of the association's Rules of Fair Practice.

The 5% markup is a general policy, and it is an extremely important one. Its importance is made clearly evident by a Securities and Exchange Commission decision covering broker-dealer markups. This SEC decision states that the sale of securities by a broker-dealer to an investor at prices that bear no reasonable relationship to the current market of those securities may constitute fraud.

The mere fact, however, that markups exceed 5% does not in and of itself prove that the prices to the customer are unfair. As noted, the 5% markup policy is intended to be used only as a general guide. It does not mean that the markup of a member may never exceed 5% of his cost. Nor does the 5% markup policy mean that a dealer is entitled to an overall average of 5% on his markup in sales to customers. Under certain conditions, markups of over 5% may be justified. For example, a dealer selling a security that he has owned for a period of time should use current market prices, rather than cost, as a basis for computing markups.

Also, in the case of certain low-priced securities (such as those selling below $10), a somewhat higher percentage may be justified under special conditions.

On the other hand, it is equally true that under certain conditions markups of *less* than 5% may be unfair to the customer. For example, when a customer buys a security by selling another security through the same *member* firm at the same time, a 5% markup or even a 3% markup on both transactions would be unfair. In such a case, the *member* should consider the purchase and sale as one transaction when determining his markup.

The most important point the broker-dealer should keep in mind when marking up securities for resale to investors is that the markup must not be *unfair*. Section 4, Article III of the NASD's Rules of Fair Practice indicates that securities will be bought from or sold to customers at prices that are fair.

If a broker-dealer's markups are *unfair*, serious repercussions may result, with appropriate action being taken by the NASD or the SEC.

GENERAL CONSIDERATIONS

Since the adoption of the 5% policy, the NASD board has determined that

1. The 5% policy is a guide, not a rule.
2. A member may not justify markups on the basis of excessive expenses.
3. The mark-up over the prevailing market price is the significant spread from the point of view of fairness of dealings with customers in principal transactions. In the absence of other bona fide evidence of the prevailing market, a member's own contemporaneous cost is the best indication of the prevailing market price of the security.
4. A markup pattern of 5% or even less may be considered unfair.
5. Determination of the fairness of markups must be based on the relevant factors of which the percentage of the markup is only one.

RELEVANT FACTORS

Some of the factors that the NASD board believes that members and the NASD committees should take into consideration in determining the fairness of the markups are as follows.

1. The type of security in the transaction—a stock would have a higher markup than a bond.
2. The availability of the security in the market—an inactive security would be harder to buy or sell than would an active security.
3. The price of the security—transactions in a lower-priced security might require more handling expense when the amount of money involved is substantial.
4. The amount of money involved—a small transaction might warrant a higher percentage markup.

5. Disclosure to the customer of commission or markup—while a factor, it does not justify a markup or commission that is unfair.
6. The pattern of markups of the member—while each transaction must be fair, the NASD board believes attention should be given to member's markups.
7. The nature of the member's business—continuing services and facilities of the member to customer might be considered in judging the markups.

Thus it is obvious that no fixed maximum markup rate can be established by the association. Further, it is equally true that a fixed definition of fairness as it relates to security markups is not possible.

TRANSACTIONS TO WHICH THE POLICY IS APPLICABLE

The 5% policy applies to all securities handled in the over-the-counter market, whether oil royalties or any other security in the following types of transactions.

1. A transaction in which a member buys a security to fill an order for the same security previously received from a customer—this transaction would include the so-called "riskless" or "simultaneous" transaction.
2. A transaction in which a member sells a security to a customer from inventory—here the amount of the markup should be determined on the basis of the markup over the bona fide representative current market. The amount of the profit or loss from market changes before or after the date of the transaction with the customer would not ordinarily affect the fairness of the markup.
3. The purchase of a security from a customer—the price paid to the customer or markdown must be reasonably related to the prevailing market price of the security.
4. A transaction in which a member acts as an agent—here the commission charged must be fair in the light of all relevant circumstances.
5. Transactions in which a customer sells securities to, or through, a broker-dealer and the proceeds are used to pay for other securities bought from the broker-dealer at about the same time—in such instances, the markup shall be computed in the same way as if the customer had purchased for cash, and in computing the markup there shall be included any profit or commission realized by the dealer on the securities being liquidated, the proceeds of which are used to pay for the securities being purchased.

THE NATIONAL ASSOCIATION OF SECURITIES DEALERS AUTOMATED QUOTATIONS SYSTEM (NASDAQ)

The NASDAQ officially began to serve the over-the-counter market in 1971. It is a nationwide hookup of computer terminals with communication facilities for market makers, investors, and regulators. Through NASDAQ terminals, market makers enter their quotations on stocks in which they make markets, for display on all the terminals of the system. They also see on their screens the quotations of all other market makers. The total number of terminals employed by market makers to enter quotations was 1,027 at the end of 1978. Daily average calls per day in 1978 were 842, 367.

The heart of the NASDAQ system is its central computer complex located at Trumbull, Connecticut. Traffic to and from this complex flows through four regional offices located in New York, Chicago, San Francisco, and Atlanta. The NASDAQ system is owned by NASDAQ, Inc. with its own board of directors. Bunker Ramo Corporation, the builder of the system, operates it under a contract to the NASD. Securities on NASDAQ numbered 2,670 at the end of 1979, with a market value of $91.7 billion. Share volume of trading amounted to 3,650,000,000 or 23.3% of the total shares traded on the national exchanges. The NYSE accounted for 60.9% the AMEX 8.3%, and the regional exchanges 7.5%.

Three levels of NASD service are available: level 1 is used largely by registered representatives, level 2 by retail traders, and level 3 by market makers.

Level 1

At the end of 1979, there were 45,000 stock and market data desk–top terminals located mainly in brokers' offices. This equipment enabled the securities salesperson to quote up-to-the-minute *the best* bid and asked prices on NASD securities to the investing public. This representative bid quotation was the median of all bid prices entered by the registered market maker. The representative asked quotation was determined by the calculation of the median spread for the security.

But by order of the SEC, after July 5, 1980 these terminals, as well as the stock tables[2] appearing in the newspapers, must reflect the *highest bid and the lowest offer* available. Thus, for the first time the customer will know the best price at which a transaction can be executed. Level 1 service is available to NASD members and under certain circumstances to others.

[2]The national NASDAQ list of 1,410 stocks is transmitted to the newspapers every business day.

Level 2

This service provides the actual current quotations of the securities made by all the market makers specializing in those issues. The market makers are identified. The service is provided by desk terminals connected to the NASDAQ system. The terminals are designed primarily for the retail trader, and they are usually located in an area devoted to trading. The service is available to NASD members and, under certain circumstances, to others.

Level 3

This service is restricted to market-making members authorized by the NASD. It provides current quotes of all the market makers in the security and allows the users to enter quotations in specific securities for which the user is a market maker. The entry and updating of quotations by a market maker is done by activating the appropriate keys.

To be an authorized subscriber to level 3 service, a member must meet certain qualifications:

1. The registered market maker shall maintain net capital in an amount of not less than $2,500 for each security in which he makes a market (unless a security in which he makes a market has a value of $5.00 or less, in which event the amount of net capital shall be not less than $500 for each such security) except that under no circumstances shall he have less than net capital of $25,000, or be required to have more than $100,000.

2. Each quotation entered by the registered market maker must be reasonably related to the prevailing market.

3. A registered market maker shall not be permitted, except under extraordinary circumstances, to enter quotations into the NASDAQ System if (1) the bid quotation entered is greater than the ask quotation of another registered market maker in the same security, or (2) the ask quotation is less than the bid quotation of another registered market maker in the same security.

4. Quotations entered by market makers will be expected to be firm at the time of entry for at least 100 shares, but will be subject to confirmation on verbal request. A pattern of continued "backing away" will be grounds for NASD disciplinary action.

5. Stabilizing bids may be entered by a registered market maker for display on level 2 or level 3. A market maker that desires to be designated as a stabilizing underwrtier must notify the NASDAQ system by 5.00 P.M.

6. Reports must be filed daily to the system on trading activity in the securities in which the dealer is a market maker. Also, monthly reports must be made.

QUALIFICATIONS FOR
AUTHORIZED SECURITIES

If a security is to be quoted in the NASDAQ system, it must meet certain qualifications. The most important of these are as follows

1. Must be within the eligible pool of securities. Generally this pool contains securities registered under the Securities Exchange Act of 1934, which requires a company to have at least 500 stockholders and $1,000,000 of assets.
2. Must have at least two market makers registered (three for ADRs and foreign securities).
3. Must have public distribution of at least 100,000 shares and $500,000 minimum capital and surplus.
4. Must be registered on a national securities exchange.
5. Must be a registered bank, investment company, or insurance companies.

MAINTENANCE REQUIREMENT

Once included in NASDAQ, the issues must maintain certain criteria to remain in the system:

1. The number of persons holding the security of record shall not be less than 300 except in the case of rights, warrants, or units.
2. This issuer's total capital and surplus shall not be less than $500,000 in the case of eligible security not yet authorized or $250,000 in the case of an authorized security.
3. The total number of shares publicly held shall not be less than 100,000.
4. Various reasons for suspension might be (a) failure to file with NASDAQ system reports, (b) failure to disclose material facts that affect the value of its securities, (c) insufficient number of market makers, and (d) failure to pay quotation fees.

ADVANTAGES OF THE NASDAQ

1. *Bid-and-asked* quotations are instantly provided to all market makers in a particular stock as well as the best bid-and-asked quotations on about 2,600 stocks.
2. *Investors* can be assured of the best execution of their orders. Some of the mystery of the over-the-counter market has been removed. This in the past kept many investors from trading there. Investors can be more sure that the traders have checked all market makers in their stock.

3. *Traders* can gauge the market more quickly and be more con-
    fident in making bids. There is less noise and confusion in the
    trading room. Work load is reduced as fewer telephone calls are
    made to check the market.
4. *Competition* is stimulated among the over-the-counter dealers
    and between the over-the-counter dealer and the exchange
    specialist.
5. *The issuing corporations* are more willing to stay in the over-the-
    counter market and not, as has been their practice, to move to the
    exchanges as soon as they can qualify financially.
6. *Information* is provided to the NASD and to the public in regard
    to volume of transactions in the over-the-counter market, on in-
    dexes of over-the-counter stocks, and on individual trades.
7. *Further automation* is possible, including the posting of actual
    prices on stocks and even the automatic execution of orders.
8. The self-regulatory program of the NASD is supplemented.

TWO WAYS TO BUY AN OVER-THE-COUNTER SECURITY

Using the NASDAQ System

Let us assume that Mr. Smith wishes to buy 100 shares of Girard Company (GIRA). This is a very active stock quoted on the NASDAQ. Accord-
ingly, Mr. Smith places the order with his registered representative, who
first checks his desk-top level 1 NASDAQ quotation unit and advises Mr.
Smith that the highest bid is 22½ and the lowest offer is 23. This would
indicate that Mr. Smith should be able to buy his stock at around 23 or
maybe slightly less. The registered representative writes a buy order for Mr.
Smith for 100 shares of GIRA at the market. He then sends it to the OTC
order room. The trader checks GIRA on his level 2 NASDAQ unit. This
unit indicates all the dealers making a market in GIRA. The OTC trader
would then contact the dealer making the lowest offered price and purchase
the shares for Mr. Smith.

Using the National Quotation Bureau, Inc. (NOB)

About 11,000 over-the-counter equity securities with a market value
of close to $50 billion are not quoted by the NASDAQ. The National
Quotation Service of the National Quotation Bureau, Inc. distributes *pink
sheets* every business day. These in the course of a year quote about 30,000

different stock issues. They also list the brokers, about 900 in all, who are making markets in these issues. Also, the NQB distributes *yellow sheets*, which contain offerings of corporate bonds.

Thus, if a customer desires to buy the stock of the PDQ Corporation, which is not quoted by the NASDAQ, he or she would ask the broker to check the pink sheets to which he subscribes. The broker would call the dealers making a market in PDQ Corporation and try to obtain the lowest asked price. This is called "shopping around" or "shopping the street." Finally when the broker is satisfied that he has obtained the lowest asked price, the broker will call back and consummate the trade for the customer.

At present there are no green or white sheets.

As mentioned, dealers' quotations consist of their bid, and asked or more often bid and offered prices. The price that a dealer will pay for a given security is called the *bid.* The price at which a dealer will sell a given security is called the *asked* price or *offer.* The difference between the bid and the asked prices in any quotation is the *spread.*

A dealer may take a *position* in a security by buying it for inventory (long position) or by selling securities that have not yet been purchased (short position).

When a customer inquires as to how a security is quoted, it is *not* sufficient if the dealer tells the customer how he is offering that security. A quotation at all times must include both sides of the market even though one side may be nonexistent, as, for example, "offered at 20, no bid" or "$20 bid, none offered."

It is not necessary for a dealer actually to have the securities he sells to his customers in his inventory at the time that the dealer sells them. A dealer may sell securities to a customer even though he does not own the securities at the time of the sale. However, once the dealer has sold them, the dealer must obtain the securities and deliver them to his customer at the agreed price regardless of how much the dealer has to pay to get them.

PUBLISHED QUOTATIONS:
THE CONSOLIDATED QUOTATION
SYSTEM (CQS)

In 1977, the Consolidated Quotation System (CQS) of the NASDAQ started to quote about 1,500 issues of the NYSE. This "consolidated tape" includes the trading done by NYSE members, by the third market dealers, and by the regional exchanges in NYSE issues. This service permits subscribers to see at a glance on the NASDAQ screen the various markets in the country for NYSE, AMEX, OTC and regional exchanges.

Quotations of over-the-counter securities have been made ever since the system started in 1971. Quotations of over-the-counter securities are as of 4.00 P.M. They are the closing bid and asked prices, with the difference given over the previous bid. These quotations do not show the retail markup or commission. An SEC rule requires all market makers to release firm quotations, good for at least a unit of trading. The rule further specifies that size can be displayed when quotations are good for more than a single unit of trading.

REVIEW QUESTIONS

1. Describe the over-the-counter market, naming eight types of securities traded in it.
2. Distinguish among a firm market, a subject market, and a work-out market. What does the term *size of the market* mean?
3. Describe in general terms the 5% markup policy. What are some of the circumstances that are considered by the NASD in determining the fairness of the markups?
4. When does the 5% markup policy apply? When does it *not* apply? What is the SEC's attitude toward the markup policy?
5. Describe the difference between a broker and a dealer.
6. What are the "pink sheets" and the "yellow sheets?" Illustrate how a broker might use them to buy a security for a customer.
7. What is the NASD policy with respect to the firmness of quotations?
8. Describe the Consolidated Quotation System and explain how it could fit in with the proposed national market.

TRUE AND FALSE QUESTIONS

1. Types of securities traded in the over-the-counter market include:

		True	False
a.	bank and insurance stocks	____	____
b.	U.S. government and municipal securities	____	____
c.	mutual funds	____	____
d.	some stocks listed on the New York Stock Exchange	____	____
e.	corporate bonds	____	____
f.	all of the above.	____	____

2. A firm market means:

		True	False
a.	prices at which a security can actually be bought or sold	____	____
b.	the same as a work-out market	____	____
c.	the opposite of a subject market.	____	____

3. When a trader quotes in the following manner bids and offers, that
    trader is quoting a *firm* market: *True*   *False*

    a.   it is quoted 70-72   _____   _____
    b.   the market is 70-72   _____   _____
    c.   it is 70-72   _____   _____
    d.   the last I saw was 70-72   _____   _____
    e.   we can trade 70-72.   _____   _____

4. The size of the market is: *True*   *False*

    a.   the commonly understood trading unit   _____   _____
    b.   the actual number of shares or bonds
         represented in the bid or offering   _____   _____
    c.   unless specified, when the firm market is
         100 shares or 5 bonds.   _____   _____

5. The 5% markup policy of the NASD was adopted: *True*   *False*

    a.   as a ceiling on markups in sales to customers   _____   _____
    b.   as a minimum spread on all transactions to
         which the broker is entitled   _____   _____
    c.   as a guide, not a rule, to all members   _____   _____
    d.   to apply in particular to sales of mutual funds.   _____   _____

6. The third market is: *True*   *False*

    a.   purchase and sale of securities between
         institutions   _____   _____
    b.   transactions by OTC dealers in NYSE
         securities   _____   _____
    c.   transactions between OTC dealers and NYSE
         members.   _____   _____

7. The advantages of the NASDAQ include all of the following *except:*
                                                                   True   *False*

    a.   traders can gauge the OTC market at a glance   _____   _____
    b.   investors can be more certain of getting better
         execution   _____   _____
    c.   the self-regulatory program of the NASD is
         greatly strengthened   _____   _____
    d.   assures a wider spread to dealers.   _____   _____

8. The qualifications for NASDAQ listing include the following:
                                                                   True   *False*

    a.   must be within the eligible pool of securities   _____   _____
    b.   must have at least two market makers   _____   _____
    c.   must have public distribution of at least
         100,000 shares   _____   _____
    d.   must be approved by the SEC.   _____   _____

10

ORGANiZEd

SECURiTiES ExCHANGES

A securities exchange is an institution that provides facilities for its members to execute transactions in securities traded thereon for their own account and risk or for the account and risk of their customers.

Securities exchanges, or stock exchanges, as most of them are called, do not buy securities from anyone, nor do they sell securities to anyone. They simply provide a convenient centralized place where member firm brokers representing buyers of securities and member firm brokers representing sellers of securities can meet and execute their customers' orders. Member firm may also execute transactions for their own account and risk.

AUCTION MARKET

The various stock exchanges around the country work on an auction basis. Bids to buy securities and offers to sell securities are made openly on the floor of these exchanges. Whenever a trade takes place, the person or institution bidding the highest for a security becomes the buyer, and the person or insitution making the lowest offer to sell a security is the seller. The prices at which such transactions take place on the New York Stock Exchange and on the American Stock Exchange are sent out to thousands of locations through the stock exchange ticker systems. These promptly and highly publicized prices give an indication to anyone interested in a particular security of the approximate price at which that security can be bought or sold.

FUNCTIONS AND SERVICES OF
ORGANIZED SECURITIES
EXCHANGES

Organized securities exchanges provide facilities in which the forces of supply and demand for a given security have an opportunity to interact and set the price at which the security trades. When a security is traded on an organized exchange, both buy and sell orders for that security are funneled to the appropriate trading area on the exchange floor. Because a large percentage of the current potential buyers and sellers is represented at that trading post, the price at which the trade takes place is likely to reflect quite clearly existing supply and demand conditions.

The securities exchanges are not in themselves a source of new equity capital. However, unless exchanges and other efficient securities markets existed, many investors would be reluctant to purchase securities at all for fear they would be unable to sell them later when they needed their cash.

Thus the *liquidity* and *marketability* added to securities by the fact that they are traded on an exchange are important factors that help facilitate the flow of new money to industry.

THE NEW YORK STOCK
EXCHANGE (NYSE)

The NYSE, founded in 1792, is the nation's largest centralized market. In 1978, it accounted for 80.3% of the volume of shares traded on organized exchanges; the American Stock Exchange accounted for 10.5%, and all other regional exchanges 9.2%.

A board of directors and a paid full-time chairman govern the exchange.[1] They have power to impose penalties for rule violations, approve listings, supervise members, and serve on many committees. There are 20 directors of which at least 10 must represent the public.

There are 1,366 members of the NYSE. These hold seats on the NYSE that carry exclusive trading privileges. These seats have sold as high as $625,000 and as low as $17,000. Currently (April 1983), they are selling at about $220,000.

In addition to the regular members, there are *allied members*. These are usually partners, senior officers, or holders of voting stock of the member firms who do not have seats. The allied members have all the privileges of the regular members except they cannot go on the floor of the exchange to execute transactions. But there are times when exceptions to this rule are

---

[1]In June 1980, John Phelan was elected the first president.

approved by the board. Allied members are subject to the same rules as regular members.

In 1977, the NYSE established two new types of membership for qualified broker-dealers: physical access to the floor on payment of annual dues of $25,000 and electronic access with dues of $13,500 annually. The NYSE also voted to allow existing members to lease their privileges of membership to qualified individuals for a stated term. In November 1979, the NYSE members voted to eliminate the annual members but not the electronic members.

Types of Broker-Dealers and Traders

There are several types of broker-dealers and traders among the members of the NYSE.

1. Commission Brokers. Commission brokers comprise approximately half of al the New York Stock Exchange members. This type of broker is the one best known to the average person because he is constantly doing business for his firm's customers. He also, of course, handles transactions for his firm and its registered representatives and partners.

The commission broker executes the orders to buy and sell securities sent in by the customers of his firm. For the performance of this agency service, the firm receives a commission.

There is no risk of security ownership involved for the commission broker, because he acts only on an agency basis in these transactions. In this important respect, the stock exchange commission broker differs markedly from the over-the-counter broker-dealer. The over-the-counter broker-dealer does not always act on an agency basis. Frequently he acts in the capacity of a principal rather than as an agent or broker.

2. Floor Brokers. These are primarily individual enterpreneurs who act as independent commission brokers. They serve a variety of clients. For example, a commission broker might be swamped with orders or might be forced to leave the floor. In these cases he might ask the floor broker to help out for a fixed commission. For years floor brokers were called "two-dollar brokers" because their commission used to be $2.00 per 100 shares traded.

3. Registered Competitive Market Makers (RCMM). This is a new category. Registered competitive market makers have specific obligations to trade for their own or their firm's accounts—when called upon by an exchange official—by making a bid or offer that will narrow the existing quote spread or will improve the depth of an existing quote. An RCMM may also be asked to assist a commission broker or a floor broker in executing a customer's otherwise unexecutable order. RCMMs must be approved and registered with the exchange. Further, the RCMM must have a minimum capital of at least $25,000. This amount must be over and above any other federal or exchange capital requirement. Perhaps most important is the requirement that all his dealings for his own account or for others are or should be reasonably calculated to the maintenance of price continuity and to minimize the effects of any temporary disparity between supply and demand.

4. Stock Specialist. The stock specialists' system is the heart of the NYSE. They, at the risk of their own capital work, to assure the maintenance of fair and orderly markets in all exchange-listed stocks. Each stock traded on the NYSE is assigned to a specialist by the exchange.

The specialist has two different major functions to perform on the stock exchange floor. One that of executing orders entrusted to him by other members of the Exchange. The other is to maintain, insofar as reasonably practicable, fair and orderly markets in stocks that he services by dealing for his own account.

Very often an investor is interested in buying or selling a particular stock only at a price different from (or *away from,* as it is often called) the current market price of that stock. When this is the case, the investor gives a limited order to his broker to buy or sell that stock.

An investor giving his broker a limited order to buy a stock sets the maximum price he authorizes the broker to pay for that security. An investor giving his broker a limited order to sell a stock sets the minimum amount he authorizes the broker to accept for that security.

If an investor gives the broker an order to buy a stock currently selling for $50 a share, but limits the price he is willing to pay for the stock to $45 a share, the order obviously cannot be executed immediately. In fact, it cannot be executed at all until the stock trades at $45, and no one knows when that will next happen.

If the stock the investor wants at $45 stays around its current price of $50 or moves upward in price, it may be many weeks or months before the investor's limited order is executed, if it is executed at all. The broker receiving this limited order cannot possibly go to the appropriate trading post on the floor and wait for the stock to drop to $45 so that he can execute the limited order. However, the broker is expected to execute the order for his customer as soon as market conditions permit; this is where the specialist in that stock comes in.

The specialist is always standing at the post where his assigned stocks are traded. Brokers with limited orders *away from* the market price give the specialist these orders. The specialist enters these orders in his specialist's books.[2] Both limited orders to buy below the current market price and

---

[2]These limited orders *away from* the market are *open orders* (or good 'til canceled orders, as they are often called). An open or good 'til canceled order (GTC) is an order entered at a specific price and is good until canceled.

limited orders to sell above the current market price are written in the book. When trading in the stock reaches the price at which these orders can be executed, the specialist takes the appropriate action.

In our illustration, the $45 limited order would be written in the specialist's books and would be represented in the market by him *when* and *if* the price reached $45. If he executes the order, the specialist receives a floor brokerage commission from the broker who gave him the order. The broker, in turn, receives the regular commission from his customer.

For the protection of the public, the specialist is prohibited by exchange rules, in transactions of the preceding nature, from buying stock for his own account at a given price while he holds an order to buy at that price for someone else. Furthermore, the specialist may not buy stock for his own account at any price while holding an order to buy that stock "at the market." He is similarly prohibited from competing with a customer he represents on the sell side.

The responsibility of maintaining a fair and orderly market for a particular stock is charged to the specialist. His job is to see that price movements of the security in which he specializes are *reasonably orderly*. The role that he plays is vital to the welfare of investors. Obviously, if stock prices typically jumped up several dollars on one transaction only to drop sharply on the next transaction, most people would be extremely reluctant to place any of their spare funds in the securities market.

To help avoid erratic price movements, the specialist is charged by the exchange with maintaining a market in his assigned stock. To do this, he often must risk his capital by buying stock for a price higher than others are willing to pay at that time. He also often has to sell that stock for less than others are willing to sell for at that time.

In performing this function, the specialist in certain respects resembles a dealer in the over-the-counter market. He makes a market in the stock in which he specializes. A specialist often makes the best bid or the best offer in a stock for his own account. At other times, he makes both the best bid and the best offer. In either case, the "spread" is narrower than it would have been without him.

When there is a large number of orders[3] to sell a given stock and few market orders, if any (or limited orders at a price reasonably close to the previous sale) to buy that stock, the specialist will normally buy to prevent the price from *dropping* too rapidly and too steeply between successive trades.

When there are a large number of market orders to buy a given security and few, if any, market orders (or limited orders at a price reason-

---

[3]A market order is an order to the broker to buy or sell a security (whichever it is you wish to do) at the best possible price.

ably close to the previous sale) to sell that security, the specialist may sell to prevent the price from *increasing* too rapidly and too steeply between successive trades.

Thus, when the market price trend of the specialist's stock is *upward*, he usually *sells* stock from his inventory or sells short.[4] When the market price trend of the specialist's stock is *downward*, he usually *buys* stock for his inventory. This type of trading action by the specialist has a *stabilizing effect*. Specialists also serve an important function in being ready to buy and sell inactive stocks if no public offers are reasonably close to the last sale.

The specialist is not expected to *prevent* a stock from declining or appreciating in price. It probably would be impossible for him to do so, even if it were expected of him. If a specialist were willing and *able* at all times to buy any and all shares of a particular company offered for sale at a fixed price, he could stop its market price from falling. If a specialist offered and was able to sell an unlimited quantity of these same shares to anyone wanting them at the same fixed price, he could stop its market price from going up. However, this activity could tie up tremendous amounts of money and would be of very little benefit to anyone.

Specialists *are* expected by their buying and selling actions to modify temporary supply and demand disparity existing in the stock exchange auction market. Their job, in other words, is to make every effort to keep the market price rises and declines fair and orderly for their securities insofar as is reasonably practical under the circumstances.

In 1979, NYSE specialists bought and sold billions of shares for their own accounts for a participation rate of 11.7% of all purchases and sales on the NYSE. Another measure of performance is the stabilization rate—that is, purchases at prices below or sales at prices above the last different price. In 1979 the specialists' stabilization rate was 90.0%. A third measure of the specialist's performance is price continuity. In 1979, 99.1% of the transactions took place at the same price as the preceding transaction, or at a variation of not more than a quarter of a point.

Each specialist at an active post must be able to assume a position of 50 trading units, that is, 5,000 shares of common, 10 units of convertible preferred, 400 shares in each 100-share-trading-unit nonconvertible preferred, and 100 shares in each 10-share-unit nonconvertible preferred stocks in which he is registered.

Further, each registered specialist in an active post must have a minimum capital requirement that shall be the greater of $100,000 or 25% of the position requirements set forth above as regards common and preferred stocks.

---

[4]A short sale refers to the sale of securities that are not owned by the seller. The seller borrows the stock to make the delivery.

A specialist at an inactive post must have at all times $50,000 in net liquid assets.

5. Odd-Lot Dealers. Odd lots, or share amounts of less than the unit of trade (e.g. usually less than 100 shares) are handled by specialists. But they must register with the exchange and pass an odd-lot examination unless waived by the exchange.

A market order to buy or sell "long" is filled at the price of the first round-lot transaction after the receipt of the order plus or minus a differential—usually one eighth of a point.

A market order to sell "short" is filled at a price of the first transaction that is higher than the last different round-lot price minus the differential.

Orders for odd lots are routed through the Common Message Switch System and executed automatically. During 1976, the exchange took over odd-lot processing from Carlisle, DeCoppet and Company. But exchange specialists assume the responsibility for the execution of the odd-lot orders.

In most stocks, a round lot is 100 shares. When this is the case, an odd lot is any number of shares from 1 to 99. Some high-priced or particulary inactive stocks have a unit of trading of only 10 shares. In such cases, an odd lot would be any number of shares from 1 to 9.

An investor buying or selling an odd lot of a security may place either a market order or a limited order.

When an odd-lot market order for a security is received on the floor of the exchange, it is not executed until after the next round-lot transaction takes place. The price at which this round-lot transaction takes place becomes the base price for the odd-lot transaction. To this base price is added the odd-lot differential in the case of a buy order. From this base price is subtracted the odd-lot differential in the case of a sell order.

6. Bond Brokers. All members of the NYSE may trade in the bond rooms. There are, however, certain members who specialize and continue to trade in bonds. In 1977, the Automated Bond System was installed. This system provides current quotations, size, volume, interest rates, yields, maturities, and last sale. By pushing a button, traders can obtain the full range of bids and offers with size for any bond on the NYSE. There are about 1,000 domestic and foreign companies and about 57 governments with bonds.

LARGE BLOCK ORDERS

During 1979, large block activity, an indicator of institutional participation, amounted to 97,509 large blocks (over 10,000 shares) for 2,164 million shares. The market value of these shares is not available but it is believed to be enormous. The total volume of shares traded on the NYSE in

1979 was 8,166 million (round lot shares). Thus, large block mostly institutional orders constitute about 26.5% of the total volume.

Mention should be made of the special methods of distribution, but as will be quickly demonstrated, they are not important in terms of dollars or volume.

Exchange Acquisition or Distribution.   The necessary orders to buy or sell a security are accumulated. Brokers often are paid a commission. The original block of orders is filled by crossing the orders on the floor in the auction market at prices between the current bid and asked quotations. In 1979, there were only two exchange distributions with 1,500,000 shares. An exchange acquisition or distribution must be approved by the NYSE director active on the floor.

Special Bids and Offers

The NYSE director must approve all special offerings and bids. The offering or bid price is printed on the ticker. For example, the tape might show SP OFF 10,000 XYZ 30 COM 1/2. This means a special offering of XYZ common at 30 with a commission for selling it of 1/2 a point or $0.50. Transactions are made on the floor of the exchange but are not a part of the auction market. In 1979, only 1 special offering with 48,000 shares was made.

Secondary Distributions

This form of distribution is used to sell very large orders. With the prior approval of the exchange, member organizations may make and participate in an over-the-counter or off-board secondary distribution of a security admitted to dealing on the exchange. For example, the holder of a large block agrees to sell securities usually below the current market. The selling group offers the shares to the buyers at a net price (no commission) at approximately the market price. A secondary distribution is sometimes advertised in the papers and usually takes place after trading hours. In 1979, there were 23 secondary distributions with 7,936,000 shares.

Specialists' Block Sales and Purchases

This brings up the long-disputed 390 Rule or Market Responsibility Rule of the NYSE. In effect, this rule states that except as otherwise provided, no member, member organization, or the like shall effect any transaction in any listed security in the over-the-counter market. The exchange has feared that, if the SEC forces the revocation of this rule, the very existence of the exchange would be threatened. There are, however, some exceptions to this rule that permit specialists to buy and sell in the over-the-

counter market. These include any purchase or sale under emergency conditions, a transaction that is part of a primary distribution, or a secondary
distribution, and a number of other circumstances. But always the exchange
must approve any over-the-counter trade in listed securities by a member.

The NYSE also readily accomodates transactions primarily for institutional investors, involving large blocks of stock. In fact, in 1978 transactions involving orders of 5,000 shares or more accounted for more than
25% of all shares traded on the NYSE. It is often assumed that the majority
of such transactions are handled as "crosses"—that is, with one broker representing both the buyer and seller, arranging the transaction for them, and
sending their orders to the exchange floor to be executed. However, a recent
(1979) study of block transactions showed that orders accounting for nearly
60% of the dollar value of such trades were handled by different agents for
their respective customers; another 23% involved "block positioning" in
which the broker acted as dealer, buying or supplying all or part of the
block being sold or bought by a customer; and only 18% involved "crosses"
in which a single broker represented customers on both sides of the trade.

LISTING REQUIREMENTS

The New York Stock Exchange has certain mathematical yardsticks
that are used to measure a corporation's eligibility for listing common
stocks. To meet these minimum qualifications for initial listing, a corporation should have

1. A minimum of 1,000,000 publicly held shares among not less than
   2,000 shareholders. Each of the 2,000 shareholders must own 100
   shares or more.
2. A demonstrated earning power before federal income taxes and
   under competitive conditions of $2,500,000 in the latest fiscal year
   and at least $2,000,000 in each of the two preceding years.
3. A market value of the shares in the over-the-counter market or on
   the regional exchanges of the publicly held shares subject to adjustment depending on the market within a maximum of
   $16,000,000 and a minimum of $8,000,000.
4. A net tangible asset value of $16,000,000. This amount is adjusted
   each July 15 and January 15 by the ratio that the NYSE composite
   index of stocks bears to the 1971 base value of the index of $55.06.
   For example, on July 15, 1975 the NYSE index was $51.25. There-
   fore the adjustment in that year would be as follows:

$$\text{Adjusted value} = \frac{\text{July 1975 Index}}{\text{base year}} \times \text{net tangible asset value}$$

$$= \frac{\$51.25}{\$55.06} \times \$16,000,000$$

$$= \$14,900,000$$

On July 13, 1979 (July 15 was on a Sunday), the NYSE composite index was $58.17. Since adjustment is made only when the index is lower than the base, in 1979 none was made. Further, the maximum adjustment that is made on the down side is 50%, or to $8,000,000.

Supplementary Materials

The NYSE also requires the applicant to supply the following:

1. the charter and bylaws
2. specimens of bond and stock certificates
3. annual reports for the past five years
4. latest prospectus and Form 10-K
5. miscellaneous date including the 10 largest stockholders, the list of holders of 1,000 shares or more, shares held in profit sharing plans, and so on.

In addition, to meet the initial listing requirements, the company must be a going concern or be the successor to a going concern.

Each company must execute a listing agreement in which it undertakes to publish interim and annual financial information, solicit proxies for stockholders' meetings, have an independent registrar, give notice of setting of record dates, give notice of changes in officers or directors, charter or by-laws, and other pertinent information.

The listing agreement between the company and the exchange calls for the distribution to stockholders of the company's annual report with financial statements certified by independent accountants at least fifteen days before the annual stockholder's meetings and not later than three months after the close of its fiscal year.

These initial listing standards are not applied inflexibly but, rather, are considered together with various compensating factors. Some of the compensating factors that are taken into consideration in determining a security's eligibility for initial listing include

1. the degree of national interest in the company
2. the character of the market for the corporation's products

Types of Orders for Securities

When an investor purchases or sells securities, the investor must make a variety of decisions regarding the type of order, or orders, he places with a broker. As noted, stocks may be purchased or sold in round lots or odd lots.

Orders may be classed according to size. For instance, a round lot is a unit of trading, usually 100 shares of stock. Only *round lots* or multiples of round lots are traded on the New York Stock Exchange auction market. *Odd-lot* orders are transacted at the effective round-lot prices plus or minus the odd-lot differential as explained on page 190. For *buy orders* no special information is needed other than the name of the security and the number of the shares wanted. A *sell order* must be marked either long or short. In general, if a customer has securities he intends to deliver, the customer will make a long sale. If the customer does not own the securities, he must borrow them to make delivery. The customer will make a short sale in the expectation that when prices decline he can buy securities to cover the short position. (Short sales are discussed in greater detail on page 199.)

A *market order* is an order to buy or sell a stated amount of a security at the most advantageous price after the order is represented in the trading crowd at the NYSE.

A *limit order* is an order to buy or sell a stated amount of a security at a specified price or at a better price if obtainable after the order is represented in the trading crowd at the NYSE.

A *stop order* is an order to buy or sell that becomes a *market* order as soon as the price of the stock reaches or "sells through" the price specified. But, because the stop order merely becomes a market order when the designated price is reached in the market, there is no guarantee that the order will be executed at that price. Perhaps, it is a misnomer to call it a stop *loss* order.

A *stop limit order to buy* becomes a limit order executable at the price or a better price if obtainable when a transaction in the security occurs at or above the stop price. This tactic might be used by an investor who wishes to curtail his loss on an existing short position.

A *stop limit order to sell* becomes a limit order executable at limit price or at a better price when a transaction occurs at or below the stop price. An investor might place a stop limit order to sell if he wished to curtail a possible loss on an existing long position or to preserve a profit.

ORDER QUALIFICATION

When a limited order is placed, a time limit is used to determine its length of life. A limited order might be for a day order, a week, a month, or GTC (good 'til canceled). A day order expires at the end of a day. A GTC order remains in effect until it is either executed or canceled. But GTC orders automatically expire at the end of the semiannual confirmation period unless renewed.

Not held (NH) orders are given to a broker to permit the broker to use his or her judgment in executing an order. (A specialist may not accept NH orders.)

An all-or-none order is a market or limited order that must be executed in its entirety or not at all. But it is not to be treated as canceled if not executed as soon as it is represented in the trading crowd.

A fill or kill order is a market or limited price order that is to be executed in its entirety, and, if not executed as soon as it is represented in the trading crowd, it is canceled.

An immediate or cancel order is a market or limited order that is to be executed in whole or in part as soon as such order is represented in the trading crowd. The part that is not executed is to be treated as canceled.

A scale order is an order to buy (sell) that specifies the total amount to be bought (sold) at specified variations.

An at the close order is to be executed at or as near the close as possible.

An at the opening order is a market or limited price order that is to be executed at the opening of the stock market or not at all, and any such order or the portion thereof not so executed is to be treated as canceled.

A sell "plus" order is a market order to sell a stated amount of stock provided that the price to be obtained is not lower than the last sale if the last sale was a "plus" or "zero plus" tick, and not lower than the last sale plus the minimum fractional change in the stock if the last sale was a "minus" or "zero minus" tick. A limited price order to sell "plus" has the additional restriction of stating the lowest price at which it could be executed. (For a detailed explanation of "plus" tick and "zero plus" tick, (see page 199.)

A buy "minus" order is a market order to buy a stated amount of stock provided that the price to be obtained is not higher than the last sale if the last sale was a "minus" or "zero minus" tick, and is not higher than the last sale minus the minimum fractional change in the stock if the last sale was a "plus" or "zero plus" tick. A limited price order to buy "minus" has the additional restriction of stating the highest price at which it can be executed.

A participate but do not initiate order is given by a customer who does not wish to become too active and upset the market for a particular stock.

A swap order is, as its name implies, a limited order to sell a stock and buy another stock at a limit.

THE INTERMARKET TRADING
SYSTEM (ITS)

The ITS is a widely regarded key building block of the national market system. ITS is a system that electronically connects the participating market centers across the country in which listed stocks are bought and sold. The exchanges linked are the American, the Boston, the New York, the Pacific and the Philadelphia. The ITS consists of a central computer facility and a network of interconnecting terminals on the floors of the participating exchanges. These quotes are flashed in each participating market center, giving the current quote for each eligible stock. These displays enable a broker representing a customer to see all the quotes in all the market centers. Thus, the broker can decide whether to execute a customer's order in the market center in which he or she is physically located or to seek an execution in another participating market center. It also enables the specialist and market makers trading for their own accounts on the floor of any participating exchange to reach out to any other exchange for an execution whenever a better price may be shown to the available. Perhaps most important, ITS provides an opportunity for any participating exchange member firm to get the best price available at any particular moment within the total nationally linked trading network.

DESIGNATED ORDER
TURNAROUND (DOT)

Introduced in 1976, DOT enables a member firm to transmit standard types of orders in virtually any listed stock from its office directly through the NYSE Common Message Switch to the proper specialist post on the trading floor. The time required is about 4 seconds. The specialist, after receiving the order, will represent it in the auction crowd and in his book. He will execute it as quickly as the market interest and activity permit. Confirmation is sent back to the originating firm over the same electronic circuit. DOT not only improves the market handling and efficiency but also provides substantial savings in execution costs.

THE SECURITIES INVESTOR
PROTECTION CORPORATION
(SIPC)

This corporation, hereinafter called the SIPC (pronounced Sip-ic), was established in December 1970 to provide financial assistance to a securities customer in the event of the failure of a SIPC member firm. (All registered broker-dealers and members of national securities exchanges are automatically members except those doing business in mutual funds, as insurance agents, or as investment advisors.)

In the event of insolvency of a SIPC member firm, the SIPC applies to the courts for a trustee. First, the trustee returns to the customer all fully paid and excess margin securities. Second, if necessary, SIPC makes advances to the trustee to pay the remaining claims of the customers up to $100,000 to cover unreturned securities and/or cash. In the case of cash, as distinct from securities, no amount in excess of $40,000 may be paid. Members are assessed on the gross income of their business. But there is a limit of 1% of gross income. It is reported that the fund at the present time (1979) has over $186 million, which is deemed adequate. But, in the event that this sum proves insufficient, the SEC has the authority to lend to the SIPC up to $1 billion, which in turn would be advanced by the U.S. Treasury. The securities industry is committed to repay any such loan by future assessments or by a transaction charge. The SIPC is run by a seven-member board of directors. Five are appointed by the president of the United States and one each by the Federal Reserve Board and the U.S. Treasury.

CAPITAL REQUIREMENTS

As a first line of defense, the customer of a failed firm has a claim of the firm's capital. If the firm is a partnership, the investor has a claim against the partners to the full extent of the general patterns' assets.

Each member or member firm must *not* have aggregate indebtedness of over 1,000% of their net capital. For example, a member firm with capital of $100,000 should not have debts of over $1,000,000. Further, if a member firm's net capital is less than 150% of its net capital minimum, it must notify the exchange and not expand its business. In addition to the net capital requirement, each member must present evidence that it has net capital of not less than $25,000.

THE NATIONAL SECURITIES CLEARING CORPORATION

The NYSE, the AMEX, and the NASD in 1977 combined to form the National Securities Clearing Corporation.

COMMITTEE ON UNIFORM SECURITIES IDENTIFICATION PROCEDURES (CUSIP)

This organization is backed by the leading exchanges, the broker-dealers, the investment banks, and even the leading commercial banks. CUSIP is a universal numbering system for securities. The actual work of assigning the numbers is handled by Standard & Poor's CUSIP Service Bureau. CUSIP greatly improves efficiency of operations in the securities industry. Instead of each house having to use its own numbering system, there is one universal numbering system for all firms. CUSIP numbers are mandatory for all National Securities Clearing Corporation members (NYSE, AMEX, and NASD members).

THE CONSOLIDATED TICKER TAPE

The consolidated tape prints all the transactions in NYSE-listed stocks on the participating markets, consisting of seven stock exchanges and two over-the-counter markets. In 1978 the NYSE's proportion of the share volume was 80.3%.

Each stock listed on the New York Stock Exchange has a symbol of one, two, or three letters. Some well-known examples are X for the United States Steel Corporation, GM for General Motors Corporation, and RCA for Radio Corporation of America. Sales are reported on the ticker tape by symbol, number of shares, and price of transaction. To simplify reporting, the number of shares is omitted when 100-share transactions are put on the ticker tape. When transactions of 100-share multiples from 200 to 900 shares take place they are shown as 2s, 3s, 4s, etc., to 9s. Sales of 1,000 shares or more generally are printed on the tape in full.

The following are typical examples of the way transactions taking place on the floor of the New York Stock Exchange would appear on the ticker tape in a brokerage company's board room:

$$T \qquad\qquad MMM \qquad KRA \qquad TA \qquad GO \qquad TXT$$
$$14{\bullet}700{\bullet}s{\bullet}57 \qquad 3s53\tfrac{1}{8} \qquad 48\tfrac{1}{4} \qquad 19\tfrac{1}{8} \qquad 27\tfrac{1}{4} \qquad 26\tfrac{7}{8}$$

A translation of this "ticker talk" would be as follows:

> 14,700 shares of American Telephone & Telegraph Company common at 57 a share
> 300 shares of Minnesota Mining and Manufacturing Company at 53 1/8 a share
> 100 shares Kraft, Inc. at 48 1/4 a share
> 100 shares of Transamerica Corporation at 19 1/8 a share
> 100 shares of Gulf Oil Corporation at 27 1/4 a share
> 100 shares of Textron, Inc. at 26 7/8 a share

Sometimes volume on the exchange is so great that only the last digit and fraction of the prices are printed. The reader is supposed to know approximately the price of the stock. For example, the tape might show simply EK 4 5/8, which would mean 100 shares of Eastman Kodak at 54 5/8.

MARGIN TRANSACTIONS

Margin transactions are of two types: (1) *short sales* and (2) *margin buying*. Both transactions require that the customer deposit with the broker a stated sum of money that represents the customer's margin.

1. Short selling. When an investor places an order with a broker to sell a security, the sell order must be marked either *long* or *short*. Ordinarily, if the investor owns the securities to be sold and intends to deliver these securities to the person to whom they are sold, the order will be marked *long*. If the investor does not own the securities, however, and must borrow them to make delivery, the sale will be marked *short*. A person sells short in the expectation that the security being sold now (and borrowing to make delivery) will decline in price so that at some time in the future he can cover his short sale and make a profit.

To illustrate, Mr. Smith sells 100 shares of Mobil Corp. at 42 1/8 marked *short*. Through his own broker, he borrows the stock to make delivery. Within a few weeks, Mobil Corp. is selling in the market at 37 1/8 a share. Mr. Smith covers his short sale by buying the stock at 37 1/8 and returning it to the lender. Mr. Smith would make a capital gain of 5 points a share, or $500 (less commissions, taxes, etc.), on such a short sale.

A further explanation of this apparently simple transaction is necessary.

First, Mr. Smith's order to sell must be marked *short* (S).

Second, no short sale is permitted except on a rising price. This is an SEC rule designed to prevent a bear raid in the stock. For example, short sales must be made at a price that constitutes a plus tick—a fractional increase in the price over the previous sale—or a zero plus tick. If sales were 42, 42 1/8, 42 1/8, we would have a zero plus tick. This would permit a short sale at 42 1/8.

Third, although the buyer of the stock does not care where the stock comes from, the broker might have to go to several sources to obtain the Mobil Corp. stock. The broker might find it in his own firm—from a customer who had given permission to lend his stock—or the broker might obtain the stock from an institution that is permitted to lend its securities. However, institutions often impose strict rules on the borrower of the stock. In any event, when the stock is located, the lender receives in cash at the then market value of the stock as security. In the past years, lenders often charged a fee of $1.00 or $2.00 a day for each 100 shares of stock borrowed. This is called lending stock at a premium. However, lenders of stock have found that the cash they receive to secure the loan of the stock is valuable, particularly in times of high interest rates, and they have been willing to pay the borrower for his deposit. This is called *lending at a rate*.

In addition, the lender of the stock is entitled to cash and stock dividends and interest of bonds loaned. If the stock should go up, it would be marked to the market (see page 222).

Also, it is possible that a customer might own shares of stock and sell them short. This is sometimes done for tax reasons. It is called selling against the box.

2. Margin Buying. A customer might have a balance in his checking account or with his broker to make a cash purchase for the full cost of his shares bought. But the customer might wish to buy more shares than he has money available. In this case the customer can put up a dollar margin and ask the broker or banker to lend him the balance to purchase the shares. The customer therefore has an *equity margin* in the shares as opposed to outright ownership, as in the case of a cash purchase. For example, if Mr. Smith buys 100 shares of XYZ Corporation for $100 a share, the total cost would be $10,000. If we assume the margin requirement is 60%, he would have to put up $6,000 initial or dollar margin. His *equity margin* would be $4,000 ($10,000 less $6,000 equals $4,000). The margin required is set by the board of governors of the Federal Reserve System under the Securities and Exchange Act of 1934. The board designates this authority under Regulation T for brokers and Regulation U for commercial banks. It has fluctuated from 40% in 1937 to 100% in 1947. In August 1979 the margin requirement for stocks, convertible bonds, and short sales was 50%. This has been in effect since 1974.

This is the *initial* margin requirement. It assures that a certain minimum initial equity will be deposited. Further, the New York Stock Exchange has ruled that no margin account may be opened unless the customer can deposit at least $2,000 in cash or securities. Withdrawals of cash or securities may be made provided that after such withdrawal the equity in the account is at least the greater of $2,000 or the amount required by the maintenance requirement. For over-the-counter margin stocks, the NASD imposes the same *initial* margin requirements. The NYSE sometimes imposes a special margin on individual issues that show a combination of unusual volume or price variation. In 1979, for the first time since 1972, the exchange placed a 75% margin requirement on six stocks.

The maintenance of margin is a regulation imposed by the NYSE and the NASD on margin stocks (see page 202) as well as by most commercial banks. Basically, it states that at no time may the margin be less than 25% of the market value of the securities (some member firms require a higher percentage). Should the value of the stocks fall below this 25% of the market value, the customer receives a *margin call* and is required to put up more money or more securities. The following example shows at what point the customer gets a margin call and how to figure when a margin call will be received:

Cost of 100 shares of PDQ Corporation at 120 a share	$12,000
Initial margin at 50% (.50 times $12,000 equals $6,000)	6,000
Loan from broker 50% (.50 times $12,000 equals $6,000)	6,000
Equity margin	$ 6,000
If the price of the stock declines to $80 a share,	
the 100 shares are worth ($80 times 100 shares)	$ 8,000
Loan from broker is still	6,000
Equity margin	$ 2,000

Because the price of the stock has reached $80 a share, a margin call will be sent to the customer. The customer must either put up more cash or securities, or he will be "sold out." Under the 25% rule, the equity of $2,000 is exactly 25% of the value of the securities (25% of $8,000 equals $2,000), a further drop of 25% of the market from $80 would wipe out the equity and the broker would have no cushion for the loan. The price at which the call notice is sent out can be determined in advance. Suppose Mr. Smith bought 100 shares of PDQ stock at 120 on margin and wished to calculate how far his stock could fall before he received a margin call. Assuming the minimum maintenance requirement of 25%, he would simply divide his broker's loan or debit balance of $6,000 by 75—the supplement of 25, which equals 80. Some brokers, however, require a maintenance of margin of 30%. In this case, Mr. Smith would receive a margin call if his stock dropped to about 85 3/4, (e.g. $6,000 ÷ 70 = 85.71). The following table summarizes these possible transactions:

Brokerage Firm	A	B
Maintenance of Margin Requirement	25%	30%
Debit Balance	75% = $ 6,000	70% = $ 6,000
Value of Account triggering call	100% = $ 8,000	100% = $ 8,571
Initial Value of the Account	$12,000	$12,000
Price When Margin Call is issued	80	85 3/4

The brokers usually check their margin accounts by simply multiplying the current market value of the account by the amount they are willing to lend. For example, broker A, willing to lend up to the maximum of 75%, would check the value of the account and multiply by 75. As long as the result was *over* $6,000, there would be no margin call (e.g. 75 × $8,000 of market value equals $6,000). Broker B, willing to lend only 70% of the market value, would issue a margin call when the stock reached about 85 3/4 (e.g. 70 × $8,571 = $6,000).

In addition to the 25% rule, the NYSE and the NASD require that ac-counts maintain $2.50 a share or 100% of market value in cash, whichever is greater, of each "short" stock with a market value of less than $5.00, and $5.00 a share or 30% of the market value in cash, whichever amount is greater, of each stock "short" in the account selling at $5.00 a share or above.

Margin customers whose equity is below the current federal initial margin requirement are considered "restricted." Retention requirements de-termine the amount of funds that restricted margin customers must apply to their debit balance following the sale of margined securities. Current (1979) retention requirements are 70% for stocks and convertible bonds. If in pre-ceding table the value of the stock PDQ had fallen to $10,000, the customer could sell $500 of his stock, withdraw $150, or 30%, and use $350, or 70%, to reduce his debit balance.

Over-the-counter margin stocks are stocks not traded on a national se-curities exchange, which the board of governors of the Federal Reserve Sys-tem have determined to have a degree of national interest to qualify under Regulation T as margin stocks. The Federal Reserve makes it quite clear that it is unlawful for anyone to claim that inclusion in this list is to imply that the Federal Reserve or the SEC has passed on the merits or approved of the stock. It simply means that the Federal Reserve has examined the compa-ny—the number of stockholders, the depth and breadth of the market of its shares, the number of market makers, the age of the company, the market value of its shares, the minimum bid price, and so forth. At the end of 1979, there were about 1,252 OTC margin stocks. On these stocks, brokers can extend credit under Regulation T of the board of governors of the Federal Reserve System (see page 381).

Nine-Bond Rule

The "nine-bond rule" (Rule 396) says, in essence, that unless the NYSE approves, all transactions of bonds for nine or less must be handled on the exchange. That is, any order for ten bonds or more may be traded in the over-the-counter market. There are, however, exceptions from this "nine-bond rule." These include an order for U.S. government or municipal secu-rities, a specific direction from a customer not to execute his order on the floor, any transaction that is part of a primary distribution of an issuer or a secondary distribution effected off the exchange, or bonds maturing within 12 months.

Active and Inactive Bonds

For years, bonds were traded by the "free crowd." These traders specialized in active bonds. Also there were the inactive bonds that were traded by the "cabinet" or "can crowd." However, in 1977, the automated bond system of the NYSE was installed. Instead of the nine-step manually operated and tedious search through cabinet files, bond traders now push a few buttons and find a full range of bids and offers with size for any bond in the system. In 1978, the 50 most active bonds were responsible for 23% of all bond volume.

Self-Regulation of the Exchange

The New York Stock Exchange has developed an extensive and complex system of rules and regulations covering all phases of its members' operations. The business customs and ethics of the securities industry have been written paragraph by paragraph, over the years, into the *Constitution and Rules of the New York Stock Exchange* and its *Company Manual* of requirements for listed companies. In addition, of course, there are many regulations required under the various state and federal securities laws that are implemented by the exchange.[5]

The conduct of member firms, both on and off the floor of the exchange, is regulated by the exchange authorities. Any member found guilty "of conduct or proceedings inconsistent with just and equitable principles of trade"[6] may be suspended or expelled.

The *Constitution and Rules*, mentioned above, deals principally with procedures and ethics in the following areas:

1. protection of the interest of customers and shareowners
2. the auction market on the exchange floor
3. exchange contracts, their clearance, delivery, and settlement.
4. personal qualifications of members of the exchange, of partners or officers of member firms, and of member firm employees representing firms with the public
5. organization of a member firm, its capital, associations with non-member firms, and business conduct.

The *Company Manual* covers the requirements for listed companies. The manual codifies good corporate practices in relations with shareowners. It presents a wide variety of requirements ranging all the way from the

---

[5]Many of the exchange's provisions were written into the Securities acts and SEC rules now having the force of law. Its provisions are paralleled, too, in many instances, in the rules and regulations of the NASD.

[6]Quoted from the original constitution of the New York Stock Exchange.

printing specifications for stock certificates to prevent counterfeiting, to the proxy requirements designed to make voting convenient and practical for all shareowners.

Floor Rules and Regulations

There are several hundred rules regulating the activities of the brokers and dealers on the floor of the NYSE. These regulations are designed to insure that securities transactions on the floor will take place at prices arrived at fairly and openly.

The hours of trading on the Exchange floor are from 10:00 A.M. to 4:00 P.M. Monday through Friday. During trading, bids and offers must be called out loud at the appropriate trading post. Bids and offers are made in multiples of the unit of trading (ordinarily 100 shares). The highest bid and the lowest bid for a given security have precedence over any other bids or offers for that security.

Regulatory Activities of the Exchange

Regulatory activities of the New York Stock Exchange include

1. reviewing all member firm legal documents
2. spot checking advertising and market letters
3. checking the business history of each candidate for membership or registration
4. checking the market performance of each specialist
5. investigating unusual market activity
6. reviewing public complaints
7. enforcing the member firm capital requirements

NEW YORK STOCK EXCHANGE EXAMINATIONS

The New York Stock Exchange requires registration of all employees of the member firms engaged in the solicitation or handling of public securities business. In determining a candidate's acceptability for registration the NYSE requires evidence of

1. integrity of high standards of business conduct
2. potential ability to perform creditably the duties of a registered representative
3. extensive knowledge of the full range of investment services offered in the securities industry

An advisory committee of the NYSE designed an examination to measure the knowledge, understanding, and skills considered most important for the registered representative to best serve the public and to meet his or her regulatory responsibility. Questions for different forms of the examination are drawn from more than 1,100 questions, which are regularly revised and updated.

The examination is given in two three-hour sessions: one in the morning, the other in the afternoon of the same day. Both parts consist entirely of multiple choice questions. In brief the main topics covered are

1. Securities industry regulations and procedures.
   a. Rules and regulations of NYSE and NASD
   b. Federal and state regulations
   c. Markets, brokerage procedures, and trading
2. Product knowledge, definitions, characteristics, and uses
   a. Common and preferred stocks and corporate and municipal bonds
   b. Government obligations and money-market instruments
   c. Investment companies
3. Economic, financial, and security analysis
   a. Capital and money-market analysis
   b. Security analysis and elements of finance
   c. Taxation
4. Servicing accounts
   a. Opening and handling accounts
   b. Customers' objectives and portfolios
   c. Tax consequences

(For further information, see the pamphlet of the NYSE, *Study Guide for the Registered Representative Examination.*)

REVIEW QUESTIONS

1. What are the main functions and services of the organized securities exchanges?
2. On what basis do the organized exchanges work? How do they differ from the over-the-counter market?
3. What are the four types of brokers or dealers on the New York Stock Exchange?
4. Describe in some detail two important roles of a specialist on the New York Stock Exchange.
5. Assume that a customer gives a broker an order to *buy* 10 shares of Continental Group, Inc. The next round-lot trade after the order arrives on the floor is 28 1/2. At what price would the odd-lot purchase take place?
6. Define and distinguish among a GTC order, a day order, a stop order, a fill or kill order, and an all-or-none order.

7. When is selling short permitted? At what price in the following sequence could a short sale be made: 47 7/8, 47 3/4, 47 5/8, 47 3/4, and 47 5/8?

8. What are the most important self-regulatory activities of the New York Stock Exchange?

9. Name three minimum financial requirements for listing on the New York Stock Exchange. What are the other considerations?

10. Describe the activities and the purpose of the Intermarket Trading System.

11. What are the most important qualifications to become a registered representative on the New York Stock Exchange?

TRUE AND FALSE QUESTIONS

1. The functions of organized exchanges are: *True*   *False*
   a. to provide a centralized place where members may meet to execute orders   _____   _____
   b. to buy from and sell to their members securities   _____   _____
   c. to enable members to buy and sell from one another for their own account and risk   _____   _____
   d. to provide new equity capital for corporations.   _____   _____

2. The main differences between the organized exchanges and the over-the-counter markets are: *True*   *False*
   a. the organized exchanges have a larger number of issues traded   _____   _____
   b. the prices (high, low, and close) of all the securities traded on the organized exchange are published; the prices of over-the-counter securities are not   _____   _____
   c. the organized exchanges work on an auction basis whereas the over-the-counter markets operate by negotiated deals.   _____   _____

3. The types of members of the organized stock exchanges include all of the following *except:*   *True*   *False*
   a. commission brokers   _____   _____
   b. stock specialist   _____   _____
   c. registered competitive market makers   _____   _____
   d. floor brokers   _____   _____
   e. money brokers.   _____   _____

4. The specialist on the New York Stock Exchange: *True*   *False*
   a. is the person who knows a great deal about the stock of one company and should be consulted before buying the stock   _____   _____
   b. executes orders entrusted to him by other brokers   _____   _____
   c. always stands at the post where his assigned stocks are traded   _____   _____
   d. must be prepared to use all his resources, if necessary, to support the market in the stock in which he specializes.   _____   _____

5. The term $2.00 broker is applied: *True*   *False*
   a. to brokers on the New York Stock Exchange who execute orders for other brokers who are too busy to handle their own orders   _____   _____
   b. to brokers who agree to execute orders for $2.00 per 100 shares   _____   _____
   c. to brokers who handle orders for members who wish to leave the floor   _____   _____
   d. to those now called floor brokers.   _____   _____

6. Assume that a customer gives an order to buy 10 shares of General Electric Co.; next round lot after the order arrives on the floor is 64. The odd-lot purchase would take place at: *True*   *False*
   a. 64   _____   _____
   b. 64 1/8   _____   _____
   c. 64 1/4   _____   _____
   d. 64 1/2.   _____   _____

7. A customer places a *stop loss* order of 55 on a stock currently selling at 60. This means that: *True*   *False*
   a. the broker should sell the stock as soon as possible to take the profit and forestall any possible loss   _____   _____
   b. the customer is guaranteed a price of 55 should the stock fall to that level   _____   _____
   c. when the stock reaches 55, the customer's order becomes a market order that might be executed above or below 55.   _____   _____

8. Given the following sequence of trades 66 7/8, 67 5/8, 67 3/4, and 67 7/8, a short sale could be made at: *True*   *False*
   a. 66 7/8   _____   _____
   b. 67 5/8   _____   _____

		True	*False*
c.	67 3/4	_____	_____
d.	67 7/8.	_____	_____

9. One of the following series of prices illustrates a "zero plus" tick at which a short sale may be made:

		True	*False*
a.	29 1/2, 29 1/2, 29 1/4	_____	_____
b.	29, 29 1/8, 29 1/8	_____	_____
c.	29 5/8, 29 1/4, 29 1/8	_____	_____
d.	29 1/2, 29 1/8, 29.	_____	_____

10. Mr. Smith buys on margin 100 shares of Union Pacific Corporation at 84. The Federal Reserve Regulation T is at 50% and the maintenance requirement of the PDQ brokerage firm is 30%. The initial amount of the margin required will be:

		True	*False*
a.	$8,400	_____	_____
b.	$5,880	_____	_____
c.	$4,200	_____	_____
d.	$2,520.	_____	_____

11. Using the correct figures in Question 10, Mr. Smith will not receive a margin call unless his stock drops to:

		True	*False*
a.	$70 a share	_____	_____
b.	$60 a share	_____	_____
c.	$50 a share	_____	_____
d.	$42 a share.	_____	_____

12. The following are some of the most important requirements for listing on the NYSE. The company:

		True	*False*
a.	must be an industrial, railroad, or public utility concern but not a bank	_____	_____
b.	must have demonstrated earning power of at least $2,500,000 before taxes and $2,000,000 in the preceding two years	_____	_____
c.	must have at least 1,000,000 shares with at least 2,000 holding 100 shares or more.	_____	_____

11

Stock and Bond

Transactions

Every investor is familiar with the stock and bond quotation sections of the large newspapers, but few are familiar with the many small symbols and letters that appear in the quotation sheets. An investor should not only follow the price changes in his stocks and bonds but also should understand the financial terms used in buying and selling securities.

STOCK QUOTATIONS

The large metropolitan papers usually publish every business day the stocks traded on the New York Stock Exchange and the American Stock Exchange. Stocks are traded and quoted in dollars a share in fractions of 1/8, 1/4, 3/8, 1/2, 5/8, 3/4, and 7/8. The table on page 210 shows a sample of quotations published in *The Wall Street Journal* of stocks traded on the New York Stock Exchange on August 1, 1979. From left to right, these quotations show for the latest 52 weeks the high and the low price of the stock traded, enabling the reader to compare the present price with the range for the year. Next is the name of the company, often in abbreviated form. Following the name of the company is the dividend rate; the yield and price-earnings ratio (see page 339); the sales volume in 100 shares; the high, low, and close for August 1; and the change between the close on August 1 and the previous trading day's close. A glance at the stock table below will show how the market behaved on Wednesday August 1, 1979 compared with Tuesday, the previous day: whether it was strong, weak, or mixed.[1]

[1]*The Wall Street Journal*, August 2, 1979.

52 Weeks			Yld P-E Sales						Net	
High	Low	Stock	Div.	%	Ratio	100s	High	Low	Close	Chg.
			—	A —	A —	A	—			
39½	29⅛	ACF	2.24	6.2	7	370	36⅞	35¾	36⅜+	⅞
23⅝	15⅜	AMF	1.24	6.9	7	353	18	17⅝	17⅞+	⅛
32⅞	13	AM Intl	.28	1.8	6	90	16	15¾	16	.....
14¾	8⅞	APL	1	10.		55	10	9¾	9¾−	¼
48⅜	33¾	ARA	1.64	4.5	7	40	36¼	35½	36¼+	⅜
31⅜	21⅜	ASA	1.40	5.6		281	25⅛	24⅝	24⅞+	¼
14⅞	8½	ATO	.48	4.4	4	54	10⅞	10⅝	10⅞+	¼
36⅛	17	AVX	.50	1.3	12	141	u38⅛	35⅞	38	+2¼
40	29½	AbbtLb	1	2.8	13	627	35¾	35¼	35¾+	⅝
23¾	16¼	AcmeC	1.20	6.0	5	14	20	19⅝	19⅞	.....

In this table, we find that ACF Industries in the last 52 weeks sold as high as 39 1/2 and as low as 29 1/8. The reported dividend is $2.24 and is based on the annualized quarterly or semiannual rate. The yield of 6.2% is calculated on the basis of the present price of the stock (see page 11). The price-earnings ratio is the current price of the stock divided by the company's latest 12 months' earnings. Thus, the stock of ACF was selling about 7 times earnings on August 1, 1979. By looking at the price-earnings ratios of other stocks, comparisons can be made. The next figure is the volume. ACF traded 37,000 shares. Finally, the high, low, close and change are shown.

The change of ACF of 7/8 of a point is the change between the closing stock price on Wednesday, August 1, and Tuesday, July 31.

At the close of 36 3/8, the price of ACF is 7.9% below its high of 39 1/2. This might be compared with a decline from its 1978 peak of only 1.7% for the New York Stock Exchange Index.

COMMISSIONS ON LISTED STOCKS

On May 1, 1975 (May Day), the fixed commissions on all listed securities that all members of the NYSE had been charging since 1792 were abandoned by order of the SEC. In other words, the members were free to make any charges that they wished to execute trades in stocks. It was feared at the time that chaos would result but the effects of free competition for brokerage business was different than expected.

First, the firms specializing in institutional business were forced to cut sharply their charges for transactions. It has been estimated that commissions were cut over 60% from the old levels. This reduction resulted in hardship for several firms that had expensive research departments serving the big institutions. Mergers and liquidations took place.

Second, small investors were not benefited, particularly if they wished to do business with a full-service firm. But, if small investors were willing to trade with a discount house, their commission costs were lower. This may be llustrated as follows:

	300 shares	500 shares
Old rate, before May 1, 1975	$ 91.50	$165.20
Average of four full-service firms	110.36	181.80
Average of four discount firms	57.97	98.90

In addition, there are New York State transfer taxes as well as Securities and Exchange Commission fees, which must be paid *by the seller* in any transaction on the stock exchanges. There is no SEC Commission fee on securities transactions in the over-the-counter market.

1.   The New York State transfer taxes are

1 1/4¢ per share under $5.00
2 1/2¢ per share between $5.00 and $9.99
3 3/4¢ per share between $10.00 and $19.99
5   ¢ per share over $20.00

The amount of taxes paid allowable as rebates is

Between 10/1/79 and 9/30/80   30% resident and 37.5% non-resident
Between 10/1/80 and 9/30/81   60% all taxpayers
After   10/1/81   100% all taxpayers

2.   The Securities and Exchange Commission fee is 1¢ for each $500 or fraction thereof.

THE UNIFORM
PRACTICE CODE

What It Is

The board of governors of the national association of Securities Dealers, Inc., was authorized to adopt a uniform practice code to make uniform the customs, practices, and trading techniques among members in the securities business. These include such matters as trade terms, deliveries, payments, rights, stamp taxes, computation of interest. due bills, and so forth.

The administration of the code has been delegated by the board to the National Uniform Practice Committee and the District Uniform Practice Committees. Any changes in the rules made by the district committees must be approved by the board. Any contract *between members* (except transactions executed on the national securities exchanges and transactions in exempt securities) is subject to the Uniform Practice Code, and the code is part of the contract unless the parties to the transactions agree otherwise. Whenever a situation arises that is not covered by the code, it is referred to the appropriate District Uniform Practice Committee for action. In the case of a controversy with respect to interdistrict trade, it is handled by the National Uniform Practice Committee.

In the following pages, we will discuss certain important sections of the Uniform Practice Code as it applies to various transactions.

Delivery of Securities (Section 4)

For each security transaction there are several dates but two dates are of particular significance: (1) the trade date and (2) the delivery date.

The *trade date* is simply the date on which the transaction between two parties takes place. All ordinary transactions must be confirmed by sending a written notice *on or before the first full business day following the date of transaction*. Confirmations of cash transactions (those in which the contract is settled on the same day the trade is made) are exchanged on the day of the trade.

The *settlement date* is simply the date on which a transaction was effected or accomplished.

The *delivery date* is the date on which the securities should be delivered to the customer. Deliveries are made for cash, regular way, and seller's option.

Cash sales means the security is sold and the contract settled on the same day that the trade is made. Cash sales usually take place if a seller wishes to meet a special situation. For example, for tax reasons an individual or a company might desire to complete a transaction before the year's end.

When a security is sold *for cash*, the following must take place *on the day of the trade:*

1. The security will be delivered to the office of the purchaser.
2. Confirmation of a cash transaction will be exchanged.
3. The security transaction is settled by payment.

Regular-way delivery means that the seller contracts to deliver the securities to the office of the purchaser on the *fifth full business day following the date of the transaction*. This means that Saturdays, Sundays, and holidays when the exchanges are closed do not count. For example, if a trade is made on Friday, the securities should be delivered by the following Friday, assuming no holidays intervene.

	Days Counted
Friday — trade day	
Saturday	0
Sunday	0
Monday	1
Tuesday	2
Wednesday	3
Thursday	4
Friday	5

If a seller delivers his or her securities before the fifth full business day, the acceptance of their delivery is up to the buyer. If the buyer declines to let the seller deliver the securities before the fifth full business day, the seller still should deliver on the fifth day.

The five-day delivery rule applies to trades in securities over the counter as well as to those on the New York and American Stock Exchanges. But exceptions are made when it is known at the time of the sale that the securities cannot be delivered on the date prescribed for a regular-way transaction. Here the seller must inform the buyer prior to the order that the securities cannot be delivered within the five-business-day period. In this case, the sale might be made for seller's option.

Regular-way delivery applies to all corporate, municipal, and most federal agency securities. *U.S. government securities* are sold for cash, that is, for delivery and payment on the day of the contract; regular way for delivery on the business day following the trade; and seller's option, not less the 2 or more than 60 days.

Seller's options for securities, other than U.S. government's, permits the seller to deliver the security at the buyer's office on the business day that the option expires (e.g., seller's 30). The seller can deliver the security prior to the expiration date, provided that one day's notice is given and provided that five business days have elapsed after the trade date.

A seller's option is often requested by sellers who have difficulty in obtaining possession of their securities for any number of reasons. For example, a person might be visiting New York City and might decide to sell his securities that are in a safety deposit box in Los Angeles, California. At the time of the sale the seller *must* advise the buyer that delivery will not be made the regular way. The buyer is not required to enter the transaction if he desires to obtain delivery regular way.

Buyer's options give the buyer the option to receive securities at his office on a specific date, when the option expires. If the seller *wishes* to deliver prior to this time, the buyer must give his permission. The refusal of such delivery by the purchaser will be without prejudice to his rights.

"Don't Know Notices" (DK Procedures)

When a party to a transaction sends a confirmation or a comparison of a trade but does not receive a confirmation or comparison, or a signed DK, from the contra broker by the close of four business days following the trade date of the transaction, the following procedure may be utilized.

1. Not later than the fifteenth calendar day following the trade the confirming member will send a Don't Know notice on the form prescribed to the contra-broker.
2. The contra-broker will have four business days after the notice is received to either confirm or DK the transaction.
3. If the confirming member does not receive a response from the contra-broker by the close of four business days, such shall constitute a DK and the confirming member will have no further liability.
4. All DK notices sent by either party must be manually signed by authorized persons.

Particular care should be taken on confirmations not only for cash sales but on all transactions. Confirmations should be compared on receipt, and any discrepancies should be checked immediately and corrected. A corrected confirmation should be sent by the party in error. Confirmations should include an adequate description of the security—if the security is a bond, the coupon rate and date of the maturity; if a stock, the class, common or preferred; and if preferred, the dividend rate. Also, it should be noted whether the confirmation is for "when, as, and if issued" or "when, as, and if distributed" securities, and the plan under which the securities will be issued or distributed should be stated.

When-issued securities, as their name implies, are usually shares of stock or of bonds that have been authorized by the corporation but have not yet been delivered or issued. Often on the stock exchanges both the old and the when-issued securities are quoted. For example, on March 23, 1980, the following appeared:

	Close
Wrigley (William Jr Company)	73 7/8
Wrigley wi	32 1/2

On January 15, 1980, the stockholders of William Wrigley, Jr Company authorized a 2 for 1 split. The new stock was not delivered until April 2, 1980. A number of other companies have authorized stock splits, and, prior to the issuance of these securities, they traded on a when-issued basis. In 1979, International Business Machines Corporation, Mobil Corporation, and Aetna Life and Casualty Company issued new securities.

All trades in when-issued securities, as well as all profits and losses, are canceled if for any reason the securities are not issued. All the trades are in contracts rather than in actual securities. When a company authorizes a split, there is very little chance that the securities will not be delivered.

The difference in price between the old and the when-issued securities is usually small, owing to the trading activities of the *arbitragers*, a highly skilled group of traders. They buy and sell the old and when-issued securities, making a short-term profit on the transactions. Often it will appear from the quotation of the old and the new securities that there is an attractive spread. Sometimes it is possible for the layman to make a profit by selling and buying those securities. But these occasions are rare, and trading of this sort is best left to the experts.

When, as, and if issued securities are delivered at the office of the purchaser on the date declared by the Uniform Practice Committee of the district in which delivery is to be effected. If no date is declared by the committee, the securities may be delivered at the office of the purchaser on the day after written notice has been delivered to the office of the purchaser. When open-market when, as, and if issued contracts in securities are being publicly offered through a syndicate, they are settled on the date the syndicate or selling group contracts are settled.

When, as, and if distributed securities will be delivered to the office of the purchaser on the date declared by the Uniform Practice Committee of the district. If no delivery date is declared, the delivery may be made by the seller on the full business day following the day on which the seller has delivered at the office of the purchaser written notice of conditions to deliver.

Dividends, Ex-Dividends, Ex-Rights (Section 5)

The *dividends* shown in the quotation sheets require some explanation. Sometimes they are shown as the annual rate, sometimes only the amount paid so far in the year, and sometimes only at the regular rate, not including extra dividends or stock dividends. In any case, these are usually explained by footnotes—a, b, c, and so on.

Each time a corporation declares a dividend there are four significant dates. These may be shown as follows:

Declaration Date	Ex-Dividend Date	Record Date	Payment Date

The board of directors of a corporation meets to *declare* a dividend on the common or preferred stock. Under most state laws, dividends can be paid only if there is a surplus.

Furthermore, in many states the directors can declare dividends on the common stock *only* from earned surplus. Some states that permit dividend payments from capital surplus require that the directors inform the stockholders of the source. But, as a general rule, dividends cannot be paid from capital. When the dividend is announced, the company designates a record date.

The *record date* is the day on which a list is made by the corporation of all the stockholders who will receive the declared dividends. As soon as a stock is purchased, the name of the buyer should be recorded on the books of the company, usually kept by a transfer agent. The charges of the transfer agent are sometimes paid by the party at whose instance the record change is made and sometimes by the company itself.

A buyer of a stock five days' prior to the record date would have time to obtain delivery of this stock the regular way and have his or her name placed on the books of the company in time to become a holder of record to receive the dividend. In other words, the term *dividend on* signifies that the buyer is entitled to the dividend declared on a security.

Ex-dividend or ex-right date is the day on and after which the buyer of a common stock is *not* entitled to a previously declared dividend or right.

In the published stock tables, an "x" before the number of shares traded indicates that the stock is trading on that day ex-dividend.

For example, on Monday December 3, 1979, the following quotation was published:

High	Low (year)		Number of Shares	High	Low	Close	Change
66 1/4	44 1/2	Kerr McGee	x 462	61	59 1/2	60 1/2	−1/8

In this case the record date was Friday, December 7, 1979. Therefore, the following will show the delivery schedule in detail:

December 3, 1979 Monday	Ex dividend date	—	Trade date
December 4, 1979 Tuesday		1 day	
December 5, 1979 Wednesday		1 day	
December 6, 1979 Thursday		1 day	
December 7, 1979 Friday		1 day	Record date
December 8, 1979 Saturday		—	
December 9, 1979 Sunday		—	
December 10, 1979 Monday		1 day	
		5 days' delivery date	

In short the buyer of the stock of Kerr McGee would not get his or her stock until the following Monday, too late to get his name on the books of the company on the record date for the payment of the quarterly dividend.

The basic rule for determining the ex-dividend date for cash or stock dividends is that securities will be ex-dividend *on the fourth full business day preceding the record date*, if the record date falls on a business day and if announced sufficiently in advance of the record date.

If the record date falls on a holiday or any day other than a full business day, the ex date is the fifth full business day preceding the record date. To repeat, a buyer of shares of Kerr McGee on or after December 3 is *not* entitled to the current dividend. It is paid to the seller. In the same manner a security might trade *ex-rights*. When a security trades *ex-rights*, the buyer does not get the rights, which remain the property of the seller. The ex-rights date is the first business day after the effective date of the registration statement. If the Uniform Practice Committee does not receive definite information sufficiently in advance of the record date, the date designated will be the first full business day practicable under the circumstances.

If definitive information concerning the issuance of *warrants* is received sufficiently in advance of the record date, then the date designated as the ex-warrants date shall be the fourth business day preceding the record date, if the record date falls on a business day, or the fifth business day preceding the record date, if the record date falls on a day designated by the committee as a nondelivery date.

Occasionally, a security is sold *before* it trades *ex-dividend, ex-rights,* or *ex-interest* but is delivered too late for the buyer to record his ownership on the company transfer records to get the dividend. Because the seller is still the holder of record, the company will pay the dividend or rights to him but the seller is *not entitled to keep it.* Under such circumstances the buyer can demand, and is entitled to receive from the seller, a promise to pay to him the distribution of dividends or rights when made. This promise is called a *due bill.*

Section 48 of the Uniform Practice Code provides that when a security is sold before it trades ex-dividend or ex-rights or ex-interest and is delivered too late for transfer on or before the record date, it must be accompanied by a *due bill* for the distribution made. Sometimes the term *due bill checks* is used. This means a due bill in the form of a check payable on the date of the cash dividend, interest, or rights.

Section 6 of the Uniform Practice Code provides that all transactions, except "cash" transactions in bonds, which are traded "flat," shall be "ex-interest" as prescribed by the following provisions.

1.   On the fourth business day preceding the record date if the record date falls on a business day.
2.   On the fifth business day preceding the record date if the record date falls other than a business day.
3.   On the fifth business day preceding the date on which an interest payment is to be made if no record date has been fixed.
4.   If notice of payment of interest is not made public sufficiently in advance of the record date or the payment date, as the case may be, to permit the security to be dealt in "ex-interest" in accordance with the foregoing provisions, such security shall be dealt in "ex-interest" on the first business day following public notice of the record date or the payment date, as the case may be.

Good Delivery

All securities transactions must be for "good delivery." This means that the security is in such form that the record of ownership may be readily transferred. In short, the ownership must be clear. There are a number of qualifications to *good delivery*. Some of these are as follows and will be discussed in detail.

1.   proper assignment
2.   good condition of security
3.   *not* in name of married women (in some states)
4.   *not* in the name of a deceased person
5.   the proper number of units
6.   *not* a called security
7.   at the proper time with taxes, etc., paid
8.   a permanent certificate if available

1. *Registered certificates* must be accompanied by an *assignment* to be good delivery. For example, if a stock certificate is registered in the name of John H. Jones, he must endorse or sign it on the back *exactly that way:* John H. Jones. The signature must correspond with the name written upon the certificate in every particular without alteration or enlargement or any

change whatever except that "and" or & Company or Co. may be written either way.

A certificate with an inscription to indicate joint tenancy or tenancy in common shall be good delivery only if signed by all co-tenants. A certificate registered in the names of two individuals or firms shall be good delivery only if signed by all the registered holders.

Sometimes the *power of substitution* is used. This may also be inscribed on the back of the certificate or as a separate power. Usually the proper signature on the certificate makes the certificate negotiable when guaranteed by a member, a member organization, or a bank. But sometimes, when there is risk of the loss of a certificate, it is desirable to designate the broker, an attorney, by *power of substitution.* This enables the broker to make good delivery. Most certificates are endorsed in blank and therefore are negotiable. Many old certificates provided space for a witness, but in recent years the witness to an endorsement has not been required. The following is an example of an assignment and power of substitution appearing on the back of the stock of the *First Investors Fund for Growth, Inc.*

For value received _____ hereby sell, assign and transfer unto
Social Security Number _____

_____
(Please print or type name and address of assignee)
_____shares
of the capital stock represented by the within Certificate, and do hereby irrevocably constitute and appoint
_____Attorney to transfer
the said stock on the books of the within named Corporation with full power of substitution in the premises.
Dated _____

Notice: The signature to this assignment must correspond with the name written on the face of the certificate in every particular without alteration or enlargement or any change whatever.

Sometimes a separate stock power is used. This is an assignment in form exactly like the one on the back of the stock certificate. It contains a full description of the security to which it may be attached, including the name of the company, the type of stock (common or preferred), its number, and the amount of shares expressed in words and numerals. Each signature to an assignment may be *witnessed* by an individual and dated. However, many transfer agents do not insist that an assignment be witnessed as long as it is guaranteed, as the guarantor thus accepts the responsibility for the authenticity of the signature. A stock power might be used by a registered stockholder who does not have the certificate available to place an assignment on its back. For example, let us assume that a farmer living in Geneseo, New York wishes to sell 100 shares of the common stock of the United States Steel Corporation. Let us assume further that this stock is held by his banker in a custody account in New York City. The farmer can simply execute a stock power and send it along with a letter of instruction to sell the stock.

Sometimes a power is used in a similar manner to transfer registered bonds. It is not advisable, as a rule, to send a signed or endorsed certificate unregistered through the mails. As an alternative, the seller might send his stock certificate in one envelope and the signed stock power in another.

2. *The bond or stock certificate must be in good condition.* If it is mutilated in any way, it must be authenticated by the proper authority. This means that the proper authority must certify that the certificate is valid in spite of the mutilation and will be accepted as representing the equity or obligation it purports to be. The proper authority might be the transfer agent on the stock, an authorized company officer, or the trustee of an issue of bonds. Each assignment, endorsement, alteration, or erasure shall bear a guarantee acceptable to the transfer agent or registrar.

3. When a sales contract is for more than 100 shares, the delivery of the stock must be made in certificates *from which units of 100 shares each may be composed* to aggregate or add up to the highest multiple of 100 shares called for by the contract. This simply means that a seller must deliver either round 100-share lots or smaller lots that add up to 100 shares. For example, a seller of 300 shares could deliver six certificates of 50 shares each. The buyer could turn around and sell the 300 shares in 100-unit lots. But the seller of 300 shares could not deliver four certificates of 75 shares each, as none of these lots add up to 100. This means that the seller of units that do not add up to the highest multiple of 100 shares must go to the company's transfer agent and perhaps *pay a fee* to have these shares consolidated.

Other examples of acceptable multiples of 100 that would be good delivery are as follows: In settlement of a 1,000-share trade by delivery of a single certificate for 1,000 shares, or by delivery of a 200-share certificate plus an 800-share certificate, or by delivery of a 900-share certificate and two 50-share certificates. Settlement of a 525-share trade is good delivery by presentation of a 500-share certificate plus a certificate for 25-share odd lot or smaller certificates equaling the odd lot. Bond transactions may be settled by delivery of bonds in denominations of up to $25,000.

Each delivery of stock should be in certificates aggregating the exact number of shares called for in the contract. Unless agreed at the time of the transaction, a certificate for more than 100 shares is not good delivery. Acceptance of any delivery not meeting the requirement explained above is at the option of the purchaser. If the purchaser accepts, a receipt should be given pending a transfer into suitable units.

4. A certificate in the name of a *deceased* person is *not* a good delivery even if properly assigned. Certificates in the name of deceased persons should be transferred by the executor to a street name before delivering it to the buyer. The transfer agent usually makes this transfer on receipt of the appropriate legal documents.

5. A *called bond* or *preferred stock* is not good delivery unless the entire issue has been called. At times there are trades in "called stock" or "called bonds," but here it is known that they are called securities and dealt in specifically as such.

6. *Drafts* accompanying the shipment of securities need be accepted only *on a full business day during business hours.* The acceptance of a draft prior to the settlement date is at the option of the drawee. Expenses of shipment, including insurance, postage, and collection charges, shall be paid by the seller. Failure to accept a draft in which no irregularities exist shall make the person on whom the draft is drawn liable for the payment of interest and miscellaneous expenses incurred because of the delay.

The securities should be *delivered* at the office of the buyer between the hours established by rule or practice in the community where the office is located. The seller, on making the delivery, will have the right to *require* that the buyer pay upon delivery of the securities by a certified check, cashiers check, bank draft, or cash.

7. *Temporary certificates* (discussed in Chapter 2) are not good delivery if permanent certificates are available.

Under Section 14 of the Uniform Practice Code, the seller must furnish the buyer at the time of delivery a sale memorandum ticket to which will be affixed canceled state transfer taxes that are required by the state in which the sale occurs, or the tax may be paid by the seller through the stock clearing corporations. (See page 211 for New York State taxes.)

A certificate with an inscription to indicate joint tenancy, tenancy in common, or in the names of two or more individuals is *not* good delivery unless signed by the co-tenants or registered co-owners.

8. Each *delivery of bonds* in coupon form shall be made in denominations of $1,000 or in demoninations of $100 or multiples thereof aggregating $1,000 (the NYSE rule 186 states multiples of $500). Registered bonds are the same as the aforesaid, except that denominations larger than $100,000 are not good delivery. When contracts for bonds are not in multiples of $100, the parties shall agree on the proper units of delivery at contract time.

Buy-In Procedures

A contract that has not been completed by the seller according to its terms may be closed by the buyer not sooner than the third business day following the date delivery was due. Written notice of "buy-in" shall be delivered to the seller at his or her office not later than 12 noon, seller's time, two business days preceding the execution of the proposed buy-in.

Transfer Fees

The party at whose instance a transfer is made will pay all service charges of the transfer agent.

Marking to the Market

Perhaps the easiest way to understand this concept is to consider what happens on a short sale. Here a customer sells a stock he does not own, hoping it will go down and he can buy it in to make delivery. Thus the customer will make a profit on the difference between what he sells the stock short for and buys it to make delivery, less taxes and commissions. However, if, after the customer has sold short, his stock goes up, then his broker will "mark the account to the market" and demand more collateral. This also occurs when there are market changes on when-issued contracts. Here trading takes place, but the settlement date is undetermined. Basically, marking to the market takes place during the period before the settlement date has been determined. If either party to the transaction is partially unsecured by reason of a change in the market, that party may demand a deposit equal to the difference between the market price and the contract price.

Computation of Interest

Interest is computed up to but not including the day of delivery. For corporate bonds, it is on a 30-day month, 360-day year. On U.S. Treasury securities, it is calculated on the basis of the *exact number of days on a semiannual basis.*

In the settlement of contracts in interest-paying securities other than for cash, there shall be added to the dollar price interest at the rate specified in the bond. In transactions for cash, interest shall be added to the dollar price at the rate specified up to but not including the date of the transaction.

Bond Quotations

Bonds are quoted on the New York and American stock exchanges in much the same manner as stocks are. Following is a sample of some bonds quoted on the New York Stock Exchange from the Wall Street Journal on August 1, 1979:

CORPORATION BONDS
Volume, $14,500,000

Bonds	Cur Yld	Vol	High	Low	Close	Net Chg.
DelPw 9⅜83	9.5	5	99	99	99	+1½
DetEd 9s99	10.	5	89⅞	89⅞	89⅞	+ ¾
DetEd 9.15s00	10.	1	90⅞	90⅞	90⅞	+ ⅞
DetEd 7⅜01	9.8	12	75½	75	75	−2
DetEd 7½03	10.	11	75¼	75⅛	75¼	+1¼
DetEd 12¾82	12.	44	104⅝	104¼	104¼	− ⅜
DiGior 5¾93	cv	11	81	80⅛	81	− ½
DialF 8¼s89	9.2	10	91	90	90	.....
Digit 4½02	cv	1	113	113	113	+ ½
Dilling 9¾499	cv	13	109	109	109	.....
Dow 7.75s99	8.8	15	88	88	88	.....
Dow 8⅞2000	9.3	2	95¾	95¾	95¾	.....
Dow 8.92000	9.4	1	95	95	95	+ ⅝
duPnt 8s81	8.2	30	97	97	97	.....
duPnt 8½06	8.9	36	95¼	93⅞	95¼	+1

Reprinted by permission of *The Wall Street Journal,*
© Dow Jones & Company, Inc., 1979. All Rights
Reserved.

It can be seen that the names of the bonds are given in abbreviated form; the quotation gives current yield; the volume; the high, low, and close; and the change from the previous day's close. For instance, Det Ed (Detroit Edison) has a coupon rate of 7 3/8%, is due in 2001, has a current yield of about 9.8%, and had a volume of bonds sold on August 1 of $12,000; it sold as high as 75 1/2, as low as 75, and closed at 75. There was a decline of 2 points, or $20, from the previous day's close.

Although a considerable number of bonds are listed and traded on the New York Stock Exchange, by far the greatest volume is done on the over-the-counter market. Prices on the over-the-counter bonds are indicated by bid-and-asked prices published by the National Quotation Bureau and distributed to the subscribing members of the National Association of Securities Dealers. These quotation sheets are not available to the public. However, markets on over-the-counter bonds as well as stocks can usually be obtained by calling a broker who subscribes to these quotation sheets.

The majority of the bonds sell *with interest,* or as sometimes stated, *and accrued interest* or *plus accrued interest.* This means that the seller of the bond receives not only the sales price but, in addition, the accrued interest from the date of the last payment of interest. This interest is calculated from the date of the last interest payment but does not include the date of delivery.

Let us assume that on Friday, July 27, 1979, an investor bought a $1,000 bond of the Detroit Edison Company with a coupon rate of 7 3/8 due 2001 at 75; the following would be the costs:

$1,000 Detroit Edison Company 7 3/8 of 2001 at 75	$750.00
Plus commission ($5.00 per bond)	5.00
Plus accrued interest (see explanation below)	31.14
	$786.14

In this case, the commission is $5.00 per bond, assuming that the bond is bought on the New York Stock Exchange. Interest on the bond, paid on March 1 and September 1, is $36.875 twice a year, or a total of $73.75 (7 3/8% of $1,000). Thus, a purchase on Friday, July 27, would not be delivered until August 3 or at the *end of five full business days.* This is the same as the regular-way delivery for stocks as explained on page 216. *But interest accrues up to but not including the date of delivery.*

The following illustrates these points.

July 27, 1979	Friday	—	Trade date
July 28	Saturday	—	
July 29	Sunday	—	
July 30	Monday	1 day	
July 31	Tuesday	1 day	
August 1	Wednesday	1 day	
August 2	Thursday	1 day	End of interest period
August 3	Friday	1 day	Delivery date
		5 days	

Interest is computed on the basis of a 360-day year. That is, every calendar month shall be considered to have 30 days or one twelfth of 360 days; every period from the date in one month to the same date in the following month shall be considered as 30 days.

In calculating the interest on the Detroit Edison bonds, the analyst should first consider that interest payments are on March 1 and September 1. Second, he should start counting each full month from the last interest payment as 30 days plus the days of the month in which the bond was sold up to, but not including, the date of delivery. The following illustrates how the count should be made on the Detroit Edison bond.

March	30 days
April	30
May	30
June	30
July	30
August	2
	152 days

In other words, the *seller* of a Detroit Edison 7 3/8 bond is entitled to 152 days' interest or 152/360 of a year's interest of $73.75, or $31.14.

No federal tax is paid by the purchaser or the seller of bonds. But a Securities and Exchange fee is charged on the *sale* of bonds if the bond is traded on the exchanges. (No fee is paid if the bonds are sold in the over-the-counter market.) The SEC fee is $0.01 per $500 of market value or any multiple thereof.

The seller of a $1,000 Detroit Edison bond would therefore receive the following.

$1,000 Detroit Edison 7 3/8 of 2001 at 75	**$750.00**
Less commission $5.00 per bond	5.00
Less SEC fee of $0.01 per $500	.02
Plus accrued interest	31.14
	$776.12

Whereas bonds of companies in sound financial condition usually sell with interest accrued, common and preferred stocks are sold without accrued dividends unless specified otherwise at the time the contract is made. In other words, they are sold flat.

Also, bonds that have defaulted on their interest payments sell flat because their future payments of interest are questionable. In other words, because the interest does not accumulate or accrue, the bonds are traded "f" or flat. There is no accrued interest, which might or might not be paid in the future.

In most cases, income bonds are traded flat. The reason for this is that the indenture of income bonds usually provides that no interest shall be paid unless and until it has been declared payable by the board of directors of the company issuing the bonds. Sometimes indentures provide that the directors may not declare the interest payable unless it has been earned.

However, there are several (about eight) income bonds listed on the New York Stock Exchange whose earnings record and surplus make declaration of interest a certainty. These bonds have been put in a special category by the exchange, which has ruled that these bonds will trade with accrued interest even though they are income bonds. Sometimes, by agreement, bonds traded over the counter may be traded with accrued interest.

Also, the payment of interest on *income bonds* is somewhat uncertain, as interest payments depend on earnings. Therefore, almost all income bonds are also quoted as flat; that is, the interest does not accrue.

On August 1, 1979, among the bond quotations appeared the following:

	High	Low	Close	
Mo Kn Tx 5 1/2 33 f	20 1/4	19	20 1/4	Change

This is the Missouri-Kansas and Texas Railroad Company 5 1/2% bonds due in 1933; they are quoted flat as shown by the "f." However, almost all bonds traded are paying interest regularly and are therefore traded "and interest." When a company pays interest on a bond that normally trades flat, the situation is the same as in the case of a payment of a dividend, discussed on page 11, except that the bonds trade ex-interest instead of ex-dividend on the fourth full day preceding the record date if the record date falls on a full business day.

Sometimes a company will be in reorganization for a long time and pays no interest on its coupons. As a result, the defaulted coupons would seem to have no value. But care should be taken of these defaulted coupons. If the bond is subsequently sold or exchanged for new securities, it must have all unpaid coupons attached (i.e., SCA—subsequent coupons attached) to be good delivery.

All government securities are traded "and interest," and U.S. Treasury bills are quoted at discounts and gradually increase to face amount at maturity.

Government securities usually are traded net. This means no commission is charged as the dealer's profit is derived from the difference between the purchase price and the sales price of the securities. Sales made the regular way require delivery the next business day.

Investment Company Securities

Concerning literature, selling dividends, breakpoint sales and so forth, see Chapter 5.

REVIEW QUESTIONS

1. What is the Uniform Practice Code of the NASD, and how is it administered?
2. Distinguish among the delivery of a common stock for cash sales, regular way, and seller's option.
3. What does it mean when a stock sells ex-dividend or ex-rights? If a stock was bought on Monday, February 12, 1979, with a record date for dividend of Friday, February 16, 1979, who gets the dividend? Explain.

4. What does good delivery mean? Name five qualifications.
5. Explain *marking to the market* as applied to a short sale.
6. Describe the calculation of accrued interest on a corporate bond.
7. What does it mean when a bond is traded flat ("f")?

TRUE AND FALSE QUESTIONS

1. A quotation of 86 3/4 for a bond and 86 3/4 for a stock:

		True	False
a.	means the same thing, that is, $86 3/4 a share for the stock, and $86.75 for the bond	_____	_____
b.	does not mean the same thing but $86 3/4 per share for the stock and $867.50 for the bond	_____	_____
c.	means that the stock is quoted in dollars per share and that the bond is in percent of par of $1,000.	_____	_____

2. Assume that a stock was sold on Friday, July 20, 1979; regular-way delivery must be made on:

		True	False
a.	Friday, July 27	_____	_____
b.	Monday, July 23	_____	_____
c.	Thursday, July 26.	_____	_____

3. Under the Uniform Practice Code, seller's option provides that:

		True	False
a.	the seller has the option to decline to sell the stock if there is a material increase in the price between the date of the sale and the delivery date	_____	_____
b.	the seller must deliver the security to the buyer's office on the business day the option expires or on one day's notice after five days have elapsed	_____	_____
c.	the delivery of all U.S. government securities is not less than 2 business days or more than 60 days.	_____	_____

4. Assume that a stock was bought on Monday, July 23, with a dividend record date of Friday, July 27; the dividend should be paid to the:

		True	False
a.	buyer	_____	_____
b.	seller.	_____	_____

5. The following are the qualifications for good delivery: *True*   *False*
   a.   proper assignment   _____   _____
   b.   good condition of the security   _____   _____
   c.   proper number of units   _____   _____
   d.   permanent certificate if available   _____   _____
   e.   all of the above.   _____   _____
6. The accrued interest on an 8% $1,000 bond bought at 95 on Wednes-
   day, January 24, 1979, with interest payable May 1 and December 1 is

                                                              True   *False*
   a. $11.50   _____   _____
   b. $13.33   _____   _____
   c. $16.10.   _____   _____
7. Assuming that this bond is sold at 95 on the NYSE, the proceeds to the
   seller are: *True*   *False*
   a. $950.00   _____   _____
   b. $958.31   _____   _____
   c. $960.80.   _____   _____
8. When a bond is traded flat, it means that: *True*   *False*
   a.   interest payments on fixed-income bonds are
        uncertain because the financial position is
        weak   _____   _____
   b.   interest is in default   _____   _____
   c.   it is an income bond with interest payments
        contingent on earnings.   _____   _____

12

Options

Options have been defined as the right to buy or sell something; this could include real estate, theatrical plays, or securities. For years options were and still are made in the over-the-counter market. Investors use the service of brokers to arrange the options. The terms of the options, including the fee or premium, are *negotiated* between the buyer and the seller. But these options are illiquid as there is no secondary market. The options must be either exercised or held to their expiration date.

In 1973 the Chicago Board Options Exchange (CBOE) and the Options Clearing Corporation (OCC) were formed. These events brought about a dramatic change in the securities industry. Options were *listed* and traded on exchanges. There was established a continuous secondary auction market in options. Further, uniform exercise prices and maturities were established, making trading possible and the market liquid. While by far the largest volume of options is traded on the CBOE, they are also traded on the American Stock Exchange and the Philadelphia, Pacific Coast, and Midwest stock exchanges. A very important role is played by the Options Clearing Corporation. The option transactions on all exchanges are cleared by the OCC. Also the OCC issues the options. Usually option certificates are not issued (except in the case of pension fund purchase of options), but records are maintained jointly by the OCC and by the brokers involved in the transaction.

There are two main types of options a call and a put. A call is a negotiable contract giving the holder at his option the right to buy a specified number of shares of underlying stock at a specified price. This price is known as the exercise or striking price. The option further specifies a time period during which the holder might buy the indicated stock. The leading newspapers publish the quotations of these options. These quotations are in effect the premiums on a per share basis that must be paid for the options. The following is a quotation from the *Wall Street Journal* of March 4, 1980 of call options to buy the stock of International Business Machines Corporation.

	April		July		October		N Y
	Vol	Last	Vol	Last	Vol	Last	Close
IBM 75	1432	5/16	411	1 5/8	85	3 1/8	62 3/4

These quotations of calls permit the buyer, for different *premiums* to purchase 100 shares of IBM stock at 75 a share for different periods. For instance, for 5/16 a share or $31.25 a customer could buy a call on IBM until April 19th, for 1 5/8 a share or $162.50 until July 19th, and for 3 1/8 a share or $312.50 until October 18th. The expiration time represents the latest time by which notice of the exercise price must be received by the Options Clearing Corporation. The day is always the Saturday following the third Friday of the expiring month. The sales volume is shown. In this case, a large volume indicates active trading. Finally, the closing price of IBM on the New York Stock Exchange is shown.

There are several factors which influence the amount of the premiums. These include:

(1) The quality of the underlying stock. Although the exchanges carefully screen the companies listing their options, there is no assurance of their investment merits. However the Options Clearing Corporation and the exchanges have agreed on uniform standards governing the selection of the underlying securities for options' trading. The most important of these include (a) a minimum of 8,000,000 shares owned by the public (b) trading volume of at least 2,000,000 shares in each of the two previous years (c) market price of at least $10 a share for 6 months prior to selection, and (d) net income of at least $1,000,000 (in 3 years).

However, in October 1977, the SEC imposed a voluntary moratorium on the expansion of listed options on all exchanges. The SEC claimed in options trading there was manipulation and deceptive practices and ordered an investigation and a report. As a result of this report the SEC and the Self Regulatory Organizations (SROs) consisting of all the options exchanges and the NYSE worked out *Uniform Proposals* for policing the options business (see page 250). In March 1980, the SEC terminated the voluntary moratorium and announced that the expansion in listed call options could begin as soon as the exchanges had submitted to the SEC a satisfactory and appropriate plan for allocating the calls among themselves. Also the SEC announced that the exchanges could expand the number of puts listed, provided that the exchanges satisfied the SEC that they had sufficient operational and surveillance capacity. The SEC asked the exchanges to provide schedules for such expansion. But the SEC deferred action on granting permission to the NYSE and the NASDAQ to trade in options.

(2) The current price of the underlying stock. As the stock moves up,

it will force the price of its option up. A downward movement in the stock will also have an adverse effect on the option price.

(3) The expiration date of an option also influences its price. An expiration date with a long time to run will afford the option holder a longer time to allow the underlying stock to appreciate in the case of a call and to decline in the case of a put.

All of these calls are *out of the money* options. The holder of any one of them could buy 100 shares of IBM at 75 a share or for $7,500. But the closing market for IBM was only 62 3/4 a share. Thus, by buying any one of the three options listed, the investor is hoping that the stock will rise before the options expire.

If, for example, the stock of IBM were selling at $77 a share, and the exercise price were still $75 a share, the option would be an *in-the-money* option. This also means that the option has an intrinsic value of $2. The intrinsic value of an option is simply the difference between the market value of a stock and its exercise price. But, if IBM were selling at $77 a share, the call option would obviously be worth much more than $2. It might be worth as much as $12 or more.

However, in most cases, call options are not exercised to acquire the underlying stocks. This involves paperwork and commissions. Instead the holder of the call sells it on one of the exchanges in a closing sale. A closing sale is accomplished by an option holder's *selling* an option having the same terms as the option he holds. (This is the opposite of a closing purchase transaction in which the maker of an option closes out by buying back an option with similar terms.) Thus, a holder or writer of an option may liquidate his position by offsetting closing transactions. Options issued by the OCC have standardized terms that include the exercise price for each series of options, leaving the premiums and the transaction costs as the only variables.

Puts

A *put* is a negotiable contract giving the owner the right to sell a specified number of shares of an underlying stock at a stated price on or before a stipulated date. A put option is usually bought by an investor who believes a stock is selling too high and that its price will decline. The following is a quotation of a put that appeared in the *Wall Street Journal* on March 4, 1980:

	April		July		October		N Y
	Vol	Last	Vol	Last	Vol	Last	Close
IBM p 60	1565	1	756	2 1/16	142	2 7/8	62 3/4

This quotation indicates that the holder of an April put costing $1.00 a share or $100 for 100 shares can sell or put 100 shares of IBM for $60 a share until April 19, 1980; that the holder of a July put costing $2 1/16 a share or a total of $206.25 can put or sell at 60 a share until July 19, 1980; and the holder of the October put costing $2 7/8 a share or $287.50 has until October 18, 1980 to sell his IBM at 60 a share.

It will be noted that the above quotations are similar to the previously discussed quotation for calls except for the designation "p" which stands for put. Trading in puts started on the exchanges in 1977, but to date relatively few are permitted to be traded. A put is basically suitable for an investor who is bearish on the underlying stock.

POSITION OF THE INVESTOR

There are many advantages to an investor in the purchase of options.

1. Options are frequently used to cover a short sale. For instance, Mr. Jones might sell short 100 shares of IBM because he believes that the recently (1979) announced delay in bringing out its new computer will hurt the stock. Therefore, he buys a call on 100 shares of IBM at 75 for 2 3/4 or $275. Because Mr. Jones has sold short his IBM at 69 1/4, the maximum loss that he can sustain if the market goes against him is 75 less 69 1/4, or 5 3/4 points, plus commissions and the cost of the call option of $275.
2. Options are used by an investor who is long on underlying stock. If Mrs. Jones, for example, wishes to protect her profit or fears a decline in a stock that she holds, she might buy a put. For example, with a stock selling at 65, she might buy a put permitting her to sell her stock at 60. As another alternative, Mrs. Jones might write a call on her stock, for say, $500. If the stock declines, the premium received for the call would not prevent the loss, but it would cushion it.
3. The purchase of calls affords the investor the advantage of leverage. Take a sample case: An investor might buy a call on IBM for $275 with an exercise price of $70. If the stock goes up to $80, the option would be worth at least 11, or $1,100. This would be a profit of $825 before commissions, or 300% on the amount invested of $275. If the investor had bought the stock, the profit of 10 points, or $1,000, would have been only 14.3% on the $7,000 cost of 100 shares of IBM.
4. By using calls an investor can buy an interest in several stocks with a relatively small amount of money.
5. A call might be used by an investor to assure the purchase price of a stock that he or she intends to purchase from the expected receipt of funds.

There are a few disadvantages of options that should be mentioned.

1. If the price of the stock stays about the same during the life of the *call* option, the call will expire without any profit to the holder. But a stock that does not move upward is ideal for an investor selling or making options. (See the next section for a discussion of writing options.)
2. Although the risk of loss to an investor buying a call is limited to the amount of the premium, still the investor can lose it all in a relatively short time.
3. There is no assurance that a secondary market will provide the liquidity needed for the holder to dispose of the call.
4. There are certain risks pertaining to writing covered and particularly uncovered calls that will be discussed in the following section.
5. Many options are never exercised.

WRITING OPTIONS

Two kinds of options are written: covered and uncovered (or naked). A *covered option* is an option that is covered or backed by an underlying security. This security may be deposited with the broker of the option seller or with a custodian bank that certifies its existence. For example, an investor might hold 100 shares of Eastman Kodak Company. The investor writes through his broker a covered call option, whereby the investor agrees, in consideration for 4 a share, or $400, to deliver at any time before the expiration of the option 100 shares of Eastman at the exercise price of 60. At the time the investor wrote the call, Eastman was selling at 55 a share. But, should Eastman go to 60 a share, the holder of the call might demand the 100 shares of Eastman. The writer of the call would have to give up his stock or make a closing purchase transaction by buying in the market an option similar to the one he had sold. Although many investors, including some pension funds, are making options to increase their return on their stocks, there is a risk of either losing their stocks or having to make an expensive closing purchase transaction.

An *uncovered, or naked, call option* takes place when an investor, or, perhaps more precisely, a speculator, writes a call option to deliver, say, 100 shares of Eastman Kodak Company at 60 between now and the time the option expires. But in this case the speculator does not have any Eastman. If, for example, Eastman goes to 70 a share, the speculator must either go out in the market and buy the 100 Eastman to make delivery or make a closing purchase transaction of a call with the same terms as the one he had written. But by this time the price of the call will have risen to a point where it would be very expensive and cause a large loss to the uncovered writer. Writers of uncovered calls must put up and maintain a margin.

In the same manner investors or speculators may write puts.

MARGINS FOR OPTIONS

For covered options carried short, it is *not* necessary to have a cash margin. But the maker must give absolute assurance that he owns the underlying stock.

Uncovered options carried short must be placed in a margin account. For short sales or the writing of uncovered calls, Regulation T of the board of governors of the Federal Reserve System at present (1979) requires cash or equity of at least $2,000. For *exchange-listed* uncovered puts and calls, the maintenance requirement is 30% of the value of the underlying security. This must be adjusted (marked to the market) as the underlying stock value relates to the exercise price. For example, for an uncovered *call* option, to the 30% margin required the investor must add the dollar amount that the market price exceeds the exercise price. Thus, as the underlying stock goes up, the margin for the uncovered call increases. Conversely, the margin requirement on the uncovered call will be adjusted downward as the price of the underlying stock declines. That is, the margin will be decreased by the amount the market price is lower than the exercise price.

For uncovered *puts*, 30% is taken of the current market value of the underlying stock. As the price of this stock drops below the exercise price, the margin is increased dollar for dollar; as the price of the underlying stock increases, the margin is decreased.

For example, let us suppose that a customer writes an uncovered call *listed* option for IBM July 70 when the market is 65.

The margin calculation would be as follows:

30% × the underlying stock $6,500	=	$1,950
Less the out of the money $7,000 − $6,500	=	500
Margin required		$1,450

If the price of IBM should go to 75 a share, the maintenance of margin would be recalculated as follows:

30% × the underlying stock $7,500	=	$2,250
Plus the in the money of $7,500 − $7,000	=	500
Margin required		$2,750

For the sale of an uncovered (naked) *over-the-counter* option the same procedures discussed above apply except the deposit must be 50% of the value of the underlying stock.

The New York Stock Exchange has a minimum margin requirement of 2 1/2 points or $250 for each short uncovered call option in a customer's account.

For example, assume that a customer wrote an uncovered call on Polaroid at 30 when its stock was selling at 24, the margin would be calculated as follows:

Strike price 30		
30% of market value of $2,400	=	$720
Less out of money of $3,000 − $2,400	=	600
		$120

However, because a minimum of $250 has to be maintained for each naked option, the margin requirement would be $250 not $120.

Let us take another case and assume that the customer writes an uncovered (naked) *put* on Manufacturers Hanover Corporation MHC July 35 when the market price was also 35. The following would be the margin required:

$$30\% \times \$3,500 = \$1,050$$

No adjustment would have to be made since the market price is the same as the exercise price. But, if the price of MHC dropped to 25, the maintenance of margin would be figured as follows:

30% × $2,500	=	$ 750
Plus the in the money of $3,500 − $2,500	=	$1,000
		$1,750

Should the stock of MHC recover to 40, the maintenance of margin would be again readjusted as follows:

30% × $4,000	=	$1,200
Less the out of the money of $4,000 − $3,500	=	500
		$ 700

COMBINATIONS AND STRATEGIES

To understand strategies, it might be advisable to review the transactions described so far. Strategies are simply a combination of the following transactions:

Mr. Jones buys a call	This gives Mr. Jones the right to buy a stock at a price during a period of time.
Mr. Jones buys a put	This gives Mr. Jones the right to sell a stock at a price during a period of time.

Mr. Jones writes a call	Mr. Jones is paid a premium and must sell or deliver a specific stock at a price during a period of time.
Mr. Jones writes a put	Mr. Jones is paid a premium and must buy a specific stock at a price over a period of time.

A Straddle

A straddle is at least one put and one call covering the same underlying security having the same exercise price and the same expiration date. An investor may buy a straddle or may write a straddle. For example, an investor buying a straddle would buy a PDQ April 45 put and a PDQ 45 call. Orders for straddles are more difficult to execute than are orders for puts and calls alone because they require the execution of orders covering different series of options at the same time. An investor buys a straddle when he believes that there will be wide fluctuations in the underlying security but is not quite sure as to the direction it might take. Through the purchase of a straddle, the investor is in a position to make a profit by selling or exercising the call component of the straddle, if the underlying security increases in value, or to make a profit by exercising or selling the put, if the price of the underlying stock goes down. Because the purchase of a straddle represents the purchase of two options, the premium for a straddle is greater than is that for a put or a call alone. This means that the price of the underlying security must rise or fall enough to permit the investor to recover the premiums paid for the straddle and the transaction costs before a profit is realized. Thus, the straddle involves all the risks of the purchase of a put or a call alone. This means that the price of the underlying security must change in value to a greater degree for the transaction to be profitable. Timing is of essence to making a profit with the straddle. The underlying security must *move* up and down, and the investor must correctly determine when to exercise or sell one or both of the components of the straddle to realize a profit. The following cases of straddle buying and straddle writing illustrate how each may be profitable and unprofitable.

Case 1: Straddle Buying. On February 8, 1980, an investor buys an IBM July 60 straddle for $1,000 with the underlying stock at 60. If the price declines to 45 before the expiration of the straddle on July 19, 1980, the investor would exercise his put or sell it in the secondary market for about $1,500. If the stock then stayed below 60, the investor would realize a net profit of $500. But, if IBM rallied to, say, 65, the investor could exercise or sell in the secondary market the call for about $500, making a total profit on the straddle of $1,000.

If IBM moved only a little during the term of the straddle, however, a loss might result. For instance, if IBM only went down to 57 and the investor exercised or sold his put in the secondary market, a profit of only $300 would be realized. If IBM later rallied to 62, the investor might realize a profit of $200 by selling the call. Thus the total profit might be only $500 compared with the cost of the straddle of $1,000, or a loss of $500 before transaction costs.

Case 2: Straddle Writing. On February 11, 1980, an investor writes an IBM July 60 straddle and receives a $1,000 premium with the underlying shares at 60. If the underlying shares subsequently go down to, say, 55, the put might be exercised, costing the investor $500. But, because the investor had already received $1,000, his net profit is $500 before transaction costs. This assumes that IBM does not go above 60 by the expiration of the straddle.

Bad timing by the investor, however, can cause serious losses. For instance, if IBM declined to 50 due to an unfavorable court decision, the put would probably be exercised, costing the investor $1,000. Further, if the stock rallied before the expiration of the option to, say, 65 the investor would have to meet the call at 60 and sustain an additional loss of $500, making a total loss of $1,500 less the premium received of $1,000, or a net loss of $500 plus transaction costs.

Straddle Margins. We have explained on page 234 the calculation of margins for writing naked puts and calls. In the case of writing straddles, the same methods are followed except that the maintenance of margin required is the *greater* of the margin required on the put or on the call. For example, if a customer writes an HR straddle July 40 for a premium of $1,000 with the market for the underlying stock of 35, the call maintenance of margin would be:

30% × $3,500	=	$1,050
Less the out of the money of $4,000 − $3,500	=	500
		$ 550

The put maintenance of margin would be:

30% × $3,500	=	$1,050
Plus the in the money of $4,000 − $3,500	=	500
Prevailing margin	=	$1,550

Walking Up and Walking Down a Stock

Walking up a stock means that an investor buys a stock that he or she believes will go up. The investor writes a call on the stock with an exercise price about the same as the current price. When the stock rises, the investor buys in the call he has previously written (at a higher price) and writes a new call on the stock with a higher exercise price. As the stock rises further, the investor again buys in the call and writes a new call at still a higher price and so on. Thus, the investor increases his income and also benefits from a higher market price of the stock.

Walking down a stock is just the opposite. The investor writes a call on his stock at about the current market price of the stock. As the stock goes down, the investor buys in his call (at a much lower cost) and writes a new call at a lower striking price (and with a higher premium). As the stock drops further, the investor again buys in the call he has written and writes a new call at a still lower exercise price. Each time, the investor collects the difference between the cost to buy in the old call and the premium received from writing the new call. Thus, walking up a stock is for bullish investors and walking down is for bearish investors.

Spread

There are two main kinds of spreads. The vertical spread which is one in which the investor buys one option and writes another option of the same class (class means both calls or both puts) on the same underlying security with the same expiration dates but with *different exercise* prices. The horizontal or time spread is one in which the investor buys one option and writes another option of the same class, on the same underlying security with the same exercise prices but with different expiration dates.

The basic strategy of an investor's executing a spread is literally to spread the risk. For example, a customer might buy in January, 1980, an April 50 call on Exxon when it was selling around 50 a share for 5 ($500). If Exxon went up, as it did, the customer would have made a considerable amount of money. However, at the time there was no certainty that Exxon would go up. If it had not risen above 50 for the life of the option, it would have expired worthless and the customer would have lost all his $500. Now if the customer was bullish on Exxon but wished to reduce his risk, he could have undertaken a vertical spread.

Vertical Spread (Price Spread)

The investor could buy an April 50 Exxon call for 5 ($500) when it was selling around 50 a share *and* write an April 55 call for 2 ($200). Thus, the investor has spread his risk. It is limited to $300 or the difference between the two premiums and compared with $500 if only a call had been bought. If the price of Exxon rises to 62, the investor would be advised to buy in the 55 call he has written which now would be around 4 or $400. Also, he could now sell the 50 call he bought for around $1,200 making a net profit of $900 ($700 on sale of April 50 option plus $200 from writing the April 55 option).

This transaction might be described as a bullish vertical spread where the investor buys the option with the striking price closest to the market price and writes the less costly option with the same expiration date but with a higher striking price.

A customer who is bearish on Exxon would execute the other side of the above spread. In other words, he would sell or write the April 50 call at 5 ($500) and buy the April 55 call for 2 ($200) with a credit balance of 3 ($300). If the stock stayed below 50 throughout the life of the option, the investor would happily pocket the $300. If Exxon went to 50 or above, and the customer was asked to deliver the April 50 call he had written, he could of course exercise his April 55 call and deliver the stock thus setting a maximum on his loss. However, the customer would undoubtedly close out the April call he had written. The cost would probably be about 5 or 6 points, because intrinsically the April 50 call would be worth about 5 points more than the April 55 call. Therefore, the maximum loss would be about 5 points or $500 less $200 received for call written or $300.

Vertical spreads both bearish and bullish can be executed with puts as well as with calls.

Horizontal or Time Spreads

As stated on page 238, a horizontal or time spread is the simultaneous purchase and sale of the same class of options, with the same underlying stock, the same exercise prices, but, different expiration months. They may be used by an investor who does not believe that the underlying stock will move sharply either up or down.

For example, if an investor in February 1980 believes that the stock of JJK Corporation selling at 51 is a so–called "dead stock," that is a stock that is not expected to fluctuate to a wide degree, he might execute a calendar or time spread. He would buy a July JJK 50 call for 5 ($500) and write a JJK April 50 call for 3 3/4 ($375) for a debit of 1 1/4 ($125). The higher July premium is explained by its more distant maturity giving the investor more time to make a profit. If, as the customer hoped, the stock sagged to around 49, the April 50 option would have no intrinsic value but might have a little time value, about 1/8th, if the option still had a few days to run. Also at the same time the July 50 option might have dropped to 3 ($300). The investor then should buy in for 1/8 ($12.50) the April 50 call option he had written and sell for 3 ($300) the July 50. Thus the investor would have a profit of

$162.50 ($300 less $125 debit less $12.50 from buying in April 50 option).

It is a general rule in writing options to write options with exercise prices as far as possible above the market price of the stock because it is the one the least likely to be exercised. If the stock drops, the investor can buy back the first option cheaply and write another option on the same stock with a lower exercise price. If the stock increases in value, he will have to pay a higher price to buy back the option but he will be able to sell others on the same stock with the same exercise price but with a later expiration date at a higher price than he paid for the old option. A key rule to successful investing in horizontal or time options might be to stick to stocks whose prices have fluctuated within known patterns in the past.

Spread Margins

The most important consideration in understanding margins for spreads is the following rule: the long option, i.e. the purchase of a call (or a put), must expire no earlier than the short option, i.e. the writing of a call or a put, if the spread is to receive special margin treatment. This means that the margin required will be the *lesser* of the adjusted 30 per cent margin for uncovered options discussed on page 234 *and* the difference between the exercise prices.

For instance, an investor in March, 1980 might write or sell a Schlumberger (pronounced Slumber Jay) May 100 for 13 ($1,300) and buy a Schlumberger May 110 for 7 ($700) with a credit balance of 6 ($600). At that time Schlumberger was selling at 107. Since the long option written expires on the same date as the short option—the option bought, the spread qualifies for special margin treatment. Therefore the margin required would be the *lesser* of the following:

30% × $10,700	=	$3,210
Plus the in-the-money of $10,700 − $10,000	=	700
		$3,910

OR

Difference between the exercise prices $11,000 − $10,000 = $1,000

Thus, the maintenance requirement spread is the lesser of the above, or $1,000. Further, the credit balance of $600 may be used to reduce the margin requirement to $400. But if this transaction is an initial one in the account, the $2,000 initial margin under regulation T must be met.

Other combinations open to investors include *straps* and strips. A strap is two calls and one put at the same exercise price, on the same security with the same expiration date. Here the investor expects the stock to go up but wants to hedge his opinion by buying one put. A *strip* is two puts and one call on the same security, with the same exercise price and with the same expiration date. In this case, the investor is bearish on a stock but wants to hedge his opinion by buying one call.

Risks of Spreads

There are a number of risks connected with spreads, but perhaps the most serious are as follows.

1. It is often difficult to execute simultaneously the purchase and writing of options within the limits desired by the investors.

2. An investor might liquidate part of his spread and thus become an uncovered or naked writer. Then a margin call would be issued as the investor would no longer be able to use the special margin requirement applicable to certain spreads.

3. There is risk of forced exercise. The writer might be forced by assignment to purchase the underlying security or to dispose of it in the case of a put, thereby upsetting his spread position.

SUITABILITY OF RECOMMENDATIONS

It is of greatest importance that before accepting an option account the broker make sure that the prospective customer understands the risks of trading options and is able to sustain a loss without seriously impairing his or her financial health.

In 1977 the SEC was concerned about the practices of the options fraternity and imposed a voluntary moratorium on the expansion of options' listing. After a lengthy study, the SEC in March, 1980 approved Uniform Proposals for the handling and for the serveilliance of options accounts. Also, the moratorium on listing of options was lifted provided certain conditions were met. (See pages 250-260.)

THE CONVENTIONAL OVER-THE-COUNTER MARKET IN PUTS AND CALLS

By far the greatest volume of options is traded in on the CBOE and the other exchanges, but there does exist an important over-the-counter market in options. Most of these over-the-counter broker-dealers have extensive communications systems and many customers. Many belong to the Association of Member Firms Options Departments, a professional group organized to service option customers.

Perhaps one of the main advantages the over-the-counter options market has over the listed markets is the fact that the over-the-counter market trades and makes markets in a number of options of secondary companies that are not listed or traded on the organized exchanges. Further, the over-the-counter market is a negotiated options market, whereas the organized option exchanges are auction markets. As mentioned before, on the organized exchanges the terms of the options are set by the exchange with the premium set by the forces of supply and demand. In the over-the-counter market the premium, the expiration date, and the exercise price are set by negotiation between the buyer and the seller.

Broker-dealers charge their customers commissions for the purchase or writing of puts and calls as well as for the exercise of an option. A typical commission might be $25 for each transaction. There is a New York State transfer tax of a few pennies a share paid by the purchaser of a call. There is no tax payable on the purchase of an over-the-counter put until it is exercised. The New York State transfer tax is gradually being phased out and will be eliminated entirely in September 1981.

All options made in the over-the-counter market are guaranteed by a stock exchange member. A member guarantee of a listed option is not necessary as they are issued and in effect guaranteed by the OCC.

ROLE OF CONVERSION HOUSES

The over-the-counter option dealer will often try to help a customer who wishes to close out his transactions by trying to find puts or calls of similar maturities, for example. The dealer might find these puts or calls from his other customers or even advertise for them. But perhaps the employment of a conversion house is of greatest help to an over-the-counter customer. A conversion house is a firm that facilitates the conversion of a put option to a call option and vice versa. For an investor who is unable to acquire the desired number of puts or calls, this technique partially overcomes the basic weakness of the options over-the-counter market; namely, its lack of liquidity. For example, let us suppose that Mr. A wishes to acquire three call options on Eastman Kodak with an exercise price of 60 for $425 each. His broker is unable to find any sellers. But he can find a seller of a *strap* (two calls and one put) on EK at 60 for $925. By buying this strap Mr. A has two calls that he wants but one put that he does not want. He therefore sells the put to a NYSE firm for a nominal fee. The NYSE firm then buys 100 shares of EK for its own account at the put option price. Next, the broker sells Mr. A a call option on EK. The NYSE broker now has a riskless situation. Should the call be exercised, he can turn over his 100 shares of EK. If the stock goes down, he can exercise his put. For carrying the 100 shares of EK, Mr. A will pay interest. Also, Mr. A has obtained his desired three options. Sometimes the use of a conversion house will result in lower costs of the options than if they were bought separately or in a group.

THE DEALER'S OWN CAPITAL

Several dealers will buy from their own customers options that the customers wish to sell. The dealers use their own capital for these purchases. They then try to resell these options to some other customer or in the market.

ADJUSTMENTS TO THE STRIKING PRICE DUE TO CORPORATE DISTRIBUTIONS IN THE OVER-THE-COUNTER MARKET

Cash dividends.   The exercise price of a put or call option is reduced by the exact amount of the cash dividend.

Stock dividend.   The total value of the contract remains constant, but the number of shares increases and the exercise price decreases in exact proportion to the value of the distribution. For example, let us assume a call option for 100 shares of EK at 60, or a value of $6,000. If Eastman declares a 10% stock dividend, the number of shares would be increased to 110 and the price would be reduced to $54.55 ($6,000 ÷ 110 = $54.55).

Subscriptions to rights. The exercise price is reduced by the exact value of the subscription rights. The value is determined on the opening sale of the rights when the stock begins to trade ex-rights.

OPTIONS ISSUED BY THE OPTIONS CLEARING CORPORATION (OCC)

To permit a secondary market in which an existing position of a holder or writer of an option may be liquidated by an offsetting closing transaction, options issued by the OCC have standardized terms that include the expiration time and the exercise price for each series of options, leaving the premium and the transaction costs as the only variables.

Exercise prices are generally fixed at 5-point intervals for securities trading below 50, at 10-point intervals for securities trading between 50 and

200, and at 20-point intervals for securities trading over 200. When trading is to be introduced in a new trading month, an exchange ordinarily selects the two exercise prices surrounding the market price of the underlying security on the day of selection. (For example, if the underlying security trades at 27 during the day the exercise prices are being selected for the new expiration month, *two* new series of options will be selected with exercise prices of 25 and 30, respectively.) It is possible that these point intervals will be changed at some future time.

Expiration dates are set by the exchanges. Each class of options is assigned one of three expiration month cycles: the January–April–July–October cycle, the February–May–August–November cycle, or the March–June–September–December cycle.

Trading in options of a particular expiration month normally commences approximately nine months earlier, so that at any given time there are generally open for trading options in each class having three different expiration months.

ADJUSTMENT TO OPTION TERMS IN THE LISTED OPTIONS

Cash dividends.   No adjustment is made to any of the terms of exchange-traded puts and calls to reflect the declaration or payment of a cash dividend. But, if the holder of a call exercises it prior to the ex date for the distribution, the exercising holder is entitled to the dividend even though the writer to whom the exercise is assigned may receive actual notice of such assignment on or after the ex date. Conversely, the holder of a put who effectively exercises it prior to the an ex date for distribution, but delivers the underlying security to the writer to whom the exercise is assigned after such exercise date, must also deliver the distribution to the writer.

Stock dividends, stock splits, and stock distributions.   When one or more shares of underlying stock are issued, the number of shares covered by the option is *not* adjusted. Instead, the number of outstanding options is proportionately increased, and the exercise price is proportionately decreased. For example, consider an option to buy 100 shares of XYZ stock at 60, or for $6,000. A 3-for-2 stock distribution would mean 300 shares for 200 shares or 150 shares for 100 shares. Thus the option would cover 150 shares, and the exercise price would be reduced to 40, to equal $6,000. With a 2-for-1 stock distribution, there would be two options covering 100 shares each with an exercise price to make $6,000. It is important to note that, after an adjustment, the new premium is determined by multiplying the premium per share by the new number of shares. For instance, if an option covers 120 shares after adjustment for a 20% stock dividend and the premium quoted is 5 a share, the aggregate premium option would be $600.

In the case of other distributions such as spin-offs, reorganizations, and so forth, the Option Clearing Corporation determines the adjustments that it considers to be fair to the holders and writers of such options.

OPTION TRANSACTIONS

After a customer has been approved by the member for options transactions, that customer may place an order with his broker in the same manner that he would for other types of securities. Orders should specify whether for puts or calls, the underlying security, the expiration month, the exercise price, the number of contracts to be purchased or written, and whether the purchase or sale is an "opening" or "closing" transaction. As soon as the broker receives the order, it is transmitted for execution on one of the exchanges on which the option is traded. As soon as the transaction is completed, the Option Clearing Corporation is advised. The clearing member for the buyer is required to pay the premium to the OCC prior to 7:00 A.M. Pacific time, 9:00 A.M. Central time, and 10:00 A.M. Eastern time of the first business day following the receipt of the report by the OCC.

CLOSING TRANSACTIONS

A *closing sale transaction* is a means whereby an investor may realize a gain in the market for his option by selling it. For example, a holder might have purchased an Eastman Kodak July 60 call in January (when EK was selling at 53 and July calls were selling at 6) for a premium of $600 plus transaction costs. Three months later EK is selling at 59 and the July 60 call is selling at 8 1/2 (or $850 per call). Here the holder could realize a $250 gain (less transaction costs) in a closing sale transaction.

Similarly, the holder of a put may realize in a closing sale transaction any gain in a put price resulting from a decline in the market price of the underlying security.

A *closing purchase transaction* is executed in the secondary market for exchange-listed option writers. In this case a writer of an option may terminate his obligation by entering into a closing purchase transaction. In such transactions the writer "buys in" the same series as the option he previously wrote. But, instead of the transaction resulting in the issuance of an option, it has the effect of canceling the writer's preexisting obligation.

TYPES OF OPTION ORDERS

A customer might instruct his option broker to execute any one of the following types of orders: market, limit, stop, or stop limit. These were discussed on page 194. But peculiar to the option business is the vertical spread (a vertical spread is the purchase of a call and the making of a call at different prices). The difference between the two, or the spread, is dictated by the customer usually on the advice of his broker. The order is placed for both sides of the transactions. Both calls must be executed at the spread indicated or the entire transaction is canceled.

POSITION OF THE OPTION CLEARING CORPORATION (OCC)

As has been stated, once the option transaction has been completed on the exchanges, the OCC issues the option. Henceforth the contractual relation between the holder or writer of the option are severed. Instead, the holders of the options look to the OCC, not to any particular writer for performance. Each time an option is issued to a buyer, there is a writer of an option of the same series contractually obligated to the OCC. Thus, the aggregate obligations of the OCC to the holders of the options are backed by the aggregate obligations that the writers of the options owe the OCC.

THE PROSPECTUS OF THE OPTIONS CLEARING CORPORATION (OCC)

The OCC from time to time issues a prospectus. This should be required reading for everyone interested in the options business. It gives in detail the function of the OCC, its operations, margin requirements, taxes, buying and writing put and call options and many other aspects of the option business.

Because it has been ruled that all options issued by the OCC are securities, they must be registered under the Securities Act of 1933. Further, a prospectus must be given to all prospective customers who are contemplating engaging in option transactions.

COMMISSIONS LEVIED ON PREMIUMS

As in the case of the over-the-counter market in options, commissions are levied on the premiums paid for calls, puts, and on the exercise of either type of option. Commissions are supposed to be set by mutual agreement between the broker and his customer, but many brokers are unwilling to negotiate modifications from the rates they establish. Other charges include a small SEC fee and for options traded on the American Stock Exchange, a New York State tax. This will be phased out in 1981 as noted earlier.

The following table illustrates the average commission charges on calls by four large brokerage houses on representative transactions:

	Premium	Money Involved	Average Commission	Per Cent
8 Calls	7/8	$ 700	$ 67	9.57
10 Calls	2 1/8	2,125	121	5.69
15 Calls	3	4,500	164	3.64
8 Calls	8	6,400	152	2.37
25 Calls	3 1/2	8,750	257	2.93

EXERCISE OF OPTIONS

The exercise of a put or call option takes place only through the OCC by timely submission of exercise instructions to the OCC by a member acting for a customer. An option may be exercised the day following its purchase or sale when and if the OCC approves the transaction.

Customers wishing to exercise options must so instruct their brokers prior to a cut-off time fixed by the exchanges. These times are: 2:30 P.M. Pacific time, 4:30 P.M. Central time, and 5:30 P.M. Eastern time on the business day immediately preceding the expiration date. On business days other than the expiration date, clearing members may tender exercise notices to the OCC between the hours of 7:00 A.M. and 1:30 P.M. Pacific time, 9:00 A.M. and 3:30 P.M. Central time, and 10:00 A.M. and 4:30 P.M. Eastern time for the exercise to be assigned on the following day.

ASSIGNMENT OF EXERCISE NOTICE

When a customer wishes to exercise a call or a put option, an exercise notice is sent to the OCC. The OCC does not deliver stock against a call or pay money against a put. But it will assign an exercise notice to a randomly selected clearing member account with the OCC that reflects the writing of an option or options of the same series as the exercised option. This clearing member is obligated to deliver the stock in the case of a call and to buy in the case of a put.

If the OCC assigns the exercise notice to a clearing member's account, the member is required to allocate the exercise notice to a customer writing an option in the account. A fair method of selection of the customer must be adopted by the clearing member. The allocation may be upon random selection basis; a first in as a writer, first out when calls are exercised basis; or any other fair method. A forced exercise of a call is most likely when the price of the underlying stock is above the exercise price and the option is near the expiration date. The unwelcome exercise of a put might be expected when the price of the stock is below the striking price. Thus, the writer of an option must be aware that he may be assigned an exercise notice at any time during the life of the option.

DELIVERY AND PAYMENT

Settlement of the purchase or sale of the underlying securities resulting from the exercise of an option is usually made through a correspondent of the OCC. But the OCC may require that contracts be settled between the assigned clearing member and the exercising clearing member before 10:00 A.M. Pacific time, 12:00 noon Central time, and 1:00 P.M. Eastern time. The day is the fifth business day following the date when the exercise notice was tendered to the OCC.

BUY-INS

If a clearing member exercises a call and does not receive the security within 30 days, that member may buy in the security at the best available price. The OCC will make up the difference between the price of the option and the actual market price the member had to pay.

If a clearing member exercised a put and did not receive payment for tendered stock on settlement date, that member can sell the stock at the best available price. The OCC will make up the difference between the amount he would have received under his put option and the proceeds of his sale of the stock.

THE STRUCTURE OF THE EXCHANGE OPTIONS MARKETS

The Chicago Board Options Exchange (CBOE) trades exclusively in options. But the other exchanges—the American (AMEX), the Philadelphia (PHLX), the Pacific Coast (PSE), and the Midwest (MSE)—all deal in securities as well as in options. On the AMEX and the PHLX, specialists similar to those on the NYSE take a position and try to maintain orderly markets as well as watch over the trading in options.

The CBOE is a membership organization headed by a board of directors. It permits only public customers to enter orders on the book. These book orders have priority over orders from the professional traders. The custodian of this public order book is called the *board broker*. He is not permitted to act as a professional trader. He keeps records of his orders and gives out information concerning the size of the markets, the quotations, and so on. Another class of broker is the *market maker*. The CBOE assigns to the various market makers certain groups of options in the same manner as does the NYSE. The market makers must maintain orderly markets in these options. Finally, the CBOE has *floor brokers* who are required to expedite the execution of orders at the best possible price. Their duties are similar to those of the floor brokers, or $2.00 brokers, on the NYSE.

TAXES ON OPTION TRANSACTIONS

Capital Gains Treatment. The Internal Revenue Service has ruled that an option is a capital asset. Gains and losses from the sale of an option are either long term or short term, depending on how long they are held. To be a long-term holding, the investor must hold a security for over one year (see page 360). Because almost all options run for less than a year, any gain or loss must be short term.

The Call Option. If a call option is allowed to expire unexercised, the expiration is treated as a sale on the expiration date. The resultant loss would be a short-term loss if the holding period was less than one year. If the option is exercised and the call holder becomes the owner of the stock, the total cost of exercising the option includes the cost of the underlying stock, the cost of the call, the commission paid on the purchase of the call, and the commission paid for buying the underlying stock. The holding period of the underlying stock does not include the time the call was held by the investor. It is measured from the exercise date, not from the time the call was bought.

The Put Option. The Internal Revenue Service has ruled that the acquisition of a put is equivalent to a short sale. Further, it maintains that the exercise, sale, or expiration of a put is a closing of a short sale. The I.R.S. considers the profit on a stock held over a year to be short term if it had been held less than a year before the purchase of the put or bought between the purchase of the put and its exercise. In other words the investor might have held the underlying stock over a year, yet any profit taken would be short term.

If a put and a stock identified with it to be used in its exercise are acquired on the same day—that is, the put is 'married to' the stock—then the I.R.S. rules that the purchase of the put does not constitute a short sale. If the put is exercised and if the identified stock is delivered, the premium paid for the put reduces the amount realized on the sale. If the put is not exercised, the premium paid for the put is added to the basis of the identified stock.

Taxes on Option Writing.   The premium received by an investor for writing a put or a call is not counted as income at the time of receipt but is carried in a deferred account until the writer's obligation expires or by the writer's selling the underlying stock to satisfy a call, to purchase the stock to satisfy a put, or to engage in a closing transaction. If the option written expires unexercised, the writer must treat the premium received as a short-term capital gain. If a put is exercised, the premium received should be treated as a reduction of cost of the underlying stock. In the case of a call, it is considered as part of the proceeds of the sale. Thus, when a put is exercised, the cost of the underlying security to the writer is the exercise price of, say, 50 (or $5,000) *less* the premium of, say, 3 (or $300), or $4,700. When a call option is exercised, the amount paid to the investor when the securities are called away includes the $5,000 *plus* the call premium of, say, 5 (or $500), or a total of $5,500.

      If a writer of an option engages in a closing transaction by payment of an amount equivalent to the value of the option at the time of payment, the difference between the amount so paid and the premium received constitutes a short-term capital gain or loss.

Spreads and Straddles.   Under the present rules of the I.R.S. both spreads and straddles are taxed according to their individual component parts—that is, as if they were simply simultaneous purchases or sales of individual puts and calls. All premium income or loss to the investor from closing purchase or expiration are usually considered as a short-term capital gain or loss rather than as ordinary income. However, the parts of the spread or straddle might be closed out in different taxable years. This might be significant to the individual investor.

UNIFORM SELF REGULATORY
ORGANIZATION (SRO)
PROPOSALS

      On March 26, 1980, the SEC approved the proposals of the Self Regulatory Organization (SRO). The SRO is composed of representatives from the NYSE, the Amex, the NASD, the Midwest, the CBOE, the Pacific Coast and the Philadelphia exchanges. In these proposals the SRO attempted to satisfy the concerns of the SEC about the options business without undue disruption or costs to the securities industry. In summary these rules are as follows:

OPENING OF AN ACCOUNT

(a) **Approval Required.** No member organization shall accept an option order from a customer unless that customer has met the information re-quirement here-in-after set forth. Based on such information, the branch office manager or other Registered Option Principal (ROP) shall approve in writing the customer's account for options trading. If the branch office man-ager is not a Registered Options Principal, the customer's approval must be approved within a reasonable time by an ROP. This approval must be based on an intensive study of the customer's personal and financial background.

(b) **Diligence in Opening the Account.** The member organization shall ex-ercise due diligence to learn the essential facts as to the customer's: (1) in-vestment objectives, (2) his or her employment status (name of employer self employed or retired), (3) estimated annual income from all sources, (4) estimated net worth (exclusive of home), (5) estimated liquid net worth (cash, securities etc), (6) marital status including number of dependents, (7) age. In addition the customer's records should contain: (a) the source of background and financial information concerning the customer, (b) any dis-cretionary authorization on file giving the name, relationship to the cus-tomer of the person holding the authority, (c) Date of the Options Clearing Corporation prospectus furnished the customer, (d) the nature and type of transactions for which the account is approved, (e) the name of the Regis-tered Representative handling the account, (f) the name of the Registered Option Principal approving the account and date, (g) the date of verifica-tion of currency of the account information. However, the member organi-zation might use the standard new account form (see page 265). Each firm can develop its own version of the new account form provided it requires from the customer the essential facts.

    If a customer refuses to answer any of the above information, it shall be noted on the customer's records. The information provided shall be con-sidered together with other information available in determining whether and to what extent to approve the option account.

(c) **Verification of the Customer's Background and Financial Information.** The information on the customer's background shall be sent to the customer for verification within 15 days after the customer's option account has been approved. If the member becomes aware of any material change in the cus-tomer's financial situation, a copy of the revised report shall be sent to the customer for verification.

(d) **Agreements to be Obtained.** Within 15 days after the approval of the options account, the customer must sign a written agreement that the account will be handled in accord with the rules of the SRO and the rules of the Options Clearing Corporation.

(e) **Prospectus to be Furnished.**   At or prior to the time the customer's account is approved for options transactions, the member organization shall supply the customer with an updated Prospectus of the Options Clearing Corporation.

MAINTENANCE OF CUSTOMERS' RECORDS

The information on approved options customers shall be maintained at both the branch office servicing the account and at the principal supervisory office having jurisdiction over that branch office. Copies of account statements of options customers shall be maintained at both places for the most recent six month period.

SUITABILITY OF RECOMMENDATIONS

No member, Registered Option Principal, or Registered Options Representative shall recommend to a customer an opening transaction in any option contract unless they have reasonable basis for believing that the customer has such knowledge and experience that he or she may be expected to be capable of evaluating the risks of the recommended transactions and is financially able to bear the risks of the recommended position. Since some types of options are speculative, the broker-dealer must be sure that the customer is able to sustain a loss without seriously impairing his or her financial health. Also, the customer should be thoroughly informed about the options business. Intensive reading of the many publications of the CBOE and the AMEX is recommended. Finally, a conference should be held with the Registered Options Principal and the customer to decide the type of options transactions deemed most suitable for the customer.

CUSTOMER COMPLAINTS AND THE MAINTENANCE OF BOOKS AND RECORDS

Every member organization conducting options business shall maintain and keep current a separate central log index or other file located at the principal place of business for all option-related complaints. This file should include (i) the identification of the complainant; (ii) the date the complaint was received; (iii) the identification of the Registered Representative servicing the account; (iv) a general description of the matter complained of; and (v) the record of what action taken by the member organization with respect to the complaint. Each option–related complaint received by a branch shall be forwarded to the office with the central file not later than 30 days after receipt.

SUPERVISION OF ACCOUNTS

(a) **A Senior Registered Options Principal (SROP)** shall develop a written program for the review of the organization's non–member customers' option accounts. The program shall be under the supervision of the SROP who is specifically identified to the SRO and who is either an officer or a partner.

(b) **A Compliance Registered Options Principal (CROP)** or an SROP with no sales function must be designated to review and propose appropriate action to secure the member organization's compliance with the securities laws and regulations in respect to options. The requirement that the CROP have no sales function need not apply to firms with less than $1,000,000 in options commissions in the last two years or that currently has less than 10 Registered Option Representatives.

DISCIPLINARY ACTION BY
OTHER ORGANIZATIONS

Every member firm is required to notify the SRO in writing of any disciplinary action, including the basis therefore, taken by any exchange, association (i.e. NASD), clearing corporation, or futures market, against a member or its associated persons. These could involve suspension, termination, fines in excess of $2,500 or any limitation of activity. The members continue to be subject to the disciplinary jurisdiction of the SRO provided written notice of the commencement of the inquiry into such matters is given by the SRO to such former member or associated person within one year of receipt by the SRO of written notice of termination of such person's status as a member or person associated with a member.

COMMUNICATIONS TO
CUSTOMERS

It is important to distinguish between advertisements and sales literature.

Advertisements include material in newspapers, periodicals, magazines as well as broadcasts over the radio and television; motion audio–

video tapes as well as bill–board advertisements are included.

Sales literature includes any written communication (not defined as advertisement) distributed or made generally available to customers. These would include any analysis, performance report, projection or recommendation with respect to options, underlying securities, or market conditions. Also included would be standard forms of worksheets, or any seminar text which pertains to options and which is communicated to customers or the public at seminars, lectures, or similar such events or any SRO–produced material pertaining to options.

(a) **General Rule.** No member, member organization, or person associated with a member shall utilize any advertisement, sales literature or other communication to any customer or member of the public concerning options which (i) contains an untrue statement or omission of a material fact or is otherwise false or misleading; (ii) contains promise of specific results, exaggerated or unwarranted claims, opinions for which there is no reasonable basis or forecasts of future events which are unwarranted or are not clearly labeled as forecasts; (iii) contains hedge clauses which are not easily identifiable or attempt to disclaim responsibility for the content; (iv) fails to meet general standards of good taste and truthfulness.

(b) **Approval by Senior Registered Options Principal.** The CROP or his designee must approve all advertisements and sales literature. Copies thereof, together with the names of the persons who prepared the material and the names of the persons who approved the material, must be kept in an easily accessible place for three years.

(c) **SRO [1]Approval Required for Options Advertisements.** In addition to the above requirement, every advertisement pertaining to options must be submitted to the Department of Sales Practice Compliance of the SRO at least 10 days prior to use for approval. If changed or disapproved, it shall be withheld from circulation until changes specified by the SRO have been made. However, SRO approval is not necessary if the advertisement has been approved by another self regulatory organization (e.g. the NASD) having comparable advertising standards; or an advertisement in which the only reference to options is contained in a listing of the services. Finally, no written material respecting options may be distributed to any person who has not previously or contemporaneously received a current prospectus of the Options Clearing Corporation.

Interpretation and Policies

The special risks attendant to options transactions and the complexities of certain options investment strategies shall be reflected in any advertisement of sale literature which discusses the use or advantages of options.

[1]This would include the NASD or any Exchange. See page 250.

All advertisements and sales literature discussing the use of options should include a warning to the effect that options are not for everyone. In the preparation of written communications respecting options, the following guidelines should be observed:

a.   Any statement referring to potential opportunities or advantages of options should also explain the risks.
b.   It should not be suggested that options are suitable for everyone.
c.   Statements suggesting the certain availability of a secondary market for options should *not* be made.

Advertisements Standards for Options

(a) Advertisements may only be used (and copies may be sent to persons who have not received a prospectus of the Options Clearing Corporation) if the material meets the requirement of Rule 134 (see page 397). Under Rule 134, advertisements must be limited to a general description of the security being offered and its issuer. Advertisements under this Rule should state the name and address of the person from whom a current prospectus of the Options Clearing Corporation may be obtained. Such advertisements may have the following characteristics: (i) The text of the advertisement may contain a brief description of such options, including a statement that the Options Clearing Corporation is the issuer of every such option. The general attributes and methods of operation of the OCC and the exchanges may be described, including how the price of the option is determined on the trading floors of the various exchanges. (ii) The advertisement may include any statement required by any state law or administrative authority. (iii) Advertising designs, including borders, scrolls, arrows, and pointers, multiple and combined logos, and unusual type spaces and lettering as well as attention getting headlines, photographs and other graphics may be used, provided such material is not misleading.

(b) The use of recommendations or of past or projected performance figures is not permitted in any *advertisement* pertaining to options.

Written communications (other than advertisements) shall conform to the following standards:

(a) Sales literature shall state that supporting documents for any claim, comparisons, recommendations, statistics or other technical data will be supplied upon request.

(b) Such communications may contain projected performance figures (including annualized rates of return) provided that: (i) no suggestion of certainty of future performance is made; (ii) parameters relating to such performance figures are clearly established (e.g. to indicate exercise price of option, purchase price of underlying stock, and its market price, option premium, anticipated dividend, etc); (iii) all relevant costs, including commission and interest charges (if applicable with regard to margin transactions) are disclosed; (iv) such projects are plausible and are intended as a source of reference or a comparative device to be used in the development of recommendations; (v) all material assumptions made in such calculations are clearly identified (e.g. "assume option expires," "assume option unexercised," etc); (vi) all risks involved in the proposed transaction are discussed; (vii) a statement that the annualized rates of return are based on at least 60 days experience, that formulas used are shown, and that annualized returns cited might be achieved only if the parameters cited can be duplicated and that there is no certainty of doing so.

(c) Communications may feature past performance of past recommendations or of actual transactions of the member organization, but not of an individual Registered Representative, provided that: (i) any such portrayal is done in a balanced manner, and consists of records or statistics that are confined to a specific "universe" that can be fully isolated and circumscribed and that covers at least the most recent 12 month period. (ii) the date and price of each initial recommendation at the transaction and at the end of the period. Also should be given the number that advanced and the number that declined, the number of items that were recommended or transacted. An offer must be made to provide the complete record on request; (iii) all relevant costs, including commissions and interest must be disclosed and, whenever annualized rates of return are used, all material assumptions used in the process of annualization must also be given; (iv) an indication of the general market conditions during the period covered must be given; (v) a Registered Options Principal must determine that the records present fairly the status of the transaction and so initial the report; (vi) a statement must be made that such communications should not and cannot be viewed as an indication of future performance.

(d) In the case of options programs (i.e., an investment plan employing the systematic use of one or more option strategies), the cumulative history or unproven nature of the program and its underlying assumptions shall be disclosed.

(e) Standard forms of option worksheets utilized by member firms, in addition to complying with the requirements applicable to sales literature, must be uniform within a member firm.

(f) If a member organization has adopted a standard form of worksheet for a particular options strategy, non–standard worksheets may not be used.

(g) Communications that portray performance of past recommendations or actual transactions and completed worksheets should be kept at a place easily accessible to the customer's sales office.

ALLOCATION OF EXERCISE
   NOTICES

Each member organization shall establish fixed procedures for the allocation of exercise notices assigned in respect to short position in such member organization's customers' accounts. The allocation shall be made on a "first-in, first-out" basis, an automated random selection basis that has been approved by the SRO or on a manual random selection basis that has been specified by the SRO. Each member organization shall inform its customers in writing of the method it uses to allocate exercise notices to its customers' accounts, explaining its manner of operation and the consequences of the system.

ALLOCATION OF EXERCISE
   ASSIGNMENT NOTICES

Each member shall preserve for three years sufficient work papers and documentary materials relating to the allocation of exercise assignment notices to establish the manner in which the allocation of such exercise notices is, in fact, being accomplished. Such records would include the record of OCC assignment, a stock record and, in the case of random selection, a computer–generated or other random number. In the case of FIFO selection, copies of the customer's statement showing the positions established.

REPORTS OF ACCOUNTS OF
   MARKET MAKERS

All registered market makers must file with the SRO (and keep current) a list of accounts in which he or she as an individual directly or indirectly controls the trading activity, exercises investment discretion, or has an interest in the profits or losses of such accounts. No market maker may engage in stock, option, or related securities trading in an account which has not been reported to the SRO.

REPORTS OF UNDERLYING
   SECURITY ORDERS AND
   POSITIONS

In a manner prescribed by the SRO, each market maker must, on the business day following the order entry date, report to the SRO every order entered by the market maker for the purchase or sale of a security underlying option traded on the SRO, or a security convertible into, or exchangeable for, such underlying security as well as opening and closing positions in all such securities held in each account. The report must include the terms of each order, identification of the brokerage firms through which the orders were entered, the times of entry or cancellation, the times reports of execution were received and, if all or part of the order was executed, the quantity and execution price.

REGISTRATION OF OPTIONS PRINCIPALS

No branch office of a member organization shall transact options business with the public unless the principal supervisor of such branch office accepting the options transaction has been qualified as a Registered Options Principal. It is provided that this requirement shall not apply to branch offices in which not more than three Registered Options Representatives are located, as long as the options activities of the branch are supervised by a Registered Options Principal.

DISCRETIONARY ACCOUNTS

(a) **Authorization and Approval Required.**   No member organization shall exercise any discretionary power in options trading in a customer's account unless the customer has given prior written authorization and the account has been accepted in writing by a Registered Options Principal. The Senior Registered Options Principal shall review the acceptance of the account to be sure that the customer really understands the risks of the proposed transactions and strategies. (The Senior Registered Options Principal maintains a written record of his findings and the reason therefor.) Each discretionary order must be approved and initialed on the day entered by the branch office manager or other Registered Options Principal. If the branch office manager is not a Registered Options Principal, his approval shall be confirmed within reasonable time by a Registered Options Principal. Discretionary accounts shall receive frequent and appropriate review by a Compliance Registered Options Principal.

(b) **Options Programs.**   Where the discretionary account utilizes options programs involving the systematic use of one or more options strategies, the customer shall be furnished with a written descriptive material concerning the nature of the risks and conforming to the requirements set forth under Communications to Customers (see page 253).

STATEMENTS OF ACCOUNTS TO CUSTOMERS

Every member organization shall send to its options customers statements of account showing security and money positions, entries, interest charges, and any special charges that have been assessed against the account during the period covered by the statement; provided, however, that such charges need not be specifically delineated on the statement if they are otherwise accounted for on the statement and have been itemized on transaction confirmations. With respect to an options customer having a general (margin) account, such statement shall also provide the mark-to-the-market price and market value of each option position and other security position in the general (margin) account; the total value of all positions in the account; the outstanding debit balance in the account; and the general (margin) account equity. The statement shall bear a legend stating that further information with respect to commissions and other charges related to the execution of listed options transactions has been included in confirmations of such transactions previously furnished to the customer, and that such information will be made available to the customer promptly on request. The statement should also request the customer to promptly notify the firm of any material change in the customer's objectives or financial situation. Statements should be sent at least quarterly to all accounts having money or security positions during the preceding quarter, and at least monthly to all accounts having an entry during the preceding month.

Interpretation and Policies

For the purpose of the foregoing rule, general (margin) account equity shall be computed by subtracting the total of the "short" security values and any debit balance from the total "long" security values and any credit balances.

SUPERVISION OF ACCOUNTS

Each member organization shall maintain at the principal supervisory office having jurisdiction over the office servicing the customer's account, information to permit review of each customer's options account on a timely basis to determine:

(i)   the compatibility of options transactions with investment objectives and with the types of transactions for which the account was approved;

(ii)   the size and frequency of options transactions;
(iii) commission activity of the account;
(iv)   profit or loss in the account;
(v)   undue concentration in options class or classes;
(vi)   compliance with provisions of Regulation T.

FRONT-RUNNING OF BLOCKS—
SRO RULING

An educational circular of the SRO presents an enforcement policy concerning "front–running blocks." Because a block transaction in an underlying security may have an impact on the market for that security or the options covering that security (or vice versa), the SRO is concerned if its members engage in the practice of trading in options or the underlying securities. In short, traders might take advantage of inside information to make a purchase or a sale in order to profit from a market movement, either upwards or downwards. (In these cases block trades are trades of 10,000 shares or more.)

The SRO considers it as conduct inconsistent with just and equitable principals of trade for a member or persons associated with a member, in respect to an account in which such a member or person has an interest, or exercises investment discretion, to cause to be executed:

(1) an order to buy or sell an option when such member or person causing such an order to be executed has knowledge of a block transaction in the underlying security, or, (2) an order to buy or sell an underlying security when such member or person causing such order to be executed has knowledge of a block transaction in an option covering that security, prior to the time information concerning the block transaction has been made publicly available.

REVIEW QUESTIONS

1. Define an put, a call, a straddle, and a spread.
2. Illustrate by example how a listed call option is quoted in the newspapers; a put.
3. Describe the factors that influence the premium on a call option.
4. How may an investor realize a profit on a listed call option?
5. What are the main advantages of buying a call option? Are there any disadvantages?
6. Explain the hazard of writing an uncovered option. What is the margin required and how is it maintained?
7. List at least four suitability requirements that an investor should meet before being allowed to have an option account.

8.   Describe how the Options Clearing Corporation handles buy-ins.

9.   What adjustments must be made to the exercise price of a listed option and an over-the-counter traded option for cash dividends, for stock dividends, and for stock rights?

10. How does the CBOE differ from the other exchanges that trade options?

11. What is meant by diligence in opening an options account? Name eight questions which should be answered by a prospective options customer.

12   What are the two most important questions an ROP must bear in mind before making recommendations to an options customer.

13. Define the difference between sales literature and advertisements.

14. Name four types of advertisements or sales literature that under no circumstances may be used.

15. Discuss the rules pertaining to written communications to customers giving performance figures.

16. What reports must market makers file with the SRO? What reports must options firms make to customers?

17. What are "front-running-blocks?" Explain the SRO ruling.

TRUE AND FALSE QUESTIONS

		True	False
1.	The over-the-counter options market:		
a.	is a negotiated market	_____	_____
b.	is an auction market	_____	_____
c.	is a restricted market	_____	_____
d.	trades only in odd-lot options.	_____	_____
2.	By purchasing a call on a stock, the investor:	True	False
a.	believes the stock will go up	_____	_____
b.	hopes the stock will go down	_____	_____
c.	protects himself from a possible large loss on a stock he is short	_____	_____
d.	is able to buy a stock at a lower commission than if he were to buy it on the open market	_____	_____
3.	An out-of-the-money call option means that:	True	False
a.	the exercise price is lower than the market price	_____	_____
b.	the exercise price is higher than the market price	_____	_____
c.	the investor has lost his entire premium	_____	_____
d.	the investor still has some hope of making a profit on the call.	_____	_____

4. A put is: *True*   *False*
    a. a means of leveraging a stock   _____   _____
    b. an insurance policy against a sharp decline in
        a stock   _____   _____
    c. a part of a straddle   _____   _____
    d. more speculative than calls.   _____   _____
5. Writing call options: *True*   *False*
    a. can give to the holder of an underlying stock
        assurance of a higher income without fear of
        losing his security   _____   _____
    b. can be the source of a large loss if the call
        option is uncovered   _____   _____
    c. can be a source of income if the underlying
        security does not fluctuate   _____   _____
    d. should be avoided entirely.   _____   _____
6. Margin regulations for options are set by Regulation T of the Federal
    Reserve Board and: *True*   *False*
    a. require a minimum equity of at least $5,000
        for short sales and uncovered calls   _____   _____
    b. for writers of uncovered listed puts and calls,
        require a margin of 30% of the underlying
        stock value adjusted as the price of the under-
        lying security changes   _____   _____
    c. for uncovered option writers in the over-the-
        counter market the margin requirements are
        the same as in the listed markets.   _____   _____
7. The CBOE and the stock exchanges handling options:
                                                               True   *False*
    a. do not encourage the general public to trade
        in options as they are too speculative   _____   _____
    b. take great care to inform the public of the
        advantages and disadvantages of options   _____   _____
    c. require an ROP or CROP to approve an
        option account   _____   _____
    d. do not worry about the public losing money
        as the amount invested in options is usually
        small.   _____   _____
8. The Option Clearing Corporation: *True*   *False*
    a. issues the underlying stocks to clearing
        members holding call options   _____   _____
    b. pays out money to holders of put options
        wishing to exercise them   _____   _____

		True	False
c.	fixes exercise prices based on the prices of the underlying securities	___	___
d.	assigns the exercise dates in one of three four-month cycles.	___	___

9. The options exchanges:

		True	False
a.	provide liquidity by enabling the option holders to close out their options without exercising them	___	___
b.	are regulated by the SEC	___	___
c.	have stimulated large public interest in options	___	___
d.	should be phased out as more people have lost money in options than have gained.	___	___

10. If a clearing member exercises a call option and does not receive the underlying stock:

		True	False
a.	he may sue the writer of the call after 60 days	___	___
b.	he may within 5 days buy in the stock and sue the writer for the balance	___	___
c.	after 30 days, he may buy in the stock and receive the difference between his call price and the price he paid for the stock from the OCC	___	___
d.	he may buy in the stock, but he has no recourse against the writer of the call.	___	___

11. A customer desiring to open an options account:

		True	False
a.	must give detailed information about his or her financial worth, income, and occupation	___	___
b.	will be denied option trading privileges if he or she declines to answer all the questions asked	___	___
c.	must agree to advise the firm if any material change takes place in his or her financial status	___	___
d.	must receive a recent prospectus of the Options Clearing Corporation.	___	___

12. The options recommendations given to the customer:

		True	False
a.	must take into account the customer's knowledge of options and his financial worth	___	___
b.	must be approved by an ROP or an ROR	___	___
c.	must not include the writing of options unless the customer owns the stock	___	___
d.	may include any type of strategy provided the customer has received a prospectus of the OCC.	___	___

13. A compliance Registered Options Principal (CROP) or Senior Registered Options Principal (SROP) with no sale function:

		True	False
a.	must be designated by every firm dealing in options to review and propose appropriate action to secure the firm's compliance with the securities laws	_____	_____
b.	may have sales function if the firm has less than $1,000,00 in options commissions and/or less than 12 Registered Representatives	_____	_____
c.	may have sales function with the approval of the SEC.	_____	_____

14. Sales advertisements:

		True	False
a.	must be approved by the SEC prior to use	_____	_____
b.	must under no circumstances contain an untrue statement or withhold a material fact	_____	_____
c.	must be approved by the SRO prior to use	_____	_____
d.	may contain records of past recommendations and projected performance under certain circumstances	_____	_____
e.	may not under any circumstances use annualized rates	_____	_____
f.	may use attention getting headlines provided material is not misleading.	_____	_____

15. Written communications to customers:

		True	False
a.	may not contain projected performances under any circumstances	_____	_____
b.	must contain all relevant costs including interest	_____	_____
c.	may feature past performance of past recommendations or actual transactions under certain circumstances	_____	_____
d.	must be accompanied by a prospectus of the OCC if not previously sent	_____	_____
e.	must discuss the risks of the proposed transaction.	_____	_____

13

Clients' Accounts

Brokerage firms have many types of customers. These include individuals, corporations, partnerships, fiduciaries, executors, guardians, receivers, and investment advisors.

INDIVIDUAL CUSTOMERS

Cash Accounts.   If a customer opens a cash account, he or she intends simply to buy and sell securities and pay for them by cash or check. Before doing even this, however, the customer must sign a signature card, give certain information on a *new account form* and finally have the account approved by an officer, partner, or principal of the firm. The information required includes: complete name, address, phone, and social security number, business, position, and business address. Business or occupation is very important. If the customer is employed by a banking, insurance, or other financial concern, it might be necessary to obtain the permission of the customer's employer to open the account. If the customer is employed by an exchange, an NASD member firm, or a stock exchange firm, not only would permission to open the account be necessary but duplicate advices of transactions must be sent to the customer's employer. Other information would include age. No minor can open an account. The manner in which the account was acquired, special instructions concerning the collection of income, the registration and delivery of the securities, or instructions to hold them in street name are important. Finally, if applicable, a New York State affidavit must be signed by individuals who do not live or work in New York State or have an affiliation with a New York firm. The affidavit entitles them to reduced tax rates on the transfer of their securities.

As for handling the account, the customer might state that orders to buy and sell securities must be placed by designated parties only, himself, wife, his banker, or his lawyer. On the other hand, he or she might give the firm the power to trade the account. The customer would then sign a trading agreement to give the broker (named in the agreement) limited power to purchase and sell securities and invest monies.

But he or she may give the broker unlimited power to trade the account *and* withdraw securities or cash. These agreements must be signed by both the customer and the designated employee who is to do the trading. Further, the firm must keep these agreements in safekeeping for at least six years. All discretionary accounts must be reviewed regularly by a partner, officer, or principal of the firm.

If the customer wishes to buy and sell options, a special option agreement must be signed.

Margin account.　All the basic information required for a cash account must also be supplied by a customer opening a margin account. In addition, a customer's hypothecation agreement must be signed. The most important parts of this agreement provide (1) That all monies, securities, and commodities shall be subject to a general lien for the discharge of all obligations of the customer to the firm. (2) That at all times the customer will maintain margins for the account as required by the firm. (As explained on pages 200-201, the *initial* margins are set by the board of governors of the Federal Reserve System, but the maintenance of margins is determined by the firm.) (3) That debit balances will be charged interest. This agreement must be signed by the margin account customer before a witness.

Below the place for the customer's signature is a *customer's loan consent*. This states that the firm shall have the right to lend to themselves, or to others, any security held for the customer on margin. If the customer agrees to this, the customer signs again before a witness. The customer also acknowledges a credit agreement letter indicating that the customer understands the method by which interest rates are calculated and charged on *net* debit balances (i.e., debit balances less free balances).

If applicable, the margin customer might also sign a trading authorization, a New York State waiver, or an option agreement.

Joint account agreement.　A joint account might be comprised of a husband and a wife or any number of individuals. But each signer of the joint account agreement has the authority to buy, sell, or sell short securities and commodities.

The firm is instructed to make deliveries on instructions personally to any of the parties.

The liabilities of the signatories of the agreement are joint and several. Also, all property held by the firm of the signatories are subject to a lien for the discharging of their obligations.

In the event of the death of any one of the signatories, a survivor must give notice to the firm. The estate of the deceased is still jointly and severally liable with the other participants in a joint account. The joint account agreement must state the intent of the parties to create an estate as *joint tenants with the right of survivorship* or as *tenants in commonn*. Joint tenants with the right of survivorship means that, on the death of one of the participants, the other or others take his or her share. Joint tenants in common means that each participant owns a share of the account. If one of the parties dies, his or her estate is entitled to that share. There might be delays until the proper documents are obtained from the executor or administrator of the estate.

CORPORATE CUSTOMERS

Cash Accounts. Corporations opening a cash account with a brokerage firm must comply with a number of regulations.

First, the *new account report form* must be filed giving basic information about the corporation. Second, a *corporation account agreement*, authorizing the opening of a security cash account, limited authority. The president of the corporation signs this document. It states that, in accord with the resolution of the board of directors, he is authorized to open an account in the name of the corporation. The president also encloses a *customer's agreement*. The secretary also signs the corporation account agreement certifying that the officers of the corporation listed by name have been duly elected and are holding office.

The secretary also certifies the resolution of the board to open the account. This resolution (1) authorizes the opening of the account with the broker, (2) empowers the secretary to certify that the company is duly organized and that its charter empowers it to transact business in securities, (3) states that no limitation has been imposed upon such powers by its charter or bylaws (a copy of the charter and bylaws are enclosed), (4) orders the secretary to advise the brokers of the persons authorized to trade the account.

Finally, the secretary, or some authorized person, sends to the broker the signature cards signed by the persons designated to give instructions to the broker.

Margin Accounts. A *corporation account agreement* authorizing the trading in securities and commodities and permitting margin transactions and short sales is signed by the president and the secretary of the corporation. This document is similar to the corporate cash account agreement just discussed.

As in the case of an individual margin account, the following must be signed: (1) a new account report form (2) a loan consent agreement, (3) a signed credit agreement, and (4) a New York State nonresident affidavit and an option agreement, if applicable.

In addition, a certified copy of the resolution of the board authorizing the corporation to buy and sell securities on margin and sell securities short is required. Copies of the charter and bylaws should also be supplied to the broker.

UNINCORPORATED ASSOCIATIONS (PARTNERSHIPS, CHARITABLE ORGANIZATIONS, SCHOOLS, COLLEGES, CHURCHES, AND INVESTMENT CLUBS)

Cash Account. Besides the usual new account form, the unincorporated association must file with the broker a certified copy of the constitution, partnership agreement, or bylaws authorizing the purchase and sale of securities. A copy of the resolution of the trustees or directors also must be filed. This designates the persons authorized to trade the account for the association. (If applicable, the New York State nonresident affidavit and option agreement must also be filed.)

Margin Account. To open a margin account, an unincorporated association must file all the documents necessary for a cash account. In addition, a signed authorization must be filed to open a margin account. These are the same as the agreements discussed under a corporate margin account.

Fiduciaries. A fiduciary is an institution or a person holding property (money, securities, real estate, etc.) for the benefit of another. It is a general term and includes trustees, executors, guardians, and receivers. Usually, a fiduciary may *not* open a margin account, grant trading authority to others, or sell short. In years past, fiduciaries were only allowed to invest in legal securities (see page 389). Today, however, most trust instruments give the trustee much more latitude in making investments. For the most part, a fiduciary is safe from surcharge if the "prudent man rule" is followed (see page 388).

Administrator and Executor of Estates. The duties of an administrator and an executor are identical. They must collect all the assets of the deceased, pay all the debts, distribute the net assets, and, finally, after accounting to the court, seek discharge. An administrator, however, is appointed by the court for a person who has died intestate. Often the administrator is a friend of the judge. An executor is appointed under the will of the deceased. This appointment, however, must be confirmed by the court.

In opening an account with a brokerage firm, both an administrator and an executor must supply (1) a new account form, (2) an inheritance tax waiver if required to transfer registered securities, and (3) affidavits of domicile and affidavits of death satisfaction.

In addition, the administrator must file with the broker a court order appointing him or her administrator of the estate. Executors must file a certified copy of the will and a court order appointing him or her executor or executrix.

Guardian.   Guardians must file with the brokers a new account form, a certificate from the court approving his or her appointment, and, if applicable, a New York State nonresident affidavit.

Receiver in Bankruptcy.   Receivers must file a new account form and a court order evidencing his or her appointment as receiver.

Investment Advisors.   Investment advisors must be registered under the 1940 act (see page 383). A special omnibus account is set up with the brokerage firm by a subsidiary or affiliate of the investment advisor. The investment advisor has power of attorney to buy or sell for his clients who are included in the omnibus account. Their names and addresses must be disclosed when the account is opened. For the omnibus account the investment advisor must file (1) a new account form, (2) supplementary documents that are required for an association account, and (3) a New York State nonresident affidavit and option agreement, if either is applicable.

Uniform Gifts to Minors Act (UGMA).   Minors are not permitted to have a brokerage account or to have securities registered in their names. A number of states have passed model UGMA laws that permit gifts of securities to minors by turning them over to a custodian. The custodian holds the securities for the minor until he or she becomes of age. A custodian account for two or more minors has no legal standing. Once securities and cash are turned over to the custodian, they cannot be reclaimed by the donor. Further, the minor cannot give the securities to anyone. The donor should not act as custodian as the funds might be included in his estate should the donor die before the minor becomes of age.

The custodian cannot buy securities on margin, lend them, sell them short, or register them in street name. The custodian can buy and sell securities and exercise rights. If profits or losses are taken, the donor's cost prevails. For example, if a father gives his son shares of Eastman Kodak which he bought 10 years ago at $10 a share, and the custodian for his son sells it for $50 a share, the cost for capital gains purposes is $10 a share. The filing of returns and the payment of taxes are the responsibility of the minor or his parent or guardian. The custodian in turn must give annual reports to the minor and receive reasonable compensation for his services.

When the minor comes of age, the custodian turns over the securities that are registered in his or her name, thus terminating the custody arrangement.

Requirement regarding Accounts of Deceased Persons. As soon as a broker learns of the death of one of the customers of the firm, all outstanding orders must be canceled. Further, the deceased customer's assets with the firm must be frozen until the necessary documents are obtained from the administrators or the executor.

If the deceased was a partner, the broker requires the appropriate documents as well as the authority of the surviving partner or partners before executing any order.

TRANSACTIONS IN CLIENT'S ACCOUNTS

Processing the Order

In entering an order, the record must include (1) the name of the customer (if a numbered account is used, the firm must have on file a written signed statement giving the customer's name), (2) a description of the security (e.g., the NYSE symbol), (3) the number of shares, (4) the par value of bonds, (5) where the security is traded, (6) the time the order was placed, (7) and the individual placing the order. The order slip must indicate the action to be taken—to buy or to sell. If the order is to sell, it must be marked either to sell long (L) or to sell short (S), depending on the client's instruction. If the orders are in options, they must be marked "buy" or "write." If the order is to write an option, it must indicate if the option is covered or uncovered (naked). Also price qualifications must be given by the customer. These might include orders at the market, at a specific price, GTC, day, week, and so on. Settlement instructions are usually given when the account is opened, but there may be special instructions for a particular transaction.

Report of Execution

Sometimes a broker will report by telephone to the customer the execution of his or her order. Usually the customer will be advised by mail the details of the transaction, giving the settlement date when the securities must be delivered or the payment received. The broker should check the statement before it is sent to the customer. Any error should not be corrected by subsequent execution without proper approval of one of the firm's officials. An NYSE member firm making an error must render a corrected report not later than 11:00 A.M. on the second business day following the transaction.

FUNCTION OF THE BACK OFFICE

The functions of the back office are indicated by their names.

The Order Department. Usually orders are written on an order form, time stamped by the order room clerk, and telephoned to the exchanges or transacted in the over-the-counter market (see page 166). In firms that have highly automated order facilities, the order might be sent directly to the trader.

The Purchase and Sales Department. The "P&S" Department has several functions. The most important is, perhaps, making out the customers' confirmation statements. These give the details of the customers' transactions including the amount of the securities sold or bought, the commissions, the price, the proceeds or cost of the securities, and the date of delivery or of payment.

The Cashiering Department. This department accepts and pays out money and securities. It holds securities in safekeeping and arranges for their transfer through the transfer agents.

The Dividend Department. This department collects the dividends and interest on the securities held by the firm in street name for the customers and credits them to the individual accounts.

The Proxy Department. For securities held in street name, annual reports, proxies, and proxy materials are sent to the brokers. These are usually forwarded to the customers. But the customers must instruct the brokerage firms of their voting intentions, as the securities are not registered in his or her name, and the brokers vote the stock usually in accord with the customers wishes.

The Reorganization Department. This department checks the call notices for bonds and preferred stocks held by the firm in street name as well as the securities of a customer for whom they manage their funds under an investment advisory contract. Also this department arranges the conversion of convertible bonds and of convertible preferred stocks.

The Stock Record Department. This department maintains the basic records of all the customers' securities held by the brokerage firm. These records include the name of the security, its owner, the location of the security, its loan status, and so on.

The Controller. The controller is usually a partner or an officer of the firm. He is in effect the office manager. The controller is responsible for the payroll; the submission of financial reports to the exchanges and to the SEC; the preparation of budgets, cost control, and financial reports to the partners and officers; and the preparation of the customers' monthly and quarterly reports.

The Margin Department.   This department keeps a close watch on the margin accounts. When they are opened, the department checks the initial margin required by the Federal Reserve Board and by the New York Stock Exchange.

As time goes on the department checks the maintenance of margin requirement of the New York Stock Exchange or the requirement of the firm which may be more strict. If the account is undermargined, it must be corrected by the customer depositing cash, securities, or the liquidation of some of the securities in the account.

REVIEW QUESTIONS

1.   Name ten questions that must be answered by a customer on a *new account report*.
2.   Why is the occupation of a customer important on a new account report?
3.   Under what circumstances may an employee of a securities firm open an account with another securities firm?
4.   What documents must a customer sign to open a margin account?
5.   In a joint account, explain the difference between a joint tenant with right of survivorship and joint tenants in common?
6.   What documents must a corporate customer file in addition to those required by an individual?
7.   Explain the duties of a fiduciary. Can a fiduciary sell short or open a margin account?
8.   What is the difference between an executor and an administrator? What documents are required by each to open a brokerage account?
9.   Describe the purpose of the Uniform Gifts to Minors Act including the duties and restrictions of the custodian.

TRUE AND FALSE QUESTIONS

1.   The *new account form* for an individual opening a brokerage account asks all of the following questions *except:*

		True	False
a.	business		
b.	citizenship		
c.	age		
d.	race.		

2. A limited trading agreement for an individual gives the broker power:

		True	False
a.	to buy and sell securities without consulting the customer	_____	_____
b.	to buy and sell securities after giving the customer notice	_____	_____
c.	to buy, sell, and withdraw securities provided the customer is notified.	_____	_____

3. A joint account agreement provides that:

		True	False
a.	either party to the agreement may trade the account	_____	_____
b.	the signators are jointly and severally liable	_____	_____
c.	the parties must be joint tenants in common.	_____	_____

4. An individual customer opening a margin account must:

		True	False
a.	sign a customer's agreement	_____	_____
b.	agree to let the firm lend his or her securities	_____	_____
c.	maintain the margins set by the firm.	_____	_____

5. A corporation opening a cash account:

		True	False
a.	must file with the firm its charter and its bylaws and the resolution of the board authorizing the account	_____	_____
b.	can only buy and sell securities for cash	_____	_____
c.	authorizes the firm to lend the securities of the corporation	_____	_____
d.	must have the signatures of the president and secretary on the corporate account agreement.	_____	_____

6. Before a partnership can open a margin account, it must file with the brokerage firm:

		True	False
a.	a new account form	_____	_____
b.	a certified copy of the partnership agreement	_____	_____
c.	a loan consent agreement, a customer's agreement, and a signed credit agreement	_____	_____
d.	a balance sheet and income statement of the partnership.	_____	_____

7. Administrators and executors:

		True	False
a.	perform the same functions	_____	_____
b.	must supply different documents when opening a brokerage account	_____	_____
c.	both must file final reports to the court.	_____	_____
d.	can open margin accounts and sell short.	_____	_____

8. Under the Uniform Gifts to Minors Act: *True*   *False*
   a.   the custodian may not sell securities, but only
        hold the securities and buy new ones with cash   _____   _____
   b.   the custodian may give the securities back to
        the donor should he prove to be in need   _____   _____
   c.   the donor should not act as custodian   _____   _____
   d.   the minor is responsible for paying the income
        taxes on the securities held by the custodian.   _____   _____

9. Numbered accounts are: *True*   *False*
   a.   forbidden by the New York Stock Exchange   _____   _____
   b.   permitted provided the broker has a signed
        statement as to the identity of the account   _____   _____
   c.   are permitted under New York Stock Exchange
        rules even if the broker does not know the
        identity of the customer.   _____   _____

14

ECONOMICS

BACKGROUND

Economists might be divided into two schools: (1) the classical production, or micro, economists and (2) the consumption Keynesian, or macro, economists.

The classical school dates back to Adam Smith (1723–1783), author of the renowned *Wealth of Nations* (1776). Smith believed that the government should let business alone. Classical economists also believed that the business cycle was a normal phenomenon of rising business activity and booming stock markets followed by a crash in the stock markets, business decline, prolonged depression, unemployment, lower costs, and finally recovery.

The concept of consumption economics goes back to Lord Lauderdale (1759–1830). But John Maynard Keynes (pronounced Kanes) revolutionized economic thought and brought consumption economics to the attention of the world by his *General Theory of Employment Interest and Money* (1936). This somewhat technical work pointed out that consumption *(C)* plus investment *(I)* equals gross national product *(Y)*. But, when savings are greater than investment, gross national product will fall.

For years, followers of Keynes and many in the U.S. government concentrated on managing total *demand* in the economy. They reasoned that, when demand weakened, the government could stimulate the economy by spending and reducing taxes. Further, they believed that, when the economy boomed, spending should be reduced, taxes raised, and debt reduced. Unfortunately, when our economy did boom, taxes were not raised and expenditures and debt were not reduced. In recent years, the economy has continued to grow but at a slow rate, whereas inflation has accelerated at an alarming rate. As a result economic thinking has shifted to the *supply* side. That is, many economists now think capital investment should be encouraged to help businesses produce more. Also labor supply, technology, and research should be slanted more to greater production. Government regulations should also be cut to enable businesses to produce more freely. Taxes should be cut not only for business but for individuals. Professor Arthur B. Laffer of the University of Southern California claims that massive income tax cuts would actually bring more revenue to the U.S. government. While there are still many in and out of government who cling to the demand (spending) side of the economy, there is an increasing number who are stressing the supply (production) side. This should bring us to an explanation of the gross national product (GNP).

The gross national product (GNP) is the sum, at market price, of the goods and services produced in the economy during a certain period. But it is also a measure of the *expenditures*, as all the expenditures of the economy would equal the income.

The GNP in current dollars in 1979 was $2,368.0 billion. But in terms of 1972 dollars it was only $1431.1 billion. This adjustment is made by dividing the current dollar GNP by an implicit price deflator. For example, the consumer price index in 1979 was about 165.5% of the level in 1972. Thus, dividing the 1979 GNP of $2,368.0 billion by the implicit price deflator of 165.5, the 1979 GNP was $1431.1 in terms of 1972 dollars.

Perhaps the easiest way to understand GNP is from the expenditures standpoint as may be seen from the following:

Total Gross National Product (billions)	1978	1979
1. Personal consumption expenditures	$1,340.4	$1,510.0
2. Gross private domestic investment	344.5	386.2
3. Net exports (excess of imports over exports)	D12.0	D3.5
4. Government purchases of goods and services	434.0	475.3
	$2,106.9	$2,368.0

Personal consumption is by far the largest item and is carefully watched by economists for any weakening or firming of the economy. It consists of about 15% for durable goods, 39% for nondurable goods, and 46% for services.

Gross private domestic investment is also important. About 66% of this amount is nonresidential structures and producers' durable equipment, 31% is residential structures, and 3% is changes in inventory. Any sharp decline in this category is a cause for concern to the economists and politicians.

Government purchases of goods and services is self-explanatory. Federal expenditures (of which health and welfare are the largest) amounts to about 35%, and state and local expenditures the balance, or 65%. It might be pointed out that the federal and local governments can increase the GNP by increasing their spending.

Net Exports is a negative item since imports to this country have been greater than exports for years. It is a source of concern to the Administration of the country as it means an outflow of dollars.

Gross national product might be stated from another standpoint:

	1978	1979
Gross national product	$2,106.9	$2,368.0
Less: Capital consumption (depreciation)	216.9	242.4
Net national product	1,890.0	2,125.6
Less: Indirect business taxes, etc.	185.9	201.4
National income (see table below)	1,704.1	1,924.2
Personal income	1,707.6	1,923.1
Less: Personal taxes and nontax payments	256.2	300.0
Personal disposable income	1,451.4	1,623.1
Less: Personal outlays	1,375.2	1,552.1
Personal savings	76.2	72.0

Net national product is a term seldom used. It is, however, the GNP less capital consumption or depreciation on plants and other property.

National income is often confused with GNP. It is the net national product less indirect business taxes and a small amount of miscellaneous items. From an income standpoint, it was as follows:

	1978	1979
Compensation of employees	$1,301.4	$1,459.1
Proprietors' income	112.9	130.9
Rental income	23.4	26.9
Corporate profits (after taxes)	160.2	178.5
Net interest	106.2	128.8
	$1,704.1	$1,924.2

Personal income is derived by eliminating corporate profits and payments of Social Security taxes and adding the dividends, interest, and Social Security payments made to individuals.

Personal disposable income is simply personal income less tax and nontax payments.

Personal savings is the amount that is left of personal disposable income after personal outlays.

BUSINESS INDICATORS

There are three types of economic indicators: the *leading*, the *coincident*, and the *lagging*. These indicators are compiled by the U.S. Department of Commerce. They are published monthly in its *Business Conditions Digest*.

The *leading* indicators are considered by far the most significant. They are supposed to forecast the future of the economy. A composite of all the leading indicators is announced monthly and often has an influence on the securities markets. For example, a decline in this index for three months often foreshadows a recession. The most important of the 12 *leading* indicators are (1) average work week, (2) new business formations, (3) layoff rate of workers, (4) contracts for plant and equipment, (5) net changes in inventories, (6) new building permits, (7) changes in liquid assets, (8) changes in security prices, (the S&P 500), and (9) changes in money supply.

The four *coincident* indicators are (1) changes in the number of employees on nonagricultural payrolls, (2) personal income less transfer payments, (3) industrial production, and (4) trade and manufacture sales.

The five *lagging* indicators are (1) the average duration of unemployment, (2) manufacturing and trade inventories (in 1972 dollars), (3) labor cost per unit of output, (4) commercial and industrial loans, and (5) average prime rate of interest.

Sources of Statistical Information (Financial)

Many large commercial banks publish monthly and bimonthly economic letters. These are usually sent free to a selected mailing list. Many of these letters contain important statistics and articles on current financial matters. Some of the best known of these letters are:

1. *The Monthly Economic Letter* (Citibank)
2. *The Morgan Guaranty Survey* (Morgan Guaranty Trust Company)
3. *Business in Brief* (Chase Manhattan Bank)
4. *The Business Report* (Manufacturers Hanover Trust Company)

The district Federal Reserve banks will also send free monthly letters. These contain statistics and articles on regional and national matters. Perhaps the most meaningful are the letters of the Federal Reserve banks of New York and of St. Louis.

The board of governors of the Federal Reserve System in Washington, D.C. publishes the *Federal Reserve Bulletin*, $20 a year (currently). This is a veritable gold mine of statistics and articles. Statistics include those on banking, production, international trade, fiscal affairs of the United States, foreign banks and so forth.

The U.S. Department of Commerce publishes monthly the *Survey of Current Business* for $22 a year. This publication has a great number of statistics on manufacturing activity, gross national product, foreign trade, and so forth. Also the U.S. Department of Commerce publishes the *Business Conditions Digest* for $40 a year. As mentioned, this publication has charts and statistics of the different indicators.

RECESSION, DEPRESSION, AND DEPRESSION, AND DEFLATION

A *recession* is a short-term decline in stock prices, business activity, and employment, as in 1948, 1954, 1957, and 1975. During these years the monetary and fiscal policies of Lord Keynes were employed to correct the recession. Taxes were cut and money, after a period of tightness, was made easy.

A *depression* is distinguished from a recession largely by its duration and intensity. A depression might last for years and result in business and financial failures, serious unemployment, sharp decline in the securities markets, and social unrest. It is hoped that, due to government aid by unemployment insurance, bank insurance by the Federal Deposit Insurance Corporation, and more particularly by more sophisticated fiscal and monetary management, a severe depression will not occur again. There has not been a real depression since the early 1930s.

Deflation occurs when demand falters and production (supply) is greater than demand. Hence prices fall. The monetary authorities often try to dampen demand by raising interest rates and imposing credit restraints. The government might even impose higher taxes. Thus, prices are deflated and money supply and costs fall. The value of money in terms of purchasing power increases. At the present time (March 1980), the monetary authorities are trying to stem inflation by a *little* deflation. The adjective little is used because the government and the Federal Reserve authorities are always afraid of bringing on a depression by making monetary policies too restrictive.

INFLATION

Inflation was a cause of concern since the beginning of the 1970s. In August 1971 President Nixon adopted an "incomes policy" when he froze wages and prices. This policy proved a failure and was abandoned after a few months. In 1978 and particularly in 1979 inflation became really serious. Prices were rising at 13% in 1979 & 19% in 1980. President Carter's attempt to impose voluntary wage and price control as did President Nixon's incomes policy met with failure.

Inflation might be defined as too many dollars chasing too few goods, with the resultant price rises. In more detail, inflation is a combination of *cost push* and *demand pull*. Cost push is a process whereby rising costs and rising prices mutually interact with a spiraling effect. This we clearly saw in the years 1966, 1972, and 1979, when there were many wage demands followed by price increases. Demand pull also contributes to inflation. Demand pull is generated when expenditures for consumption, for investment in capital goods, and for government purchases are in excess of the nation's capacity to produce. Closely allied to the demand-pull theory of inflation is the belief of many economists that the most important element in our present economy is the *money supply*. These economists believe that, as the U.S. government has large deficits, more money is printed and hence prices rise. Therefore, the best answer to inflation is to balance the budget and, if possible, to reduce the money supply. Then we will not have too much money chasing too few goods.

Stagflation occurs when business and employment decline but prices continue to rise. For example, between 1967 and 1974 industrial production moved from 100.0 to 129.9, and consumer prices during the same period went to 147.7. But in 1975 industrial production dropped sharply to 117.8, and the consumer price index increased to 161.2. Industrial production recovered in the later 1970s to 152.0 in February 1980, an increase of 29.1% from the 1975 level, but prices rose faster, to 233.2, a gain of 44.6%. Currently (1980) many fear that this country may be headed for an even more severe period of stagflation.

MONETARY POLICIES OF THE
FEDERAL RESERVE SYSTEM

The Federal Reserve System is a regional central bank. It consists of a main office in Washington, D.C. and twelve district Federal Reserve Banks located throughout the country. There are about 5,400 member banks holding about 73% of total commercial bank deposits. The system is managed by seven governors appointed by the president of the United States. The Federal Open Market Committee (FOMC) manages the credit of the country. It consists of the aforementioned seven governors plus five of the twelve district Federal Reserve bank presidents. These presidents alternate on the FOMC with the exception of the New York president who has a permanent seat.

With this brief introduction to the Federal Reserve System, we shall move to its important role in the determination of interest rates and its attempts to control the money supply and inflation.

In simple terms, it would appear that interest rates might be determined by the demand and the supply of loanable funds. For example, if the supply of loanable funds increases faster than the demand, interest rates should fall, and vice versa. But there have been many times when this has not been true. This has been due to the intervention of the Federal Reserve System.

On Fridays each week, the Federal Reserve reports the monetary aggregates. In February 1980, the Federal Reserve gave new definitions of money supply.

M1-A includes all demand deposits of commercial banks excluding demand deposits of foreign banks and official institutions *and* currency in circulation.

M1-B includes M1-A plus all deposits subject to check including NOW accounts, credit unions and demand deposits of savings banks. M2 includes M1-B plus savings and small time deposits, money market funds, overnight repurchase agreements and overnight Euro-dollar deposits.

M1-3 includes M1-2 plus large denomination time deposits at commercial banks, savings banks, savings and loan associations and long-term repurchase agreements.

L stands for liquidity and includes M3 plus liquid assets held by individuals which include U.S. savings bonds, Treasury bills, bankers acceptances and Euro–dollars; in fact, all assets that can be easily converted into cash.

During recent years and particularly during 1979 and 1980, the money supply figures showed rapid increase. At the same time interest rates rose to new peaks. The prime rate on April 3, 1980 rose to 20%, the commercial paper (dealer) rate to 17 7/8% and the brokers' loan rate to 18 1/2%.

This apparent paradox is caused largely by attempts of the Federal Reserve authorities to restrict bank reserves and to control the growth of the money supply. The ultimate aim is to control inflation.

TOOLS OF THE FEDERAL RESERVE SYSTEM

The most effective tool of the Federal Reserve System is the Federal Open Market Committee (FOMC). The FOMC determines the credit policy of the system. For example, if the FOMC decided to tighten credit, it would instruct the manager of the FOMC account in New York to *sell* U.S. government securities. This would reduce the reserves of the member banks at the reserve banks. It would tend to cause interest rates to rise. Conversely, the purchase of U.S. government securities would increase member bank reserves and hence tend to lower interest rates. In times of recession the FOMC has made money easier in this manner to encourage business by stimulating borrowing.

Another tool of the Federal Reserve System is the discount rate. This is the rate that the Federal Reserve district banks charge their member banks for short term borrowing. By raising the rate as it did in 1980 to an all–time peak of 13%, it hoped to discourage borrowing from the Federal Reserve banks. When the discount rate is raised, it is in effect a warning to the member banks to "go easy" on lending.

The most drastic tool of the Federal Reserve System is perhaps the power to raise and lower the reserve requirement of the member banks. By raising the reserve requirement the Federal Reserve can immediately "mop up" the member bank reserves. This has been called the "meat ax" technique. Conversely, lowering the reserve requirement can immediately make money easy. This has been done during periods of bad business just as increasing reserve requirements was implemented to stem inflation in 1979.

The board of governors of the Federal Reserve System can raise or lower the margin requirement against secured loans made by brokers to customers under Regulation T, by commercial banks to their customers under Regulation U, and by others under Regulation G. But this tool has not been too effective. When margins have been raised, the market for a time goes down, but shortly resumes its upward course. Regulation Q sets a ceiling on interest on time deposits of commercial banks. There is currently much agitation for the removal of this regulation. Regulation W concerns installment buying. It is not in effect at the present time, but it could be reactivated if inflation becomes much worse than at present (1980).

Finally, there is moral suasion, sometimes called the "open mouth technique." By public speeches before and letters to bankers, the officials of the Federal Reserve caution or encourage. The member bankers are able to learn to some extent how the Federal Reserve feels about inflation, credit conditions, lending policies, and so forth.

Thus, the Federal Reserve System can restrict credit and hopefully contain inflation by (1) selling U.S. government securities, (2) raising the discount rate, (3) raising the reserve requirement, (4) raising margin requirements, and (5) warning bankers to restrict loans.

In 1979, the Federal Reserve adopted most of these policies. If, on the other hand, the Federal Reserve wished to stimulate business, the reverse of all these actions might be employed. In an ideal world, monetary and fiscal policy should provide stable prices, economic growth, full employment, and balance-of-payments equilibrium. But government fiscal policy is also very important.

In any event, the chief aim at present (April 1980) is to control inflation. This the Federal Reserve hopes to accomplish by reducing bank reserves, which would force the banks to curtail loans that in turn would
create deposits. This would reduce the growth of the money supply (M1 and
M2). On the other hand, if we have a serious recession and unemployment increases, the Federal Reserve may have to reverse its policies and increase the bank reserves, which would increase the money supply as well as
cause interest rates to fall. In this event, we may have a bad case of stagflation. That is, business would continue to decline but prices would continue
to rise.

FISCAL POLICIES OF THE FEDERAL
GOVERNMENT

Under the Full Employment Act of 1946, it was set forth that it should
be the policy of the U.S. government to seek *maximum employment*. This
does not mean that the whole work force in the United States should be employed. There will always be fractional unemployment. This is caused by
people changing jobs, by people who do not want to work, or by some who
cannot work due to disabilities. Probably the nation's work force could be
considered fully employed if there were only 4% unemployed.

In 1982 total revenues of the U.S. government were $618 billion and
total disbursements were $728 billion with a deficit of $110 billion. This is
one of a long line of deficits and is one of the main causes of inflation. At
present (July, 1983), the Administration is making valiant efforts to balance
the budget in 1984. But in 1983, it is estimated that the expenditures will be
about $808 billion and the receipts only $598 billion, leaving a deficit of
$210 billion.

For the last 45 years, the U.S. government and the monetary authorities (largely under the influence of Keynes) have tried to minimize the
swings of the business cycle. In periods of recession or depression, monetary and fiscal policy has been coordinated. Taxes have been lowered,
money supply has been made easy, and government expenditures have been
expanded.

AUTOMATIC STABILIZERS

In periods of declining business activity, it is a difficult and lengthy
process to get relief legislation through Congress. But there are automatic
stabilizers that come into play as business declines. As unemployment rises,

unemployment insurance payments are made to those out of work; as farm
and other commodity prices decline, price support payments are made;
Social Security payments increase due to the addition to their rolls of those
seeking early retirement; the defense department increases or expedites its
orders. All these actions will bring about a larger cash flow to the economy.
But, unfortunately, they will also cause greater deficits and, hence, inflation
potential. Finally, private savings are perhaps the best stabilizer. In the beginning of a depression, savers lose confidence in the economy and increase
their savings. But, as the public saves more, less is spent on consumption
and capital investment. Therefore, the GNP declines along with savings.
This is called the *paradox of savings or thrift*. That is, increased savings
causes an actual reduction in the volume of savings and investment. On balance, the administration has some discretionary power as far as spending
for defense, public works, and so forth, but congress maintains strict control over taxing power.

DEVALUATION

Basically, devaluation is undertaken to lower the parity of a currency.
For years the currencies of the world were set in terms of gold. Between
1933 and 1971 the price of gold in the United States was set at $35 an ounce.
But the dollar was not convertible into gold, nor could any individual buy
or even hold gold. Not until 1977 could individuals trade in gold.

During World War II, currencies were rigidly controlled. In 1945,
after the war, the International Monetary Fund (IMF) was formed and currency parities for all members were set. But in the subsequent years many of
the currencies of the members were subject to strain and parities had to be
adjusted. The dollar, already in short supply was being sent all over the
western world. Under the Marshall Plan new plants were being built by
U.S. funds to help restore war-torn economies.

In 1971 President Nixon ended the convertibility of the dollar and allowed it to go free. A crisis developed in Europe as a result. In December of
that year, the international bankers met at the Smithsonian Institute. They
set approximate parities for all the leading currencies. The price of gold was
set at $38 an ounce. (In February 1973 it was raised to $42.22.)

In 1973 the Organization of Petroleum Exporting Countries (OPEC)
raised the price of oil fourfold. This brought about a world crisis. Many
countries who were dependent on oil had to borrow to finance their current
deficits. In the Arab–Israeli War, OPEC cut off the shipment of oil to the
West for months. Further, OPEC has on frequent occasions raised the price
of oil and will probably continue to do so in the foreseeable future.

As a result of the world economic confusion, many countries, particularly those in the West, came to the conclusion that the parities of their currencies could not be sustained. The West German mark, the Swiss franc, and the Japanese yen in the late 1970s were particularly strong but the U.S. dollar was very weak. Therefore, many countries came to the conclusion that, by allowing their currencies to float, they could best control their money supply and hence inflation.

As far as the United States was concerned, in 1976, 1977, and 1978 and again in 1979, imports exceeded exports by a substantial amount. In other words, the *balance of trade* was unfavorable. Dollars went abroad in a veritable flood. The value of the dollar in terms of other currencies declined. Here it might be explained that there is no actual quotation for the dollar. But, in terms of other currencies, the value of the dollar rises and falls. For example, on September 19, 1979, the dollar could buy 1.8073 German marks compared with 1.8088 on the previous day and 2.3401 four years ago. As the United States has larger and larger balance-of-payments deficits, the dollar's purchasing power will decline, and inflation in this country will increase.

Also it should be pointed out that the balance of payments is divided into two main categories: the current account and the capital account.

The current account includes merchandise exports and imports (sometimes referred to as the balance of trade). Also included are net military transactions, net investment income, other service income transactions, remittance, pensions, and U.S. government grants.

The capital account reflects the increase or decrease in the net debtor or net creditor status of the United States. That is, it reflects the changes in private assets held abroad and the changes in foreign private assets in the United States.

The *gold*, or *U.S. official asset account* is carried as a memo item in the balance-of-payments statement. At the end of 1979, U.S. reserve assets amounted to $18.9 billion, of which $11.2 billion was gold, $5.0 billion was foreign currencies and reserves at the International Monetary Fund, and $2.7 billion was Special Drawing Rights (SDRs).

SPECIAL DRAWING RIGHTS (SDRs)

The idea of Special Drawing Rights was first suggested by J. M. Keynes. The International Monetary Fund believed that SDRs would add to the monetary base of world currencies and contribute to greater stability. The first SDRs were issued in 1970.

Essentially an SDR is an asset created by the IMF based on gold and a "basket" of foreign currencies held by the IMF. A weighted average of 16 currencies is used. The IMF allocates the SDRs to various members. Countries use the SDRs in the same way that U.S. banks use the Federal funds market—to tide over temporary shortages.

The Incomes Policy

This is a policy of controlling prices and wages by government fiat. It is the same as if a housewife clamps the lid on a pressure cooker. The boiling water in the cooker is the insistent demands of labor for higher wages coupled with the attempts of the corporations to offset these demands with higher prices. Both attempt to force up the lid. The lid is the government, which tries to keep prices and wages down. However, when the lid is removed, watch out! Governments have learned from experience that when controls are removed, prices rise rapidly.

VALUE ADDED TAX (VAT)

The value added tax (VAT) has been an efficient means of raising revenue in a number of European countries, notably France, for a number of years. Furthermore, it is being considered as a means of raising as much as $60 billion by the current administration.

Although in theory the VAT is a flat percentage paid on the value added to a product or a service at each stage of production or distribution, actually it would probably be a flat percentage of the total sales at each stage of the production or distribution process. Also, the manufacturer is allowed to credit against his tax liability the total amount of the VAT that he paid to his suppliers. For example, assuming a 10% VAT rate and sales of a steel company of $10,000,000, the VAT liability would be $1,000,000. But, assuming the mill purchased $3,000,000 of iron ore, coke, and sulphur, the credit would be $300,000, or the VAT paid by the supplier. Therefore, it will be extremely important for the suppliers to record on their bills of sale the VAT they have paid so that the buyer may take credit.

It is believed that the VAT would help our export balance, as rebates would be given for exports and a border tax would be imposed on imports. Furthermore, the VAT would be ideal for revenue sharing with the states and municipalities; it would help finance education; it would eliminate burdensome sales taxes; it would permit reductions in personal and corporate income taxes.

At the present time (1980), congressional committees seem to be in favor of some form of VAT. It is estimated that as much as $150 billion a year could be collected with a 10% tax rate. This money could be used to offset a rollback of Social Security taxes and a substantial reduction in federal income taxes. The new tax would be added to the price of goods. It would therefore be easy to collect. Further, it would be a tax that would be hard to evade. It has been estimated that substantial taxes have not been paid. These would be picked up by the VAT.

REVIEW QUESTIONS

1. What is the difference between the *classical* and the *consumption* schools of economics?
2. Describe the expenditure components of the gross national product.
3. Name the leading indicators, the coincident indicators, and the lagging indicators. Which of these is followed most closely and why?
4. Define inflation and stagflation. What are the possible remedies for inflation?
5. Describe the tools that the Federal Reserve might use to make money easy or tight.
6. Distinguish between a depression and a recession. What actions have the U.S. government taken to alleviate their bad effects?
7. Define devaluation. What were the events that led up to our present currency problems?
8. Describe the components of our balance of payments. Why does the United States have such large deficits.
9. Explain how the value added tax is supposed to work.

TRUE AND FALSE QUESTIONS

		True	False
1.	Keynesian or consumption economics aims to:		
a.	stimulate consumption	____	____
b.	encourage spending by the government and business	____	____
c.	favor individual free choice	____	____
d.	reduce government control.	____	____
2.	Business cycles such as occurred in the years 1929–1933 are perhaps a thing of the past because of:	True	False
a.	massive government action	____	____
b.	intelligent business planning	____	____
c.	labor unions	____	____
d.	the Council of Economic Advisors.	____	____
3.	The gross national product is:	True	False
a.	the sum of the sales of all the industrial corporations in the United States	____	____
b.	the same as the national income	____	____

c. the sum at market price of the goods and   *True*   *False*
    services produced by the economy during a
    period   _____   _____
d. the expenditures for consumption, for private
    domestic investment, for government pur-
    chases, and for miscellaneous items.   _____   _____

4. The difference between depression and recession is that:

                                                      True   *False*

a. a depression is a prolonged period of low busi-
    ness activity with unemployment, depressed
    stock prices, and low profits   _____   _____
b. a recession is the same but for a shorter period _____   _____
c. a depression is a thing of the past, but
    recessions are still possible   _____   _____
d. depressions have been eliminated, or at least
    greatly modified, by possible government
    spending policies.   _____   _____

5. Inflation might be defined as a condition in which: *True*   *False*
a. rising costs push up prices   _____   _____
b. demand for goods is greater than production   _____   _____
c. too many dollars chase too few goods   _____   _____
d. stock prices of industrial companies rise
    sharply.   _____   _____

6. The balance of payments means: *True*   *False*
a. summary statement showing the receipts from
    and payments to foreign countries to the
    United States during a calendar year   _____   _____
b. a favorable balance of payments will always
    occur when exports are greater than imports,
    and vice versa.   _____   _____

7. Companies hurt by inflation would include all the the following *except:*

                                                      True   *False*

a. electric public utilities   _____   _____
b. petroleum-producing companies   _____   _____
c. railroads   _____   _____
d. industrial companies with large debt.   _____   _____

8. Inflation might be cured by: *True*   *False*
a. lowering the general rate of interest   _____   _____
b. the U.S. government's balancing the budget
    and cutting the increase in the money supply   _____   _____
c. wage and price controls   _____   _____
d. increasing production.   _____   _____

15

Technical Analysis
of The Stock Market

FUNDAMENTAL ANALYSIS VERSUS
TECHNICAL ANALYSIS

Security analysts have been divided for years into two schools of thought: the fundamental and the technical. The *fundamental analyst* considers the qualitative factors of a company, such as its outlook, its management, its research, as well as the quantitative factors, which include its earnings, its balance sheet, its price, its dividend, and any number of ratios. The *technical analyst* is interested primarily in the action of the stock market in general and the price action of the particular company that the analyst is following. These price actions are recorded on charts.

In recent years a number of security analysts have been using the computer to evaluate stocks and portfolio policies. This might be called the quantitative school, as complicated mathematical formulas are used.

Some analysts have been successful with one method, others with the other. But success seems to depend on the individual's interpretation of the data or charts. It is believed that a keen analyst should be well grounded in the fundamentals of a company but should not ignore the technical factors. The reason is that many follow the technical approach, so when a certain formation appears on the charts, mass buying often follows if the formation is favorable, and mass selling if it is unfavorable.

STOCK AVERAGES

One of the best ways to follow the day-to-day changes in the market as a whole is to watch one of the several stock averages. Perhaps the most generally used is the Dow Jones average of 30 industrial stocks. Less well known are the other Dow Jones averages. These are the 20 transportation companies, the 15 utilities, and the 65 composite average. Others are the Standard & Poor's, the American Stock Exchange price index, the NASDAQ, and the New York Stock Exchange indexes.

The following table shows these indexes as they appeared in *The Wall Street Journal* on Friday, September 21, 1979 (based on prices as of September 20, 1979).

DOW JONES CLOSING AVERAGES

	1979	— THURSDAY — — Change — 1978			Yr. Ago Chg.
Industrials.........	893.69 +	17.24	+	1.97%	861.14 + 3.78%
Transportation.....	264.37 +	1.22	+	0.46%	242.01 + 9.24%
Utilities...........	107.00 +	1.49	+	1.41%	105.99 + 0.95%
Composite	313.13 +	4.45	+	1.44%	298.78 + 4.80%

OTHER MARKET INDICATORS

	1979	— Change —		1978
N.Y.S.E. Composite	62.85 +	1.09	+1.76%	57.36
Industrial	70.65 +	1.55	+2.24%	62.73
Utility	38.13 +	0.02	+0.05%	39.60
Transportation	52.82 +	0.38	+0.72%	48.20
Financial	67.37 +	0.46	+0.69%	62.08
Amer Ex Mkt Val Index	227.61 +	3.74	+1.67%	166.48
Nasdaq OTC Composite	150.20 +	0.76	+0.51%	132.10
Industrial	167.90 +	1.14	+0.68%	145.89
Insurance	163.24 +	0.73	+0.45%	137.05
Banks	114.19 −	0.06	+0.05%	109.06
Stand. & Poor's 500	110.51 +	2.23	+2.06%	101.90
400 Industrial	123.56 +	2.80	+2.32%	112.86

The most recent of these indexes is the NASDAQ, the oldest is the Dow Jones. Perhaps the most comprehensive is the index developed by the New York Stock Exchange in 1966. As may be seen from the preceding tabulation, it consists of five indexes as follows:

1,109 issues of Industrial Companies (manufacturing, merchandising, mining, and service)
  71 issues of Transportation Companies (airline, motor transport, railroad, and shipping)
 189 issues of Utility Companies (operating and holding companies)
 212 issues of Finance Companies (banks, closed-end investment companies, real estate, and savings and loan companies)
1,581 issues of Composite Companies (all of the above)

The basis is 50, or the average price of all stocks as of December 31, 1965.

Stock splits and dividends have the effect of reducing the per share price and are compensated for by simply increasing the number of shares divided into the value of the stocks, which are calculated every half-hour of a trading day.

The advantages of this index are two: first, it is much broader than any of the other indexes because it covers many more stocks; second, it tends to play down the wide swings of the other averages, in particular the Dow Jones Industrial average of 30 stocks. For example, on September 20, 1979 the press and brokers made much of the Dow Jones average's rise of 17.24 points in one session. It ignored the New York Stock Exchange composite index that gave a more accurate picture of the market. It is the Dow Jones 30-stock average that gets the publicity.

The NASDAQ (National Association of Securities Dealers Automated Quotation System) commenced operation in May 1971. Through its automated quotation system, which is connected directly to the wire service computers, the NASD provides daily, monthly, and weekly stock price indexes for over-the-counter securities in different industry categories. All domestic over-the-counter stocks listed are included in the indexes. The system adjusts daily for capitalization changes, such as stock splits, as well as listings and delistings. The indexes are updated at five-minute intervals and are available to three levels of NASDAQ subscribers (see page 177 for details on levels), the wire services, and the newspapers. Each index has been assigned a base value that was derived from the prevailing market price on February 5, 1971.

At the end of 1979, 2,670 securities were quoted by the NASDAQ system. From these quotations, NASDAQ compiles seven indexes. They are the composite index of all stocks, the industrial index (consisting of about 65% of the total), the insurance and bank stocks (about 5% each), the finance company stocks (about 14% of the total), and the public utility and transportation stocks, which combined represented about 11% of the total.

Standard & Poor's Corporation publishes a daily index of a composite of 500 stocks and individual indexes for each component. These are 400 industrials and 20 transportation, 40 public utilities, and 40 finance companies. *Barron's* publishes weekly a 50-stock average along with other statistics, such as the projected per share earnings for the total 50 stocks, five-year average earnings for the group, price-earnings ratios, and earnings for the year just ended.

Dow Jones Bond Average is a weekly index of 20 bonds—10 utility and 10 industrial bonds. Also individual indexes are published for each of these categories.

AMEX Exchange Market Value Index System measures the changes in the aggregate market value of shares, ADRs, and warrants. Market value is the share prices of about 800 listed share prices of Amex issues multiplied by the number of shares outstanding of each company. At the close of August 31, 1971, the level of the market value index was set arbitrarily at 100.00, which represented the aggregate market value of all AMEX stocks, warrants, and ADRs on that day. It is called a weighted index because each issue exerts an influence on the level of the index in proportion to the number of shares it has outstanding.

THE DOW THEORY

The average that is followed by many is the Dow Jones average of 30 industrial stocks. This average is reported every half-hour during the trading time from 10:00 A.M. to 4:00 P.M. It is constructed by taking the market price of the 30 stocks and dividing the total by a divisor. This divisor is adjusted downward for stock dividends and splits over the years. As of November 30, 1979 it stood at 1.465.

From the Dow Jones average many market technicians attempt to predict the future of the stock market by the so-called *Dow theory*. Some of the principles of the Dow theory are

1. When the market is in a basic upward trend, the market will rise and fall in intermediate swings, *but the peak of each swing will be higher than the preceding peak.* But it is impossible to determine when the peak of the cycle has been reached. See upper portion of the illustration that appears below.

2. When the market is in a basic downward trend, each decline will be followed by a recovery in price. But each recovery will not be as high as the preceding peak. Here again, however, history has shown that it is not possible to determine when the bottom has been reached. This might be illustrated by the falling, irregular curve shown in the graph.

3. At times another average, such as the Dow Jones average of 20 transportation issues, confirms the upward trend of the 30 industrials. If it does confirm the upward movement, it is a signal that a further upward movement may be expected. If the industrial average goes up above its preceding peak but the transportation average does not rise above its preceding peak or declines, this is a signal that the industrial rise is false and will turn into a decline.

Many investors have charted these averages for years back and have attempted to work out theories like the one explained. On the basis of these theories, many have endeavored to forecast the future course of the stock market. Some have been moderately successful, but the woods are full of people who have lost money trying to forecast the future of the stock market. It is believed that the averages are useful and interesting in showing the course of the market and for measuring changes, but not for forecasting the future.

THE ODD-LOT THEORY

Another method of market forecasting is the *odd-lot theory*. As explained, the buyers of odd lots and the New York Stock Exchange are buyers of 1–99 shares or less than the unit of trading. The theory is that the odd-lot buyers are uninformed and are therefore wrong. For example, when odd-lot purchases exceed sales, the theory holds that the market will go down, and vice versa. The odd-lot purchases and sales are reported daily by the New York Stock Exchange.

A simple ratio may be constructed by dividing the sales of odd lots by the purchases. If sales exceed purchases, the index will rise and indicate a bullish trend, and if purchases exceed sales, the index will fall. However, care should be exercised in using this index, as the "uninformed small investor" is *often right*. For instance, during the long declines in the market in 1970 and in 1971 the "uninformed odd lotters" were heavy sellers on balance. In fact during most of the 1970s, odd-lot holders have been sellers.

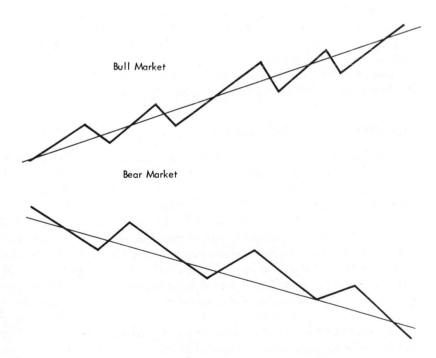

Bull Market

Bear Market

THE ADVANCE-DECLINE THEORY

Some market technicians place greater faith in the *advance-decline* theory. This in effect measures the strength of a market's rise or fall. Each day *The Wall Street Journal* reports the number of issues that advance and the number that decline. A simple index may be made by dividing the number of stocks that advanced by the total issues traded. For instance on September 20, 1979, 918 stocks advanced out of 1,885 traded. An index can be calculated by dividing the stocks that advanced, or 918, by the total traded, or 1,885, which equals 48.7%. This is not a good percentage and may indicate that the 17.24-point gain of the Dow Jones 30 industrials on that day was a false move.

This index should be plotted on the same chart as some stock index. If the advance-decline index rises faster than, say, the Dow Jones Industrial Average, the market could be said to have relative strength. In other words, the market is broad and therefore a rise might be expected. But, if the market rises rapidly and the advance-decline index rises less rapidly or even falls, this indicates that the stock market may fall.

TRADING VOLUME THEORY

Closely related to the advance-decline theory is the trading volume, which is watched by some technicians. For example, traders like to see heavy volume in a rising market and dislike it in a declining market. Also, in a sharply declining market, if the volume does not increase, the feeling is that the selling will dry up and the decline may not continue. There are a number of chartists who follow the volume of transactions on individual stocks as well as for the market as a whole.

THE SHORT INTEREST THEORY

There are many technicians who watch the short interest position as reported in the middle of the month by the New York Stock Exchange. This is the total of the shares sold *short* on the exchange. It is helpful to compare the total short interest with the average volume for the month and arrive at a ratio. For example, on March 14, 1980, customers were short 49,150,000 shares and the average volume for the month was 47,411,000 shares. Dividing the short interest by the average volume equals 1.04. As a general rule technicians consider a ratio of 2.00 as bullish, 1.50 as neutral, and 1.00 as bearish. The theory behind a heavy short interest compared with volume is that when a rally does occur, the short sellers will become anxious and seek to cover or buy in their stock. Thus a large short interest will cause a rally in the market to be more steep as the shorts run to cover. Short interest figures are available not only in the aggregate but for individual stocks.

THE CONFIDENCE INDEX

This is a ratio of the yield on Barron's 10 high-grade bonds to the yield on the Dow Jones 40 bonds (high and medium grade). For example, in the week ended March 24, 1980, the average yield on *Barron's* best-grade bonds was 12.18% and the average yield on *Barron's* intermediate-grade bonds was 13.25%. The Confidence Index was calculated by dividing 12.18 by 13.25 or 91.9. The Confidence Index appears every week in *Barron's* under the heading of Market Laboratory. The theory behind the Confidence Index is that, as the so-called smart-money investors switch from stocks to high-grade bonds, the rates on high-grade bonds will go down. As the rates on high-grade bonds go down, the Confidence Index will fall. When this happens it is a signal according to some that the market will fall. Conversely, when the smart money is confident of the future, purchases are made of the lesser quality bonds, which drives the medium-grade rates down and hence the Confidence Index rises. At times, particularly from 1946 to 1961, the Confidence Index was a good guide to future market action. But due to the recent upsets in the money and capital markets, the Confidence Index has lost some of its value. Another criticism of this index is the fact that it does not take into consideration the large shifts in the demand and supply of capital.

CASH POSITION

Cash position refers to the customers' funds at brokerage firms available for investment in common stocks. In December 1979, brokerage customers' net free credit balances in margin and cash accounts amounted to $5,130 million compared with $2,700 million in 1977 and $2,440 million in 1976. Thus customers' free balances have been showing an upward trend since 1976.

Investment companies, exclusive of money-market funds, reported a cash position of $4,988 million at the end of 1979, or 10.3% of total assets of $48,613 million. In addition there were about $61,100 million of money-market funds that could be liquidated. Also the pension funds are currently (1980) reported to have large holdings of cash assets (i.e., short-term Treasuries, commercial bank CDs, and so forth).

It is clear that the stronger the cash position of investors, the more vigorous the rally in a stock market can be. Holders of cash become restive as the stock market starts up and soon cannot resist the temptation to "get aboard" the market with their cash, thus further stimulating the rally. On the other hand, if investors' cash is low, there is less of a cushion to a declining market.

INSIDERS' TRANSACTIONS

Every month *The Wall Street Journal* publishes the purchases and sales of stock of officers and directors and holders of 10% or more of the stock of their company. Although these transactions should be noted with care, it does not always mean that something is wrong if an officer is selling the stock of his company. For instance, an officer might be selling his stock to pay off a mortgage, some other debt, or to raise money to buy an annuity. An officer might be transferring the stock to his children. Conversely, the officer might be buying stock to exercise rights given to management. Nevertheless, when an officer sells his stock, it might or might not foreshadow bad news for the company; also, the purchase might augur good news. At all events the analyst should investigate any large transaction by an "insider."

SEASONAL PATTERNS

Too great reliance should not be placed on any statement that certain days or months are good or bad ones to trade stocks. But there are certain factors that normally influence the market in the absence of disturbing political or business news. For example, there is an expression that a trader should be a four-day bull. This means that the market will go up on the last day of the month and the first three days of the following month because of the investment demand for dividends that will be paid on the first of each month. All of January is believed by some to be a good month for the market because the year-end extra plus the regular dividends will have to be invested. April may not be so good a month because many will be selling stocks to raise money to pay taxes. In May and June there will be selling to raise money to pay for summer vacations. Often there is a summer rally. There is an old rule followed by some traders: "Buy stocks after the fourth of July and sell them after Labor Day and pay for your vacation." October, November, and December are usually not good months because many are selling for tax purposes. To repeat, too great dependence should not be placed on these seasonal factors as something almost always occurs that upsets the pattern.

DAILY PATTERNS

Almost all technical analysts who watch the tape believe that there are certain daily patterns. But few can agree what they are and, more important, how to use them to advantage. Almost all will caution investors that none of these patterns is reliable. For example, many feel that all things being equal the market in the first hour of trading will sell higher than in the last. If this be so, it might be a good idea for a buyer of stocks to make purchases in the closing hour and sales in the opening hour. But this is often not the case. For instance, when in the closing hour of a day there is heavy selling and a decline in the market, it is often the case that on the following trading day the market continues its decline.

Mondays are frequently bad days and have been christened "Blue Mondays." This is often caused by the announcement of bad news on the weekend. Customers thinking over this bad news are inclined to sell stocks.

The stock market seems to exhibit trends lasting weeks and even months rather than days. When the market is in one of these trends, either up or down, it is easy to predict the daily movements. For example, in early 1970 money was very tight, large firms were failing, business was bad. Hence every day, almost without interruption, the market went down. Conversely, when good news turns the market around, it will go up day after day.

In general money is not made on a day-to-day basis but by careful selection of the stock of a good company and sitting with it until it appears that it is overpriced.

CHART INTERPRETATIONS

One of the charts frequently used by technicians is the *point and figure* chart. Point and figure charts are constructed by marking with an X every time a stock moves up an interval, say, a point and an O every time it goes down. Whenever a stock changes directions (moves up or down), the new mark is moved to the right. No account is taken of time or of volume. Basically, point and figure charts reflect the supply and demand for stocks. The chartist is particularly interested in sidewise price trends, as they claim there is a relation between the lateral price movement and the subsequent vertical movement. The following is an example of a bullish triple top formation:

Stock Price					
29					
28					X
27	X		X		X
26	X	O	X	O	X
25	X	O	X	O	
24		O			

Starting at 25 the stock moves up to 27, then declines to 24, then moves back to 27, declines to 25, then back to a *triple top* at 27, and then moves upward.

Individual Formations

These are used to forcast both the averages and the individual stocks.

The head and shoulders tops with a declining neckline is one of the most common. In this case the line chart would look as follows and indicate a *bearish* trend:

A bullish formation would be the reverse or a head and shoulders bottom and look as follows:

In both cases, the volume of buying and selling is watched. In the head and shoulders tops, for example, if the buying volume is weak on the up side and strong on the down, the formation is particularly unfavorable.

Another formation is a chart that shows a resistance point or support level. This is illustrated as follows:

All these phenomena are interesting and should be understood because when they occur there are many who notice them and often take action in the securities market. Unfortunately, there is no technique yet discovered that can, with uniform accuracy, predict the market.

REVIEW QUESTIONS

1. Explain the difference between fundamental, technical, and mathematical analysis of stocks.

2. Describe the different stock indexes and averages. What are the advantages of the New York Stock Exchange average over the Dow Jones average?

3. What is the Dow theory? What is meant by confirmation of averages? Head and shoulders formation?

4. Explain the odd-lot theory. How would you follow this theory?

5. What is the advance–decline theory and what does it measure? What is the importance of trading volume?

6. According to the short interest theory, what would be the significance of a short interest of 48,619,000 shares and an average volume of 25,291,000?

7. Under normal circumstances, what is the best time of a trading day to buy a stock? To sell a stock?

TRUE AND FALSE QUESTIONS

		True	False
1.	In fundamental appraisal of a stock, the analyst would consider all of the following *except*:		
	a. research	___	___
	b. management	___	___
	c. price action	___	___
	d. outlook.	___	___
2.	The best approach to the analysis of a stock is:	True	False
	a. the fundamental	___	___
	b. the technical	___	___
	c. both technical and fundamental.	___	___
3.	The Dow theory:	True	False
	a. assumes major trends, intermediate swings, and minor movements	___	___
	b. predicts the future of the stock market	___	___
	c. shows the past course of the market and measures changes.	___	___
4.	The odd-lot theory:	True	False
	a. assumes that, when the public is buying odd-lot shares on balance, the market will go up due to increased demand	___	___
	b. assumes that, when the public is selling odd lots on balance, the market will go up	___	___
	c. is an infallible theory because the public is *always* wrong about the market.	___	___
5.	The advance–decline theory:	True	False
	a. measures the strength of the advance of the stock market	___	___

		True	False
b.	indicates the market will rise if the advance–decline index moves up faster than the Dow Jones index of 30 stocks	____	____
c.	is affected in great part by trading volume.	____	____

6. The short interest theory:

		True	False
a.	is the relationship between the short interest and daily average trading volume for a month	____	____
b.	forecasts a bullish market when short interest is equal to the average volume for the month	____	____
c.	forecasts a bearish market when short interest is two times the average volume for the month.	____	____

7. A support level is:

		True	False
a.	the price level at which a company will guarantee its stock	____	____
b.	the price at which a stock has sold for a long time; then rises and falls will be supported at the price at which many buyers are reluctant to sell	____	____
c.	the price at which the stock will tend to stop on a decline, but when it falls below this level it is called a breakthrough.	____	____

16

Industry Analysis

Industry life cycles might be described as (1) the invention or early development stage; (2) the growth cycle as the industry becomes established; (3) the stabilization or mature, cycle; and (4) the declining cycle. Examples of industries that have completed these cycles are textiles steel and perhaps automobiles.

There are three types of industries: defensive, growth, and cyclical.

Defensive Industries

These industries usually report steady earnings and dividends even during a recession. But in good times they show only moderate gains in earnings and dividends. Generally included in this category are the telephone, electric public utility, food, and beverage industries.

Growth Industries

These are industries that grow year after year at a steady rate of, say, 7% or better. Their dividends are usually low in comparison with earnings. Their expenditures for research and capital equipment are large. In the 1970s, good growth industries included the electronics, computer, oil drilling, drug, and photographic industries.

Cyclical Industries

The earnings, dividends, and stock prices of cyclical companies fluctuate widely during business cycles. The stocks in cyclical industries should not be held as long-term investments but may be used as trading vehicles— to be bought at the bottom of the business cycle and sold at the top. Cyclical industries include the steel, nonferrous metal, railroad, automobile, and automobile supply industries.

FACTORS AFFECTING INDUSTRY PERFORMANCE

Comparison of Industry Sales with GNP

This method of analysis is particularly useful for a large company that sells consumer products. For example, a comparison can be made by taking a percentage of the sales of Sears, Roebuck and Company to the GNP. This will show whether Sears is gaining or losing its position over the years relative to the economy. Also, comparisons can be made between companies of an industry to indicate any shift in market share.

Production and Inventory Statistics

A decline in the ratio of sales to inventories in an industry indicates a possible undesirable accumulation in inventories. The Department of Commerce publishes monthly a ratio of new orders to inventories for the country. This ratio is keenly watched by economists, particularly if a recession is threatened.

Wage Ratios

These are particularly important in labor-intensive industries such as steel. The ratio of wage costs to net sales can be used to show the relative vulnerability of a steel company to a wage increase. For example, Inland Steel Company has a much lower wage ratio than does Bethlehem Steel Company. Labor relations are particularly important in all industries. Some have particularly good relations, such as the office equipment and photographic industries. Some have fair labor relations, such as automobile and steel, and some have poor relations, such as textiles and coal.

Price Levels

In periods of inflation and spiraling costs, managers of businesses must be able to raise their selling prices. Regulations of public service companies make this very difficult and at times impossible to accomplish. But in many industries prices can be adjusted upward to preserve profit margins. Industries dependent on a particular commodity, such as the copper or aluminum processors, usually carry a large inventory in the commodity. Depending on the method of inventory valuation (see page 312), the profits of the corporation may reflect a substantial gain or loss that in turn affects dividend payments.

Sales and Deliveries

Sales growth is important and can mean larger profits and dividends. But the analyst should note the rate of growth. Steady growth is better than wide fluctuations of sales. Some companies have large sales and small profits, however. The Great Atlantic & Pacific Tea Company reports large sales but very small profits. Several companies are in trouble despite sales in the billions. Sales growth of a company is fine as long as it is translated into wider profit margins.

Profit Margins

This is the *percentage of net sales* remaining after all costs and expenses other than of nonoperating costs (such as interest and federal income taxes) have been deducted. Stating it another way, the operating profit is divided by net sales to obtain the operating profit margin. Trends in operating profit margins indicate to the investor the company's control over operating expenses. Further, in analyzing a company's profit margin, it should be compared with other companies' or an industry average. Industries with high profit margins include the computer, electronic, oil, and chemical industries. Profit margins are sometimes calculated by dividing net income by net sales. But we prefer the former method.

Growth Forecasts

Economists will often give forecasts of the possible future growth of their industries. Officers of companies from time to time give speeches before security analysts societies in various cities. Almost always they give forecasts of the future of their companies. Sometimes they also forecast earnings. But management in general is reluctant to make forecasts to individual security analysts for fear of censure by the SEC. Ironically, the SEC is considering the imposition of rules to require management to make forecasts, particularly in new security offerings. Management, however, is reluctant to do this for fear of lawsuits if the forecasts prove substantially wrong.

Management Performance

One of the most important reasons one industry or one company in an industry moves forward is good management. Management in industries that are highly regulated have little opportunity to be innovative. But, in unregulated and highly competitive industries, superior management can have an important influence. Even in industries that in general have good managers there are some laggards. Well-managed industries are thought to be the electronics, computer, drug, and chemical groups. The steel, nonferrous metal, and textile industries are generally regarded as being poorly managed.

It is often difficult for an outsider to evaluate management. Yet there are certain guidelines that are obvious or should be sought out by direct questioning of the broker or security analyst recommending the stock. Some of these questions might be

1. Who are the chief executive officers? Have they trained successors? What about their training program? Do they have an obsessive desire for their company to succeed? (This has been said about the management of International Business Machines Corporation.)
2. What are the personal relationships of management with its employees, its customers, its stockholders, trade groups, and the public?
3. Where are the plants located? Has management endeavored to correct environmental problems?
4. What are the relations of management with the regulatory authorities?
5. Does management make judicious use of debt?
6. Has management promoted growth internally or by wise mergers?
7. Has the company acquired unrelated or unprofitable companies?

SOURCES OF INDUSTRY STATISTICS

The monthly *Federal Reserve Bulletin* publishes the quarterly sales, profits, and dividends of eight important industries. The Department of Commerce publishes monthly the *Survey of Current Business*, which contains detailed production statistics on a number of industries including chemical, food, electrical equipment, and metals as well as foreign trade and GNP. It also contains profits data.

Standard & Poor's Corporation has two publications devoted to industries: *Industry Surveys* and *Statistical Service. Industry Surveys* are detailed basic analyses of a number of industries. Areas covered include order backlogs, sales by products, problems, and detailed financial statistics. Also there are current analyses of each industry giving up-to-date developments. *Current Statistics* is a large loose-leaf volume with many monetary and economic as well as industry statistics going back many years.

The *financial press* includes: *The New York Times, The Wall Street Journal,* and *The Journal of Commerce* (all dailies). Weekly publications are *Business Week, Barron's, Forbes,* and *U.S. News and World Report.* Monthly publications are *The Financial Analysts Journal, Fortune, Harvard Business Review,* and *The Journal of Finance.* A most important annual (January) publication is the *Annual Report of the President* prepared by the Council of Economic Advisors.

Trade publications are *Aviation Week, Ward's Automotive Report, Chemical Week, Electrical World, Oil and Gas Journal, Rubber Age,* and *Iron Age.* In the regulated industries, there is the *Public Utility Fortnightly* and *Railway Age.*

NEWER APPROACHES

The Efficient Market Theory

Many large-capitalization stocks such as General Motors, IBM, AT&T, and Exxon can be bought and sold in large volume, with small transaction costs and with little change in prices. Therefore, in general, investors that wish to buy or sell according to the news may get into or out of these stocks easily. But investors don't always sell on receipt of bad news. For example, they may be reluctant to take large capital gains or they may wish to hold the stock for sentimental reasons. Also the market for some stocks on the national exchanges and particularly on the over-the-counter market is far from efficient. An order to buy or sell a few thousand shares of a stock might cause a wide fluctuation in price. This fluctuation would be due to market reasons and not to many acting on information. With these exceptions, those who believe in an efficient market hold that stocks properly reflect the true or intrinsic value of the individual stocks. The efficient market theorists reject fundamental and technical analysis as a waste of time. Rather, they believe there is no such thing as an overvalued or an undervalued stock.

The Random Walk Hypothesis

The random walk hypothesis was developed by Professor Eugene F. Fama in 1965. It relates the price performance of a stock to an aimless, or random, walk. Stocks rise and fall, aimlessly blown up and down by the desires of supposedly informed investors. As good news about a stock is learned, purchases are made and the stock rises, and vice versa for bad news. The random walk theory assumes that all important information about a stock is known to its investors and that the market price is close to the intrinsic value. Random walk theorists also believe that the past history of a stock has no influence on its future price performance.

Performance Benchmarks— Beta and Alpha Factors

The beta (Greek letter β) represents the variation or volatility of a stock relative to the market in general. For example, a stock that fluctuates up and down the same as the general market (as measured by some index) would have a beta coefficient of 1.00. If the fluctuation of a stock is less than the average—that is, if it is more stable—the beta would be less than 1.00. The beta can be used to select stocks that should be bought at different phases of the market. For instance, when it is believed that the general market is too high, the high-beta stocks should be sold and the low-beta stocks bought. But in a period of depressed markets, the investor might buy the high-beta stocks if he thinks that the market will rise. *Value Line Investment Survey* gives betas on every one of its company reports. *Value Line* betas well below 1.00 include the electric public utilities, railroads, and some banks. High betas, well above 1.00, include the air transport, electrical equipment, and aerospace stocks. Stocks with betas of about 1.00 are General Motors and IBM.

The alpha factor (the Greek letter α) is seldom used by analysts. However, according to Professor Harry C. Sauvain, the alpha is the average rate of return from the individual stock for the period of measurement relative to the rate of return from the stock price index, both measured by the investment performance relatives. An alpha of $+5\%$ means that the rate of return was five percentage points greater than was that of the index; if alpha is -5%, the rate was five percentage points less.[1]

Monitoring Performance

Finally, the investor should carefully monitor his portfolio. No stock or bond should be bought and then put away and forgotten. Things change rapidly in industries and in companies. If the fortunes of a company start to deteriorate, its security should be switched to another company with a more promising outlook. There is an old rule: "Cut your losses and let your profits run." Further, an investor should appraise his portfolio at least once a month. Every quarter the investor should review his portfolio with his financial advisor. Particularly toward the end of the year, the portfolio should be carefully reviewed for tax switches.

[1]See Harry C. Sauvain, *Investment Management*, 4th ed. (Englewood Cliffs, N.J.: Prentice-Hall, 1973), pp. 206–207

READING THE FINANCIAL NEWS

Newspaper Security Quotations

The most complete quotations are found in *The Wall Street Journal* and *The New York Times* (financial section). Out-of-town papers quote the leading stocks and some bonds. Found in *The Wall Street Journal* and the *Times* are the following quotations:

Stocks

1. The consolidated tapes of the New York and the American stock exchanges
2. The NASDAQ over-the-counter stocks
3. The important investment company stocks
4. Options traded on the Chicago Board of Options, and the AMEX, the Midwest, and the Philadelphia exchanges

Bonds

1. Corporate bonds—only a few on the New York and American stock exchanges (see over the counter, page 166)
2. U.S. government and agency bonds, notes, and bills
3. Municipal bonds—only a few revenue securities (see *Blue List*, over-the-counter, page 65)

Miscellaneous Quotations

1. Regional exchanges
2. Foreign stock markets and foreign exchange
3. Commodities

Both papers give in summary form the quarterly and annual *earnings statements*. Also a section in *The Wall Street Journal* is devoted to *dividend* payments. *Tombstone* advertisements (see page 71) give little information except the size of the issue and its price and, in the case of a bond, its coupon rate and maturity. A list of the leading underwriters is given. *Tender offers* are usually explained in detail. These offers were made frequently in the 1970s when large companies were trying to take over smaller concerns, sometimes over the objections of the smaller company's management and even the Federal Trade Commission. On occasion, a company will make a tender offer to buy in some of its own outstanding stock at prices above the market. *Redemption* notices of bonds and preferred stocks are published in both papers. It is important for the investor holding convertible bonds and convertible preferreds to take note of these as he could own convertible securities that are selling above their call prices.

REVIEW QUESTIONS

1. Define defensive, cyclical, and growth industries. Give an example of a company in each.
2. What factors affect industry performance?
3. How are profit margins calculated? What is their significance?
4. Name at least five criteria you would consider in evaluating management.
5. What are the most important government and private sources of information for industry statistics and trade information?
6. What is meant by the random walk hypothesis? Can it be used to predict the future prices of a stock.
7. Explain the beta factor and illustrate how it may be used to trade stocks.
8. What does the industry approach to security analysis mean? Select and give reasons for your choice of three industries that have a favorable outlook and three that have an unfavorable outlook.

TRUE AND FALSE QUESTIONS

1. An industry life cycle means:

		True	False
a.	the number of years that a company is in existence	_____	_____
b.	pioneering, growth, mature, and decline periods	_____	_____
c.	the cyclical fluctuations of a company's sales over the years.	_____	_____

2. Profit margins may be calculated by taking the percentage of:

		True	False
a.	operating profits to sales	_____	_____
b.	net income to sales	_____	_____
c.	net income to units of production.	_____	_____

3. Good management has been effective particularly in the following industries:

		True	False
a.	electric public utilities	_____	_____
b.	railroad	_____	_____
c.	computer	_____	_____
d.	drug.	_____	_____

4. The beta factor is:

		True	False
a.	a measure of the volatility of a stock compared with an average of stocks	_____	_____
b.	less important than the alpha factor	_____	_____
c.	a good guide to the trader in stocks.	_____	_____

5. The random walk hypothesis: *True*   *False*
    a. stresses the importance of past history of a
        stock   _____   _____
    b. relates the price performance of a stock to a
        random, or aimless, walk   _____   _____
    c. assumes that all important information about
        a stock is known to investors.   _____   _____

17

SECURITIES ANALYSIS I
THE BALANCE SHEET

The balance sheet shows the financial condition of a company on a particular day, usually the last day of the year. We call it a balance sheet because all the assets equal, or balance with, all the liabilities plus the stockholders' equity. The balance sheet shows a fixed condition of the company; the income statement shows where the money came from, how it was spent, and what is left. Although the balance sheet is related to the income statement, it is distinctly separate from it.

A simple balance sheet is presented here. The *assets*, listed on the left-hand side, include cash, inventory, accounts receivable, and property, making total assets of $1,000,000. The *liabilities*, listed on the right-hand side, include the debts of the company to bondholders, the U.S. government, the trade, and the long-term creditors. These debts total $700,000.

Now, we have assets of $1,000,000 and liabilities of $700,000. Clearly, the assets do not balance with the liabilities. The difference of $300,000 belongs to the stockholders. We call this *stockholders' equity*. In other words, if all the assets were sold for $1,000,000 and the creditors were paid the $700,000 due them, the owners or stockholders would get $300,000. The $300,000 is a liability in that it is due the stockholders, but it is also a *balancing item* between the assets and the liabilities. Thus, a balance sheet is intended to show the financial position of a business as of a certain date by listing the items owned, the items owed, and the equity of the owners.

Table 17-1 illustrates how these items balance.

It is suggested that the reader look at the more detailed balance sheet of the Lobuck Corporation (page 321) and keep in mind the three main categories: assets, liabilities, and stockholders' equity. We will now discuss the items of this balance sheet in detail.

310

TABLE 17-1

Assets		December 31, 1979	Liabilities
Cash	$ 200,000	Taxes	$ 200,000
Accounts receivable	100,000	Accounts payable	200,000
Inventory	200,000		
Property	500,000	Bond	300,000
			700,000
		Stockholders' equity	300,000
Total assets	$1,000,000		$1,000,000

ASSETS

The assets of a business are the items of value it owns. There are three main types of assets: current assets, fixed assets, and other assets.

Current assets usually include cash on hand, or in banks, U.S. government securities, marketable securities, accounts receivable, sometimes notes receivable, and inventories. We call them current assets because they can be turned into cash in the normal course of business, usually within one year.

The statement of Lobuck Corporation (Table 17-3) shows the following current assets:

Item		
1	Cash	$ 100,000
2	U.S. government securities	500,000
3	Accounts and notes receivable	500,000
4	Inventories	400,000
5	Total current assets	$1,500,000

Cash (item 1) is clearly a current asset. But intelligent corporate treasurers keep cash in their banks at a minimum. They place as much as possible of their liquid funds in cash items such as Treasury bills, CDs and the like. Municipal and other marketable securities are held by financial concerns but seldom by industrial companies. It is reassuring to see on a company's balance sheet a large amount of cash and marketable securities in relation to the amount of current liabilities. This means that a company can easily pay its current debts. Also, a company with large cash resources can expand its own business or even buy another business.

Accounts receivable (item 3) is the amount of money due to a company from its customers. Companies often sell goods to customers in return for promises to pay. The evidence of such a promise is the order, either verbal or in writing. Sometimes customers do not pay their bills promptly or default on their payments. To cover an actual or possible loss, a reserve is set up for bad debts; this amount is deducted from the accounts receivable, and only the net is carried as a current asset. In good times, the losses on accounts receivable are small, and a company usually has little difficulty in turning the accounts receivable into cash. Sometimes *notes receivable* appear as a current asset. Here the customers have signed papers or notes promising that their debts will be paid. This is usually done when the terms for payment are long, running into several months.

Inventories (item 4) include (1) raw materials that the company has purchased (e.g., steel, lumber, cloth); (2) goods in process or partly finished products; and (3) finished products (e.g., automobiles, furniture and suits, etc.). Inventories are usually the least current of the current assets. Trouble often occurs when a company is unable to sell its old inventory. We can spot this if the inventory over the years increases, when compared with current assets or sales. Comparison should only be made with companies in the same fields, as in some businesses companies traditionally carry high or low inventories.

The cost of inventories may be determined by a number of different methods, but the most common are *last in first out*, or LIFO, and *first in first out*, or FIFO.

Under the LIFO method, all sales are *assumed* to be made from inventories acquired most recently, and the value of the inventory left on hand is prorated back to the earliest purchases.

Under the FIFO method, all sales are *assumed* to be made from inventories acquired during the earlier periods, and the inventory left on hand is prorated back to the most recent purchases.

Thus, in a period of rising prices the LIFO method is the conservative, since it understates the profits and inventory value. The reverse is true with the FIFO method.

The following table illustrates how cost of inventories is determined under the LIFO and FIFO methods:

TABLE 17-2

Inventory Determination

LIFO Inventory Cost Determination
(assume sales of 30 units @ $100 per unit = $3,000

Inventory for Sales Assumed to Be Taken from the Most Recent Purchases

December 10	Purchase 10 units @ $90 per unit	$ 900
November 15	Purchase 10 units @ $70 per unit	700
October 12	Purchase 10 units @ $60 per unit	600
		$2,200
Balance		$ 800

FIFO Inventory Cost Determination

Inventory on Hand Prorated Back to the Earliest Purchases		
Sept. 10	Purchase 10 units @ $60 per unit	$ 600
July 8	Purchase 10 units @ $50 per unit	500
July 5	Purchase 10 units @ $55 per unit	550
Inventory value		$1,650
Balance		$1,350

But under FIFO the opposite would be true. The inventory taken for sales would be valued at $1,650 instead of $2,200, giving a balance of $1,350 ($3,000 − $1,650 = $1,350) instead of $800 under LIFO.

The inventory left under FIFO would be $2,200 instead of $1,650 under LIFO.

Quick assets are a little different from current assets in that they *exclude* inventory. In other words, *quick assets* include cash, marketable securities, and accounts and notes receivable.

Fixed assets usually include property, plant, buildings, and equipment. Companies sometimes show these items separately but more as a single figure, as in the Lobuck Corporation, item 6:

Item		
6	Property, plant, and equipment	$1,400,000
7	Less reserve for depreciation	700,000
		$ 700,000

The property, plant, and equipment are the assets from which the company obtains its main source of income. Sometimes companies own valuable patents or copyrights that yield a substantial income in the form of royalties.

It is difficult to evaluate fixed assets. Almost all companies carry their plant and equipment *at cost*, which means the amount of money the plant and equipment cost the company either to build or to buy. But the cost figure may be meaningless if the plants were built when prices were much lower. Every year, a prudent management customarily writes off, by a charge against income, a part of the cost of the plant, builings, and equipment. The charge to income is called depreciation. Depreciation as well as depletion and amortization will be discussed on page 331-332. At all events, the sum of all these annual charges to depreciation for the Lobuck Corporation is $700,000. As shown in the preceding table, this reserve for depreciation is carried as a deduction from a fixed asset. Thus, the net property, building, and equipment is figured by deducting the accumulated reserves for, or provision for, depreciation from the cost of the fixed assets. The actual value of the fixed asset might be much more or less than the net amount.

Other assets usually include investments in subsidiaries, and intangible assets such as trademarks and patents. The other assets of the Lobuck Corporation are as follows:

Item		
8	Investments in subsidiaries	$174,000
9	Patents, trademarks, and goodwill	20,000

Investments in subsidiaries or intermediate assets (item 8) usually include investments in operations that complement those of the parent company. For example, General Motors Corporation owns a subsidiary called General Motors Acceptance Corporation. This subsidiary handles the financing of automobiles and other products of the parent company.

Also, many companies, such as Ford Motor Company and International Harvester Company, have large investments in subsidiary companies operating in foreign countries.

Intangible assets include patents, trademarks, brand names, and goodwill. They are usually not a large item. Many companies carry them on the balance sheet at $1. A *patent* (item 9) is an exclusive right given by the U.S. government to a device or process. For example, Sanford L. Cluett some years ago invented a process for preshrinking linen before it was tailored. The patent had considerable value to Cluett, Peabody & Co., Inc.

A *trademark* (item 9) is a picture, drawing, or design used by a manufacturer to distinguish his goods. A trademark does not have a legal life and can be used by a company as long as it is in business. A well-known trademark is the flying red horse of the Mobil Corporation.

A *brand name* is simply a special name given by a company to one of its products to make it better known. Thus American Brands, Inc. hopes that the public will ask for a "Lucky Strike" cigarette.

Goodwill (item 9) often appears on the balance sheet of a company that has bought another company at a price in excess of its book or net asset value.

Sundry deferred charges (not shown) are sometimes called prepaid expenses. Examples are fire insurance premiums or rent paid in advance.

LIABILITIES

Liabilities are the amounts owed by a business and include current liabilities and long-term liabilities. Although stockholders' equity is carried on the liability side of the balance sheet, it is not strictly a liability that must be paid. The stockholders receive their equity only if the company is liquidated and after all creditors are paid.

Current liabilities are called "current" because they are debts that usually must be paid by the corporation within one year. They include accounts payable, dividends payable, notes payable, bank loans payable, taxes payable, wages payable, and long-term debt due within one year.

Current liabilities of Lobuck Corporation are as follows:

Item		
11	Accounts payable	$200,000
12	Notes payable	150,000
13	Accrued taxes	250,000
14	Accrued salaries and wages	25,000
15	Other current liabilities	75,000
16	Total current liabilities	$700,000

Accounts payable (item 11) are the amounts owed for goods received or for services rendered. They are usually paid promptly.

Notes payable (item 12) are often necessary when a company must borrow from a bank to purchase inventories or supplies or to pay wages over a seasonal peak. When the finished products are sold, the bank loans are paid. Almost all bank loans are short term. That is, they are due within one year. Sometimes a company will buy supplies and equipment and give notes to the manufacturers.

Accrued taxes or *reserve for accrued taxes* (item 13) are one of the most important of the current liabilities. Corporations, like most individuals, must pay income taxes to the U.S. government. For most large corporations this amounts to about half their income after expenses. The companies calculate the taxes that will be due based on estimated earnings. In addition, most companies owe money for state taxes and local real estate taxes. Clearly, all these liabilities must be paid within a year. Also, payroll taxes, frequently substantial, are carried as a current liability.

Accrued salaries and wages (item 14) are, as the name indicates, the amount of money due the employees of the company. Most of the employees are paid on a weekly or semimonthly basis. Thus the accumulated wages are usually not large.

Other current liabilities (item 15) includes interest accrued on bonds, dividends declared but not paid, and installments on long-term debt due within one year. Accrued interest and dividends declared are usually not large amounts, but debt installment can be an important item. Often industrial companies issue bonds and agree to pay off a substantial part of these bonds every year.

For example on December 31, 1978, the American Brands, Inc. had outstanding $556,791,000 of debt of various maturities and interest rates. But a substantial part of this debt was due in one year. At the end of 1978, the current portion of this long term debt was $160,314,000, which sum was carried as a current liability.

As we have mentioned, current liabilities are debts that the corporations must pay within a year. Long-term liabilities, or funded debt, are debts that are not due until after a year's time. They usually include all types of bonds: mortgage, debenture, and refunding bonds as well as equipment trust certificates and serial bank loans. They do not include reserve for depreciation or common or preferred stocks. A more complete discussion of these bonds is given in Chapter 2. Essentially, a bond is a written promise of the corporation to pay a fixed sum in the future, usually over five years, plus interest. From item 17 we see that Lobuck Corporation on June 1, 1996 must pay $400,000 on first-mortgage bonds. In the meantime, it must pay interest at the rate of 8% a year or $32,000 (8% $\times$ $400,000). Bonded debt is also called funded debt. Bonds are sold by corporations to buy land, build plants, purchase equipment, and so forth.

As was explained in Chapter 2, par or stated value of a bond is $1,000. Thus it is often important for an analyst to break down a bond account into number of bonds. For example, a $50,000,000 bond issue would be 50,000 of $1,000 bonds. If we assume interest on these bonds at 8%, the dollar interest charges would be $80 $\times$ 50,000, or $4,000,000.

We also class term loans of commercial banks and insurance companies as long-term liabilities. Here the company may borrow from banks or insurance companies to buy fixed assets, to add to current assets, to retire debt, and so forth, but the company agrees to pay the term loan in installments over a period of from three to five years.

STOCKHOLDERS' EQUITY OR NET WORTH

Stockholders' equity usually consists of capital stock and retained earnings or surplus.

The capital stock is the preferred and common stock originally subscribed by the stockholders. When a corporation is formed, a stated number of common shares is authorized, and sometimes preferred shares are authorized. A part or all of these authorized shares may be issued and sold. The authorized but unissued shares are not part of the capitalization but are held in reserve for a future time. Common and preferred shares usually have a par or stated value.

The net worth of Lobuck Corporation is as follows:

Item		
18	Preferred stock — 3,600 shares — 5% — $100 par	$360,000
19	Common stock — 100,000 shares — $4 par	400,000
20	Retained earnings (earned surplus)	434,000
21	Capital surplus	100,000

The *preferred stock* (item 18) on the balance sheet has a par value of $100, which is the usual par value for preferred stocks. The number of shares outstanding can be obtained by dividing the par value into the dollar amount outstanding. Because our balance sheet shows $360,000 of preferred stock outstanding, the number of shares would be $360,000/100 or 3,600 shares. Par value of $100 does not mean that the stock is worth $100. Also, the company is in no way obligated to pay $100 a share on the preferred (see page 11).

The *common stock* (item 19), like the preferred, is usually carried at a *par value* or *stated value*. As in the case of the preferred stock, the number of shares may be obtained by dividing the dollar amount of the common stock by the par or *stated value*. This would be $400,000 divided by $4.00 par value or 100,000 shares. As was explained in detail in Chapter 1, the par value has no relation to the market or intrinsic value of the stock. Par value is simply an arbitrarily assigned figure.

However, there is a distinction between par value and stated value. *Par value* is the arbitrarily assigned amount at which the stock is carried on the financial statement. It is sometimes called face value. It is also the amount that the company must receive for each share of stock issued. Most state laws provide that this par value—$1, $5, $10, or $100—has to be fully paid when the original or new stock is sold for the company to have fully paid and nonassessable stocks. High par values make it difficult for companies to sell new stock, particularly if business has declined and the market value is below the par value.

Hence, *no-par* laws have been passed in a number of states. These laws permit corporations to issue no-par stocks without face value, but they require that such stock have a *stated* or *assigned* value, usually at least $1.

Under no-par law, assigned value has to be paid into the corporation, and any excess can be called surplus.

The analyst should practice converting the book value of a common stock account to the number of shares given the par value. For example, if the common stock account is carried at $10,000,000 and the par value of the stock is $10, the number of shares would be 1,000,000.

Retained earnings or *earned surplus* (item 20) is the accumulated earnings over the years that have not been paid out to the stockholders in dividends. These earnings have been "plowed back" into the company. That is, the officers of the company might have used these excess earnings to buy more inventory, to add to plant, to buy more equipment, and so forth. For this reason, the investor should not take the term "retained earnings" too literally. These retained earnings are not held in cash that can be paid out to the stockholder. In almost all cases, the retained earnings are invested, wisely or unwisely, in the business. Sometimes a company may have a large retained earnings account but, due to poor earnings or a weak financial condition, can pay only small dividends to the stockholder. An example of this situation is the case of the old New York Central Railroad Company. This railroad reported *surplus* (retained earnings) of $369,943,000 at the end of 1964 but could pay only a small dividend. The New York Central Railroad Company used the term surplus instead of retained earnings. This is the older form and is still followed by some companies. The American Institute of Certified Public Accountants prefers the term *retained earnings*. Sometimes companies use the terms "reinvested earnings," "earnings employed in the business," or "earnings retained."

Capital or *paid-in surplus* (item 21) occurs when the stockholders pay to the company for stock at the time of issuance an amount in excess of par or stated value of the stock. This excess amount is carried as capital surplus on the liability side of the balance sheet but is invested in the business just as earned surplus is. For example, Lobuck Corporation might start with 100,000 shares of $4 par value, or $400,000. The subscription price of the stock might be $5, or a total of $500,000 (100,000 shares times $5). This would mean that $400,000 would be carried as the capital and $100,000 as capital or paid-in surplus. Sometimes managements wish to start their companies with extra surplus. This gives the company a chance to get started and to absorb initial losses without invading the capital stock account. Normally, operating losses are not charged to capital surplus or paid-in surplus but, rather, to earned surplus. It will help the investor to keep in mind that *retained earnings* is a balancing item between all the assets on the one hand and the liabilities plus stocks (common and preferred) on the other. It is not a store of available funds.

The *capital structure*, or the *capitalization* as it is sometimes called, is the total amount of funds invested in the business. The buyers of the bonds when they were first sold supplied funds to the corporation. The subscribers to the common and preferred stocks also supplied funds to the corporation. But only those initial subscribers to the bonds and stocks supplied capital. To buy a bond or stock in the market adds nothing to the funds of the company after it has been sold initially. In short, the capitalization or the capital structure of a corporation is the stocks (common and perhaps preferred), the bonds, the retained earnings (or earned surplus), and the capital surplus. The authorized but unissued stock is *not* part of the capitalization.

The capitalization of Lobuck Corporation (Table 17-3) is the funded debt, the preferred and common stock, and the surplus, as follows:

Item		
17	First-mortgage bonds—8% due June 1996	$ 400,000
18	Preferred stock—3,600 shares—5%—$100 par	360,000
19	Common stock—100,000 shares—$4 par	400,000
20	Retained earnings (earned surplus)	434,000
21	Capital surplus	100,000
	Total capitalization	$1,694,000

Sometimes a corporation will set up *reserves* for contingencies. This entails segregating funds from the surplus account for possible loss, possible plant addition, and so forth. Although this sum is not an actual liability, as is a *reserve* for federal income taxes, it earmarks the surplus in a sense and prevents its being paid out in dividends.

The *book value*, net asset value, or net worth of a common stock is the theoretical amount per share that a stockholder could receive if the corporation went out of existence by distributing all its assets less debts to the stockholders. In other words it is the liquidating value. This assumes that the assets can be liquidated at book value, which is often not the case.

We figure that the theoretical book or liquidating value of Lobuck Corporation equals $9.34 a share as follows:

Item		
19	Common stock—100,000 shares—$4 par	$ 400,000
20	Retained earnings (earned surplus)	434,000
21	Capital surplus	100,000
	Total equity for common stock	$ 934,000
	Per share of common equals $934,000 divided by 100,000 shares of common equals $9.34	

It should be stressed that this is the *theoretical* book value. Book value as such is not an accurate figure because of the difficulty in determining the intrinsic worth of many assets. Furthermore, in almost all cases the book value of a stock bears *no* relation to its *market* value. For example, at the end of 1979, Xerox had an estimated book value of $39.00 a share compared with a market value on March 24, 1980 of $55 a share. But the United States Steel Corporation on the same dates had an estimated book value of $53.16 a share compared with a market price of $17 a share. *Liquidating value* means the amount a stockholder could realize if the company were liquidated—that is, the assets sold and the debts paid. This amount could be more or less than the book value. It is largely a theoretical concept, because a company is almost never liquidated unless it is in difficulty. In this event, the amount realized in liquidation is almost always substantially less than the net worth or book value as shown on the balance sheet.

Treasury stock is not shown in the illustration but is important and was discussed on page 2.

ANALYSIS OF THE BALANCE SHEET

Perhaps the easiest way to analyze a balance sheet is by the use of balance sheet ratios. A balance sheet ratio is the relationship of one part of the balance sheet to another.

The *current ratio* is the relationship of current assets to current liabilities—it is the current assets divided by the current liabilities. In our balance sheet following, total current assets (item 5) are $1,500,000 and current liabilities (item 16) are $700,000. Thus the current ratio is $1,500,000 ÷ $700,000, or 2.14. Usually we like to see a current ratio of 2.00 or more, depending on the type of business. In the case of a public utility or a railroad, a current ratio is not particularly important. Also we should always look at the proportion of current assets. For example, if inventories have been increasing over the years, it may mean that a large part of the current assets are in illiquid inventories. This would mean that a company might not be able to meet its current liabilities as they mature. In a similar manner, accounts or notes receivable might increase sharply and become illiquid.

Cash items to current liabilities[1] is a useful comparison. It shows how much cash and government securities the company has available to meet its current debts. In the following table, cash (item 1) of $100,000 plus U.S. government securities (item 2) of $500,000 equals $600,000.

---

[1]Sometimes called *liquidity* ratio.

TABLE 17-3

The Lobuck Corporation Balance Sheet

Assets		December 31, 1980
1	Cash	$ 100,000
2	U.S. government securities	500,000
3	Accounts Receivable	500,000
4	Inventories	400,000
5	Total current assets	$1,500,000
6	Property, plant, and equipment	1,400,000
7	Less Reserve for Depreciation	700,000
		$ 700,000
8	Investments in subsidiaries	174,000
9	Patents, trademarks, and goodwill	20,000
10	Total assets	$2,394,000

Liabilities and Stockholders' Equity		
11	Accounts payable	$ 200,000
12	Notes payable	150,000
13	Accrued taxes	250,000
14	Accrued salaries and wages	25,000
15	Other current liabilities	75,000
16	Total current liabilities	$ 700,000
17	First-mortgage bonds—8%—due June 1, 1996	400,000
18	Preferred stock—3,600 shares—5%—$100 par	360,000
19	Common stock—100,000 shares—$4 par	400,000
20	Retained earnings (earned surplus)	434,000
21	Capital surplus	100,000
22	Total liabilities and Stockholders' Equity	$2,394,000

We should compare this with current liabilities (item 16) of $700,000. Thus, cash items of $600,000 divided by current liabilities of $700,000 gives a ratio of 0.86. Usually a satisfactory cash items ratio is between 0.50 and 0.75.

Working capital, net working capital, or *net current assets* is simply the excess of *current* assets over *current* liabilities. In Table 17-3 it would be current assets (item 5) of $1,500,000 less current liabilities (item 16) of $700,000, or $800,000. Large working capital, or net current assets as it is sometimes called, means that the company has free liquid funds. These funds can be used to acquire new assets to improve credit standing by making prompt payments to creditors or by paying funded debt.

Net current assets, or working capital per share, is calculated by subtracting current liabilities from current assets and then dividing by the number of shares. In Lobuck Corporation's balance sheet, current assets were $1,500,000. Subtracting the current liabilities of $700,000 would leave net current assets, or working capital, of $800,000. Dividing this amount by 100,000 shares of common would result in a net working capital of $8.00 a share. Some security analysts recommend a stock when it is selling below its net working capital per share, that is, provided other factors are favorable. In a recent study (1979) 27 well-known listed stocks were selling below their working capital per share.

Most companies in their annual reports give their stockholders a statement of the *sources* and *uses* of funds, which explain the changes in working capital for the fiscal year. For example, the following is a sources and uses statement:

TABLE 17-4

Sources & Uses of Funds Sources of Working Capital	December 31, 1979–1980 1980
From operations	
Net income	$169,650
Depreciation	50,900
Proceeds from sale of debt	20,500
Sale of property	7,800
Deferred taxes	3,000
Total sources	$251,850
Uses of Working Capital	
Purchase of plant	$105,860
Cash dividends	70,150
Reduction of long-term debt	10,600
Total uses	$186,610
Increase (decrease) in working capital	$ 65,240

The *working capital-to-debt ratio* is the relationship between the net working capital and the debt—in this case, working capital of $800,000 divided by debt of $400,000 (item 17), or 2.00. This is a very satisfactory ratio. Customarily, in an industrial concern we like to see at least a ratio of 1.00. This means that working capital is equal to debt. This should not be considered a hard-and-fast rule. Companies in the aluminum and aviation fields have a low ratio of working capital to debt. These companies are expanding through sales and earnings at a rapid rate and can support large debt. Nevertheless, a low working capital-to-debt ratio should be investigated.

The *quick assets* provide a good test of the ability of a business to satisfy its obligations or meet contingencies. They are the *total current assets less inventory.* The inventory of a company is usually a substantial portion of the current assets, and, although given a cash value, it is more difficult to convert the inventory into cash than other current assets such as marketable securities or accounts receivables.

The *net quick assets* are the current assets less the inventory and less the current liabilities.

The *quick,* or *acid-test, ratio*[2] of a balance sheet is the ratio of current assets *less* inventory or quick assets to current liabilities. In our balance sheet, it would be current assets of $1,500,000 less inventory of $400,000 equals $1,100,000 divided by current liabilities of $700,000, or 1.57. Usually a satisfactory acid-test ratio is about 1.00. This is called the acid test because inventory is the current asset which fluctuates the most. Inventory can be old and very illiquid. Therefore, to exclude it from current assets leaves cash, U.S. government securities, which clearly are liquid, and accounts receivable, which *usually* are liquid. These can be tested by the income account, as will be shown in Chapter 18.

The inventory as a percentage of current assets is obtained by dividing the inventory by the current assets. For example, the inventory of Lobuck Corporation of $400,000 divided by the current assets of $1,500,000 indicates that the inventory is 26.6% of current assets. Should the percentage increase over the years, it might be a danger signal. At the end of 1979, leading corporations in the United States reported inventories of $468 billion, or 40.0% of current assets of $1,170 billion.

Still a better way of testing inventory is to use the *inventory turnover ratio,* also discussed on page 336. Suffice it to say here that it is obtained by dividing the year-end inventory into the annual sales to see how many times the inventory turns over in a year. If this turnover *slows down* over the years, it might indicate that the inventory is not moving and that old and perhaps unmarketable inventory is accumulating. Some analysts prefer to divide to average inventory over the year into the cost of sales.

The accounts receivable appearing on the balance sheet should also be tested by the so-called *collection ratio.* One way of obtaining this ratio is by dividing the total sales for the year by the number of days in a year and dividing this figure into the dollar value of the receivables. If we assume

---

[2]Sometimes called the net quick asset ratio.

sales (as we do later in this book) of $5,000,000 and accounts receivable of $500,000 the result will be:

$$\text{Accounts receivable} \quad \div \quad \frac{\text{Sales}}{365} \quad = \quad \text{Collection ratio}$$

$$\$500,000 \quad \div \quad \frac{\$5,000,000}{365} \quad = \quad \$500,000 \quad \div \quad \$13,700 \quad = \quad 36.5\%$$

An alternate method of calculating the age of the receivables or the collection ratio is discussed on page 337. However, it should be stressed that an increase in the age of the receivables usually indicates that the company is having difficulty in collecting its bills.

The *percentage of debt to the total capitalization* is another measure used to determine the strength of the company. Usually, in an industrial concern, we like to see debt amounting to no more than 33% of the total capitalization, in electric public utilities 55%, in natural gas companies 65%, and in railroads 40%. If a large part of the capitalization is debt, it means that the bondholders are putting up most of the funds for the business.

The debt percentage in the case of Lobuck Corporation may be calculated by referring to page 319, which shows total capitalization of $1,694,000. The debt–capitalization percentage is figured by dividing the debt of $400,000 by the capitalization of $1,694,000, giving 23.6%.

The following is a summary and a review of the most important terms and ratios described in the preceding chapter:

1. *Working capital or net working capital:* Current assets of cash, U.S. government securities, accounts and notes receivable, inventories, and deferred charges minus current liabilities of accounts and notes payable, accrued taxes (reserve), and accrued wages.—No standards.
2. *Current ratio:* Current assets/current liabilities.—Standard 2 to 1.
3. *Quick assets:* Current assets minus inventory.
4. *Net quick assets:* Current assets minus inventory minus current liabilities.
5. *Quick asset ratio* (sometimes called acid-test ratio): Quick assets/current liabilities.—Standard 1 to 1.
6. *Cash items ratio:* Cash and government securities/current liabilities.—Standard 0.50 to 0.75.
7. *Working capital–debt ratio:* Working capital/debt.—Standard 1 to 1.
8. *Book value:* Common stock, plus surplus, plus undivided profits *or* stockholders's equity/number of shares of common.

9. *Percentage of debt of total capitalization:* Debt/debt plus preferred plus surplus or retained earnings. Standard maximum for industrial, 33% debt of total capitalization; for public utility 55%.

10. Exercise in determining number of shares from capital stock account.

Capital Stock Account	Par Value	Number of Shares
$10,000,000	$ 20	500,000
15,000,000	10	1,500,000
20,000,000	50	400,000
30,000,000	100	300,000

11. Exercise in determining the number of bonds from bond account.

Bond Payable	Par Value	Number of Bonds
$100,000,000	$1,000	100,000
20,000,000	1,000	20,000

REVIEW QUESTIONS

1. Distinguish between current assets and current liabilities. Mention four possible current assets and four current liabilities.

2. Explain the difference between FIFO and LIFO in determining the cost of inventories. In a period of rising prices, which is the more conservative? Explain.

3. Distinguish among a patent, a trademark, and a brand name. What is the general term for these assets?

4. What are the most important fixed assets? How are they carried on the balance sheet of a corporation?

5. Distinguish between par value, no par value, and stated or assigned value of common stock.

6. Explain how the following are calculated, giving in each case the desired ratio:
   a. current ratio
   b. cash items ratio
   c. debt–working capital ratio
   d. acid-test, or quick, ratio

7. Describe in detail the components of stockholders' equity. How is the book value of common stock calculated? What is the relation of book value to market value? Illustrate.

TRUE AND FALSE QUESTIONS

1. Current assets include all of the following *except:*   *True*   *False*
   a. cash   _____ _____
   b. short-term U.S. government securities   _____ _____
   c. investments in subsidiaries   _____ _____
   d. accounts receivable   _____ _____
   e. inventories   _____ _____
   f. fixed plant and equipment.   _____ _____
2. Current liabilities include: *True*   *False*
   a. accounts payable   _____ _____
   b. notes payable due within one year   _____ _____
   c. accrued income taxes   _____ _____
   d. all of the above.   _____ _____
3. In a period of rapidly rising prices, it might be best for a company to
   determine the cost of inventory by the: *True*   *False*
   a. FIFO method   _____ _____
   b. LIFO method.   _____ _____
4. Patents, trademarks, brand names, and goodwill are usually classed
   as: *True*   *False*
   a. other assets   _____ _____
   b. intangible assets   _____ _____
   c. miscellaneous assets.   _____ _____
5. Net quick assets are: *True*   *False*
   a. cash   _____ _____
   b. cash and U.S. government securities   _____ _____
   c. current assets less inventory and current
   liabilities.   _____ _____
6. Fixed assets are usually plant and equipment carried at:
      True   *False*
   a. cost   _____ _____
   b. replacement value   _____ _____
   c. arbitrary value set annually by auditing firm.   _____ _____
7. A long-term funded debt of a corporation includes: *True*   *False*
   a. bonds due in over a year's time   _____ _____
   b. reserve for depreciation   _____ _____
   c. preferred stock.   _____ _____
8. Par value is all of the following *except:*   *True*   *False*
   a. an arbitrarily assigned amount at which the
   stock is carried on the books of the company   _____ _____
   b. a good indication of the market value of the
   stock   _____ _____
   c. usually fully paid up when stock is sold.   _____ _____

9. The book value of a corporation is: *True*   *False*
    a. the value of net assets or theoretical amount a
        stockholder would receive if the company
        went out of business   _____   _____
    b. the liquidating value of the corporation   _____   _____
    c. the common stock at par value plus the sur-
        plus (earned and capital)   _____   _____
    d. a good indication of market value.   _____   _____
10. The book value per share of common stock is calculated by:
                                                                True   *False*
    a. adding to common stock the earned and
        capital surplus and dividing by the number of
        shares   _____   _____
    b. dividing the common stock account by the
        number of shares   _____   _____
    c. dividing the common stock and earned
        surplus by the number of shares.   _____   _____
11. The capitalization or capital structure includes: *True*   *False*
    a. debt, plus preferred, plus common at par,
        plus earned and capital surplus   _____   _____
    b. preferred and common stock at par   _____   _____
    c. preferred and common stock at par plus
        surplus.   _____   _____
12. The current ratio is: *True*   *False*
    a. the relation between the cash and U.S. gov-
        ernment securities and the current liabilities   _____   _____
    b. the relation between all current assets and all
        current liabilities   _____   _____
    c. the relation between current assets and debt.   _____   _____
13. The satisfactory current ratio should be: *True*   *False*
    a. at least 1.00 times   _____   _____
    b. at least 1.50 times   _____   _____
    c. at least 2.00 times.   _____   _____
14. The acid-test ratio is: *True*   *False*
    a. current assets less inventory to current
        liabilities   _____   _____
    b. the current assets less reserves for bad debts
        and for inventory deterioration   _____   _____
    c. current assets less inventory to bank and
        trade debt.   _____   _____
15. Working capital or net working capital is: *True*   *False*
    a. the total amount of money that is working
        for the corporation   _____   _____

b.   the difference between the current assets and   *True*   *False*
     current liabilities   _____   _____
c.   an indication, if a large amount, that the
     company has free liquid funds to acquire new
     assets, to improve credit, and even to pay
     funded debt.   _____   _____

16. The desired percentage of debt to total capitalization of an *industrial*
     corporation is: *True*   *False*
     a.   not over 75%   _____   _____
     b.   not over 50%   _____   _____
     c.   not over 33%.   _____   _____

17. A security analyst can find from a balance sheet all of the following
     except: *True*   *False*
     a.   net worth   _____   _____
     b.   net income   _____   _____
     c.   working capital   _____   _____
     d.   inventories.   _____   _____

18

Securities Analysis II
The Income Statement

As we have seen in the preceding chapter, the balance sheet shows the financial strength and the general condition of the company on a stated date. The statement of income and expenses, frequently referred to as a *profit and loss* statement, shows where the money comes from, how it was spent, and what remains for the owners or stockholders for the period of a *fiscal* year. The *fiscal* year may be the same as the calendar year, ending December 31. Sometimes the fiscal year is based on the normal business year for the industry. For example, the *fiscal* year for the retail trade industry ends on January 31 and for the U.S. government on September 30.

Every income and expense statement, no matter how complicated, may be divided into three parts: revenues, costs, and net earnings. To examine the income and expense statement of Lobuck Corporation, see the table following:

Item		
1	Revenue	$5,000,000
2,3,4,5,6	Costs	4,424,550
7	Net income	575,450

It is easy to see that the company has earned $575,450 on sales of $5,000,000, or 11.5%. This appears to be a good profit margin, but it should be compared with the profits of other companies in the same field and with previous years' profits of the same firm. In this way we can see if the affairs of the company are improving or getting worse. Although past earnings are not an infallible guide to future earnings, the buyer of a security of a company with improving past earnings feels more confident than if the earnings were declining or remaining steady.

A more detailed discussion of the items of the income statement of Lobuck Corporation might be helpful:

Item		
1	Net sales	$5,000,000

Net sales (item 1) is the amount of money that the company has collected by cash sales or expects to collect by credit sales. The term *net sales* means the net amount collected or due after allowance for discounts and for returned goods. On rare occasions a company will report both gross and net sales. But the difference between gross and net sales is usually small. A few industrial concerns, such as the oil companies, as well as all railroad and public utility companies, use the term *operating revenues* instead of sales.

Item		
2	Cost of goods sold	$3,430,000
3	Selling and administrative expenses	300,000

Cost of goods sold (item 2) includes wages, cost of materials, and maintenance of plant and equipment. These are called the basic costs of operating the business. Clearly, labor must be paid, materials must be bought, and equipment must be maintained. If the cost of goods sold increases faster than the sales, it is possible that management is not alert to rising costs. Perhaps the company should increase the price of the product or control expenses more carefully.

Sometimes a company will list separately its cost of materials and supplies, its salaries and wages, its maintenance, and even its research costs. But the usual practice is to lump them in one item: cost of goods sold or cost of sales.

Selling and administrative expenses (item 3) include all the expenses of selling the goods and services. Some of the more important items are the training of sales personnel and their salaries or commissions. A well-trained and alert sales force can be an important growth factor. One of the reasons for the success of the International Business Machines Corporation is its highly trained and active sales force. Another important selling expense is advertising.

Item		
4	Depreciation	$208,000

Depreciation (item 4) is the means by which the cost of plant, build-ings, and equipment is recovered. Let us assume a manufacturer has bought a piece of equipment worth $15,000. Because the manufacturer expects this equipment to last for five years, the cost of this machinery must be recov-ered over its life. The manufacturer sets aside an equal amount each year in the form of a depreciation reserve, or $3,000 each year; this is the straight-line method of depreciation. The reserve is used to reduce the cost of the fixed asset (see Lobuck Corporation, item 7, in Chapter 17). Depreciation is sometimes called a noncash charge. The manufacturer may use this money in the business. Depreciation should not be confused with earnings; the money is simply set aside to recover the cost of the fixed asset over the years. But almost never are these funds kept in cash, nor are they available to the stockholder. They are, to repeat, used in the business. Such use would include the purchase of new equipment and plant construction. De-preciation is treated as an expense of operating a business. It is thus a deduc-tion before federal and state income taxes.

Besides the straight line method of calculating depreciation, there are a number of other methods. But the best known are the sum of the years' dig-its and the double declining balance. These methods are explained in detail on pages 141-142.

All of these methods of depreciation are based on the historical costs of assets. Due to inflation, plant equipment, and even some inventories are greatly under-valued. Depreciation charges based on historical costs are too low. Therefore, in 1980 the Financial Accounting Standards Board (FASB) required about 1,200 large companies to supply to their stockholders with supplementary income accounts adjusted by the current cost or the constant dollar methods. *Current cost* adjusts for price changes of specific assets of the corporation whereas the *constant dollar* method adjusts for the increase in the general price level. The following shows the net income before and after adjustments of four well known companies:

TABLE 18-1

1979 Net Income (In Millions)			
	Historical	Constant Dollar	Current Cost
General Electric	$1,409	$1,064	$ 986
General Motors	2,899	1,780	1,800
Union Carbide	566	390	400
Xerox	563	350	420

Depletion is a term—and a tax allowance—generally used by natural resources companies whose assets are constantly being exhausted or depleted. Under the federal tax laws, these companies can make charges against income to allow for the wasting of these assets. For example, the independent oil producers were permitted a 22% depletion in 1980, but this will decline gradually to 15% in 1984 and thereafter. To a lesser extent, the copper, sulfur, clay, asbestos, and brick companies also can make depletion charges.

Amortization means to set aside money regularly to retire debt or write off an asset. The most frequent use is to retire or amortize debt through sinking fund payments. That is, regular payments, usually semiannual, are made by the company to a trustee who retires the bonds either by purchase in the market or by drawing by lot according to the numbers on the bonds. Assets usually retired by amortization include intangible assets (see page 314).

Obsolescence is the process by which an asset becomes out of date or obsolete. It might be losing its value due to technological changes. For example, a new type of machine to make rubber tires might lead to the obsolescence of the old machines.

Item		
5	Interest	$32,000

Interest (item 5) includes the interest paid by a company on its bonds, on its long-term payable notes, and on its bank loans. In railroads, the term *fixed charges* is used and includes not only interest on the railroad's own debt but interest on guaranteed bonds, dividends on guaranteed stocks, and rentals for leased lines and properties. In an industrial company, interest charges are usually not an important item. But, if interest charges are high compared with the operating income, the company may be operating on a thin margin. This means it is vulnerable to a general decline in business activity. As we explained in Chapter 2, the operating profit should be several times the interest or fixed charges. Interest charges of public utility companies are a large item in the income statement, but the revenues of these companies, due to their nature, are more stable than are those of most industrial concerns. Interest or fixed charges is an expense of operating a business and, therefore, is a deduction before taxes.

Item		
6	Taxes, federal	$454,550

Taxes (item 6) generally include income taxes paid to the U.S. government. In addition, companies pay substantial real estate taxes to the city or town as well as to the state in which the properties are located.

For Lobuck Corporation the federal income taxes are calculated as follows:

Item		
(B)	Operating profit	$1,062,000
5	Less: Interest on bonds — 8% — $400,000	32,000
	Taxable income	$1,030,000
	Federal income taxes	454,550

Federal income taxes in 1979 on corporations ranged from 17% to 46%. For most large corporations, the rate is about 46%. The federal income taxes of Lobuck Corporation are calculated as follows:

17% on the first	$ 25,000	$ 4,250
20% on the next	25,000	5,000
30% on the next	25,000	7,500
40% on the next	25,000	10,000
46% on amount over $100,000	930,000	427,800
	$1,030,000	$454,550

There are times when corporations pay less than 46% of their taxable income. This happens if corporations have tax losses from previous years that are carried forward and used to reduce current taxes. Also, a corporation might have holdings of municipal securities. As was explained in Chapter 4, the interest on these securities is exempt from federal income taxes.

Other income sometimes appears on the income statement of companies. It includes income from securities, from real estate not used for operations, and from investments in subsidiary and affiliated companies. In most cases, other income of industrial companies is not large.

Item		
7	Net income	$575,450

Net income is the most interesting item on the income statement. It is the amount that results from deducting all the expenses from the net sales. It is also *in theory* the amount available to the stockholders. We say in theory because the stockholder rarely receives *all* the net income. The amount the stockholder receives in dividends depends on decisions by the board of directors.

From net income, however, the analyst can determine the amount earned per share of *preferred*, if there is preferred stock outstanding. After deducting the preferred dividends from the net income, the analyst can also calculate the earnings per share of common stock.

TABLE 18-2

Lobuck Corporation Income Statement, 1979

Item		
1	Net sales	$5,000,000
2	Cost of goods sold	3,430,000
3	Selling and administrative expenses	300,000
(A)	Gross operating profit	$1,270,000
4	Depreciation	208,000
(B)	Operating profit	$1,062,000
5	Interest on bonds	32,000
(C)	Taxable income	$1,030,000
6	Federal income taxes	454,550
7	Net income	$ 575,450
8	Dividends on preferred stock	18,000
9	Dividends on common stock	300,000
10	Retained earnings	$ 257,450
11	Earned per share preferred	$159.85
12	Earned per share common	$5.57
13	Dividend per share preferred	$5.00
14	Dividend per share common	$3.00
15	Number of shares preferred	3,600
16	Number of shares common	100,000

From the income statement of Lobuck Corporation (Table 18-2), the net income per share on the *preferred* stock is calculated as follows:

Item		
7	Net income	$575,450
11	Per share preferred stock:	
	$575,450 ÷ by 3,600 shares = per share	$159.85

Because Lobuck Corporation had net income of $575,450, the earnings per share of preferred are figured by dividing the net income by the number of shares of preferred. Although Lobuck Corporation earned $159.85 per share of the preferred, this does not mean that each share of preferred is entitled to $159.85. The maximum amount the preferred stockholders of Lobuck Corporation could receive each year is $5 a share (5% ×

$100 par = $5). As shown in Chapter 1, the per share earnings are merely one indication of protection or coverage of the preferred dividend. The maximum dividend paid depends on the stated rate, which in this case is $5.

The earnings per share of common are obtained by dividing the net income by the number of shares of common, *after deducting the preferred dividend* as follows:

Item		
7	Net income	$575,450
	Less: Preferred dividend:	
	3,600 shares of preferred times $5.00 =	18,000
	Balance for common	$557,450
12	Per share common:	
	$557,450 ÷ 100,000 shares =	$5.57

Thus, the per share earnings of the common stock of Lobuck Corporation are $5.57 per share.

The dividend paid on the common amounted to $3.00 a share, or 54% of the net income of $5.57 per share. This is usually called the *dividend payout ratio*, or sometimes simply the payout ratio. The dividend payout ratio is the dividends paid as a percentage of earnings. Some companies such as the leading automobile companies pay out a large proportion of earnings. Others such as the drug and the electronics companies pay out a smaller proportion of earnings. In 1978, leading U.S. corporations paid in dividends the equivalent of about 42% of their profits after taxes.

Finally, we have *retained earnings* (item 10) of $257,450. This is the net income that the company has not paid out to stockholders. It is retained in the company and is added to the surplus or retained earnings account in the balance sheet. It might be used to buy more inventory, to buy equipment, or to expand plant. For Lobuck Corporation, retained earnings are figured as follows:

Item		
7	Net income	$575,450
8	Less: Dividends on preferred stock	18,000
9	Less: Dividends on common stock	300,000
10	Addition to retained earnings	$257,450

IMPORTANCE OF FOOTNOTES

In particular the analyst should note the inventory policies (FIFO or LIFO), depreciation policies, (straight line), and any unusual charges against income such as losses on foreign exchange transactions. On some occasions, large charges are made to write off antiquated plants.

Convertible securities should be used to calculate fully diluted earnings. This means that the investor should assume that the convertible securities *are* converted to stock giving a new number of shares outstanding. These are divided into the actual net income to obtain the so called fully diluted earnings.

The SEC and the American Institute of Certified Public Accountants (AICPA) require companies with convertible securities and warrants to report earnings on a fully diluted basis as well as on the basis of the actual shares outstanding. Also the analyst should note the warrants and options given to key employees.

ANALYSIS OF THE STATEMENT OF INCOME AND EXPENSES

The analyst can make a number of comparisons between the items in the income statement. Comparisons with previous years' statements are particularly helpful. They enable the analyst to see the progress or deterioration of the company. Some of the parts of the income statement that the analyst should examine and compare not only with previous years but also with other companies include net sales, operating profit, and net income.

Net sales growth is very significant. A steady year-to-year increase in sales is usually a good sign. Also, a consistent decline in sales is almost always a bad sign. A company must sell its goods and services to make profits. The growth of sales can be measured and compared in several ways.

A simple percentage of the growth of sales in the most recent year, say, 1980 compared with 1975 or compared with an average of the sales for a period of three years such as 1975–1977 is often a useful calculation.

Sales may be used to measure the efficiency of capital expenditures of a company. For instance, the dollar growth in sales over a period of years might be compared with the dollar capital expenditures during the same period.

In particular, sales may be used to measure the turnover of inventory and the age of receivables.

The *turnover of inventory* is often measured by taking net sales divided by inventory. For Lobuck Corporation, net sales of $5,000,000 divided by inventory of $400,000 would be 12.5 times. Any slowing of this turnover would indicate that inventory is accumulating faster than sales. Also, it might indicate that some of the inventory is getting old and less marketable.

The *age of accounts receivable* is measured somewhat in the same way. Net sales are divided by the accounts receivable and then translated into number of days. For example, net sales of $5,000,000 are divided by accounts receivable of $500,000, or 10 times. This amount in turn is divided *into* 365 days giving 36.5 days as the age of the accounts receivable. An increase in the number of days of accounts receivable indicates that the accounts receivable are becoming less liquid and collections are slowing up.

Operating profit is an important item in the income statement. It shows the amount of money the company has made on its sales before taxes and interest. For Lobuck Corporation, Table 18-2, operating profit is figured as follows:

Item		
1	Net sales	$5,000,000
2	Less: Cost of goods sold	3,430,000
3	Less: Selling and administrative expenses	300,000
4	Less: Depreciation	208,000
	Total operating expenses	$3,938,000
	Operating profit	$1,062,000

Here we deduct from sales of $5,000,000 operating expenses of $3,938,000 to obtain the operating profit of $1,062,000. Sometimes the sales of a company will increase, but at the same time the operating expenses will increase at a faster rate. As a result, the operating profit may remain the same or in some cases decline. This may mean that the company is taking on more business but is cutting prices. Also it may mean that the expense of obtaining the orders or producing the goods has increased.

But when sales expand it is encouraging to see the operating profit expand at a faster rate. This reflects maintenance of selling prices and control of expenses in the face of expanding volume.

Sometimes a company will be so inefficiently operated that it will report an operating deficit. In other words, it cannot earn enough to pay its out-of-pocket operating expenses. This might be a temporary situation due to prolonged strikes such as have taken place in the airlines or in the newspaper field. On the other hand, the analyst should avoid a company that, for no explained reason other than inefficiency or inherent weakness, reports deficits.

The *operating margin,* or margin of profit, is the relationship between operating income and net sales. It shows, in effect, the percentage of net sales that is brought down to operating income. On the basis of the preceding figures, the operating margin may be obtained by dividing the operating profit of $1,062,000 by the net sales of $5,000,000, giving 21.2%. Thus, on every dollar of sales the company has an operating profit of 21.2 cents. Again we stress that trends are important. An improving operating margin is obviously to be favored over a declining margin. Also, comparisons might be made with similar companies *in the same industry*. In this way, the analyst can obtain an appraisal of relative efficiency.

Perhaps a better way to measure the operating efficiency of a company is to determine the operating profit *before* depreciation, federal income taxes, and interest. This may be done by subtracting from net sales *only* the cost of goods sold and the selling and administrative expenses. The net amount then can be divided by the net sales to show the percentage earned on sales.

Referring to Lobuck Corporation, Table 18-2, the percentage earned on sales *before* depreciation, federal income taxes, and interest would be figured as follows:

Item		
1	Net sales	$5,000,000
2	Less: Cost of goods sold	$3,430,000
3	Less: Selling and administrative expenses	300,000
	Total operating expenses	$3,730,000
	Operating profit before depreciation, federal income taxes, and interest	$1,270,000
Percentage earned on sales	($1,270,000 divided by $5,000,000)	equals 25.4%

This method enables the analyst to compare more accurately the relative operating efficiencies of companies before special charges. For example, one company might arbitrarily make higher depreciation charges than another. Thus, all things being equal, the company making higher depreciation charges might show a lower profit margin after depreciation than a company that was not so conservative and is writing off the cost of its assets over a longer period.

Depreciation on an income statement should be examined to determine if the company is under- or overdepreciating its fixed assets. One way to obtain a rough comparison of depreciation policies is to relate dollar depreciation charges to net sales. Care must be taken to relate depreciation to net sales of companies in the *same industry*. For example, in 1978 General Electric Company reported depreciation of $576 million, or 5.4% of its net sales of $10,653 million. For the same year Westinghouse Electric Company reported depreciation of only 2.2% of sales. This is a rough measure but, when there appear wide differenes between companies in the same field, a closer analysis should be made of their respective depreciation policies. (See page 140 for a further discussion of depreciation.)

Net income is perhaps the most important item on the income statement. A study of the growth of net income in capsule form indicates the progress of the company. Furthermore, it is a reasonable means of forecasting its future. If a company is showing a good trend in net income over the years, it is reasonable to assume that it has good management, that its capital expenditures have been wise, and that its expenses are controlled.

We can measure net income growth by comparing a recent year with a past year or an average of three years in the past in the same way as we measured sales on page 336. For instance, Pfizer & Company Inc. A leading ethical drug company, in 1979 earned $3.26 a share, a gain of 68.9% over $1.93 in 1975.

TABLE 18-3

Selected Per Share Earnings and
Price Data for Three Ethical
Drug Companies in 1979

	3/24/80 Price	Dividend	Per Share Yield	Earnings	% Earnings gain over 1975	Dividend Payout Ratio	Price/ Earnings Ratio
Pfizer & Co	33¼	$1.44	4.33%	$3.26	68.9%	44%	10.2X
Merck & Co	61¼	$2.30	3.72%	$5.08	67.7%	45%	12.2X
Squibb Corp	31	$1.14	3.68%	$2.52	11.5%	45%	12.3X

The Table 18-3 shows that all three companies have reported good earnings growth since 1975. But Pfizer has shown the best growth and Squibb the poorest of the three. But these figures do not show that Squibb is developing Captopril, a drug that is supposed to help people suffering from high blood pressure.

The price–earnings ratio of Pfizer is also the lowest. This is obtained by dividing the price of the stock, 33¼, by the current earnings of $3.26, or 10.2 times. In comparing companies of equal merit, the one with the lower price–earnings ratio may be the more attractive.

However, a high price/earnings ratio, as in the case of Squibb, may indicate a favorable factor in the outlook for the company and that the company has special support. At all events, a high price/earnings ratio should be investigated to determine its justification. The same is true of a low price/earnings ratio which may not always indicate a cheap stock.

The payout ratios of all three drug companies are about the same (i.e., about 45%. This means that the companies are following a conservative policy on dividends to devote more money to research.

The net income to stockholders' equity is obtained by dividing the net income of a corporation by the stockholder's equity. As we saw on page 319, the stockholders' equity of Lobuck Corporation was $934,000 (capital stock of $400,000, capital surplus of $100,000, and retained earnings of $434,000). To obtain the rate of return on equity, the analyst divides the net income after preferred dividends of $557,450 by the stockholders' equity of $934,000, or 59.6%. This is an unrealistically high figure, but it is given for illustration purposes to tie in with the balance sheet of Lobuck Corporation.

The same result might be obtained by dividing the book value per share (book value was explained on page 319) and dividing it by the net income per share. For example, we calculated the net income of Lobuck Corporation (on page 335) at $5.57 a share and the book value (on page 319) at $9.34. Therefore the rate of return on stockholders' equity would be $5.57 divided by $9.34, or 59.6%.

The *percentage earned on sales* is another useful means of comparing companies. In the case of Lobuck Corporation this amount is calculated by dividing the net income of $575,450 by the sales of $5,000,000 to equal 11.51%. Comparisons should be made with percentages earned on sales in previous years with other companies in the same line of business. In this way it can be determined if the percentage is increasing or decreasing.

Times interest earned is calculated by dividing the balance of income available after costs and taxes for fixed charges (interest, etc.) by the fixed charges. For example, the balance available for interest of Lobuck Corporation was the operating profit of $1,062,000 less federal income taxes of $454,550 or $607,450. Interest on bonds was $32,000. Therefore the times interest earned would be $607,450 divided by $32,000 or 18.98 times.

Times preferred dividend coverage is usually figured on an overall basis. That is, the amount available for fixed charges is divided by the interest plus the preferred dividend requirement. For example, Lobuck Corporation's $607,450 available for fixed charges would be divided by fixed charges of $32,000 plus preferred dividends of $18,000, or $50,000, to equal overall coverage of the preferred dividend of 12.2 times.

The leverage or debt-to-equity ratio is the percentage of debt to the total capitalization. In periods of good business a high debt-to-equity ratio can mean higher profits for the stockholder but greater risks in bad times. For Lobuck Corporation, the debt was $400,000 and the total capitalization was $1,694,000 (see page 319). Therefore, the debt-to-equity ratio is $400,000 divided by $1,694,000, or 23.6%. This is a reasonably conservative ratio for an industrial company.

Cash flow is simply the sum of the net income plus the depreciation charges. In the case of Lobuck Corporation, the following would be the cash flow calculation:

Depreciation	$208,000
Net income	575,450
Total cash flow	$783,450

Some security analysts use the term *cash flow earnings* incorrectly and reduce it to a per share figure. This should be done with great caution if at all. Most analysts consider depreciation a method of recovering the cost of an asset and not available as earnings to the stockholder.

In our analysis, we have assumed that the earnings as reported are accurate. One of the best ways to check this is to be sure that the accounts are audited by a recognized firm of certified public accountants. This is true of almost all large concerns. There are, however, different ways of treating depreciation, taxes, and inventories, which might change the net income of a company. Therefore, the security analyst should always check these items when comparing one company with another in the same field.

The following is a summary of the most important terms and *ratios* discussed in the preceding chapter:

1. *Net sales:* Gross sales less discounts, returns, and allowances.
2. *Operating income:* Net sales less cost of sales, selling, administrative expenses, and depreciation.
3. *Net income:* Operating income less interest and taxes.
4. *Operating ratio:* Cost of sales, selling, and administrative expenses and depreciation charges/net sales.
5. *Margin of profit:* Operating income/net sales.
6. *Dividend payout ratio:* Dividends paid/net income.
7. *Earning power test:* Net income plus interest/capitalization (bonds plus preferred, plus common, plus surplus or retained earnings).
8. *Capital expenditures test:* Capital expenditures/sales growth (over a period of years).
9. *Depreciation adequacy test:* Depreciation/net sales.
10. *Percent earned on Net Sales:* Net income/net sales.
11. *Rate of return:* Net income per share/book value per share *or* net income/capital stock, surplus, and undivided profits (stockholders' equity).

REVIEW QUESTIONS

1. Define net sales, cost of goods sold, and selling and administrative expenses.
2. What is depreciation? Explain in detail two methods by which it may be calculated (see pages 140-141).
3. Distinguish among depletion, amortization, and obsolescence.
4. Given a taxable corporate income of $2,000,000, calculate the federal income taxes.
5. After you have calculated the taxes in problem 4, *find the net income per share of common stock,* assuming 100,000 shares of 5% $100 par preferred and 200,000 shares no-par common stock.

6. Why is the growth of net sales significant? How can sales growth best be measured and compared?

7. How is operating margin or margin of profit calculated? In what way may it be used by the analyst?

8. Describe cash flow. In what way should the term *not* be used?

TRUE AND FALSE QUESTIONS

		True	False
1.	An income account is *not*:		
	a. referred to as a profit and loss statement	_____	_____
	b. a statement of income and expense	_____	_____
	c. a measure of the solvency of the company.	_____	_____
2.	The fiscal year is:	True	False
	a. always the same as the calendar year	_____	_____
	b. based on normal business year for the industry.	_____	_____
3.	Depreciation is a method by which:	True	False
	a. the cost of plant and equipment are recovered over their useful life	_____	_____
	b. the value of plant and equipment are measured over their useful life	_____	_____
	c. the cost of plant and equipment less salvage value are recovered over useful life.	_____	_____
4.	Straight-line depreciation is:	True	False
	a. treated as an expense and is tax deductible	_____	_____
	b. a noncash charge	_____	_____
	c. an equal amount set aside each year in the form of a depreciation reserve.	_____	_____
5.	Depletion is:	True	False
	a. a noncash charge	_____	_____
	b. a tax deduction	_____	_____
	c. used to write off a wasting asset of a natural resource company	_____	_____
	d. all of the above.	_____	_____
6.	Operating profit is:	True	False
	a. a good measure of efficiency of a company	_____	_____
	b. calculated by deducting from net sales the cost of goods sold, the selling and administrative expenses, and the depreciation	_____	_____
	c. should be used as a percentage of sales to measure efficiency	_____	_____
	d. all of the above.	_____	_____

7. Net income is: *True*   *False*
    a.   usually larger than operating profit because it
         includes other income   _____   _____
    b.   usually smaller than operating income be-
         cause it is calculated after taxes and interest
         on debt.   _____   _____
8. Federal income taxes are roughly 46% of taxable income. Therefore, a
    company reporting a substantially lower percentage: *True*   *False*
    a.   is failing to pay taxes due and might be sub-
         ject to penalties   _____   _____
    b.   might have a tax-loss carryover from previ-
         ous years   _____   _____
    c.   might have holdings of municipal bonds   _____   _____
    d.   might be reporting higher depreciation to the
         government than to stockholders.   _____   _____
9. Dividends paid to stockholders: *True*   *False*
    a.   may not exceed net income   _____   _____
    b.   should not exceed 50% of net income   _____   _____
    c.   should be conservative if a company is either
         expanding rapidly or in weak financial condi-
         tion.   _____   _____
10. The security analyst can test the inventory: *True*   *False*
    a.   by dividing the net sales by the inventory at
         the end of the year   _____   _____
    b.   by taking the percentage of depreciation to
         inventory.   _____   _____
11. The age of the receivables is usually calculated: *True*   *False*
    a.   by dividing the cost of goods sold by the
         amount of the receivable   _____   _____
    b.   by dividing the sales by the accounts re-
         ceivable   _____   _____
    c.   by dividing the sales by the accounts receiv-
         able and dividing the result into 365 days.   _____   _____
12. Cash flow is: *True*   *False*
    a.   the net income after preferred and common
         dividends   _____   _____
    b.   "the sum of the depreciation charges plus net
         income   _____   _____
    c.   a good measure of the earning power of a
         company when calculated on a per share
         basis.   _____   _____

13. All of the following are a good measure of the growth of a company
     except: *True*   *False*
     a.   the growth of income per share   _____ _____
     b.   increasing percentage of net income to sales   _____ _____
     c.   the growth of total assets   _____ _____
     d.   increasing percentage of net income to cap-
          italization.   _____ _____

19

Investment Risks and Portfolio Policies

Construction of Investment Policies

It cannot be stated too often that it is necessary for the registered representative or whoever is advising customers to know that customer's ability to lose principal or income, as well as many other facts detailed on pages 265 and 351. This information should help determine the relative mix of conservative and speculative securities being bought for a particular client.

Kinds of Investment Risks

Any investor faces any number of investment risks; that is there is no such thing as a riskless investment.

1. financial risk

Bond investors hope for a continued stream of certain income and the payment at maturity of $1,000 per bond. But, if the issuer runs into difficulty, the interest and principal payments could be reduced or eliminated.

Stockholders hope for increased market prices of their shares as well as increased dividends. They too can be disappointed if the company falls on hard times.

For some investors, an aggressive policy might be taken. The investor might, for example, concentrate on a few companies, taking a large position in each. Here the investor must make or have made a careful investigation into the affairs of the companies. An example would be buying an interest in a takeover prospect.

On the other hand, *diversification* for the average investor is perhaps the best policy. Diversification is one of the main selling points of many investment companies. It is the basic philosophy behind the index funds (see page 88). But diversification should never be random. A careful study of the outlook for each industry and the companies in that industry must be made. Some investors try to diversify by buying the stock of a conglomerate company that controls several companies in different lines of business. Good examples of conglomerate companies are Gulf and Western Industries, Inc. and Textron, Inc.

The client's ability to hold securities during wide market fluctuations is an important consideration. If the customer holds securities on margin, he might be wiped out if he is not able to put up the additional margin that may be required. Also the emotional make up of the client is important. Does the investor panic in a down market or become overenthusiastic in a rising market?

The quality of investment management should be high. Commercial banks and investment counsel firms offer the most expensive advice, but it is not always the best. On the other hand, such advisors are usually conservative, whereas investment management by brokerage firms is generally more aggressive. Investment management is particularly important when investments are concentrated in a few issues and/or when speculative issues are held.

2. interest rate risk

The inverse correlation between interest rates and bond prices was discussed in detail on page 34. There is, however, less inverse correlation between interest rates and stock prices. At times they move in the same direction.

The greatest risk to investors of fixed-income bonds is the fluctuation in prices of long-term bonds. This is serious if the investor is for any reason compelled to liquidate during a period of high interest rates. If, however, the bonds are of investment grade, the interest and principal will ultimately be paid. But there is no appreciation of principal or interest; hence no inflation protection.

Short-term securities are good for stability of principal, but they do have some disadvantages. In periods of high interest rates, short-term U.S. government securities yield a high and safe return. However, when interest rates drop sharply, as they sometimes do, the investor finds himself with cash that must be invested at substantially lower rates.

Perhaps the best compromise is the policy of *spaced maturities*. This policy is used by many bank portfolio managers to handle the securities of their banks. To illustrate, an investor with $500,000 might buy $100,000 of 5-year Treasury notes, $100,000 of 4-year, $100,000 of 3-year, $100,000 of 2-year, and $100,000 of 1-year. Each year a note matured, the investor would buy a new 5-year note. Thus the investor would receive an average yield of roughly the high and the low for the period.

Some sophisticated investment managers attempt to ride the yield curve, but mostly with indifferent success.

3. market risk and marketability risk

Market fluctuations of the prices of both bonds and of stocks can be influenced by external causes that have nothing to do with the individual company. Further, general investor enthusiasm or pessimism often exaggerates the swings of individual securities. For example, the stock of a good company might be driven to unrealistic heights or depressed below intrinsic value.

For the holder of a large-capitalization stock, there is no problem of marketability on the NYSE, the AMEX, or the NASDAQ. But there are stocks with thin markets on all these exchanges particularly for small companies. Shares of these companies might have to be sold at several points below the asked prices and bought well above the bid price. The size of the spread between the bid price and the asked price is a measure of the stock's marketability.

In the selection of the securities in a portfolio of a client, marketability must always be considered. For example, is the client able and willing to hold a security for a long time? Does the client have possible future demands for money such as heavy tax payments? Also, is the client emotionally constituted so that gradual liquidation of his investments is not a disturbance?

4. purchasing power risk

This is particularly true of bondholders who are often paid at maturity in depreciated dollars (see inflation, page 279). Some stocks in the past have partially protected the investor against inflation by increasing their dividends and market prices faster than the rate of inflation. This has been true of the stocks of some of the natural resource, high technology, and gold mining companies. But the stocks of many companies, particularly the electric utilities, have been severely hurt by inflation and have declined sharply.

Convertible bonds and convertible preferred stocks have been bought by some investors as a hedge against inflation and against recession or depression. They believe that in a period of bad business the holder of a convertible security would have senior securities that would continue to pay their interest and preferred dividends, whereas in an inflationary period the companies would prosper and the value of the convertible securities would rise (see pages 13 and 27).

Therefore, investors seeking to protect themselves from the ravages of inflation must reconcile their policies with regard to financial risk with the policies designed to minimize the loss of purchasing power. As protection against inflation an aggressive investor might buy South African gold mining stocks, gold bullion, or possibly stocks of small companies that have shown good growth, are in sound financial shape, and have a good outlook.

5. taxability risk

Generally speaking, all income from corporate bonds and stocks is fully taxable by the U.S. government and by most state governments. But there are exceptions. Dividends paid from capital are considered return of capital and are exempt from income taxes. This is true of many public utility stocks. Corporations holding preferred and common stocks of other corporations may exclude for tax-purposes 85% of the dividends received. This is particularly true for fire and casualty companies that hold a large amount of preferred stocks.

Municipal securities, as explained on page 60, are exempt from federal income taxes but in some cases are subject to state and even city taxes (see page 61).

6. callability of bonds and preferred stocks

Almost all bonds and preferred stocks may be called by the issuer (see page 36). At present this is not a risk, as almost all the bonds and preferred stocks are selling below their call prices. The exceptions are some convertible bonds and preferred stocks. In these cases a potential profit would be lost if the investor failed to convert or sell the securities before the call date (see page 36).

7. economic risk

Economic and social risks that might upset the market include (a) sharp increases in oil prices by the OPEC nations; (b) the collapse of a large company or bank; (c) continued large deficits in the U.S. balance of payments, (d) continued deficits of the U.S. government, (e) left-wing government, (f) deep depression and extravagant spending by the government; and (g) any number of international crises.

The Risk-Reward Concept

This concept means that some investors are willing to assume a higher risk provided the rewards are commensurate. For example, an investor might take a large risk by buying a stock such as Lockheed Aircraft Corporation in 1970 when it reported a deficit of $7.60 a share. The risk would have been great, but the reward was enormous as the stock recovered from about 7 to 32 by 1979.

Investment Counseling

Many investors try to improve their chances of making profits, or avoiding losses, by employing investment counsel firms. But most of these firms require a minimum value of funds to be managed of several hundred thousand dollars. They usually charge an annual fee of about 3/4% of the principal, scaled down as the amount of the fund exceeds the minimum.

These firms employ many highly paid specialists in securities. Their recommendations are coordinated by account managers who in turn run the individual accounts. Many commercial bank trust departments and a few brokerage firms manage for a fee the funds of their customers.

Policies with Respect to Buying and Selling of Securities (Trading)

Whereas trading in the stock market is good for the brokerage business, it is often better for the investor to buy and hold sound securities until such a time as the company ceases to grow or a better opportunity presents itself. A few experts in stock market technique are able to time purchases at or near the start of a rise in the stock market or in a particular stock and to sell or sell short near the top. But these transactions are risky and often misfire. They are particularly risky if done on margin (see page 199).

Another consideration is commissions. Many traders have found that profits from trading are substantially eaten up by commissions. Also several so-called experts buy call options if they think the market is going up and sell short or write calls if they believe the market is going down (see pages 229-233). All these trading practices are only for the skilled investor who can afford to take a loss.

Defensive Policies

Some authorities have stated that a good stock should be brought without regard to market changes. But more knowledgeable security analysts believe that at no time should the market price be ignored. They point out that, before any stock is purchased, it should be carefully analyzed for its intrinsic value as well as for its prospects. Once the investor has decided on the worth of the security, the investor should go ahead and buy it, not waiting for minor fluctuations.

A defensive policy toward purchasing power risk might include a *balanced portfolio*. But, as always, the portfolio should be tailored to the background, age, and financial condition of the client (see page 352). Generally speaking, the investor should not hold all cash (or money-market funds), all stocks, or all fixed-income securities. Rather, a balanced portfolio is suggested. This might consist of 50% of medium-term U.S. government notes or money-market funds, good-grade convertible bonds, and convertible perferred stocks and possibly some long-term high-grade bonds. If the client is in a high tax bracket, municipal securities should be considered. These fixed-income securities should give the client downside protection in the event of a depression. The other 50% might be invested in well-selected common stocks as a partial hedge against inflation. Stocks in this category might include oil, natural gas, and sound companies that have shown growth over the years, such as electronics, computers, drugs, and so forth.

Time Diversification

Of all the formula timing plans, perhaps the most successful is the *dollar-cost-averaging plan*, which was discussed in detail on page 101. Under this plan, periodic purchases are made of a fixed dollar amount of stock regardless of price. For years the New York Stock Exchange provided facilities through its M.I.P. (monthly investment plan). But more recently, the NYSE turned over its M.I.P. facilities to Merrill Lynch, Pierce, Fenner & Smith, Inc. This firm now provides facilities whereby a customer can make small periodic purchases on certains stocks quoted on the NYSE, on the AMEX, and on the NASDAQ through their Share Builders' Plan. Although the dollar-cost-averaging plan has much to recommend it, as it has enabled many to build up a substantial fund, it is not a riskless form of investment.

It should be stressed that dollar-cost averaging should not be confused with *share averaging*, as when a customer buys more of a stock that has depreciated in value. The latter practice might be dangerous as there might be a good reason for the decline of the stock.

Then there is the *constant-ratio, or equalizing, plan*. Here the investor or his or her advisor sets a fixed percentage of fixed-income securities to equities, say, 50:50. These percentages are kept relatively constant. For example, if the stock market rises so that stocks are 60% of the total portfolio, the proportion of the stocks will be cut back to 50% If the stock market declines, the percentage of stocks will be increased to restore the 50:50 balance.

Another plan is the *variable-ratio plan*. In this case the investor or his advisor changes the percentage of fixed-income securities to equities in relation to some stock index. As the index goes up, the proportion of stocks to bonds will be reduced. Thus at the peak of the market, the lowest amount of stocks will be held. On the other hand, as the market index declines, the stock fund will be increased so that the investor will be able to take advantage of any recovery in the stock market.

Finally, there is the *constant dollar* plan. Here the investor sets aside a *fixed dollar* amount for stocks. When and if stocks appreciate, the dollar amount of the gain is transferred to the fixed-income account. Thus the common stock dollar account remains constant. If the market declines, the bonds are sold, and the stock account is built up to its constant dollar amount.

All these plans have had a somewhat unsatisfactory record except the dollar-cost-averaging plan. The basic weakness has been that nobody has been able to consistently tell the high or low point of the stock market. For example, in the past, several plans were sold out of stocks, and the market continued to go up several hundred points.

INVESTMENT OBJECTIVES OF CUSTOMERS

Financial Planning

First, the customer should have adequate savings, say, enough to support his family for at least six months in case of job loss. Second, the customer should have sufficient insurance—enough to take care of his family in case of death.

In making recommendations, the registered representative should always bear in mind that the securities must be *suitable*. This is one of the most important of the NASD Rules of Fair Practice (see Article III, Section 2.) Especially when the registered representative opens a new account, he should endeavor to find out as much as possible about the background of his customer. In particular, the registered representative should try to find out the customer's ability to stand the loss of principal, the ability to stand loss of income, the tax position, the need for marketability, and the necessity for protection against inflation. (This applies largely to an institutional customer such as fire insurance company.) In more detail, the registered representatives should try to learn the following about his customer:

Personal
  Age and health
  Dependents, their age, and educational status
  Present employment, its stability and prospects
  Temperament and knowledge of investments
Present Portfolio
  Type of securities
  Balance of fixed income and equities
  Cash and savings
Financial
  Salary
  Other income
  Tax position
  Insurance
  Mortgage and other debts
  Surplus earnings available for investment
  Real estate or other investments
  Possible inheritance
Miscellaneous
  Pensions and profit sharing
  Keogh or IRA plans
  Projected changes in financial status
  Amount available for investment

The registered representative may have to use tact in finding out all this information. Some customers are reluctant to disclose too much of what they consider their private affairs. But the registered representative should point out that the more information he has, the better he can advise the client.

Objectives or goals should be determined by mutual agreement between the customer and the registered representative. Almost all customers are interested in *appreciation* of their portfolio; some are interested in *tax exemption*; many are interested in *income*; some in protection against *inflation* and almost all are interested in *protection of principal*. Nobody likes to see his capital diminish. It is obviously impossible to combine all these objectives. But it is the duty of the registered representative to *tailor* the investment program as nearly as possible to the particular objectives of the customer, taking into consideration his personal and financial background.

Starting with the objectives of the *senior citizens* (the retired and widowed), the registered representative should try to obtain as high an income as possible consistent with safety. Investments might incluce corporate or municipal bonds, the latter if the client is in a high tax bracket, and sound common stocks with good yields and comfortable coverage.

The *businessperson*, if he or she had a large salary or other substantial income, might be encouraged to buy municipal securities and growth common stocks. Growth stocks have been defined as having an average growth of net income over the years of about 7% as well as other charactertics.

The *young person starting out* in business should first be encouraged to have a backlog of savings and ample insurance. Second, the registered representative and the customer should determine how much can be set aside for *growth* common stocks.

Develop a Perspective on Overall Economic Outlook.

This is somewhat difficult, as even the msot learned economists and the brightest stock market technicians cannot agree on the outlook for the economy and the stock market. But the investor should try to keep informed by reading regularly at least *The New York Times, The Wall Street Journal*, and *Business Week* and *Barron's*.

Selection of Specific Investments in Appropriate Industries.

This means to select the best company in an industry that has shown steady growth and has a favorable outlook. The aim should be to obtain moderate long-term appreciation, adequate income, and if possible protection against inflation. Classical examples of growing companies in expanding fields are IBM in the computer, Hewlett-Packard in the electronics, General Electric in the electrical equipment, Owens-Corning Fiberglas in the building supply, Merck in the drug, du Pont in the chemical, and Exxon in the oil.

REVIEW QUESTION

1. What are the most important financial risks? Discuss the ways in which an investor might reduce them.
2. Why does an increase in interest rates mean a decline in the bond market? How best may a fixed-income investor protect his or her investment.
3. What does the wide spread between the bid and the asked price of a stock indicate to a prospective seller?
4. Name the stocks you think might afford moderate protection against inflation.
5. Is there any disadvantage in holding a coupon convertible bond? A convertible preferred stock?
6. What are the most important economic events which could cause a serious loss to the investor? Name three.
7. Distinguish between an aggressive and a defensive investment policy.
8. What are the conditions for a successful dollar-cost-averaging program? Why have other formula plans been unsuccessful?
9. What information in particular should a registered representative find out about a prospective customer. Name eight facts.

TRUE AND FALSE QUESTIONS

1. The best way to reduce the interest rate risk is by: *True*   *False*
   a. spaced maturities   _____   _____
   b. buying long-term bonds   _____   _____
   c. buying short-term securities   _____   _____
   d. buying high-yielding medium-grade bonds.   _____   _____

2. Marketability of a stock is: *True*   *False*
   a. more important than the company's earnings record or its prospects   _____   _____
   b. an essential criterion for an investment-grade company   _____   _____
   c. not necessary for some investors   _____   _____
   d. the ability of an investor to convert his securities into cash within a few days.   _____   _____

3. Purchasing power risk can be reduced by: *True*   *False*
   a. aggressive investing   _____   _____
   b. buying long-term high-yielding bonds   _____   _____
   c. buying some common stocks   _____   _____
   d. buying discount bonds.   _____   _____

4. Economic and social risks include: *True*   *False*
    a.   the breakup of the OPEC cartel   _____   _____
    b.   the balancing of the federal budget   _____   _____
    c.   continued large balance-of-payments deficits   _____   _____
    d.   continued extravagant U.S. government
         spending.   _____   _____

5. The speculator who trades in and out of the stock market:
                                                                True   *False*
    a.   is sure to come out ahead in the long run   _____   _____
    b.   obtains diversification by holding many
         securities   _____   _____
    c.   usually would do better by holding a fewer
         issues   _____   _____
    d.   should only buy and sell investment-grade
         stocks.   _____   _____

6. An investor attempting to gain protection against inflation should buy
    the stocks of: *True*   *False*
    a.   oil and natural gas companies   _____   _____
    b.   electric public utilities   _____   _____
    c.   drug companies   _____   _____
    d.   railroad companies.   _____   _____

7. Dollar-cost averaging: *True*   *False*
    a.   is the same as shares averaging   _____   _____
    b.   has enabled many to build a substantial
         fund over the years   _____   _____
    c.   is more sound than the constant-or
         variable-ratio plans   _____   _____
    d.   does not require continuous buying.   _____   _____

8. The most important facts a registered representative should learn
    about a prospective client are: *True*   *False*
    a.   financial position   _____   _____
    b.   objectives and goals   _____   _____
    c.   dependents and obligations   _____   _____
    d.   college.   _____   _____

9. The registered representative should recommend to a young executive
    making a good salary: *True*   *False*
    a.   a backlog of savings and ample insurance   _____   _____
    b.   U.S. Treasury securities and municipal
         bonds   _____   _____
    c.   speculative securities with growth prospects   _____   _____
    d.   if in the high tax bracket, a balanced
         program with fixed-income securities—U.S.

		True	False
government notes and municipals—and growth stocks.			

10. A retiree aged 65 without dependents and $1,000,000 from the sale of his business should invest the proceeds

		True	False
a.	all in high-priced growth stocks		
b.	half in corporate bonds and half in "blue chip" common stocks		
c.	half in municipal securities and half in investment-type stocks with growth potential.		

20

TAXES

Tax laws are so complicated that great caution should be taken in advising customers. There are many competent professionals (lawyers and accountants) to whom problems should be referred. There are, however, some basic rules that might be kept in mind, particularly when advising customers on security trades.

WHO MUST FILE

For tax years beginning after 1978, the gross income levels at which individuals must file an income tax return are: (1) *single* with an income of $3,300 or more ($4,300 if over 65) and (2) *married* with joint-return income of $5,400 ($6,400 if one spouse is over 65, $7,400 if both over 65). A short form 1040A may be filed if wages, tips, dividends, interest or interest from self-employment are less than $400.

Records

Every taxpayer should maintain such records as will enable him to prepare a complete and accurate tax return. These will enable the taxpayer to give proof of income and expenses in case the Internal Revenue Service makes an audit of the return.

The records that should be kept include:

1. Tax and income withholding statement, Form W-2.
2. Dividend payments reported by corporations as paid taxpayer, Form 1099.
3. Other income such as fees, bank interest, savings interest, trust income, rents, and royalties.
4. Brokerage reports of purchase and sale of securities.

5. Charitable contribution receipts or canceled checks.
6. Business expenses: travel, hotel, and restaurant expenses that are necessary in the performance of employment. Other expenses that are deductible from ordinary income include state transfer taxes, safety deposit boxes, and like costs used for business or investment purposes. Federal transfer taxes, brokerage commissions, and other costs are considered a part of the purchase price or selling costs.
7. Federal, state, and real estate tax receipts or canceled checks.
8. Interest payments on mortgages, etc.
9. A clear copy of each tax return filed.
10. Receipted medical bills.

It should be stressed that medical expenses are deductible only to the extent that they exceed 5% of adjusted gross income, and drugs are counted only to the extent that they exceed 1%.

These records should be kept for as long as they may be material in the administration of the internal revenue law. Ordinarily, the statute of limitation for a return is three years from the date that the return was due. However, the Internal Revenue Service cautions that there are instances in which a taxpayer should retain his records indefinitely. As a practical hint, it is suggested that a large envelope be used for each year and the return and all the receipts and records of contributions, taxes, security purchases and sales, and so on for the year be enclosed in separate smaller envelopes. Thus, if the taxpayer is called for an audit, the return can be easily assembled and verified.

PERSONAL INCOME TAXES ARE PROGRESSIVE

The larger the income, the higher the tax. The following sample of tax rates for married couples filing joint returns illustrates clearly this point.

TABLE 20-1

Taxable Income for Married Couple — 1984				
Over	Not Over	Pay +	Tax Rate	On Excess
$ 20,200	$ 24,600	$ 2,644	23%	$ 20,200
60,000	85,600	16,014	44	60,000
85,600	109,400	27,278	48	85,600
109,400	---	38,702	50	109,400

This table is applied after deductions. For example, a married couple filing a joint return with a net taxable income of $65,000 would pay

On $60,000	$16,014
On $5,000: (44% × $5,000 =	2,200
Total Tax	$18,214

TAX TREATMENT OF INTEREST ON DEBT SECURITIES

The interest on all U.S. government obligations is subject to federal income taxes but is exempt from state taxes. State and municipal obligations are *exempt* from federal income taxes but not from all state taxes. Interest on all corporate obligations are fully taxable at the federal and state levels.

TAX TREATMENT OF DIVIDENDS FROM CORPORATE STOCK

As pointed out on page 333, for all practical purposes corporations pay taxes on their taxable income of about 46%. After these taxes are paid, corporations report net income. From this net income dividends are usually paid. (There are exceptions when a corporation pays dividends—even if there are no earnings.) Thus the stockholder, being an owner of the corporation, in effect pays 46% of the taxable income to the government and in addition must report and pay taxes on his dividends. This is regarded as double taxation of the stockholder.

The only recognition of this situation is the fact that taxpayers are allowed to *exclude* $100 from their dividends received. If a wife receives dividends, she also can exclude up to $100. But if one spouse has dividends of $100 or more and the other has none, the exclusion is only $100. One spouse may not use the amount not used by the other.

In March 1980, Congress passed a law permitting individuals to double their exemptions for dividends *and* interest (for the first time interest may be deducted) for the years 1981 and 1982. Thus, an individual in those years may claim an exemption for dividends and/or interest on the first $200 and on a joint return, $400.

STOCK DIVIDENDS

Usually stock dividends of shares identical to the old shares are not taxable as income. But, if the investor has a choice of receiving a dividend in cash or in stock or if the stock dividend discharges the dividend arrearages, *then* they are treated as regular income and are taxed.

But, if the stock dividends are *sold* by the investor, he can use a simple formula to arrive at an adjusted cost basis.

For example, let us suppose a customer bought a share of the XYZ Company at 45 and it advanced to 60 in a year. At this point the company declares a stock dividend of 10%. The customer sells the 10% stock dividend at 60. The investor must figure the cost of the old stock on an adjusted basis as follows:

$$\frac{\$45 \text{ Old cost}}{1.00 + .10 \text{ Dividend}} = \frac{\$45}{1.10} = \$40.909 = \text{Adjusted cost}$$

If at a later time the company pays, for example, a 5% dividend, the investor's new adjusted cost will be calculated as follows, using the last adjusted basis:

$$\frac{40.909}{1.00 + .05} = \frac{40.909}{105} = 38.952$$

STOCK RIGHTS

Stock rights are treated the same as stock dividends. They are not usually taxable as income unless the stockholder has the option of receiving cash or other property.

WAYS OF EASING THE TAX BURDEN

As explained in Chapter 4, the income from municipal bonds (bonds of states, cities, towns, and authorities, etc.) are exempt from federal income taxes. Income from bills, certificates, notes, and bonds issued by the U.S. government are *not* exempt from federal income taxes but are exempt from the state income taxes.

Some investors can invest in oil wells and real estate ventures. These are speculative and only for the rich and well informed. They do offer tax advantages, as heavy depreciation and depletion charges can be taken (see Chapter 7).

Some companies pay dividends that are entitled to special tax treatment and are sometimes called *tax-free* dividends. One group consists of companies holding a large amount of high-cost stock. Such companies sell these shares and establish losses that offset other income. To the extent of the offset, earnings are paid tax free to stockholders. Some companies own large mineral resources that require many depletion charges. Some of these companies pay dividends that at least in part are considered a return of capital.

Some public utilities pay dividends that in part are considered tax free.

This comes about through these companies' paying dividends in excess of the income reported for tax purposes.

Perhaps the best known method of easing the tax burden is by switching securities. In switching securities, the investor can often accomplish a double purpose: (1) take a tax loss reducing the tax liability and (2) improve his portfolio by selling the stock of a company with unsatisfactory outlook and buying one with a more favorable outlook.

TAX TREATMENT OF SECURITIES TRANSACTIONS

Capital gains are essentially profits on the sale of capital assets, which include stocks and bonds. There are short-term and long-term capital gains. A short-term capital gain is one taken on a security held 12 months or less. A security held more than 12 months is a long-term capital gain. To determine the holding period, the date of the month, not the number of days, is used. For example, a security bought on January 21, 1980 and sold as late as January 21, 1981 would be a short-term gain or loss. But the sale would be considered a long-term gain or loss if it were made on January 22, 1981. If, however, the security were purchased on the last day of the month, it would become a long-term transaction on the first day of the thirteenth month. For example, a security purchased on March 31, 1980 must not be sold before April 1, 1981 to be considered a long-term capital gain.

The Trade and Settlement Dates

To establish a capital loss, the *trade* date must be on or before the last day of the year. To establish a capital gain, the settlement date must be no later than the end of the year. For example, in 1979 the last day to sell a security to qualify for capital gains tax treatment was Friday, December 21. Securities could be sold to establish a capital loss as late as Monday, December 31.

COMPUTATIONS OF CAPITAL GAINS AND LOSSES

The following assumptions might be made

1. A long-term capital gain of $6,000. *Result*: 60%, or $3,600, of the amount is deducted, and the balance, or $2,400, taken into income and taxed in bracket.
2. A long-term capital loss of $6,000. *Result*: 50%, or $3,000, is used to reduce taxable income. (It is not possible to reduce taxable income dollar for dollar of long-term losses. All short-and long-

term capital losses are grouped together, and total loss deductions
may not exceed $3,000 a year. If there is more than $3,000 of
losses, the unused balance may be carried over indefinitely.)

3. A short-term capital gain of $6,000. *Result*: The entire amount is
taken into taxable income and taxed in bracket.

4. A short-term capital loss of $6,000. *Result*: The entire amount
may be used as a reduction of income spread over the years, with
a maximum of $3,000 each year.

5. A net long-term capital gain of $200 and a net short-term capital
loss of $500. *Result*: The difference between the short-term loss of
$500 and the long-term gain of $200 is $300, or a net short-term
loss. Therefore, the $300 may be used to reduce taxable income.

6. A net short-term capital gain of $1,200 and a net long-term capital
loss of $3,000. *Result*: Combining the two, the balance is $1,800
of long-term loss. Therefore, 50%, or $900, may be used to re-
duce taxable income.

7. A net short-term capital gain of $300 and a long-term capital gain
of $400. *Result*: The amount of $300 is added to taxable income
from short-term gains, and 40% of long-term gains of $400, or
$160, is also added.

Care must be taken, however, to offset short-term capital gains before
they become long-term capital gains, *because long-term capital gains must
be matched with long-term capital losses first.*

Let us assume the following:

Short-term capital gain *taken*	**$2,000**
Short-term capital loss on paper but *not taken*	**$2,000**
Long-term capital gains *taken*	**$2,000**

The taxpayer should take his or her *short-term loss* before it becomes
long term. In this case, the short-term gain would be offset by a short-term
loss and the taxpayer would pay a tax on only 40% of his long-term capital
gain of $2,000, or $800.

However, if the taxpayer allows the short-term loss to go over 12
months and become a long-term loss, then the taxpayer *must match* this
long-term capital gain. If in the former case, if the taxpayer is in the 50%
bracket, half, or $5,000, will be left of the profit. In the second case, the fol-
lowing would result (assuming no change in the gain of $10,000):

The taxpayer with a short-term profit of, say, $10,000 might be faced
with two alternatives: to sell and take a short-term profit, which is carried
to income and taxed in bracket, or to hold the security until it becomes a
long-term capital gain. If in the former case, if the taxpayer is in the 50%
bracket, half, or $5,000, will be left of the profit. In the second case, the fol-
lowing would result (assuming no change in the gain of $10,000):

Capital gain	$10,000
Less: 60%	6,000
Taxable as income	4,000
50% tax.	2,000

Here the tax on capital gains is reduced from $5,000 to $2,000. But the taxpayer cannot be sure that the $10,000 will remain the same. On the basis of tax bracket the taxpayer can estimate how far the gain can decline before it is equally advantageous to take the short-term profit or wait until the profit is long term.

For instance, assume a decline of 37 1/2% in the profit; it would be equally advantageous to take the short-term profit or wait and take the long-term gain.

37 1/2% decline in profit to	$6,250
Less: 60% of long-term gain	3,750
Taxable as income	$2,500
Taxes for individual in 50% bracket	1,250
Profit on long-term sale	6,250
Less: Tax	1,250
Break-even point	$5,000

As the tax bracket of the individual rises, the break-even point declines. For a taxpayer in the 60% bracket, the trade-off point would be a decline of about 47.5%.

IDENTIFICATION OF SECURITIES

Let us assume an investor holds shares of the same stock bought at different times and at different prices. The investor decides to sell part of his holdings. The investor must assume, if he cannot identify the cost basis and holding period, that the stock sold was his earliest purchase (i.e., first-in, first-out). It is obvious therefore that the investor should preserve his records with care to establish identification.

WASH SALE RULES

A wash sale is essentially a sale that is not a sale. A wash sale takes place when an investor sells a security to establish a tax loss. At the same time the investor hopes to buy it back after the required interval.

But the Internal Revenue Service has ruled that

1. the investor must have held the security for at least 30 days prior to the wash sale.
2. when sold the security must *not* be bought back for at least 31 days. Thus the total period between acquisition, sale and repurchase should cover at least 61 days.
3. the investor during the 30-day period prior to the wash sale or 31 days after has not bought or agreed to buy a substantially identical security. (These requirements apply to all types of investors including corporations and banks unless dealers.)[1]
4. securities sold to establish a *gain* may be repurchased at once. For example, a security holder might wish to mark up the cost of his securities. This is sometimes done by some institutional portfolio managers.

TAX TREATMENT OF SHORT SALES

A short sale usually results in a short-term gain or loss. This is true when the investor does *not* hold the stock he is selling short. When the investor covers the short sale by buying in the stock and delivering it to the lender, the time interval is usually a few days and is well below the year specified as the time limit for a short-term gain or loss.

When the taxpayer *does* own the stock he is selling short, the tax treatment depends on the length of time the security has been held. If held less than 12 months the gains are short term; if held more than 12 months (1 year plus 1 day) the losses are treated as long term.

Dividends on stocks sold short must be paid by the borrower to the lender. They may be considered a nonbusiness expense by the borrower.

Short sales are sometimes used to assure a profit and at the same time defer payment of taxes. For instance, let us assume that, some time in November 1979, an investor has a profit of $2,500 in the ABC Company. He desires to take this profit but does not wish to add to an already high 1979 tax bill. Accordingly, the investor sells short "against the box" his shares of ABC Company but borrows an equal amount to make delivery. On January 2, 1980, the investor delivers his own stock to close out the

---

[1]The term "substantially identical" requires a little explanation. Apparently, the I.R.S. does not consider the securities of different corporations to be identical. For instance, an investor might sell at a loss Westington Electric and buy General Electric. Also, different types of securities of the same corporation are not considered substantially identical. An investor could sell the common and buy the preferred stock of a company. Bonds and notes issued by the same government agency are not considered substantially identical if the issue dates, the interest rates, and the maturity dates are different.

deal. Thus the investor has taken a profit of $2,500 and does not have to pay a tax on it until April 15, 1981.

TAX DEDUCTIONS AVAILABLE TO THE INVESTOR

Expenses available include

1. custodian, investment counsel, accounting, and legal advisory or tax consultant fees
2. rental of safety deposit box
3. secretarial and office expense in relation to investments
4. interest paid on margin accounts or bank collateral loans (The exception here is that interest paid or expenses to carry tax-exempt securities are *not* an allowed deduction.)
5. Payments on Keogh or IRA plans (see page 127)
6. State and local transfer taxes are charged against ordinary income

OTHER TAX DEDUCTIONS

The most important other tax deductions are as follows:

1. real estate taxes on home
2. contributions to recognized charities
3. prescribed drugs in excess of 1% of gross income
4. medical expenses plus the above net drug deductions (after 1% deduction) *less* 5% of gross income
5. state income taxes
6. state sales taxes except license fees and gasoline taxes
7. business expense—moving expenses and courses of study when job related
8. finance and interest charges
9. credit of 15% of first $2,000 spent for qualifying energy conserving expenditure (maximum credit: $300); for solar and wind equipment, 30% of first $2,000 of expenditure and 20% for next $8,000, with a maximum of $2,000
10. entertainment expenses that are directly related to trade or business
11. in 1979 personal exemptions of $1,000 each, for the taxpayer, his spouse, and for each dependent and additional exemption when each spouse is over 65
12. the standard deduction used by taxpayers who did not itemize their deductions became the *zero-bracket amount* (ZBA). In 1982 it equaled $3,400 for married persons, $2,300 for a single head of the household, and $1,700 for a single person.

MINIMUM TAX PREFERENCE ITEMS

The tax preference items for individuals include (1) the difference between the market value of a stock and the price at which a qualified stock option is exercised, (2) accelerated depreciation on real estate in excess of straight-line depreciation (see page 143), and (3) intangible drilling costs in excess of oil and gas income.

No tax is due by individuals on tax preference items provided they do not exceed the greater of $10,000 or 50% of their regular income taxes. The excess, however, is subject to a tax of 15% as follows:

Mr. Jones and wife in 1979 had an income of $162,400. Their income tax would be $81,464 (see page 357). Their tax preferences were $130,000. Their *minimum tax on tax preferences* would be

Tax preferences	$130,000
Less: 50% of taxes of $81,464	40,732
	$89,268
Minimum tax: 15% of $89,268	13,390

Individuals may have to pay an alternative minimum tax if this tax exceeds their regular tax. The most important tax preference item is the untaxed portion of capital gains. For instance, 40% of long-term capital gains are carried to income and are taxed in bracket, but the balance, or 60%, is a tax preference item. The gains from the sale of main residences are *not* considered tax preference items. The alternative minimum tax is graduated and based on alternative minimum taxable income. The tax is 10% on income over $20,000 up to $60,000, 20% over $60,000 and up to $100,000 and 25% on the excess over $100,000.

ESTATE AND GIFT TAXES

Neither a tax return nor a tax is required if a gift to any one person does not exceed $10,000 a year. A wife, a husband, or both may give each of their children as much as $20,000 a year. Either could give the $20,000 but both must consent, and a return must be filed with the government. But no tax would be due. Except for these annual gifts, all gifts are included in the estate of the donor. The Unified Tax Rate Schedule for years 1977 and thereafter applies to both gifts and to estates. There is, however, a credit allowed by the government against federal income taxes. This credit amounts to $79,300 in 1983 and in 1987 and thereafter to $192,800. Thus, an individual dying in 1987 and leaving a net taxable estate of $600,000 on which taxes would be $192,800 would pay no tax as the credit allowed by the government is exactly that amount. In 1987, and thereafter with a uniform credit of $182,800, the net taxable estate could be as high as $600,000 without having to pay any federal tax. Some state estate taxes are fairly high, but state taxes are in part at least deductible.

One of the main advantages of making gifts prior to death is that the donor can be reasonably sure that his or her heirs have the money and that the transfer will not be held up by the delay and expense of administration. Nevertheless, in spite of the tax credit explained above, the gift and estate taxes are very progressive as may be seen from the following:

Table 20-2		1983		
A Taxable Estate Equal to or More than	B Taxable Estate Less than	Tax on Amount in Column A	+	Rate on Tax in Excess over the Amount in A
$ 250,000	$ 500,000	$ 70,800		34%
500,000	750,000	155,800		37
1,000,000	1,250,000	345,800		41
3,000,000	or more	1,290,800		57

According to this table, an estate of $300,000, for example, would pay a federal tax of $70,800 plus 34% of the excess over $250,000 of $50,000, or $17,000, making a total of $87,800. But a deduction should be made from the amount of a credit of $79,300 allowed in 1983 (and $96,300 allowed in 1984), making the net tax due of $8,500.

This estate tax must be paid in cash nine months after the date of death. It may be calculated on the basis of the net taxable estate valued either on the date of death or six months thereafter, whichever is lower.

MARITAL DEDUCTION

It is often advisable for married couples to take advantage of the so-called marital deduction provision of the federal income tax law. This simply means that one spouse may leave half (50%) outright to the other, and it will for tax purposes not be included in his or her estate. However, it must be clearly stated in the spouse's will and must be an outright bequest without any conditions. The balance of the spouse's estate could be set up as a trust for the benefit of the surviving spouse. In the case of small estates, the marital deduction may be as much as $250,000, regardless of the amount of the estate. Further, the marital deduction provision was changed in 1979 to permit lifetime transfers between spouses of up to $100,000.

1. Who should file income tax returns? What records should be kept?
2. Explain the double taxation of dividends.
3. Describe three ways in which a wealthy person might ease the burden of federal income taxes.
4. Distinguish between a short-term and a long-term capital gain. How are the holding periods calculated?
5. Explain how a gain or loss must be established in year-end transactions.
6. What is the required procedure in establishing a loss and buying the security back?
7. How should stock dividends be treated if held by stockholder? If sold?
8. What are the general principles of the corporate income tax? (See Chapter 18).
9. What are tax preference items? How are they taxed?
10. Name at least six tax deductions available to the investor.

TRUE AND FALSE QUESTIONS

1. Filing of tax returns is required of: *True* *False*
   a. every U.S. citizen _____ _____
   b. every U.S. resident regardless of citizenship _____ _____
   c. every single person in the United States with income of $3,300 or more if under the age of 65; if over 65, income of $4,300. _____ _____

2. Medical expenses: *True* *False*
   a. may not be deducted from taxable income _____ _____
   b. are a deduction from taxable income up to 100% _____ _____
   c. may be deducted to the extent that they exceed the excess of the 1% of gross income allowed for drugs plus 5% of gross income. _____ _____

3. As far as dividends and interest are concerned: *True* *False*
   a. the taxpayer in 1980 is allowed to exclude $100 from dividends only and in 1981, $200 from dividends and interest _____ _____
   b. the amounts in excess of the above must be included in taxable income _____ _____
   c. the dividends are in effect subject to double taxation as the corporation also pays taxes. _____ _____

4. A taxpayer with a high income: *True*   *False*
   a. cannot do anything except pay the taxes in
      a high tax bracket   _____   _____
   b. can reduce the taxes by buying municipal
      bonds   _____   _____
   c. can reduce taxes by taking tax losses.   _____   _____

5. If a taxpayer buys a stock on February 7 and sells it at a profit on
   February 7, it is: *True*   *False*
   a. a short-term gain   _____   _____
   b. a long-term gain.   _____   _____

6. A taxpayer in the 50% bracket who has a long-term gain of $20,000
   must pay a federal income tax of: *True*   *False*
   a. $10,000   _____   _____
   b. $8,000   _____   _____
   c. $5,000   _____   _____
   d. $4,000.   _____   _____

7. A taxpayer in the 50% bracket with a long-term loss of $6,000 may
   deduct from taxable income: *True*   *False*
   a. $6,000 in the first year   _____   _____
   b. $3,000 in first year and $3,000 in the second   _____   _____
   c. $3,000 in the first year only.   _____   _____

8. As far as year-end transactions are concerned: *True*   *False*
   a. to realize a gain the current year, the stock
      must be delivered on or before the last busi-
      ness day of the year   _____   _____
   b. to realize a loss, the stock may be sold on
      the last business day   _____   _____
   c. to establish a loss and buy back, the
      security holder must have held the security
      30 days and not repurchase until 31 days
      after sale.   _____   _____

9. Stock dividends: *True*   *False*
   a. are not taxable if held   _____   _____
   b. are not taxable if sold at a profit from ad-
      justed cost   _____   _____
   c. taxable if sold at a profit from adjusted cost.   _____   _____

10. A net taxable estate of $650,000 of an individual dying in 1987 would
    pay a federal estate tax of: *True*   *False*
    a. $182,800   _____   _____
    b. $100,000   _____   _____
    c. $87,500   _____   _____
    d. $18,500.   _____   _____

21

FEDERAL AND STATE
SECURITIES REGULATION

The securities business is one of the most highly regulated industries in the United States. A wide variety of federal and state legislative acts have been enacted to govern the activities of the individuals and institutions engaged in this economic area. The products handled by the securities business (stocks and bonds) are regulated from the cradle to the grave, so to speak. The services supplied by the individuals and institutions in the securities business are subject to this same intensive and extensive regulation.

From the time a corporation gives birth to a new security issue until the time that issue dies (through refunding or retirement, merger, consolidation, reorganization, or dissolution of the corporation) the issue is watched, controlled, studied, observed, evaluated, checked, and double checked. Furthermore, all individuals and institutions involved in its conception, birth, active life, old age, and death are subject to codes, rules, regulations, laws, and restrictions of many types and from many sources.

In addition to the regulatory details spelled out by the federal and state statutes, securities and security issuers, underwriters, brokers, dealers, and salespersons are subject (when applicable) to the extensive regulations, rules, and codes of

1. National Association of Securities Dealers, Inc.
2. New York Stock Exchange
3. American Stock Exchange
4. various regional securities exchanges
5. the orders and interpretations of a variety of regulatory agencies, such as
   a. Securities and Exchange Commission
   b. Interstate Commerce Commission

    c.   Federal Power Commission
    d.   Federal Reserve System's board of governors
6. individual firms in the securities business
7. various securities associations and institutes

FEDERAL SECURITIES REGULATION

Any securities business being conducted on an interstate basis is subject to the provisions of the federal securities laws. Generally speaking, the federal securities laws are more comprehensive and more stringent than are their state counterparts. However, some state laws appear in certain respects to be more restrictive and detailed than the various federal provisions designed to regulate the same general area. In some cases, it appears obvious that the state legislative bodies have not provided statutes governing a given area of the securities business because of their feeling that the federal securities laws were already adequately supplying any needed restrictions in that area.

The Securities and Exchange Commission

The Securities and Exchange Commission (SEC), organized July 2, 1934, is the U.S. government agency that administers the federal securities laws. The commission consists of five men appointed by the president for five-year terms.

The act of Congress that created the SEC is called the Securities Exchange Act of 1934.

The commission administers nine major pieces of federal legislation, all of which relate to the nation's securities business. These are the

1. Securities Act of 1933[1]
2. Securities Exchange Act of 1934
3. Public Utility Holding Company Act of 1935
4. Trust Indenture Act of 1939
5. Investment Company Act of 1940
6. Investment Advisors Act of 1940
7. Securities Acts Amendments of 1964
8. Investment Company Amendments Act of 1970
9. Securities Reform Act of 1975

The SEC also serves as an advisor to the federal courts in the corporate reorganization proceedings under Chapter X of the Nationl Bankruptcy Act.

[1]This act was administered by the Federal Trade Commission until September 1934.

Securities Act of 1933

The Securities Act of 1933 was the first of a series of federal legislative acts passed to regulate the interstate activities of the securities business. This act has two basic objectives:

1. "to provide full and fair disclosure of the character of securities sold in interstate and foreign commerce and through the mails."
2. to prohibit certain fraudulent acts and practices in the sale of securities generally and to prohibit statements, acts, and practices that tend to misrepresent the facts or deceive the investor.

The Securities Act is often referred to as the "truth in Securities Act" and attempts to assure that the investing public will have adequate information with which to make an accurate informed evaluation of a security being offered for sale.

Registration of Securities

One of the main provisions of the Securities Act of 1933 deals with the registration of securities. The act requires registration with the SEC of all securities covered by the act before these securities may be offered for public sale by an issuing company or by any person in a "control" relationsip to such a company.

To meet this registration requirement, specified information dealing with many aspects of the corporation must be presented in detail in a registration statement and filed by the issuer with the SEC.

Exempted Securities

Certain securities issues are exempt from registration with the SEC. Some of the major exemptions are

1. securities issued or guaranteed by the U.S. government or its agencies
2. securities issued by states, municipalities, or public authorities
3. issues of domestic banks or trust companies
4. commercial paper or bankers' acceptances
5. securities issued by railroads, airlines, and trucking companies
6. offerings under Regulation A of the SEC[2]

[2]Although Regulation A offerings are exempt from registration with the SEC, it is necessary for the issuer to file a circular or specified content with the commission at least 15 days before the proposed date of offering. Also, an offering circular generally must be used in connection with the sale of such securities and their sale is subject to the Rules of Fair Practice of the NASD. See page 376.

7. miscellaneous offerings that include securities of building and loan companies, farmers' cooperatives, receivers' or trustees' certificates, and religious, educational, and charitable institutions (insurance policies or variable annuities and variable life policies are *not* exempt from SEC registration)

Exempted Transactions

Transactions that are exempt from SEC registration requirement include

1. transactions between private individuals
2. brokers' transactions executed on unsolicited customers' orders
3. private placements that do not involve a public offering (see page 375)
4. transactions by securities dealers with the following *exceptions* (that is, the following must be qualified with the SEC):
    a. those representing the unsold allotment or subscription by a dealer participating in the distribution
    b. those following an effective registration that are traded within
        (1) 90 days of issuance of the primary or initial offering
        (2) 40 days of a subsequent or secondary offering by the issuer

The Registration Statement

The registration statement filed with the SEC generally contains much more information about the issuing company than the typical investor will take time to read. Ordinarily, the registration statement contains information about the type of business, the purpose of the securities issue, comparative balance sheets and income accounts, statements about suits pending against the corporation, compensation of the promoter, the underwriting spread, and the price at which the security will be issued, among numerous other things.

Under the Securities Act of 1933, an abbreviated form of the registration statement (called a prospectus) must be delivered to all initial buyers of registered securities. The act also states that every written communication soliciting an order of open-end investment company shares must be accompanied or preceded by a prospectus. The prospectus contains the most important information covered in the registration statement.

When the SEC examines the registration statement covering a particular security issue, it looks primarily for false or misleading statements (or omissions) of a material nature. The act provides penalties of fine or imprisonment or both for any such misleading statements or omissions. All persons signing the registration statement are liable for misleading statements or omissions of fact. Criminal penalties of five years in prison and/or $5,000 fine may be imposed. Civil suits may be brought for recovery within three years of offering, and one of discovery.

It is important to remember that the SEC does *not approve* securities registered with it and offered for sale. In fact, the SEC does not even guarantee the accuracy of the disclosures made in a prospectus or registration statement. Nor does it pass on the merits of a particular security covered by a registration statement. The individual investor, not the SEC, must make the ultimate decision concerning the value or worth of the security.

To make certain that the role of the SEC in reviewing the registration statement of a new issue is not misunderstood, the Securities Act requires a statement on each prospectus indicating the limitation of the SEC's authority. This statement, which must be printed in heavy type on the prospectus cover, is as follows:

THESE SECURITIES HAVE NOT BEEN APPROVED OR DISAPPROVED BY THE SECURITIES AND EXCHANGE COMMISSION NOR HAS THE COMMISSION PASSED UPON THE ACCURACY OR ADEQUACY OF THIS PROSPECTUS, ANY REPRESENTATION TO THE CONTRARY IS A CRIMINAL OFFENSE.

Effective Date of the Registration Statement

A 20-day waiting period (or cooling-off period as it is often called), must elapse between the filing date and the date on which the registration statement becomes effective. Once the registration statement becomes effective, the securities may be sold. This minimum interval, which may be extended or shortened by the SEC, is necessary to give the commission time to examine the registration statement and call for any additional required information from the issuer. The SEC asks for this supplementary material by issuing a deficiency letter that outlines to the company any additional information needed and any changes that must be made. When the additions and changes called for by the deficiency letter have been prepared, they are presented in an amended registration statement and filed with the SEC.

A stop order suspending the effectiveness of a registration statement can be entered by the SEC whenever it appears that the registration statement contains any untrue statement of a material fact or any misleading omission of a material fact. An opportunity is given for a hearing before the stop order is imposed. For a summary of the Securities Act of 1933, see page 456.

Preliminary Prospectus

Until the registration statement becomes effective, no confirmation of a sale may be made. However, during this waiting period, a preliminary prospectus (referred to in the past as a red-herring prospectus) may be used. A preliminary prospectus is one that is complete except for amendments as to price and any additional required information. It may be used to acquaint potential investors with essential facts to obtain indications of interest prior to the effective date of a registration statement.

The outside front cover of the preliminary prospectus must bear the caption "Preliminary Prospectus" in red ink. It must also show the date the prospectus was issued, and must have the following statement printed in prominent type:

> A registration statement relating to these securities has been filed with the Securities and Exchange Commission but has not yet become effective. Information contained herein is subject to completion or amendment. These securities may not be sold nor may offers be accepted prior to the time the registration statement becomes effective. This prospectus shall not constitute an offer to sell or the solicitation of an offer to buy nor shall there be any sale of these securities in any state in which such offer, solicitation or sale would be unlawful prior to registration or qualification under the securities laws of any such state.

The public offering price and the underwriting spread are not decided until shortly before the actual offering. When they are decided, a final amendment (setting forth the public offering) is filed with the SEC. If everything is acceptable to the commission, the registration statement will be ordered effective and the securities will be released for actual sale.

Delivery of Final Prospectus

The final prospectus is essentially the preliminary prospectus plus the final amendment. The final amendment contains the offering price and the underwriters' spread or commission.

A final prospectus must be given to all buyers of the issue. If a customer has not previously been given a preliminary prospectus (red herring) and the receipt of the prospectus is the first opportunity to study the issue, the customer may cancel his purchase order.

The final prospectus must be given to *all* buyers by both the underwriters and, if formed, the members of the selling group. The time limit for the required prospectus is 40 days after the effective date the issue is sold, provided the issue has previously registered securities for sale. It is 90 days if the issuer has never registered before.

Private Placements (Rule 146)

Private placements generally mean the direct sale of an issue of securities to a relatively few large, well-informed, and wealthy investors. These would include substantial individuals, foundations, insurance companies, pension funds, trust companies, commercial and savings banks. A simple rule might be that the buyers must be *smart and rich*. In more detail, the SEC rules that the buyers must be adequately informed. The issuer must provide the buyers with the same information as would be available in a full registration statement. Usually the buyers get more information than that, however. In fact, they are often told facts that the company is reluctant to put in a registration statement. Further, the SEC insists that the buyers be experienced investors who will express in writing their intention to hold the securities as investments. The transactions must be negotiated. Promotional advertisements are not permitted. Finally, the number of informed buyers should be limited—to about 35. To ensure that the purchasers are not acting on behalf of another and that they do not intend immediately to reoffer the securities, the offerees must sign an investment letter. Hence the name *letter stock* has come into being. If in the future it becomes necessary or desirable to reoffer the security, the investors must follow Rule 144 (see page 376).

There are a number of advantages in selling securities directly to institutions (e.g. life insurance companies, savings banks, pension funds, and so forth). Speed is perhaps the most striking advantage. There are no lengthy registration delays with the SEC. The deal can often be arranged in a matter of days between sophisticated individuals. Also there is privacy, as no prospectus is issued that might contain information the company might not wish to disclose to competitors. In the event the issuer might wish to amend the loan agreement in later years, the lender is usually more understanding. It is not necessary to get the approval of many security holders. Finally, there is no fear of minority suits from disgruntled security holders. There are a few disadvantages to private placements. Often the rate of interest paid by the borrower is higher than would have been paid had the issue been sold by competitive bidding. At times, the sinking fund provisions of the institutional borrowers have been more restrictive. Also, it is not possible for a borrower to buy his securities in the market at a discount for sinking fund purposes because there is no public market for the bonds. But in 1979 about 46% of the total bonds issued were privately placed. The role of the investment banker in private placements is important. Often the issuers wish the investment banker to sit in on the negotiation and advise them on the fairness of the terms. Also, in a number of cases the investment banker will find an institution that is willing to lend to its corporate client.

Intrastate Offerings (Rule 147)

Offerings of securities by issuers chartered in a state to investors in that state are exempt from registration with the SEC. The issuer, however, must do the bulk (80%) of its business and have the bulk of its assets in the mother state. The purchasers must also make written statements that they are residents of the state in which the issuer conducts the majority of its business. Resales within nine months must be made only to residents.

Regulation A Offerings

Regulation A offerings may be made up to $1,500,000 by filing a short offering circular with the regional sales offices of the SEC. The circular must be filed at least 15 days prior to the offering date. The main advantage of Regulation A filing is the exemption from the requirement for filing an audited statement and periodic financial reports once the securities are sold. This is true unless the company has assets of $1,000,000 and 500 shareholders.

Also the SEC permits subsidiaries of companies, particularly of public utilities, to issue securities under Regulation A up to $1,500,000. In short a Regulation A filing is easier and less expensive in terms of legal and filing fees.

In March 1979, the SEC approved a rule that would permit companies with less than $1,000,000 in assets and 500 stockholders to make initial stock offerings up to $5,000,000 with the abbreviated registration with only two years of financial statements. This new form, however, cannot be used by the oil, gas, or mining companies or by limited partnerships (i.e., as tax shelters).

Sales of Restricted or Controlled Securities (Rule 144).

Restricted securities (as described earlier) are essentially private (unregistered) placements as well as stocks acquired by employee stock options. They are sometimes called letter stock.

Control securities are securities held by any individual who dominates a company. He or she might not own the majority of the company's stock but own a sufficient amount to have an important voice in the management of the company. He or she might be an officer, a director, or simply a stockholder.

If either of these categories of investors wishes to sell their stock, the SEC has laid down strict rules.

First, these securities can only be sold if there is ample public information concerning the company. This would include annual and quarterly reports and the fact that the company is a *reporting company*. This means that the company has filed the necessary reports with the SEC for at least 90 days prior to the proposed sale.

Second, the holder of the restricted stock must have held it at least two years before sale is possible. There is no holding period for control stock unless it is also restricted stock. In this case, the two-year holding period applies.

Third, if the securities are traded on a national exchange 1% of the shares outstanding may be sold in a three-month period *or* the average weekly volume of the shares of that stock traded on all national exchanges and on NASDAQ during four calendar weeks, before the notice of sale.

Fourth, no notice of sale need be given to the SEC if the total shares are 500 or less and the dollar amount does not exceed $10,000. Three copies must be filed with the SEC and one with the exchange on which the stock is listed.

Fifth, the investor or his broker must not actively solicit buy orders or make any extra payment to execute sell orders. The broker acting on a regular commission basis may make inquiries of other brokers who are known to be familiar with the securities being sold.

Sixth, a recent amendment effective November 1978 provides that an investor may sell *all* his restricted stock if listed on a national securities exchange or traded on the OTC *and* quoted by the NASDAQ and owned for three years. If traded on the OTC and not quoted on the NASDAQ, the holding period is four years. The securities sold must be of reporting companies, and all sales must take place in a three-month period. This amendment applies to investors that are not affiliates or control persons of the issuer. A control person of the issuing company must wait at least three months after the status as a control person has been ended before selling all his securities.

Release of Publicity and Offering Material on New Issues

During the prefiling period, no offers whatsoever of the securities may be made. In the interval between filing and the effective date of an issue (1) the preliminary prospectus is given to all prospective buyers, (2) the underwriters sound the market (i.e. do their homework), (3) the underwriters might circle amounts that prospective indicate that they might buy, and (4) the underwriters do not project the company's prospects but may answer unsolicited inquiries.

When the registration has become effective, orders are solicited, sales are made, and closing payments are made to the issuer some days later. The final prospectus must accompany every sale confirmation.

The Securities Exchange Act of 1934

The Securities Exchange Act of 1934 is one of the most important federal statutes regulating the securities business. It was enacted following a number of congressional investigations that uncovered the existence of a variety of undesirable and improper practices in the securities markets of the early 1930s. The Exchange Act became law on June 6, 1934, its express objective being to establish and maintain fair and honest markets for securities.

As a result of the stock market crash in 1929, and the confusion that followed, American investors generally lost confidence in securities as a safe and profitable investment medium. Such a situation is a calamity in a capitalistic society, which depends on private capital for the machines required to sustain industrial health and promote economic growth. Congress knew it was essential that this lost confidence be restored as quickly and as completely as possible.

The Securities Act of 1934 was the statute Congress offered to help the securities business place its house in order and keep it in order. Its provisions were designed to outlaw the misrepresentations, manipulations, and other abusive practices that had been preventing the functioning of just and equitable principles of trade in the securities markets. From its provisions and amendments, the Securities Exchange Commission and the National Association of Securities Dealers, Inc. were created to help with its enforcement.

Exchange Registration. The Securities Exchange Act of 1934 provides for the registration and regulation of securities exchanges and the registration of the securities listed on such exchanges. To ensure fair and orderly markets, all exchanges, unless exempt, must register with the SEC.[3] Under the securities acts amendments of 1964, the Exchange Act also provides for the registration and regulation of certain securities traded over the counter (see pages 384 and 385).

One primary objective of Exchange Act is to provide the investing public with reliable information regarding securities listed on national securities exchanges and the corporations that issued such securities. To provide this information, detailed registration statements must be filed by each corporation *listing* it shares on an exchange. The Exchange Act forbids trading in any nonexempt security on a national exchange unless the security is registered. Data contained on the registration form must include all pertinent material facts and must set forth in such a manner so as not to be misleading. The Exchange Act establishes financial and other reporting requirements for issuers of securities registered under the act.

[3]A detailed discussion of the organization, operation, and regulation of registered securities exchanges is presented in Chapter 10.

Prohibitions Against Manipulative and Deceptive Devices

Concerning insider transactions the Exchange Act also establishes reporting requirements and imposes trading restrictions on the directors, officers, and principal securities holders of corporations whenever such persons are trading in the securities of their own companies. Principal securities holders subject to these provisions are those shareholders who are beneficial owners of more than 10% of the outstanding securities of a registered class of stock. Under the regulations, all such "insiders" must report their initial holdings to the SEC and must report any change that takes place in their beneficial ownership within ten days after the end of each calendar month in which any change occurs.

Corporate insiders, by virtue of their position, may have information of a company's condition and prospects that is unavailable to the general public. This inside knowledge may be used by such persons to their personal advantage in trading in the company's securities. Thus, regulations have been promulgated that remove the profit incentive in short-term trading by permitting the corporation or its stockholders to bring suit for the recovery of profit from insiders on transactions completed within six months. "Short" sales and "sales against the box" are also prohibited by such persons by the Exchange Act regulations. (See short sales, page 199.)

Several sections of the Securities Exchange Act contain provisions that specifically prohibit manipulation of securities prices and fraudulent and deceptive practices in the securities markets.

Securities transactions designed to give a misleading appearance of active trading are illegal. Two such prohibited fictitious practices are:

1. "Wash sales," in which one person purchases and sells the same stock at about the same time to give the impression of activity in the stock, and
2. "Matched orders," in which transactions between individuals acting in concert to "paint the tape" record a price and give the impression of delivery without a true change of ownership.

The Exchange Act also prohibits pool devices used to manipulate markets and the spreading of rumor or false information.

In this connection, the SEC has stated, for example, that:

1. Predictions of specific and substantial increases in the price of a speculative security are inherently fraudulent and cannot be justified.
2. A recommendation to a customer to purchase a speculative security without having made a reasonable inquiry as to its current financial condition and business operations is contrary to the basic obligation to deal fairly with the investing public.

For securities that are exempt from regulation (i.e., U.S. governments, etc.) by the SEC, any irregular or fraudulent transactions can be prosecuted under the antifraud laws of the various states. Other sections of the Securities Exchange Act include a prohibition against *trading* by persons interested in the distribution of the same securities. The exemptions to this prohibition include unsolicited customer orders, stabilizing bids by the manager of the underwriting group (see page 161), and market-making transactions ten busness days prior to the distribution.

Over-the-Counter Markets — Registration of Broker-Dealers

The Exchange Act of 1934 also requires the registration of all securities brokers and dealers. Unless a securities broker-dealer is registered with the SEC, he or she is denied the mails or any instrumentality of interstate commerce to effect any securities transaction. (See page 171 for a more detailed discussion on this point.)

Proxy Solicitations

The Exchange Act also concerns itself with proxy statements and the regulation of proxy solicitations of issuers of securities registered under the act. Under provisions of the act, the SEC insists that all proxies must be detailed and truthful and must avoid false or misleading statements of material fact. Furthermore, the proxy statement must not omit any material fact necessary to make statements already made not false or misleading. The proxy statement must disclose all pertinent information concerning the matter to be decided by the proxy vote, and a place should be provided on the proxy to enable the shareholder to vote yes or no.

Personnel Records

Under the provisions of the 1934 act, certain records are required to be kept by brokers and dealers who are registered with the SEC. Beginning in 1962, such brokers and dealers were required to maintain personnel records showing the following information for each of their registered representatives:

1. name, address, Social Security number, and the starting date of employment or other association with the member, broker, or dealer
2. date of birth
3. the educational institutions attended and degree or degrees granted
4. a complete, consecutive statement of all business connections for at least the preceding ten years, including the reason for leaving

each prior employment, and whether the employment was part-time or full-time

5. a record of any denial of membership or registration and of any disciplinary action taken or sanction imposed upon the registered representative by any federal or state agency, or by any national securities exchange or national securities association, including any finding that he was a cause of any disciplinary action or had violated any law

6. a record of any denial, suspension, expulsion, or revocation of membership or registration of any member, broker, or dealer with whom he was associated in any capacity when such action was taken

7. a record of any permanent or temporary injunction entered against the representative or any member, broker, or dealer with whom he was associated in any capacity at the time such injunction was entered

8. a record of any arrests, indictments, or convictions for any felony or other misdemeanor, except minor traffic offenses of which he has been subject

9. a record of any other name or names by which the registered representative has been known previously or which he has used in the past

Credit Extension to Customers
By Brokers and Dealers (Margin Requirement)

The board of governors of the Federal Reserve System prescribes the regulations that determine the amount of credit brokers and dealers may extend to their customers. These regulations are contained in the Federal Reserve Board's *Regulation T*. Regulation T was adopted by the Fed's board of governors under the provisions of the Securities Exchange Act of 1934 (as amended).

Regulation T relates to the extension of credit to customers by brokers and dealers doing business through the medium of a member of a national securities exchange. Initial margin requirements are established under Regulation T and have ranged from 40% to 100%.

Regulation T also permits extension of credit on certain OTC margin stocks that are deemed by the Federal Reserve Board to have a degree of national interest, depth of market, availability of information respecting the stock issues, and character and permanence of the issues to warrant the stocks inclusion on the list. (Margin stocks are discussed in more detail on page 202.)

Regulation T is considered one of the most important federal regulations affecting the day-to-day activities of registered representatives. The *special cash account of* Regulation T concerns *cash* transactions of customers. It is understood that they will be settled *promptly,* that is, within two or three days required by the usual transmittal facilities.

Customers purchasing securities must make full payment within seven full business days after the trade date. If not, the broker must cancel or otherwise liquidate the transaction or any unsettled portion thereof.

The following are *exceptions* to this rule:

1. when the amount involved is under $100
2. when the security purchased is an unissued security, the period of seven full business days runs from the date on which the security was made available by the issuer
3. when there is a delay in shipment, additional days of delay are granted up to seven full business days
4. when the purchase is made by the customer with the understanding that payment is to be made on delivery (COD)

When the account is not settled within 7 full business days, that account must be frozen for 90 calendar days.

Citing unusual circumstances, a customer might appeal, with success, to the NASD or to the exchanges for a limited extension of time. (Forms are available at the NASD district office.)

Regulation U applies to the extension of credit on registered securities by banks. It deals with loans by banks for the purpose of purchasing or carrying registered stocks.

Regulation G, first promulgated in 1968, applies to the extension of credit on registered securities by firms *other than* brokers, dealers, and banks. It includes to a large extent small finance companies and individuals called unregulated lenders prior to this regulation.

Restriction on Borrowing by Members, Brokers, and Dealers

Section 8 of this act stipulates the *net capital rule*. It sets limits on the amount of indebtedness that a firm may contract in relation to its net capital (for a detailed discussion, see page 461).

Hypothecation of Customers Securities

Essentially the 1934 act prohibits lending of customers' securities without their consent or commingling them with securities of the firm (for a more detailed discussion, see pages 266 and 437).

Trust Indenture Act of 1939

The Trust Indenture Act, passed in 1939, established specific statutory standards for trust indentures. A trust indenture (or deed of trust, as it is often called) is a contractual agreement between a corporation issuing bonds and a trustee or trustees representing the investors who own the bonds. The trust indenture indicates in detail the rights and privileges of the bondholders and how these may be enforced. It also gives a detailed description of rights, privileges, and liabilities of the debtor corporation. Under a trust indenture, the trustee (generally a bank or trust company) represents all of the bondholders and deals with the corporation on their behalf.

The Trust Indenture Act applies only to those trust indentures under which more than $1,000,000 of securities may be outstanding at any one time. Most debt securities, such as mortgage bonds, debentures, notes, and so on, are issued pursuant to a trust indenture.

SEC studies made prior to the passage of the Trust Indenture Act disclosed that many trust indentures failed to provide the minimum protection needed to prevent losses to debt security holders. In addition, the studies revealed that many corporations neglected to provide an independent trustee to protect the bondholder's investment. The act was specifically designed to prevent losses brought about by these conditions. For details of the Trust Indenture Act of 1939, see the appendix.

INVESTMENT ADVISERS ACT OF 1940

The Investment Advisers Act of 1940 sets the statutory standards that govern the activities of individuals or organizations who engage in the business of advising others (either directly or in writing) with respect to their securities transactions. Unless exempt from the act, all organizations and individuals who receive compensation for giving such advice must register under this act. The basic purpose of the act is to protect investors from practices based on fraud or deceit.

The major points of control established by the act are as follows:

1. It is unlawful for registered investment advisers to engage in fraudulent or deceitful practices in connection with clients or potential clients.
2. Investment advisers are required to disclose the nature of their interest, if any, in transactions executed for their clients.
3. Investment advisers are prohibited from entering into profit sharing arrangements with clients. (This means that an investment adviser may not base his compensation upon a share of the capital gains or appreciation of his client's funds.)
4. Investment advisers are not allowed to assign investment advisory contracts without their client's consent.

Most investment counselors and securities services are covered by the act; however, certain exemptions exist, such as

1. newspapers
2. magazines of general circulation
3. brokers and dealers giving gratuitous and incidental advice
4. banks and government security houses
5. individuals such as attorneys, accountants, engineers, and teach- ers who are giving advice that is purely incidental

For details of the Investment Advisers Act, see the appendix.

THE INVESTMENT COMPANY ACT OF 1940 WITH 1970 AMENDMENTS

The Investment Company Act of 1940 is the most important piece of federal legislation relating to investment company activities. The act provides for the registration and regulation of companies primarily engaged in the business of investing, reinvesting, owning, holding, or trading in securities.

The organization, operation and regulation of investment companies is discussed in detail in Chapter 22. For a summary of the Investment Company Act of 1940, see pages 457 and 460.

The Securities Investors Protection Act of 1970

The Securities Investors Protection Corporation (SIPC) was formed under this act. It is a federally chartered, non-profit, membership corporation that provides protection for accounts of customers of broker-dealers and of members of the national securities exchanges who get into financial difficulty. (For further details, see page 196.)

"OTC Registered" Securities (see Securities Amendments)

Unless specifically exempted by the 1964 amendments, the new provisions apply to those nonlisted companies engaged in interstate commerce with assets in excess of $1,000,000 and with 750 or more shareholders of record in one class of their stock. Such companies must file a registration statement with the SEC. Securities of issuers registered under the new requirements are referred to as *OTC registered.* During the course of the first year in which the 1964 amendments were in effect, over-the-counter issuers filled a total of 1,508 registration statements with the SEC.

On July 1, 1966, the OTC registered securities requirements were extended to include nonexempted corporations engaged in interstate commerce with total assets in excess of $1,000,000 and with 500 or more shareholders of record in one class of their stock. Under the terms of the 1964 amendments, corporations are considered to be engaged in interstate commerce if they are in a business affecting interstate commerce or if their securities are traded by use of the mails or by any other means or instrumentality of interstate commerce.

Fingerprinting

Every person who is a partner, officer, director, or employee of a member firm who is engaged in the handling of securities or has acess to securities must be fingerprinted. Fingerprints are forwarded to the U.S. attorney general for processing.

Securities Reform Act of 1975

This act is an amendment to the Securities Exchange Act of 1934. It mandated basic changes in the entire securities industry. The most im r-tant are

1. The Congress of the United States directed the SEC to facilitate the establishment of a *national market system.* Drawing on all possible techniques of data processing, all security markets—the over the counter, the national exchange, and the NASDAQ—should be linked to trade in qualified securities.
2. The SEC was directed to appoint a National Market Advisory Board by December 1, 1975, of 15 members drawn by diverse geographical areas. This board was directed to make recommendations to the SEC in regard to the National Market System. Also, the board was instructed to study the possible need for a National Regulatory Board to regulate the National Market System.
3. The National Market System would regulate *securities information processors.* Securities information processors are persons distributing or publishing information with respect to transactions in or quotations for any security (except an exempt security). This would include ticker tape, terminal displays, and the like.
4. The creation of a *Municipal Securities Rule Making Board.* This is a self-regulatory organization for the municipal securities industry. The initial board of 15 members was appointed by the SEC. (Five were from the industry, five from the banks—bank representatives—and five were from the public of which one was from the issuers and one was from the investors.)
5. No national securities exchange may fix commissions after the date of the act.
6. Periodic reports must be made to Congress by the SEC and the National Advisory Board.

As of November 1979, the securities industry seems to be divided as to what is the best form of National Market System. Merrill Lynch, Pierce, Fenner & Smith have their own automated system called Merrill Lynch Best Price Selector. This system, which is only for the firm's own customers, automatically routes a customer's order to the best market on any national exchange.

The New York Stock Exchange is sponsoring the Intermarket Trading System (see page 195), which links up several national exchanges, but to date it accounts for only a small part of the total stock volume. The NASDAQ is also a system that the NASD has expressed intentions to extend to a national market system.

Finally, there is a Cincinnati Stock Exchange System (CSE). This is a central computer with many video display terminals. Buy and sell orders are automatically matched and executed. This system is violently opposed by the NYSE but is supported by Merrill Lynch, Pierce, Fenner & Smith.

State Regulation of the Securities Business

State governments in the United States have been regulating various aspects of securities for well over 100 years. Massachusetts, for example, had a statute attempting to control the stock and bond issues of common carriers in that state as early as 1852, long before any federal government attempts were made to regulate the securities industry. Federal securities legislation of general applicability did not appear until 1933, by which time 47 states had laws governing the activities of the securities firms operating within their boundaries.

Miminum capital requirements exist in many states. Often the state simply requires that the firm meet the standards of the SEC. A few states have rules that, instead of prescribing a fixed minimum capital, follow the formula of the SEC and some stock exchanges in prescribing a ratio of 15 to 1 or 20 to 1 between the aggregate indebtedness and the net capital. Also, *suitability rules* require that recommendations and investment advice given to prospective investors be compatible with the needs and circumstances of the customer.

Blue-Sky Laws

State statutes regulating the offering and sale of securities within the jurisdiction of the respective states are commonly referred to as *blue-sky laws*. "The name that is given to the law," said Justice McKenna in *Hall* v. *Geiger-Jones Co.*, 242 U.S. 539, 550 (1917), "indicates the evil at which it is aimed; that is, to use the language of a cited case, 'speculative schemes which have no more basis than so many feet of blue sky.' "

All states except Delaware have some type of blue-sky law in force. There is no local blue-sky law in the District of Columbia. Securities transactions there are governed by the federal statutes.

The first blue-sky law was adopted by Kansas in 1911. During the next several years, many other states adopted similar laws. The variations in state laws, however, made it difficult for investment bankers to market issues on an interstate basis. Consequently, in 1929, a Uniform State Securities Act was approved by the Conference of Commissioners on Uniform State Laws and by the American Bar Association and served as a basis for numerous new state securities laws.

The Investment Bankers Association prepared three model blue-sky laws in 1948, which brought the 1929 Uniform State Securities Act up to date and coordinated it with the existing federal securities laws. As a result, a new Uniform State Securities Act was approved in 1956 by the Conference of Commissioners on Uniform State Laws and the American Bar Association.

Although space does not permit individual treatment of all state blue-sky laws in this book, broker-dealers and registered representatives are urged to become fully cognizant of the securities regulations of the state in which they operate, as their professional lives may very well depend on such knowledge. Furthermore, registered representatives might advise customers to consult with legal counsel with respect to the interpretation of the technicalities of certain state laws and their application in individual circumstances.

Although the provisions of the 49 blue-sky laws vary widely, they generally utilize three distinct types of regulatory devices.

1. The blue-sky laws in at least 41 states have antifraud provisions, which prohibit deceitful and fraudulent securities activities. Laws that do *not* have antifraud provisions generally have provisions prohibiting misrepresentation or misleading statements.
2. All but a few states require the registration of certain persons engaging in the securities business in their respective state. Aproximately half the states require some form of registration or licensing of investment advisors. It is important for a registered representative to remember that registration or licensing as a salesperson in the state in which you conduct your principal activities does not automatically permit you to make sales in other states where registration is required. Similarly, registration of a broker-dealer under the Securities Exchange Act of 1934 or its amendment does not exempt that broker-dealer from state registration requirements.
3. Most states have provisions in their blue-sky law calling for the registration of licensing of nonexempt securities.

State registration may be affected by

1. *Notification.* Under this method, registration statements for se-
    curities that meet certain specified standards become effective af-
    ter a long period of time unless the registration is denied by the
    state security administrator (permitted in 36 states).
2. *Coordination.* Under this procedure, copies of the prospectus
    filed under the Securities Act of 1933 may be filed with the appro-
    priate state security administrator in lieu of a state registration
    statement. State registration becomes effective at the same time
    federal registration become effective (permitted in 20 states).
3. *Qualification.* Under this method, a registration statement must
    be filed with the appropriate state security administrator who in
    turn must approve or disapprove the registration statement. In
    many states the security administrator has broad authority to re-
    fuse to permit particular security offerings for a variety of rea-
    sons. This broad power of the state administrator to approve or
    disapprove a specific security issue can be more restrictive than
    the SEC power under the Securities Act of 1933, as the federal law
    is primarily a "disclosure" statute rather than an "approval"
    statute.

Registration of securities under the Securities Act of 1933 does not
automatically exempt a security from state registration requirements.

General Corporation Laws

Most corporations operating in the United States are incorporated
under the general corporation law of some state. These state laws are important to individuals in the securities business, because the conduct of an
individual business firm's corporate affairs will be determined, in part, by
the corporate laws of the state from which it received its corporate charter.

Because a corporation is an artificial person created by the state, its
whole character and most of its activities depend on the conditions of its
charter. The amounts and kinds of securities that may be issued by a corporation will be indicated by its charter.

"Prudent Man" Rule

In 40 states or more, trustees operate under some form of "prudent
man rule." Under this rule, trustees are relatively free to select the securities
they feel are best for their customers. No specific group of securities are designated as legal investments for trustees in "prudent man rule" states.

The term *"prudent man rule"* stems from a Massachusetts court decision in 1830 that stated in part that "all that can be required of a trustee . . . is that he shall conduct himself faithfully and exercise a sound discretion. He is to observe how men of prudence, discretion and intelligence manage their own affairs, not in regard to speculation, but in regard to the permanent disposition of their funds, considering the probable income as well as the probable safety of the capital to be invested."

A trustee operating under the "prudent man rule" obviously must be careful in his selection of securities. The task of such a trustee is much more difficult than is that of a trustee operating in a state in which authorized trusteed investments are specifically designated by the state's "legal list."

Legal Lists

Some states designate classes and groups of investments that may legally be purchased by a trustee operating in that state. This compilation of eligible securities is known as a *legal list*.

In legal list states, the state banking department, or commission, annually publishes a list of securities (often called "legals") considered eligible for investment by instutional investors such as life insurance companies, mutual savings banks, commercial banks, trust companies, and restricted trust funds operating in that state. Traditionally, the investments of such institutions have been limited, by the legal lists, to high-grade bonds, high-grade preferred stocks, and well-secured first mortgages on real estate. In recent years, however, many states have moved toward a liberalization of investment practices. These states now permit a portion of restricted trust funds to be invested in common stocks and permit some investment in the shares of investment companies by these funds.

Partial control is exercised over the investment practices of fire and casualty insurance companies in some states. Typically, these regulations call for the investment of an established portion of the institutions' funds in high-grade bonds, while permitting remaining funds to be invested at the discretion of the company management.

Ordinarily, unrestricted trust funds, endowments of educational institutions and philanthropic foundations, and the funds of investment companies are not subject to state control insofar as investment portfolio holdings are concerned.

The Law of Agency

Basically, this law as it applies to registered representatives requires that they be *loyal* to their employers as they act as the employers' agents. That is, they are to serve employers with all their skill, judgment, and discretion and to keep the employers informed of all facts coming to their knowledge that affect their employers' business rights and interests. This obligation arises from the relationship between registered representatives and their employers. They are the employers' agents. The principal-agent relationship is based on good faith under the law, with each having responsibilities to the other. For example, the employee may not act adversely to the interests of his employer by acquiring a private interest of his own in opposition to the interest of his employer. He could not, directly or indirectly, have an interest in the subject matter of the agency without the consent of his principal. Nor could he act for a third person whose interests are contrary to those of his principal.

On the other hand, employers have certain responsibilities to their agent. Employers are obligated to compensate their agents for services rendered in their behalf. Employers are liable to their agents for their own conduct as well as to third parties for the conduct of their agents as long as their agents are acting within the scope of their duties.

Uniform Gifts to Minors Act (UGMA)

A detailed discussion of this act appears on page 269.

Clifford Trusts

One way to help a minor build up a college fund is by means of a Clifford trust, named after George B. Clifford who first devised the idea of a short-term trust. For example, a parent can set up a trust with an amount of, say, $10,000 or $12,000. (An amount smaller might be used, but trustee costs might make it not worthwhile.) The trust must be for more than ten years and for the *child's college education only.* It cannot be used for camp, an educational trip to Europe, or normal support. Otherwise, the trust would be disallowed and the income taxed with the donor's income. The income from the trust may be accumulated, but, it is taxable to the child. However, because each individual has an exemption of $1,000, the tax should be minimal. By the end of the ten-year period, the fund could easily double. A Clifford trust is particularly advantageous to parents in a high tax bracket who find it difficult and expensive to save.

REVIEW QUESTIONS

1. List at least five acts now administered by the SEC.
2. Under the Securities Act of 1933, what is the purpose of the registration statement and what does it include?
3. What is a preliminary prospectus (red herring prospectus) and how does it differ from a final prospectus?

4. List the most important type of securities that are exempt from registration. What types of transactions are exempt?

5. Describe the basic rules that must be followed to effect a private placement (Rule 146). Can a private placement ever be reoffered?

6. Mention the advantages of a Regulation A offering.

7. Describe some of the deceptive and misleading devices forbidden under the Securities Exchange Act of 1934. Name four provisions of this act.

8. Explain how Regulation T controls credit. How does the special cash account of Regulation T work?

9. Under the Trust Indenture Act of 1939, what are the liabilities, the rights, and the privileges of (a) the issuing corporation, (b) the trustee, and (c) the bondholders?

10. What is the significance of the *Securities Reform Act of 1975* to the New York Stock Exchange and to the municipal securities industry?

11. Discuss the importance of blue-sky laws in the distribution of securities.

12. What is the "prudent man rule" and how does it relate to the legal lists?

TRUE AND FALSE QUESTIONS

1. The Securities and Exchange Commission administers the:

		True	False
a.	Securities Exchange Act of 1934	_____	_____
b.	Investment Company Act of 1940	_____	_____
c.	Uniform Gifts to Minors Act of 1956	_____	_____
d.	Banking Act of 1935	_____	_____
e.	Trust Indenture Act of 1939.	_____	_____

2. The Securities and Exchange Commission, after a waiting period, allows the registered securities to be sold; this means that:

		True	False
a.	the Securities and Exchange Commission has approved the securities	_____	_____
b.	the Securities and Exchange Commission has examined the registration statement and has passed on its accuracy	_____	_____
c.	the securities are not speculative, but considered investments	_____	_____
d.	severe penalties may be imposed on the underwriters for material misleading statements	_____	_____
e.	all of the above are true.	_____	_____

3. An offering of all of the following securities are exempt from
   registration: *True*   *False*
   a. railroad   _____   _____
   b. municipal   _____   _____
   c. public utility   _____   _____
   d. U.S. government.   _____   _____
4. A private placement is: *True*   *False*
   a. a direct sale of an issue of securities to a
       few well-informed wealthy investors   _____   _____
   b. only a small percentage of the total
       securities offered   _____   _____
   c. a security that once placed can never be
       reoffered   _____   _____
   d. much quicker than a public offering.   _____   _____
5. A preliminary prospectus: *True*   *False*
   a. has almost all the material contained in a
       final prospectus except the price and un-
       derwriting spread   _____   _____
   b. shall constitute an offer to sell when sent to
       a prospective buyer   _____   _____
   c. is usually called a red herring prospectus.   _____   _____
6. The important provisions of the Securities Exchange Act of 1934
   include: *True*   *False*
   a. registration and regulation of the securities
       exchanges   _____   _____
   b. filing of detailed registration of corporations
       listing their shares   _____   _____
   c. registration of all brokers and dealers   _____   _____
   d. regulations on proxies   _____   _____
   e. restrictions on insider trading   _____   _____
   f. all of the above.   _____   _____
7. Regulation T. under the Securities and Exchange Act of 1934, provides
   that the board of governors of the Federal Reserve System shall
   prescribe: *True*   *False*
   a. the amount of credit extended by banks to
       brokers and dealers   _____   _____
   b. the amount of credit extended by banks to
       their individual customers   _____   _____
   c. the amount of credit that brokers and
       dealers may extend to their customers   _____   _____
8. The Trust Indenture Act of 1939:   *True*   *False*
   a. protects bondholders by requiring the
       trustees to guarantee the principal and
       interest of the bonds   _____   _____

b. requires that the trustees check the per-
    formance of the covenants of the indenture   _____ _____
c. provides that the trustee can be sued for
    negligence   _____ _____
d. provides that the trustee must authenticate
    the bonds.   _____ _____

9. Under the securities acts amendments of 1964, the *new provisions*
    require the registration, periodic reporting, proxy rules, and trading
    provisions of the Securities Exchange Act of 1934 to: *True*   *False*
    a. apply to all publicly-owned securities   _____ _____
    b. include only nonlisted, over-the-counter
        securities of companies engaged in interstate
        commerce with assets of over $1,000,000
        and with over 500 stockholders   _____ _____
    c. include only fire, casualty, and life in-
        surance companies with assets of over
        $1,000,000 and over 750 stockholders.   _____ _____

10. State statutes regulating the offering and sale of securities within the
    state: *True*   *False*
    a. are called blue-sky laws   _____ _____
    b. are in force in all states including the
        District of Columbia   _____ _____
    c. are uniform throughout the country   _____ _____
    d. need not be complied with if the securities
        are registered with the SEC.   _____ _____

11. The state banking departments sometimes publish a list of securities
    called "legals" that are usually: *True*   *False*
    a. bought by fire and casualty companies   _____ _____
    b. bought by national banks   _____ _____
    c. bought by mutual savings banks and
        restricted trust funds   _____ _____
    d. made up of only fixed-income securities.   _____ _____

22

Investment Company

Regulation

Investment companies in the United States are very closely regulated at both the federal and state levels. State blue-sky laws are applicable to the activities of investment companies as are the general corporate statutes of the various states. At the federal level, a variety of statutes and regulatory agencies govern the operations of investment companies. These include the

1. Securities Act of 1933
2. Securities Exchange Act of 1934
3. Federal Reserve System—Board of Governors
4. Investment Company Act of 1940
5. Investment Company Amendments Act of 1970
6. Investment Advisers Act of 1940
7. Internal Revenue Service
8. Securities and Exchange Commission
9. National Association of Securities Dealers', Rules of Fair Practice

INVESTMENT COMPANY REGISTRATION AND PROSPECTUS REQUIRED UNDER SECURITIES ACT OF 1933

The purpose of the *Securities Act of 1933* (see page 371) is to provide the public with complete and accurate information regarding the offering of new securities (including investment company securities). Its main aim is to prevent fraud. The SEC, which administers this legislation, imposes severe penalties (civil and criminal) for misstatement or withholding a material fact on the required registration statement of the company, including investment companies. It cannot be repeated too often that the SEC does not ever *approve* a registration statement or prospectus; it simply allows it to become effective.

Open end funds issue new shares continuously (see page 78), and shares must be properly registered with the SEC before they are offered for public sale. A prospectus is an abbreviated registration statement, and a copy of this must be given to a potential open end fund customer before, or at the time, he purchases the fund shares. At least every 14 months, a new registration must be filed and a new updated prospectus issued.

The mutual fund prospectus contains a great deal of information of vital importance to the potential investor and should be read carefully. The law requires an investment company to define clearly its fundamental investment policy in its registration statement and in its prospectus. This policy cannot be changed without stockholder approval. Some of the important items in the prospectus that should be observed by the potential investor include the following, in order of importance: (1) the statement showing the per share growth and capital changes over the years; (2) the portfolio of investments. Often the prospectus will give not only the individual securities by industries but also their quantity, cost, and market value; (3) the management of the fund. This includes the officers and the directors of the fund and their affiliations; (4) the sales charges and the fee schedule for quantity purchases; (5) the right of accumulation; (6) the investment manager and or advisor—his fee and background; (7) the exchange privileges into other funds managed by the same group including fees if any; (8) miscellaneous items might include the income expense account of the fund, giving the expense ratio, the balance sheet of the fund, automatic withdrawal plans, redemption privileges, and the auditor's report.

ADVERTISING BY INVESTMENT COMPANIES

For about 30 years the Statement of Policy (SOP) of the Securities and Exchange Commission, administered by the NASD, determined the contents of all mutual fund advertisement, sales literature, and tombstone advertisements. But, after long study, in SEC, in March 1979, *withdrew* the Statement of Policy entirely as expression of its views on advertising by mutual funds.

Instead, it announced that henceforth neither the SEC nor its staff would give detailed interpretive rules concerning sales literature prior to use. The investment company industry was told to assume the responsibility for determining the development of sales literature that was not *misleading*. The SEC and its staff would make spot checks on the literature that must be filed with the SEC. The SEC staff and the commission would publish advisory views on issues of particular significance as the need arose. Although the SEC discontinued giving interpretive opinions on investment company advertisements to the NASD, it promised to continue to work with the NASD and to give formal and informal assistance. Generally speaking, the intent of the SEC was to liberalize the iron-clad rules of the SOP by issuing Rules 156 and 434 and amending Rule 134 of the Securities Act of 1933.

Rule 156: Investment Company Literature

This rule reiterates the basic tenet of the SEC that sales literature must not be *misleading*. It will be misleading says the SEC if it (1) contains an untrue statement of a material fact or (2) omits to state a material fact necessary to make a statement in the light of the circumstances of its use, not misleading. The new Rule 156 of the Securities Act of 1933 describes in general language misleading material in an advertisement.

Whether or not a particular description is misleading, weight should be given to all the pertinent factors. (1) A statement could be misleading because of (a) other statements being made in connection with the offering or sales of securities, (b) the absence of explanations, qualifications, limitations, or other statements necessary or appropriate to make such statements not misleading, or (c) general economic financial conditions or circumstances. (2) Representations about past or future performances could be misleading because of statements or omission of material facts including situations in which (a) portrayals of past income gains or growth of assets convey the impression of net asset results achieved by an actual or hypothetical investment that would not be justified under the circumstances or (b) representations, whether expressed or implied, about future investment performance or including representations as to security of capital, capital gains, and increased income based on increased income realized in the past. (3) A statement involving a material fact about the characteristics or attributes of an investment company could be misleading because (a) statements about possible benefits connected with or resulting from services to be provided or methods of operation that do not give equal prominence to discussion of the risks and limitations, (b) exaggerated or unsubstantiated claims of management or techniques or characteristics of the investment company, the security of investment funds, and the effects of government supervision, (c) unwarranted or incompletely explained comparison with other investment vehicles or indexes.

For the purpose of this section, sales literature shall be deemed to include any communication whether in writing by radio or by television used by any person to offer to sell or induce the sale of securities of any investment company. Communications among issuers, underwriters, and dealers are included if they can reasonably be expected to be communicated to investors.

Rule 434: Published Advertisements

This rule permits investment companies to publish advertisements containing a broader range of information than was permitted in the old tombstone advertisements under Rule 134, thereby assisting investors in considering alternate investments.

Under Rule 434, the advertisements of registered investment companies may be considered a prospectus if

1. it appears in a bona fide newspaper or magazine or is used on radio or television
2. it contains information the substance of which is included in the prospectus
3. it states where a prospectus may be obtained and that it should be read carefully before investing
4. the advertisement is used prior to the effective date of the registration, it must contain the statement that the registration statement has not yet become effective (see red herring, page 374)
5. the limit to the number of words, of which an advertisement may consist has been removed

Advertisements need not be filed with the SEC as part of the registration statement.

Rule 134: Tombstone Advertisements

Over the years this rule has been broadened and liberalized to permit tombstone advertisements to contain more information about investment companies. These include growth characteristics, net asset value, officers, and so forth. Also, the advertisements must suggest that the reader request a prospectus for more complete information. Rule 134 was amended to allow tombstone advertisements by investment companies to contain certain information prior to the effective date of the registration.

Rule 135A: Generic Advertisements

If no reference is made to specific securities, explanatory information relative to securities of investment companies and the investment company industry may be discussed. Explanatory information may be given relative to investment companies, their objectives, their services, and so forth.

A Caution

The SEC does not want the withdrawal of the SOP to be considered as a repudiation of the content because many of the SOP's principals still appear valid in the light of the commission's regulatory experience. Therefore, it behooves the industry to bear in mind some of the abuses that the SEC criticized. These include (1) implication or claim of a fund that the custodian gave added respectability, security, or management skill to the fund, (2) government, and state regulations that are not adequately explained, (3) representation that investment company securities are better than U.S. government securities, insurance, and the like without full explanation, (4) claims that investment company securities are a source of new capital, (5) incorrect calculation of rate of return on investment company securities, (6) use of the phrases "dollar averaging" or "averaging the dollar" instead of dollar-cost averaging and failure to explain the drawbacks of dollar-cost averaging.

The NASD and Advertising Literature

All advertising literature of investment companies must be filed with the NASD within three days of use. The NASD eliminated the five-day requirement for filing of all other advertising material and implemented a spot check procedure. Advertising on options have a ten-day filing requirement. However, materials in these last two categories would not be subject to either filing or spot check if reviewed by the exchange having substantially the same standards as the NASD.

The advertising department of the NASD reviews all advertising submitted to it and will comment thereon. The NASD has set forth a number of guidelines for advertising literature in Section I, Article III of the Rules of Fair Practice. These rules are discussed in detail on page 421. In summary of the high points of this rule, the sales literature should be based on the principles of fair dealing and good faith and should provide a sound basis for evaluation of the facts about any particular security. No material fact should be omitted nor should an untrue statement be made. Exaggerated, unwarranted, or misleading statements should not be made. A member must have a reasonable basis for making any recommendation and have a file of informative material to back it up. Testimonials used must state the expertise of the author and his compensation if any.

The Investment Company Institute (ICI)

Almost all investment companies are members of the ICI. The ICI represents the investment companies before federal and state legislatures. It is in effect a trade association; it sponsors conferences of industry members; it acts as a clearinghouse for information, and it sets guidelines for industry ethical standards. Although it does not enforce rules, it encourages and codifies high standards of business practice.

The Securities Exchange Act of 1934 has mainly to do with the regulation of the national stock exchanges and the trading practices of their members. But under it the SEC and the NASD were established. These play key roles in regulating the investment company industry. Furthermore, the act required the registration of all broker-dealers with the SEC and the regulation of proxies and insider trading. The Board of Governors of the Federal Reserve System under the Securities Exchange Act of 1934 administers Regulation T. This applies to margins on brokers' loans and to investment company activities as well. Regulation T does not permit the extension of credit on unlisted securities by brokers and dealers.[1] Because the shares of an open-end investment company are not listed on national securities exchanges, the prohibition against extension of credit applies to transactions in mutual fund shares. The effect of Regulation T is to bar brokers and dealers from granting credit or arranging for credit to enable customers to buy or carry the securities of any open-end investment company.

Section 3 — Certain Definitions Under the Act

This section defines a *broker* as a person engaged in the business of effecting transactions in securities for the account of others. A *dealer* is one who is engaged in buying and selling securities for his own account. A *security* is defined as a stock, a bond, a debenture, a certificate of interest in a profit-sharing oil and gas lease, and a voting trust certificate. Currency, notes, drafts, and bankers' acceptances if under nine months' maturity are not considered as securities.

Section 10 — Regulation of the Use of Manipulative and Deceptive Devices

This section is a regulation against the use of manipulative or deceptive devices and is aimed largely at exchange members. *For the Securities Investors Protection Act* (SPIC), see page 196.

THE INVESTMENT COMPANY ACT OF 1940 AND THE 1970 AMENDMENTS

This act provides for the registration and regulation of companies engaged in the business of investing, reinvesting, owning, and holding or trading in securities. An important purpose of the act is to provide complete and accurate information about the background and character of the management of investment companies, their investment policies, their financial strength, and their holdings of securities.

[1]With the exception of OTC Margin stocks. See page 202.

Section 2(a) — General Definitions

Affiliated persons are described as those holding the power to vote 5% or over of the outstanding securities. Sales load, principal underwriter, periodic payment plan certificates, separate account, and redeemable securities were also defined.

Sections 3(a) — Definition of an Investment Company

An investment company is a concern that holds itself out as being engaged in the business of investing and reinvesting in securities.

Section 4 — Classification of Investment Companies

Face amount, unit investment trusts, and management companies were all discussed on pages 76 to 77.

Section 5 — Subclassification of Investment Companies

As was noted in Chapter 5, an open-end investment company is a management company that offers for sale or has outstanding redeemable securities for which it is an issuer (see page 78). A closed-end investment company is any management company other than an open-end company (see page 79).

Management companies are further divided into diversified and non-diversified companies. A diversified company is a management company that meets the following requirements: At least 75% of the value of the total assets is represented by cash, cash items, including receivables government securities, other securities, and securities of other investment companies. Not more than 5% of the investment company's assets may be invested in one company. Thus, one part of the fund must amount to 75% of the assets invested to qualify as a diversified fund. The other 25% need not be diversified and might in fact be invested in a single issue. Also, the fund may not have more than 10% of the voting power in a single company. Nondiversified means any management company other than a diversified company.

Section 10 — Affiliations of the Directors

The board of directors of an investment company must not have more than 60% of its members who are interested persons of such investment company. Interested persons include officers and employees of the fund, its investment advisers, its banker, and its principal underwriter. This does not mean that they cannot serve on the board but that outside directors must constitute at least 40% of the board.

Section 12(a) — Functions and Activities of Investment Companies

Under this section, it is unlawful for the investment company to purchase securities on margin or to participate in a trading account except in connection with an underwriting in which the fund is a participant. Also, it is unlawful to effect a short sale except in connection with an underwriting in which such registered company is a participant.

Section 13 — Changes in Investment Policy

No registered investment company shall, *unless authorized by a majority vote of the outstanding shares,* change the subclassification from diversified to nondiversified investment company, borrow money, issue senior securities, underwrite securities issued by other persons, purchase or sell real estate, deal in commodities, make loans, or deviate from its policy in respect to the concentration of investments in any particular industry or group of industries recited in the company's registration statement.

Section 15 — Investment Advisory and Underwriting Contracts

Contracts with investment advisers must be approved by a majority of the outstanding shares. The stockholders must be advised in advance of the cost and other details. The initial contract runs for two years. Continuance depends on annual approval by the board of directors or the stockholders. The contract may be terminated with 60 days' notice.

Section 16(a) — Changes in the Board of Directors

Directors must be elected by the shareholders at the annual or special meetings. If the terms of the directors are by class, no term shall be less than one year or longer than five. One class must expire each year. Vacancies between meetings may be filled by a vote of two thirds of the board.

Section 17 — Transactions of Certain Affiliated Persons and Underwriters — Conflict of Interest

It is unlawful for any affiliated person, promoter, or principal underwriter knowingly to sell any security or other property to such registered company, unless such sale involves solely securities that the buyer is the issuer or that the seller is the issuer. Further, no loans may be made to the aforementioned parties. However, exceptions might be granted by the SEC if application is made in the proper form.

Section 18 — Capital Structure

Closed-end. It is unlawful for any registered closed-end company to sell senior securities (bonds) unless the assets cover the debt by 300%. No dividends (except stock) may be paid unless the debt is covered by 300% after the dividend payment. Preferred stock may be issued if asset coverage is 200%.

Open-End. An open-end investment company may not issue bonds or preferred stock. But it may borrow from a bank with 300% collateral coverage. If the coverage of a bank loan falls below 300%, the investment company must within three days reduce the loan to restore the 300% coverage. Capital adequacy is provided in that $100,000 of net worth required to start an investment company.

Section 19 — Dividends

No dividends shall be paid by any registered investment company except from accumulated, undistributed net income as determined according to good accounting practices for the current or preceding year unless the statement adequately declared the source. Long-term capital gains may not be distributed more often than once every 12 months. A statement must be made showing the source of payments.

Section 21 — Loans

Loans may not be made by the management companies to the investment company if the investment policies in the registration statements do not permit it.

Section 22 — Distribution, Redemption, and Repurchase of Securities

The NASD may prescribe rules or methods of computing the minimum price at which a member may purchase shares of investment companies. No registered investment company may sell redeemable shares except at the current public offering price as described in the prospectus. This policy is currently under attack in the U.S. Congress with some members demanding free pricing and open competition. Under this section the NASD was instructed to study the question of the load charged to investors in investment companies. By February 14, 1972, they had to set the maximum load that might be charged on sales of mutual funds. This they set at 8½%. If accumulation rights are not provided, the maximum is 8%; if dividend reinvestment is not free, 7.25%. See page 463.

No registered investment company shall suspend the right of redemption or postpone the day of payment for more than seven days after the tender of the security to the company or its agent. The exception to this rule might be in the event of a national emergency, the closing of the NYSE, or an order by the SEC.

Section 27 — Periodic Payments

The maximum sales load for total payments of a periodic payment plan is 9%. However under the 1970 amendment to the 1933 act, the purchaser of a periodic plan could select either of the following options:

1. Pay 50% of the sales load in the first year but with the options (a) to rescind the entire transaction within the next 45 days or (b) within 18 months to request the sponsor to refund the value of the account plus 85% of the gross payments of the commissions.
2. Pay 20% of the load each year for three years but not more than 64% in the first four years (16% average each year). Regardless of the alternative followed, the customer is entitled to a refund of the value of his account plus the sales charge if he cancels his plan within 45 days.

Section 30 — Periodic and Other Reports

Periodic reports must be made to the shareholders and to the SEC at least once a year. These reports must be detailed and certified by an independent public accountant.

Section 34 — Unlawful Representations and Names

No investment company or anyone connected with it shall sell shares or attempt to sell shares based on the representation that they are sponsored, guaranteed, recommended, or approved by the U.S. government or its agencies.

Section 35 — Breach of Fiduciary Duty

The SEC is authorized to bring action against anyone who has engaged within five years or is about to engage in a breach of a fiduciary duty. Action may be brought against the officers, the directors, the investment advisers, and the advisory board. An example of the breach of fiduciary duty would be the case of a member who is a trustee, paying agent, or transfer agent using improper information as to the ownership of securities for the purpose of soliciting purchases, sales, or exchanges except at the request and on behalf of the issuer.

Section 36 — Larceny and Embezzlement

Action may be brought by the SEC against anyone who steals, abstracts, or willfully converts assets of an investment company.

Other Provisions of the Investment Company Act

1. The investment company may not buy a security if any one of its employees owns 1/2 of 1% of the securities or combined employees own 5%.
2. The investment policy must be in the prospectus that should be updated at least every 14 months.
3. The SEC regulates all proxies.
4. The securities of the fund must be kept by a bank, a broker, or a member of a national securities exchange.
5. The management fee must be fair. Damages may be assessed.

THE INVESTMENT ADVISERS ACT OF 1940

This act is one of the weakest of the securities acts. It was discussed in detail on page 383. In summary it requires all professional advisers with the exception of those with less than 15 clients or doing only intrastate business to register with the SEC. They must give information about their education, operations, and qualifications. But they do not have to take any examination nor does the SEC have any power to discipline the investment advisers.

INVESTMENT COMPANIES AND THE RULE OF FAIR PRACTICE (INVESTMENT COMPANY RULE) — SECTION 26

Discounts to dealers may be given under certain conditions. But no member may *purchase* at a discount from a public offering price any security of an open-end investment company from an underwriter unless he is an NASD member. Furthermore, no member who is an underwriter shall *sell* to any dealer or broker who is not a member. The sales agreement must set forth, among other things, the concession to be received by the dealer.

Sales charges are regulated. No member shall offer or sell any open-end investment company or any "single payment" investment plan if the offering price is excessive, taking into consideration the relevant circumstances. The maximum sales charge on any transaction should not exceed 8.5% of the offering price. Furthermore, dividend reinvestment shall be made available at net asset value. Under certain circumstances, an investment company might make a reasonable charge for reinvesting dividends, but in no case is it to be more than 7.25% of the offering price (see page 463).

The right of accumulation (cumulative quantity discounts) shall be made available to "any person" for a period of not less than ten years from date of first purchase in accord with a schedule of quantity discounts (see page 99).

The offering price of mutual funds shall be as outlined in the prospectus. No member shall offer or sell the shares except at this price. Underwriters are required to calculate the offering price at least once a day, usually at 4:00 P.M.

Withheld orders of customers so as to benefit members are forbidden.

Conditional orders for securities or open-end investment companies shall not be accepted on any basis other than at a specified price.

Dealer purchases of open-end investment company shares may be done only to cover purchase orders already received from customers or for their own investment.

Execution of investment company portfolio transactions is a most important section of the Rules of Fair Practice. No member shall directly or indirectly influence the distribution of shares of any investment company on the basis of brokerage commissions received.

The antireciprocal rule provides that no member shall provide salespersons or branch managers any incentive or additional compensation for sale of investment company shares. However, under the *reciprocal brokerage rule* portfolio, transactions may be made by members even though they also sell the shares of the investment company. The choice of the broker should be on the basis of the value and the quality of the brokerage service, not on the sales of investment company shares.

Selling dividends is a means of inducing an investor to buy investment company shares just before a dividend distribution. No advantage accrues to the buyer of the investment company shares by purchasing them just before a dividend distribution. Before it is distributed, the amount of the dividend is included in the price the investor pays for the shares. When the distribution is paid out to the share holders, the shares decline in price (on their ex-dividend date) by the amount of the distribution.

Rates of return on investment company shares should not be based of actual or prospective capital gains.

Breakpoint sales, discussed on page 99 are sales of investment company shares of about $1,000 below the point at which the sales load drops. Investment company underwriters and sponsors as well as dealers have the responsibility for preventing this abuse.

Special deals are considered inconsistent with the just and equitable principles of trade. It is a violation of the Rules of Fair Practice for a principal underwriter or his associates in connection with the sale of investment company shares to make any gift of *material value* to a member or registered representative. Anything of material value would be a gift worth over $25.00.

Prompt payments must be made by all members for shares of investment companies. Members are required to transmit payments to underwriters promptly after the date of the transaction. If the underwriter does not receive payment within ten days following the date of the transaction, the underwriter must notify the district office of the NASD.

REVIEW QUESTIONS

1. Enumerate the federal acts, state laws, and various other governmental and nongovernmental regulations under which investment companies are regulated.
2. What are the important purposes of the Investment Company Act of 1940?
3. What is the purpose of the *outsiders* provision of the Investment Company Act of 1940?
4. Why are advisory contracts regulated under the Investment Company Act of 1940?
5. Is it possible under the act for an *open-end* investment company (a) to issue bonds, (b) to borrow from banks, (c) to issue preferred stock? What about a *closed-end* investment company?
6. Explain the terms *breakpoint* sales and *letter of intention* as applied to the sales of open-end investment companies (see Chapter 5).
7. What in particular does the prospectus of a mutual fund contain? About how often must a prospectus be revised?
8. What is the *investment company* rule?
9. Explain the term *selling dividends* as applied to investment companies.
10. What is the interpretation of the NASD board of the Rules of Fair Practice in regard to *special deals?*
11. What was the general policy and aim of the SEC in withdrawing the Statement of Policy? Has the SEC abandoned all regulation of the investment company industry? Explain.
12. What are the important provisions of Rules 156 and 434 of the Securities Act of 1933?

TRUE AND FALSE QUESTIONS

1. Open-end investment companies are regulated by all of the following
   except: *True*   *False*
   a.   the Securities Act of 1933   _____   _____

	True	False
b. the Securities Exchange Act of 1934		
c. the Investment Company Act of 1940		
d. the Internal Revenue Service		
e. the New York Stock Exchange		
f. the Securities and Exchange Commission		
g. the National Association of Securities Dealers, Inc.		

2. The purpose of the Investment Company Act of 1940 is:

	True	False
a. to ensure the stockholders of investment companies against fraudulent acts of the management		
b. to reduce selling abuses		
c. to assure availability of adequate factual information about investment companies.		

3. The outsiders provision of the Investment Company Act of 1940 is to assure that the public will be represented. On each board of directors of an investment company, nonaffiliated directors shall constitute at least:

	True	False
a. 30%		
b. 40%		
c. 60%.		

4. Under the Investment Company Act of 1940, the investment advisory contract:

	True	False
a. must be approved by a majority vote of the directors and by the stockholders		
b. is approved initially for two years and thereafter renewed annually		
c. may not be canceled except on renewal date.		

5. Under the Investment Company Act of 1940, an open-end investment company:

	True	False
a. may not issue bonds		
b. may not issue preferred stocks		
c. may not borrow from banks.		

6. Under the Investment Company Act of 1940, a closed-end fund:

	True	False
a. may not issue bonds		
b. may not issue preferred stocks		
c. may not borrow from banks		
d. may issue bonds if covered by collateral of 300% and may issue preferred stock with 200% asset coverage.		

7. Under the Investment Company Act of 1940, a mutual fund may not
    purchase securities if its officers and investment advisers:

                                                                 True   *False*
    a. own individually 2% or together 4 % of the
        securities of the company.   _____   _____
    b. own individually 1% or together 3% of the
        securities of the company   _____   _____
    c. own individually 1/2 of 1% or together 5%
        of the securities of the company.   _____   _____

8. The Investment Company Act of 1940 provides that shares must be
    redeemed by the company: *True*   *False*
    a. within seven days at net asset value   _____   _____
    b. without any redemption fee   _____   _____
    c. within the regular delivery period (e.g., five
        business days).   _____   _____

9. The maximum load on contractual plans under the Investment Com-
    pany Act of 1940 is: *True*   *False*
    a. 7% of asset value   _____   _____
    b. 8% of offering price   _____   _____
    c. 9% of asset value   _____   _____
    d. 9% of offering price.   _____   _____

10. The investment company rule provides that the underwriter or
    sponsor of an investment company may execute sales agreements:

                                                                 True   *False*
    a. with any security dealer   _____   _____
    b. with any security dealer registered with the
        SEC   _____   _____
    c. with any security dealer provided he is a
        member of the NASD.   _____   _____

11. Selling dividends: *True*   *False*
    a. is the process whereby a stockholder, who
        wishes to have his money promptly, may
        sell his dividend at a discount between the
        period it is declared and paid   _____   _____
    b. is a violation of the Rules of Fair Practice of
        the NASD   _____   _____
    c. refers to the process whereby investors are
        induced to buy investment company shares
        just before a distribution of a dividend.   _____   _____

12. Special deals mean: *True*   *False*
    a. that a dealer will offer to a customer
        quantity discounts   _____   _____

b.   an underwriter, to facilitate distribution,   *True*   *False*
     makes a gift of material value to a
     registered representative   _____   _____
c.   that gifts of under $25.00 may be made be-
     cause that amount does not constitute
     material value.   _____   _____

13. Rule 156 of the Securities Act of 1933 provides that investment
     company advertisements *must:*   *True*   *False*
     a.   not be misleading   _____   _____
     b.   be approved by the SEC   _____   _____
     c.   assure the investor a safe return   _____   _____
     d.   contain an estimate of future earnings based
          of the company's past record.   _____   _____

14. Rule 434 of the Securities Act of 1933 provides that investment com-
     pany advertisements may be considered a prospectus *if:*
                                                           True   *False*
     a.   it is limited to 600 words   _____   _____
     b.   it contains information that is also included
          in the prospectus   _____   _____
     c.   the advertisement is filed with the SEC as
          part of the registration statement.   _____   _____

23

THE

NATIONAL ASSOCIATION of

SECURITIES DEALERS, INC.

The National Association of Securities Dealers, Inc. is a registered national securities association. It was created pursuant to the provisions of federal law to adopt, administer, and enforce rules of fair practice in connection with over-the-counter securities transactions.

The NASD became a registered national securities association in August 1939. It was organized under the Maloney Act, an amendment (Section 15 A) to the Securities Exchange Act of 1934.

The Maloney Act provides for the registration with the Securities and Exchange Commission of national securities associations and establishes standards for such associations. According to the act, the rules of these associations must be designed to promote just and equitable principles of trade and to meet other statutory requirements. The act also empowers these associations to require their members to maintain high standards of commercial honor.

The National Association of Securities Dealers, Inc. is the only association registered under the Maloney Act.

The act calls for the NASD to function as "a mechanism of regulation among over-the-counter brokers and dealers operating in interstate and foreign commerce or through the mails."

The Securities and Exchange Commission supervises the NASD operations. The SEC is authorized to review all disciplinary actions and decisions of the association. It has the right to review the action taken on applications for membership and also to review any changes that are made in the rules of the NASD.

NASD RULES STRESS ETHICAL
AS WELL AS
LEGAL CONDUCT

Through the NASD, the over-the-counter securities market is regulated in a way that would be difficult, if not impossible, to accomplish under straight governmental control. Government regulations generally concern themselves with the *legality* or *illegality* of a particular situation or action. The ethical conduct of the individual or of an organization, as contrasted to legal conduct, is generally considered outside the scope of governmental supervision.

The NASD is able to enforce ethical as well as legal standards among its members. Ethical standards are enforced by the simple method of denying membership in the association to any broker-dealer operating in an unethical or improper manner. Generally, loss of NASD membership prevents a broker-dealer from operating profitably in the over-the-counter securities market. Thus through the association a more sensitive type of control can be exercised than would be possible under direct SEC supervision.

In adopting the legislation under which the NASD was organized, Congress permitted the association to adopt rules that, among other things, preclude a member firm from dealing with a nonmember firm except on the same terms and conditions as the member firm deals with the investing public. These rules were provided by Congress as an incentive to membership in national securities associations. *More important, however, is the fact that these rules are essential and basic to the effective enforcement of ethical standards by the NASD.*

Because of these rules, membership in the NASD is a prerequisite to profitable participation in almost all underwriting and most over-the-counter trading. Only association members have the advantage of price concessions, discounts, and similar allowances. Loss or denial of membership in the NASD due to unethical business practices thus imposes a severe economic sanction on an organization.

PURPOSES

The NASD was originally established for the purpose of cooperating with the government in its efforts to prevent improper transactions in the securities business. To help provide effective guildelines for its operations, the NASD has indicated the functions it expects to perform and has formulated the objectives it hopes to attain. In the NASD Certificate of Incorporation, the association's functions and objectives are indicated as follows:

1. To promote through cooperative effort the investment banking and securities business, standardize its principles and practices, promote high standards of commercial honor, and observe federal and state securities laws.
2. To provide a medium through which its membership may be enabled to confer, consult, and cooperate with governmental and other agencies in the solution of problems affecting investors, the public, and the investment banking and securities business.
3. To adopt, administer, and enforce the Rules of Fair Practice and rules to prevent fraudulent and manipulative acts and practices, and in general to promote just and equitable principles of trade for the protection of investors.
4. To promote self-discipline among members and to investigate and adjust grievances between the public and association members, and between association members themselves.

BOARD OF GOVERNORS

The board of governors, comprised of 27 members (including 5 at large and the president of the NASD) administers and manages the affairs of the association. Overall policy-making functions of the association are granted to the board, and it has full power to act on behalf of the association in most matters.

In the exercise of its powers, the board of governors may:

1. adopt, for submission to the membership, any new bylaws or Rules of Fair Practice, or any changes or additions to existing bylaws or Rules of Fair Practice that it deems necessary or appropriate
2. make any regulations, issue any orders, resolutions, interpretations, and directions, and make any decisions that it deems necessary or appropriate
3. prescribe maximum penalties for violations of the provisions of the bylaws or the rules and regulations of the corporation; or for neglecting or refusing to comply with orders, directions, and decisions of the board of governors or any duly authorized NASD committee

Each district is represented on the board of governors by one or more members who are elected for a three-year term by the membership in the district they represent.

Both the board of governors and the district committees have the right to hold meeting whenever they feel it is necessary. Also, action may be taken by mail, telephone, or telegraphic vote.

Both the board of governors and the district committees do not receive any pay for the work they do for the association. However, they are reimbursed for any out-of-pocket expenses incurred by them in the affairs of the association. Without this voluntary contribution of time and effort on the part of the many elected board members and committee members, the Association could not operate.

DISTRICT COMMITTEES

There are 13 district committees elected by the member firms in their respective areas. They supervise NASD programs in the districts and serve as business conduct committees that review the reports of NASD examiners, investigate complaints against members, conduct disciplinary proceedings, and impose penalties for violations of federal and state laws and NASD's Rules of Fair Practice. The chairman of each district committee also serves as an advisory council to the board of governors.

BYLAWS

1. membership registration

Membership in the association is open to *all properly qualified* brokers and dealers, whose regular course of business consists in actually transacting any branch of the investment banking or securities business in the United States under the laws of the United States.

For NASD membership purposes, any individual, corporation, partnership, association, joint stock company, business trust, unincorporated organization, or other legal entity is a

1. "broker" if engaged in the business of effecting transactions in securities for the account of others but does not include a bank.
2. "dealer" if engaged in the business of buying and selling securities for his own account through a broker or otherwise but does not include a bank or any person who buys or sells securities for his own account other than as part of a regular business.

Banks by definition are not broker-dealers and thus are not eligible for membership in the association.

Who May Not Become a Member of the NASD

Not everyone wishing to engage in business and selling securities is eligible for membership in the NASD.

One of the main purposes of the NASD has always been to promote high standards of commercial honor in the securities business. Obviously, with this basic objective, anyone convicted of a violation of the federal or state securities laws is barred from the NASD membership, unless admittance is directed by the SEC.

Broker-dealers are denied NASD membership under the following conditions, unless the Securities and Exchange Commission specifically approves and orders such membership:

1. A broker-dealer who has been suspended or expelled from a registered securities association or from a registered national securities exchange for acts inconsistent with just and equitable principles of trade.
2. A broker-dealer whose registration with the Securities and Exchange Commission has been revoked or denied.
3. An individual who has been named a "cause" of a suspension, expulsion, or revocation, or one whose registration as a registered representative has been revoked by the association or by a registered national securities exchange.
4. An individual who has been convicted within the preceding ten years of any crime:
   a. arising out of the securities business.
   b. involving embezzlement.
   c. involving fraudulent conversion.
   d. involving misappropriation of funds.
   e. involving the abuse or misuse of a fiduciary relationship.
5. A broker-dealer with any partner, officer, or employee who is not qualified for membership under any of the limitations of the bylaws of the association.
6. A broker-dealer with officers, partners, or employees who are required to be registered representatives, but who have not become registered representatives.

Broker-dealers must be registered with the SEC and the state authorities, if required by law, to be eligible for membership in the NASD.

2. registration of branch offices

A branch office of an association member is an office, other than the main office, located in the United States that is owned or controlled by the member and that is engaged in the investment banking or securities business.

Members are required to notify the NASD board of governors immediately upon opening or closing any branch office. All branch offices of an association member must be registered with the NASD, and a fee must be paid for each branch office.

The NASD board of governors has established a number of standards for use in determining whether an office of a member firm or the operations of one or more of its registered representatives or principals constitutes a branch office operation and consequently require registration as a branch office.

In determining whether an office or the activities of a person associated with a member in an area constitutes a branch office of a member, the following standards will be used:

1. It shall be considered a branch office if the member directly or indirectly contributes a substantial portion of the operating expenses of any place used by a person associated with a member who is engaged in the investment banking or securities business, whether it be commercial office space or a residence. Operating expenses, for purposes of this standard, shall include items normally associated with the cost of operating the business, such as rent and taxes.
2. It shall be considered a branch office if the member authorizes a listing in any publication or any other media, including a professional dealer's digest or a telephone directory, which listing designates a place as an office or if the member designates any such place with an organization as an office.

A branch office is not an "office of supervisory jurisdiction" unless it has been designated as such and has had specified supervisory activities assigned to it under the member's written procedures. If an office falls within the definition of both an office of supervisory jurisdiction and a branch office, it must be designated to the NASD in each category.

3.   registration and qualification of principals

The NASD board of governors in September 1965 established a second category of registration for individuals associated with member firms. This new regulation required all persons associated with NASD member firms (unless exempt) to register either as a "registered representative" or as a "principal."

The NASD further indicated that all persons associated with an NASD member who were designated as principals were required to pass a "Qualification Examination for Principals" before their registration could become effective. "Principals" were identified as those persons associated with an NASD member who are actively engaged in the *management* of the member's investment banking or securities business. Included were those involved in supervision, solicitation, the conduct of business, or the training of persons associated with the member firm.

"Principals" include such persons as:

1. sole proprietors
2. officers
3. partners
4. managers of offices of supervisory jurisdiction
5. directors of corporations

Any person who was registered with the NASD on or before October 1, 1965, and was designated as one of the above principals, was not required to pass the Qualification Examination for Principals unless his most recent registration had been terminated for a period of two years or more immediately preceding the filing of a new application.

Any individual associated with an NASD member firm as a registered representative whose duties are changed by the same member firm after October 1, 1965 so as to require his classification as a principal is allowed a reasonable period of time following such a change to pass the principal's examination.

Effective September 1, 1972, every broker and dealer making application for admission to membership must designate with the NASD an officer, partner, or himself or herself as "financial principal." The duties of the financial principal shall include the preparation and/or approval of the financial statements, the computation of capital, and supporting schedules.

4.   registration of registered representatives

As noted, every officer, partner, director, or manager of an office of supervisory jurisdiction of an NASD member firm must register as a registered principal. In addition, all other persons associated with member firms who are engaged in the management, supervision, solicitation, trading, or handling of transactions in listed and unlisted securities are required to be registered with the association. Every employee engaged in the solicitation of subscriptions to investment advisory or to investment management services furnished on a fee basis must also become registered. Registration is also required of anyone to whom has been delegated general supervision over foreign business or who is engaged in the sale of listed or unlisted securities on an agency or principal basis. Employees of member firms who are not involved in any of the above activities need not become registered representatives. Thus, those whose duties are solely clerical and ministerial need not become registered.

The NASD warns that a member must not permit any person to transact any branch of the investment banking or securities business as its representative unless such person is registered with the NASD as a registered representative or registered principal of that member. This is a significant restriction in that it prohibits the use of unregistered trainees and office personnel as order takers or salespersons and in client contact assignments.

Representatives must be registered to offer variable annuity contracts. A variable annuity is a retirement contract developed by the life insurance industry in recent years and was discussed in more detail in Chapter 6.

Registration is not required of employees who are engaged solely in the handling or selling of

1. exempted securities, including federal, state, and local government obligations
2. cotton, grain, or other commodities, provided they are registered with a recognized national cotton or commodities exchange
3. securities on a national securities exchange, provided they are registered with a national securities exchange
4. persons associated with a member whose functions are related solely and exclusively to the member's need for nominal corporate officers or capital (i.e. limited partners)
5. persons whose functions are solely and exclusively clerical or ministerial

By resolution of the board of governors, the NASD has determined that any member who fails to register as a qualified employee may be suspended from the NASD.

a. qualifications of a registered representative

Individuals who become, or are associated with, an NASD member firm may become registered representatives if they:

1. possesses all the qualifications for membership in the Association
2. have passed the NASD qualification examination for registered representatives

Before new employees may become registered representatives, the member firm must certify to the adequacy of the training and the experience of these new employees. This certification must be based on adequate investigation.

A member who employs a registered representative must have reason to believe, upon the exercise of reasonable care, that the individual hired is qualified by training or experience to perform the functions and duties to which he is assigned.

The determination of the training and experience of the registered representative is solely the responsibility of the member. Improper or unwarranted certification by a member constitutes conduct contrary to high standards of commercial honor and may result in disciplinary action.

A registered representative of a member firm does not have to devote his entire time during business hours to the business of the member. A large number of registered representatives sell securities on a part-time basis.

The *restrictions* on applicants for registration are essentially the same as those set forth on page 414 as applying to NASD membership. Each member is responsible and has the duty to ascertain by careful investigation the good character, business repute, experience, and ability of each person prior to his or her application.

b.   examinations for registered representative

The examination for qualification as an NASD registered representative is now a 125-question, two-hour, multiple-choice examination. There
are several forms of this examination, each of which requires equal
knowledge. This examination is not scored on the curve, and all questions
are given equal weight. The subject matter covered in the examination is
presented in a booklet entitled "Study Outline for Qualification Examination for Registered Representatives and Registered Principals" as well as
the NASD *Training Guide*. Both of these booklets are available from the
NASD headquarters, 1735 K Street, N.W., Washington, D.C. 20006.

Registered representative applicants taking the NYSE full registration
examination should use the *NYSE Study Outline*. Examinations are
coordinated with the full and limited registration examinations of the New
York, the American, and the Pacific Coast stock exchanges. An applicant
for registration with a firm having membership in any combination of these
four organizations may qualify for registration with all at a single
examination session.

c.   examinations for registered principals

For principals there is a 170-question, three-hour examination of
multiple-choice questions, all of which are given equal weight. Applicants
should use the *Study Outline* as well as the *NASD Training Guide*. Principals' examinations are also coordinated with those of the NYSE, the American, and the Pacific Coast exchanges in the same way as the examination
for registered representatives.[1]

d.   results of the examinations

The results of the examination are reported to the applicant's firm
in the following manner. If the applicant passes the examination, the
member firm will receive notice of the applicant's registration. This notice
will give the examination grade as either A (excellent), B (good), or C (fair).
If the applicant fails the examination, a notice of failure will be sent to the
member firm along with an analysis of the examination paper.

e.   close supervision required after registration

After new employees have become registered representatives, the
member firms must supervise their purchase and sales methods. This
supervision should be detailed and methodical. Each member is responsible
for all the transactions made by employees. A responsible official of a
member firm must approve in writing every transaction made by the
registered representatives. The office of supervisory jurisdiction means any

[1]The NASD examinations are coordinated to a varying degree with certain state
examination programs.

office designated as directly responsible for the review of the activities of registered representatives.

Also, each member shall review the activities of each account to detect irregularities. Further, each office of the supervisory jurisdiction shall make at least one annual inspection.

f. termination of registration

Registered representatives of member firms may voluntarily terminate their registration at any time, but only by formal resignation in writing addressed to the board of governors. Upon receipt of such a request, the board of governors immediately notifies the member firm involved. The resignation does not take effect until 30 days after it is received by the board, or so long as there is any complaint or action pending against the registered representative. Registered representatives are not permitted to transfer their registration.

Members, Branches, and Registered Representatives

At the end of 1979, there were 2,801 member firms as compared with 4,118 at the end of 1972, a decline of 32%. But these firms had 6,935 branches at the end of 1979, compared with 6,619 at the end of 1972, an increase of 4.8%. Registered representatives and principals totaled 191,319 at the end of 1979, as compared with 201,805 at the end of 1972, a decline of 5.2%.

How to Become a Member of the NASD

It is a relatively simple matter to apply for membership in the NASD. Any broker or dealer desiring to join who is *lawfully* engaged in the investment banking or securities business may do so by completing and filing the necessary forms and paying the necessary fees. Requests for the necessary forms should be addressed to the National Association of Securities Dealers, Inc., 1735 K Street, N.W., Washington, D.C. 20006.

When the association sends the forms to the applicant, they also forward information about the obligations of membership. All NASD applicants are urged to read this material carefully. The completed forms should be returned to the NASD office in Washington, D.C. for processing. After admission to membership, the applicant will be billed for the assessment and branch office fees.

In addition to the filing of these NASD forms, all NASD broker-dealers operating in interstate commerce are required to file a registration form with the SEC. This form, known as Form BD, is required in connection with registration under the Securities Exchange Act of 1934.

Form BD must be executed and filed, in duplicate, with the Securities and Exchange Commissions, Washington, D.C., 20549. This form is customarily included by the NASD when it sends application forms to firms applying for Association membership. Registration with the SEC is required before NASD membership can be granted.

REVENUE FROM ASSESSMENTS
AND DUES

The bylaws of the NASD provide annually for assessments by the board of governors to cover operating expenses. The board estimates each year how much money it will need to carry on the work of the association. On the basis of this estimate, it determines the dues and charges to be assessed against the members.

After October 1979 the following assessments were made:

1. a basic membership fee of $300.00 a year
2. 0.21% of gross income from state and municipal securities
3. 0.25% of gross income from the over-the-counter securities
4. for each principal and each representative, $5.00 a year
5. for each branch office, $30.00 a year
6. each member will be assessed a fee of $50.00 for each application for registration of a principal or registered representative as well as an examination fee of $40.00
7. Each applicant for membership shall be assessed $500.00 in connection with the filing of an application for membership in addition to any dues or fees otherwise payable
8. other fees are assessed for examining documents in regard to corporate financing deals, late filing
9. A large amount each year from NASDAQ for user service fees

THE RULES OF FAIR PRACTICE

The NASD board of governors, under Article VII of the association's bylaws, had adopted, and the members have approved, a series of regulations called the Rules of Fair Practice. These rules are designed to promote and enforce just and equitable principles of trade in the securities business. The Rules of Fair Practice constitute a guide to members in the ethical conduct of their business as distinguished from the legal conduct of business.

The NASD board of governors is empowered to make and issue interpretations of all Rules of Fair Practice. The board also determines procedures with respect to complaints of violation of the rules and prescribes the penalties for such violations.

Thirty specific rules are set forth in Article III of the Rules of Fair Practice. All the rules are designed to carry out the original intention of the Maloney Act.

Business Conduct of Members (Section 1)

Most basic of the Rules of Fair Practice is Section 1, Article III, which sums up the fundamental philosophy of the association. It states, "A member, in the conduct of his business, shall observe high standards of commercial honor and just and equitable principals of trade." Under Section 1, the board of governors had adopted an interpretation of the Rules of Fair Practice relating to *free riding* in connection with the distribution of original offerings of securities. (See page 427.)

NASD Member Firm Advertising

The advertising practices of NASD member firms are regulated by the association's board of governors through an interpretation of Section 1, Article III of the Rules of Fair Practice. This interpretation provides principles to be used by the membership as a guide in the preparation and utilization of their advertising material.

For many years, the NASD board members were aware that certain advertising practices existed in the securities business that employed "come-on" techniques and contained statements that misled or tended to mislead investors. Consequently, a special committee was appointed by the chairman of the board to make a study of the advertising practices employed by the association's members.

Ultimately, the board of governors adopted the following interpretation of Section 1 of Article III of the Rules of Fair Practice with respect to advertising:

> It shall be deemed a violation of Section 1 of Article III of the Rules of Fair Practice for a member, directly or indirectly, to publish, circulate or distribute any advertisement, sales literature or market letter that the member knows, or has reason to know, contains any untrue statement of a material fact or is otherwise false or misleading.

The NASD encourages the proper use of advertisements, sales literature, and market letters by their members to interest and inform the public concerning securities and available investment services. They also encourage the proper use of recruiting advertisements to publicize the existence of career opportunities within the securities business.

The NASD stresses the importance of basing all advertising, sales literature, and market letters on the principles of fair dealing and good faith. The material should be presented in such a way as to provide a sound basis for evaluating the facts in regard to any particular security or type of security. Furthermore, it should provide a sound basis for evaluating the facts concerning any industry that is discussed or any service that is offered. No material fact or qualification may be omitted from the presentation if the omission in the light of the context of the material presented would cause the advertising or sales literature to be misleading.

Exaggerated, unwarranted, or misleading statements or claims are prohibited in all advertising, sales literature, market letters, and recruiting material sponsored by NASD members. In preparing such literature, members should keep in mind the fact that the risk of fluctuating prices, uncertainty of dividends, and uncertainty of rates of return and yield are inherent in the investment process.

Since this interpretation has been adopted, any NASD member using such prohibited advertising material, or employing such undesirable promotional practices, has been subject to disciplinary action by district business conduct committees under the Rules of Fair Practice.

As previously noted, NASD members may use the association's name on advertising only to the extent authorized by the NASD board of governors. Specifically, members are prohibited from using the name of the association in advertising or on the letterhead of letters that carry a discussion of a particular security or type of securities.

Definitions of Advertisements

The NASD board of governors has determined for the purpose of administering this interpretation that *advertisements* will be considered to be *"any material for use in any newspaper, or magazine, or other public media, or by radio, telephone recording, motion picture or television."* The board has also determined that *sales literature* and *market letters* will be considered to include notices, circulars, reports, newsletters, research reports, form letters, or reprints or excerpts of the foregoing, or reprints of published articles.

Advertisements, sales literature, and market letters will be considered as coming under this interpretation if they involve

1.   the offering of any security or type of securities or relate to or recommend the purchase or sale of any security or type of securities or
2.   the offering of any securities analysis or communication referred to above or contain any securities analysis or investment advice or offer investment advice or any other service with regard to securities

Advertising designed to recruit sales personnel must also conform to the board's interpretation of Section I, Article III of the Rules of Fair Practice. Consequently, also included within this interpretation will be any communication that offers employment as a registered representative or registered principal by a member.

Excluded Material

The NASD board indicates that certain types of material are excluded from this interpretation. For example, letters addressed to an individual concerning only recommendations or advice relating to that individual, or others for whom he or she may be acting, would not come under this interpretation. Also excluded would be material addressed by a member to its branch office or material that is not distributed to members of the public but is just used internally by a member organization.

Tombstone advertisements that do no more than identify the NASD member and/or identify an offered security, state its price, or offer literature about the security also are exempted from the interpretation.

Announcements relating solely to changes in the personnel of member organizations also are excluded. Material published in a prospectus or a preliminary prospectus that satisfies the rules of the SEC also are excluded, as are advertisements and sales literature subjected to the SEC Statement of Policy.

All advertising material perpared by the NASD member should contain the name of the member, the person, or the firm preparing the material if other than the member firm. It should also include the date on which the material was first published, circulated, or distributed, and if the information contained in the advertising material is not current, this fact should be stated.

The NASD indicates that, when a member firm makes a recommendation (whether or not it labels the material as a recommendation), the member must have a reasonable basis for making such a recommendation and that the following facts must be disclosed:

1. the price at the time the original recommendation was made
2. that the member usually makes a market in the issue, if such is the case
3. that the member intends to buy or sell the securities recommended for the firm's own account and ownership if such is the case
4. the existence of any options, rights, or warrants to purchase any security of the issuer whose securities are recommended, unless the extent of such ownership is merely nominal

The member must also provide or offer to furnish upon request available investment information supporting the recommendations. And, in December 1971 the SEC issued a rule prohibiting market makers from publishing a quotation on their stocks without having in file extensive financial and other data on the stock.

NASD members may use material referring to past recommendations if the material sets forth all recommendations as to the same type, kind, grade, or classification of securities made by the member within the last year. Longer periods of time may be covered in referring to past recommendations only if the years cited are consecutive and include the most recent year. When such material is used it must also name each security recommended, the date it was recommended, and whether the customer was told to buy the security or to sell it. Additional information required in such a presentation includes the price at the time the recommendation was made; the price at which, or the price range within which, the recommendation was to be acted upon; and whether the period involved was one of a generally rising market or one of a generally declining market.

Advertisements, sales literature, or market letters of NASD members must not contain promises of specific results, exaggerated or unwarranted claims, or unwarranted superlatives or give opinions for which there is no reasonable basis. Any forecasts presented by a member must be clearly labeled as forecasts and must not include any unwarranted statements. References to past specific recommendations may not imply that the recommendations were profitable to any person, or would have been profitable to any person, and that they are indicative of the general quality of a member's recommendations.

Testimonial material concerning the NASD member or concerning any advice, analysis, report, or other investment or related service rendered by the NASD member must make clear that the experience cited in the testimonial is not necessarily indicative of future performance or results to be obtained by others. Testimonials must also state whether any compensation was paid to the maker directly or indirectly for giving the testimonial. If the testimony implies that the person making the statement is an expert and that his opinions are experienced or specialized, the qualifications of the person giving the testimonial should be given.

When an NASD member offers free services to his customers, he may not refer to the services as free services unless they are in fact entirely free and without condition or obligation. Consequently, the NASD member should not make a statement to the effect that any report, analysis, or other service will be furnished free unless this is actually the case.

NASD members may not claim or imply that they have research or other facilities beyond those that they actually do possess or have reasonable capacity to provide.

NASD regulations do not permit the use of cautionary statements or *caveats* (often called hedge clauses) if they could mislead the reader or are inconsistent with the contents of the material.

Advertisements in connection with the recruitment of sales personnel must not contain exaggerated or unwarranted claims or statements about opportunities in the investment banking or securities business.

Filing Requirements

A separate file of all advertisements, sales literature, and market letters, including the name or names of the person or persons who prepared them and or approved their use, shall be maintained for a period of three years from the date of each use, for the first two years in a place readily accessible to examination or spot checks.

Each item of advertising and sales literature and each market letter shall be approved by a signature, or initial, prior to use by an officer, partner, or official of the NASD member designated to supervise all such matters.

Prior to 1979, each NASD member was required to file each "advertisement" for review with the executive office of the NASD in Washington, D.C. (within five business days after initial use). But in 1979, the NASD eliminated this five day requirement and implemented spot check procedures. However, investment company literature must still be filed within three days of use with the NASD.

EXECUTION OF RETAIL TRANSACTIONS IN THE OVER-THE-COUNTER MARKET (SECTION 3)

The board of governors of the NASD, under its obligation to "remove impediments to and perfect the mechanism of a free and open market," has made a review of practices that can affect the price of shares paid for by customers in retail transactions. The following is an interpretation of the board's review:

1. In any transaction for a customer, a member shall use reasonable diligence to ascertain the best interdealer market for the subject security and buy or sell in such market so that the resultant price to the customer is as favorable as possible under the prevailing market conditions. Among the factors which will be considered by the business conduct committee in applying standards of reasonable diligence are: (a) the character of the market for the security- e.g. price, volatility, relative liquidity, and pressure on available communications; (b) the size and the type of the transaction; (c) the number of primary markets checked; and (d) the location and accessibility to the customer's broker–dealer of primary markets and quotations sources.

2. In any transaction for a customer, no member shall interject a third party between the member and the best available market except in cases in which the member can demonstate that, to his knowledge at the time of the transaction, the total cost or proceeds was better than the interdealer market for the security. In other words, a member's obligation to his customer is not fulfilled when he channels transactions through another broker-dealer unless that broker-dealer can show that by so doing he has reduced costs to the customer.

PROMPT RECEIPT AND DELIVERY OF SECURITIES (SECTION 4)

No member shall accept a customer's purchase order for any security unless that member has first ascertained that the customer agrees to receive the securities against payment. Further, no member shall execute a *sell* order unless he has reasonable assurance that

1. the customer has in his possession the security
2. the customer is long in his account with the member
3. the customer will deliver the security in good deliverable form within five business days
4. the security is on deposit in good deliverable form with an NASD member, a broker-dealer registered with the SEC, or any other organization subject to state or federal banking regulations.

To satisfy the requirement of reasonable assurance, the broker-dealer or registered representative taking the order should note on the order ticket his conversation with the customer as to the present location of the securities in question.

FORWARDING OF PROXY AND OTHER MATERIALS (SECTION 5)

Members should forward promptly to their customers, for whom they hold stock in a street name, all material periodically sent to them from the issuer. These include annual reports, quarterly reports, and proxy materials. Failure to do so would constitute conduct inconsistent with the high standards of commercial honor of an NASD member. A corporation soliciting proxies shall timely furnish the member with sufficient copies of the soliciting material and satisfactory assurance that the member will be reimbursed by the soliciting corporation. The board of governors of the NASD has suggested a guide to members of a minimum for all sets mailed of $3.00.

FREE RIDING (SECTION 6)

When a member firm of the NASD is participating in an initial public offering of securities, it is required to make a bona fide offering of the securities at the price specified in the prospectus. A member firm functioning as an underwriter or a member of a selling group is not permitted to set aside any of the firm's total allotment for himself or the firm's account for the purpose of speculation. Any NASD member retaining his allotment of an initial public offering for himself, family, his partners, or employees—instead of making a bona fide public offering of these securities—is said to be *free riding*. Fundamentally, free riding is a dealer's holding back portions of *hot issues* for the benefit of himself or favored customers, instead of making bona fide efforts to distribute the new securities to the public. Hot issues are new securities issues that are expected to go to an immediate premium as soon as they are issued and traded over the counter or on an exchange. The hot issues, of course, are the ones usually involved in free-riding situations.

Free riding violates the basic rule that a member in the conduct of his business should observe high standards of commercial honor. In greater detail, it is considered a violation of Article III Section I if a member or his associates

1. continue to hold any of the securities so acquired in any of the member's accounts
2. sell any of the securities to any officer, director, general partner, employee, or agent of a member or of any other broker/dealer, or to a person associated with a member or with any other broker/dealer, or to a member of the immediate family of any such person
3. sell any of the securities to a person who is a finder in respect to a public offering or to any person acting in a fiduciary capacity to the managing underwriter, including among others attorneys, accountants, and financial consultants, or to a member of the immediate family of any such person
4. sell any of the securities to any senior officer of a bank, of an insurance company, or of any other institutional type of account or to any person in the securities department of or whose activities involve or are related to the function of buying or selling securities for these institutions or to the immediate families of such persons
5. sell any securities to any account in which any person specified under paragraphs (1), (2), (3), or (4) hereof has a beneficial interest.

Provided, however, a member may sell part of its securities acquired as described above to: (a) persons enumerated in paragraphs (3) or (4) hereof; (b) members of the immediate family[2] or persons enumerated in paragraph (2) hereof provided that such person enumerated in paragraph (2) does not contribute directly or indirectly to the support of such member of the immediate family; and (c) any account in which any person specified under paragraphs (3) or (4) or subparagraph (b) of this paragraph has a beneficial interest, *if* a member is prepared to demonstrate that the securities were sold to such persons in accordance with their normal investment practice with the member, that the aggregate of the securities so sold is insubstantial and not disproportionate in amount as compared with sales to members of the public, and that the amount sold to any one of such persons is insubstantial in amount.

A member may not

6. sell any of the securities at or above the offering price to any other broker-dealer *unless* he or she receives from the latter in writing assurance that the purchase would be made to fill orders for bona fide customers, other than those enumerated in paragraphs (1) through (5), at the public offering price as an accommodation to them and without compensation for such.
7. sell securities to a bank or branch of foreign bank without assurance that buyers are not persons enumerated in paragraphs (1) through (5) and that the securities would not be sold in a manner inconsistent with paragraph (6).
8. sell securities to foreign broker-dealers unless they agree not to sell to persons enumerated in paragraphs (1) through (5). *The obligations of members to make a bona fide public offering applies equally to registered representatives.*

RECOMMENDATIONS TO CUSTOMERS (SECTION 2)

Section 2 of Article III states that recommendations to customers concerning the purchase, sale, or exchange of securities should be based upon reasonable grounds and that such recommendations are *suitable* for the customer.

A securities transaction should not be proposed to a customer unless the proposed transaction appears to serve the customer's best interest. The interest of the customer should be the controlling factor, not the interest of the sales representative or the interest of the broker-dealer.

[2]The term "immediate family," for purposes of this interpretation, is defined as the parents, mother-in-law or father-in-law, husband or wife, brothers or sisters, children, or any relative to whose support the NASD member, persons associated with the member, or other persons in categories (2) and (3) above contribute directly or indirectly.

The decision concerning the advisability of making any specific recommendation to a customer should be based on the facts concerning the customer's general financial situation and needs. Particular attention should be paid to the amounts and types of other securities the customer owns. Without this information, an intelligent decision concerning changes in a customer's security account is not possible.

Whenever a member recommends to his customer that a certain security should be purchased or sold, all essential information about that security must be supplied to the customer. However, a sale representative does not completely discharge his obligation to his customer simply by disclosing all essential information about the security being recommended. The sales representative, as noted, must consider and disclose all other pertinent factors when making a recommendation to his customer.

NASD district business conduct committees and the board of governors have taken disciplinary action and imposed penalties in many situations in which members' sales efforts have exceeded the reasonable grounds of fair dealing.

Some practices that have resulted in disciplinary action under the Rules of Fair Practice and that clearly violate the member's responsibility for fair dealings are set forth below:

1. *Recommending speculative low-priced securities to customers without knowledge of the customers' other securities holding, their financial situation, and other necessary data.* The fact that such information is not always readily available does not relieve the NASD member from his obligation to obtain adequate information about his customers' financial circumstances before he recommends speculative low-priced securities to the customer.
2. *Excessive activity in a customer's account, often referred to as "churning" or "overtrading."* There are no specific standards to measure excessiveness of activity in customer accounts because this must be related to the objectives and financial situation of the customer involved (see page 431).
3. *Trading in mutual fund shares, particularly on a short-term basis.* It is clear that normally these securities are not proper trading vehicles and such activity on its face may raise the question of rule violation.
4. Numerous instances of fraudulent conduct have been acted upon by the association and have resulted in penalties against members. Some of these activities include
    a. Establishment of fictitious accounts to execute transactions that otherwise would be prohibited. Examples would be the purchase of hot issues or disguised transactions that are against firm policy.
    b. Transactions in discretionary accounts in excess of those

authorized by customers or without actual authority from customers.

c. The execution of transactions that are unauthorized by customers or the sending of confirmations to cause customers to accept transactions not actually agreed upon.

d. Unauthorized use or borrowing of customers' funds or securities.

e. Transactions by registered representatives that are concealed from their employers, or securities transactions outside registered representatives' regular employment, even if disclosed to their employers, if such transactions are in violation of federal or state law.

5. *Recommending the purchase of securities in amounts that are inconsistent with the reasonable expectation that the customer has the financial ability to meet such a commitment.*

Under Section 1, Article III of the Rules of Fair Practice, the following transaction would be improper.

You offer to one of your customers, a country bank, a block of ABC Corporation notes at 100 (quoted 99–100), suggesting that the bank sell an equal amount of XYZ Corporation notes at 102 (XYZ notes being quoted 102–102 1/2). The banker talls you he would like to make the switch, but the XYZ notes cost him 104 and he doesn't want to show a loss on his books. He suggests that if you will pay him 104 for his XYZ notes, he will buy your ABC notes at 102, which will give him the same differential as your suggested exchange.

A great deal depends on the specific circumstances of a particular situation. However, the following examples appear to violate NASD rules as written and interpreted or federal securities laws and administrative rules and regulations:

broker-dealer buys 100 shares of LMN common on Monday@100 1/8, on Friday he sells to customer@103, when the market if 92 bid, offered @ 95."

A salesman urges his customer to purchase shares of XYZ Mutual Fund as a "good buy" solely because a dividend has been declared and will be paid to holders of record shortly.

A broker-dealer tells a new customer, "The price of this stock is going up quickly—you can buy today for $10 a share. Next week when payment is due I will sell the stock you buy today, deduct the purchase price, and send you my check for the difference."

A broker-dealer's salesman offers to pass back one half of the sales charge on XYZ Mutual Funds as an inducement to the customer to buy.

A dealer sells 100 shares XYZ Corp. common over the counter for 85 at 10:01 A.M. His confirmation states, "As Dealer (Principal) and for our own account, we confirm Sale to you of 100 shares XYZ @ 95."

The following example does not appear to violate NASD rules as written or interpreted or federal securities laws and administrative rules and regulations as written and interpreted.

A dealer who has no position in the security sells 100 shares of XYZ Corp. common @ 95 to customer at 11:05 A.M. and confirms. He buys 100 shares XYZ Corp. common for 94 at 11:10 A.M.

The following statements are examples of the type of comments that may properly be made by security sales representatives, assuming there are no contradictory facts:

We feel this security has excellent speculative features.

My firm is the only firm making a market in this security so we know more about the market than anyone else. The market this morning is 26 bid, 27 offered.

While this security has some speculative features, we feel the higher return available due to its present low price makes it attractive for long-term investment.

The following statements are examples of the type of comments that may never be properly used by security sales representatives regardless of the circumstances:

We will refund your purchase price if you wish to sell out when the market value is below the purchase price.

This security will be issued in one week. Give me your order today before allotment is sold out.

Get in on the ground floor. I know the price of this security will double in three months.

"CHURNING" CUSTOMERS' ACCOUNTS

Churning is the improper practice of encouraging investors to make frequent purchases and sales of securities without adequate or proper jurisdiction. Churning or excessive activity in customers' accounts by brokers for the purpose of earning additional commission is subject to disciplinary action under the NASD Rules of Fair Practice.

Excessive activity of customers' accounts is particularly questionable when investment company shares are involved. Investment company shares are designed for long-term investment purposes, not for short-term speculation. As noted, nothing about investment company shares makes them proper instruments for in-and-out trading.

Sometimes, of course, it is in a customer's best interest to sell part or all of the securities in his account and purchase other securities or temporarily hold a cash balance. When there is no clear-cut advantage to the customer by taking such action, however, the securities in the customer account should be retained.

CHARGES FOR SERVICES
PERFORMED (SECTION 3)

Section 3 of Article III of the Rules of Fair Practice states that charges made by members for services performed must be *reasonable* and not unfairly discriminatory between customers.

Services performed by member firms for their customers include such things as

1. collection of monies due for principal, dividends, or interest
2. exchange or transfer of securities
3. appraisals of securities
4. safekeeping or custody of securities

FAIR PRICES AND COMMISSION
(SECTION 4)

Section 4 of Article III of the Rules of Fair Practice states that members buying securities for, or selling securities from, their own accounts shall buy or sell at prices that are fair. Furthermore, members will not charge customers more than a fair commission when acting as their agent. See Chapter 9 for a detailed discussion of this regulation.

THE MARKUP POLICY

For a complete discussion of the 5% markup policy, which is basically a guide not a rule, see Chapter 9 page 174.

PUBLICATION OF PURCHASES
AND SALES (SECTION 5)

Section 5 of Article III of the rules provides that no member of the association shall circulate information based upon fictitious transactions or quotations. According to the rule, only bona fide securities transactions should be reported. Also, quotations of bid-and-asked prices must be clearly marked as *nominal quotations*, unless they are known to be bona fide bids and offers.

Section 5 also states that it is improper to circulate misinformation about securities transactions or quotations by communications of any kind, including by notice, circular, advertisement, newspaper article, or investment service. See Chapter 21 for a detailed discussion.

MANIPULATIVE AND DECEPTIVE
QUOTATIONS (SECTION 18)

NASD members must not be responsible in any way for the publication or circulation of any report of any securities transaction unless such a member knows, or has reason to believe, that such transaction was a bona fide transaction, purchase, or sale. To do so would be inconsistent with Sections 1, 5, and 18 or Article III of the NASD Rules of Fair Practice.

Similarly, it would be inconsistent with the above-cited sections for the member to be responsible in any way for the publication or circulation of any quotation for any security without having reasonable cause to believe that such quotation is a bona fide quotation, is not fictitious, and is not published or circulated for any fraudulent, deceptive, or manipulative purpose.

POLICY WITH RESPECT TO THE
FIRMNESS OF QUOTATIONS
(SECTION 6)

Members make trading decisions and set prices for customers on the basis of telephone or wire quotations as well as from the National Quotation Bureau sheets. No member shall offer to buy from or to sell to any person any security unless such member is prepared to purchase or sell at such price and under such conditions as are stated at the time. Sometimes dealers who place bids in sheets have been unwilling to make firm bids and offers on inquiry as to constitute "backing away." Members, of course, change interdealer quotations constantly, but, when a member makes a firm trading market, that member is expected to at least buy or sell the normal unit of trade unless designated as not firm, less than the unit of trading, or subject. Thus every member has the obligation to identify correctly the nature of his quotation.

DISCLOSURE OF PRICE AND
CONCESSIONS (SECTION 7)

Section 7 of Article III of the rules states that selling syndicate agreements or selling group agreements shall set forth the price at which the securities are to be sold to the public or the formula by which such price can be ascertained and shall state clearly to whom and under what circumstances concessions, if any, may be allowed.

SECURITIES TAKEN IN TRADE
(SECTION 8)

Section 8 of Article III of the rules provides that, whenever an NASD member firm is a member of a selling syndicate or a selling group, it shall purchase securities taken in trade at a *fair* market price. The purchase price (of the securities taken in trade) shall be determined by conditions existing at the time at which the NASD member purchases such securities.

USE OF INFORMATION
OBTAINED IN FIDUCIARY
CAPACITY (SECTION 9)

Section 9 of Article III of the rules forbids use by an NASD member of any confidential information acquired by a member while acting in the capacity of paying agent, transfer agent, or trustee or in any other similar capacity.

Information obtained by association members (while acting in any of the above capacities) as to the ownership of securities will under no circumstances be used for the purpose of soliciting purchases, sales, or exchanges of such securities except at the request and on behalf of the issuer.

INFLUENCING OR REWARDING
EMPLOYEES OF OTHERS
(SECTION 10 AND SECTION 11)

Under Section 10 of Article III of the rules, members are forbidden to give anything of value to the employee, agent, or representative of another person as a reward in relation to the business of the employer of the recipient without the prior knowledge and consent of the employer.

Association members are not permitted to attempt to influence the business decisions of the employees of others, either directly or indirectly.

Section 11 deals with influencing or rewarding the employees of others in connection with published material about securities. Information about a security placed in newspapers, investment services, and the like, often is intended to have an effect on the market price of that security. Under such circumstances, it is highly improper to attempt to influence the decision concerning the desirability of publishing certain data.

Section 11 does not apply to published material that is clearly distinguishable as paid advertising.

DISCLOSURES REQUIRED (SECTIONS 12, 13, AND 14)

Section 12 of Article III of the rules requires a member acting as a broker or dealer to notify customers in writing at or before the completion of each transaction whether he is

1. acting as the customer's broker
2. acting as a dealer for his own account
3. acting as a broker for some other person
4. acting as a broker for the customer and also for some other person

When acting as an agent, a broker-dealer is required to disclose to his customer the source and amount of any commission or other remuneration received. Also, upon request a broker-dealer must disclose the date and time of the transaction and the name of the person from whom the security was purchased or to whom it was sold.

A member, when acting as a dealer (principal), is not required to disclose to his customer the amount of profit he made on the transaction.

Section 13 of Article III of the rules requires the disclosure to the customer of any control existing between an association member and an issuer of a security. The disclosure should be made in writing by the member before entering into any contract with, or for, a customer for the purchase or sale of a security.

Section 14 of Article III of the rules requires a member participating in (or having a financial interest in) a primary or secondary distribution to give a written notification of this fact to customers under the following conditions:

1. when the member acts as an agent for the customer *or* receives a fee from him for financial advice
2. when the customer is purchasing the security in which the member is participating or has a financial interest

The written notification of the member's participation or interest must be made *before* the completion of any such transaction with the customer.

DISCRETIONARY ACCOUNTS (SECTION 15)

A discretionary account is an account in which the customer gives the broker or dealer discretion, either complete or within specified limits, as to the purchase and sale of securities, including selection, timing, and the price to be paid or received.

Section 15 of Article III of the Rules of Fair Practice states that members vested with discretionary power over a customer's account must not make security purchases or sales that are excessive in size or frequency in view of the financial resources and character of the customer's account. No NASD member, registered representative, or principal are permitted to exercise discretionary power in a customer's account at all, unless the customer has given prior written authorization and the account has been accepted in writing by a properly designated representative of the member firm.

Each discretionary order must be approved in writing by an authorized official of the member firm. Furthermore, all discretionary accounts must be reviewed at frequent intervals to detect and prevent transactions that are excessive in size or frequency in view of the financial resources and character of the account.

OFFERINGS "AT THE MARKET" (SECTION 16)

Section 16 of Article III of the rules states that a member having a financial interest in the distribution of an over-the-counter security may not say he offers the security "at the market" when that member or his associates maintain the only active market in the security without disclosing that fact.

SOLICITATION OF PURCHASES ON AN EXCHANGE TO FACILITATE A DISTRIBUTION OF SECURITIES (SECTION 17)

No member participating or financially interested in the primary or secondary distribution of any security of any issuer shall pay in any way to any person compensation for soliciting another to purchase any security of the same issuer on a national securities exchange or for purchasing any security of the same issuer on any exchange for any account other than the member's. Further, no member shall sell or induce an offer to buy such security if, in connection with such distribution, the member has paid or has agreed to pay compensation for soliciting another to purchase any security of the same issuer on any national securities exchange. This provision shall not apply to any salary paid by a member to his or her regular employees whose duties might include solicitation or execution of orders on a national securities exchange.

USE OF FRAUDULENT DEVICES (SECTION 18)

Section 18 of Article III of the rules proibits the use by NASD members of any manipulative, deceptive, or fraudulent device or contrivance to effect or induce the purchase or sale of securities. For more details on fraudulent devices, see pages 428-431.

HYPOTHECATION OF CUSTOMER'S SECURITIES (SECTION 19)

Section 19 of Article III of the rules states that members will not make improper use of a customer's securities or funds.

Members may not borrow a customer's securities without first securing written permission. A member is also required to obtain written authorization from a customer before he may lend a customer's securities to anyone or use the customer's securities in any other way.

Regardless of the nature of the agreement between the member and his customer, the member is never justified in pledging more of a customer's securities than is fair and reasonable in view of the indebtedness of the customer to the member.

Hypothecation is the practice of pledging customers' securities as collateral by brokers and dealers to obtain loans. There are a number of important SEC rules concerning hypothecation practices that have been adopted under the Securities Exchange Act of 1934.

Basically, these rules provide that a broker or dealer may not hypothecate or pledge securities carried for the account of their customers.

1. in such a way as to permit the securities of one customer to be *commingled* with the securities of other customers unless he first obtains the written consent of each such customer
2. under a lien for a loan made to the broker or dealer in such a way as will permit such securities to be *commingled* with the securities of any person other than a bona fide customer

The rules further provide that a broker or dealer may not hypothecate securities carried for the account of his customers in such a way as to permit the liens or claims of pledges thereon to exceed the aggregate indebtedness of all such customers in respect of securities carried for their account.

In addition, this section prohibits guarantees against loss and indicates the extent to which a member may share in the profits or losses in an account with a customer.

INSTALLMENT OR PARTIAL PAYMENT SALES (SECTION 20)

Section 20 of Article III of the rules prohibits members from carrying accounts for, or conducting transactions for, customers if payments are made on an installment basis except under the following conditions

1. When acting as an agent for the customer, the member must actually buy the security for the account of the customer, take delivery in the regular course of business, and maintain possession or control of the security for as long as he remains under obligation to deliver the security to the customer.
2. When acting as a principal, the member must actually own the security at the time of such transaction and must maintain possession or control of the security for as long as he is under obligation to deliver the security to the customer.
3. The member must satisfy any applicable provisions of Regulation T.

Under these types of transactions, the member must not pledge or hypothecate any security involved for any sum larger than the amount the customer owes him.

REQUIRED BOOKS AND RECORDS (SECTION 21)

Section 21 of Article III of the rules indicates that each member must maintain books and records in accordance with all applicable federal and state laws.

Each member will maintain accounts of customers in such form and manner as to show the following information: name, address, and whether the customer is legally of age; the signature of the registered representative introducing the account and the signature of the member or the partner, officer, or manager accepting the account for the member. If the customer is associated or employed by another member, the fact should be noted. In discretionary accounts, the member should also record the age or aprpoximate age and occupation of the customer as well as the signature of each person authorized to exercise discretion in such account.

A *record of complaints* will be kept in each office of supervisory jurisdiction in a separate file of all written complaints of customers and the action, if any, taken by the members. Or the broker-dealer might keep a separate record of complaints and a clear reference to the files containing the correspondence connected with such complaint as maintained in such office.

Records required of NASD member firms are specified by the Securities and Exchange Commission. These records are also required of all members of national securities exchanges and any broker or dealer transacting a business in securities through such members. The books and records described below under 1, 2, 3, and 5 must be preserved for at least six years, the first two in an easily accessible place; items 4, 6, 9, and 10 must be preserved three years with two years' available.

These required books and records are

1. Blotters (or other records of original entry) containing an itemized daily record of
   a.   all purchases and sales of securities
   b.   all receipts and deliveries of securities (including certificate numbers)
   c.   all receipts and disbursements of cash
   d.   all other debits and credits
   e.   the account for which each transaction was effected
   f.   the name and amount of securities
   g.   the unit and aggregate purchase or sale price (if any)
   h.   the trade date
   i.   the name or other designation of the person from whom purchased or received or to whom sold or delivered
2. Ledgers (or other records) reflecting all assets and liabilities, income, and expense and capital accounts
3. Ledger accounts (or other records) itemizing separately
   a.   each cash and margin account of every customer and of such member, broker, or dealer and partners thereof
   b.   all purchases, sales, receipts, and deliveries of securities and commodities for such accounts
   c.   all other debits and credits to such accounts
4. Ledgers (or other records) reflecting
   a.   securities in transfer
   b.   dividends and interest received
   c.   securities borrowed and securities loaned
   d.   monies borrowed and monies loaned (together with a record of the collateral thereof and any substitutions in such collateral)
   e.   securities failed to receive and failed to deliver

5. A securities *record* or *ledger* reflecting separately for each security as of the clearance dates all "long" or "short" positions (including securities in safekeeping) carried by such member, broker, or dealer for his account or for the account of his customers or partners and showing the locations of all securities long and the offsetting position to all securities short and in all cases the name or designation of the account in which each position is carried

6. A memorandum of each brokerage order, and of any other instruction, given or received for the purchase or sale of securities whether executed or unexecuted. Such memorandum will show

   a. the terms and conditions of the order or instructions and of any modification or cancellation thereof
   b. the account for which entered
   c. the time of entry
   d. the price at which executed
   e. to the extent feasible, the time of execution or cancellation

Orders entered pursuant to the exercise of discretionary power by such member, broker or dealer, or any employee thereof, shall be so designated.

The term "instruction" shall be deemed to include instructions between partners and employees of a member, broker, or dealer.

The term "time of entry" shall be deemed to mean the time at which such member, broker, or dealer transmits the order or instruction for execution or, if it is not so transmitted, the time at which it is received.

7. A memorandum of each purchase and sale of securities for the account of such member, broker, or dealer showing the price and, to the extent feasible, the time of execution

8. Copies of confirmation of all purchases and sales of securities and copies of notices of all other debits and credits for securities, cash, and other items for the account of customers and partners of such member, broker, or dealer

9. A record in respect of each cash and margin account with such member, broker, or dealer containing the name and address of the beneficial owner of such account and, in the case of a margin account, the signature of such owner; in case of a joint account or an account of a corporation, such records are required only in respect of the person or persons authorized to transact business for such an account

10. A record of all puts, calls, spreads, straddles, and other options in which such member, broker, or dealer has any direct or indirect interest or which such member, broker, or dealer has granted or guaranteed, containing, at least, an identification of the security and the number of units involved

11. A record of the proof of money balances of all ledger accounts in the form of trial balances; such trial balances shall be prepared currently at least once a month
12. A questionnaire or application for employment executed by an associated person (partner to registered representative) must be approved by an authorized person of the member firm and must contain certain basic information about the applicant.

Members of a national securities exchange are not required to make or keep such records of transaction cleared for such member by another member as are customarily made and kept by the clearing member.

Brokers or dealers registered pursuant to Section 15 of the Securities Exchange Act of 1934, as amended, are not required to make or keep such records reflecting the sale of U.S. savings bonds.

Such records shall not be required with respect to any cash transaction of $100 or less involving only subscription rights or warrants that by their terms expire within 90 days after the issuance thereof.

The following material must be preserved by registered broker-dealers for a period of not less than three years, the first two years in an easily accessible place:

1. all checkbooks, bank statements, canceled checks, and cash reconciliations
2. all bills receivable or payable (or copies thereof), paid or unpaid, relating to the business of such broker or dealer as such
3. originals of all communications received and copies of all communications sent by such broker or dealer (including interoffice memoranda and communications) relating to his business as such
4. all trial balances, financial statements, branch office reconciliations, and internal audit working papers relating to the business of such broker or dealer as such
5. all guarantees of accounts and all powers of attorney and other evidence of the granting of any discretionary authority given in respect of any account and copies of resolutions empowering an agent to act on behalf of a corporation
6. all written agreements (or copies thereof) entered into by such broker or dealer relating to his business as such, including agreements with respect to any account

Every such broker-dealer must preserve for a period of not less than six years after the closing of any customer's account any account cards or records that relate to the terms and conditions with respect to the opening and maintenance of such account.

Every such member broker-dealer must preserve during the life of the enterprise (and of any successor enterprise) all partnership articles or, in the case of a corporation, all articles of incorporation or charter, minute books, and stock certificate books.

After a record or other document has been preserved for two years, a photograph thereof on film may be substituted therefore for the balance of the required time.

Any person required to keep the records required must continue to preserve the records for the period of time specified, even if he discontinues operating as a securities broker or dealer.

A questionnaire or application for employment filled out and signed by each associated person must be retained by the firm in a readily available place. This questionnaire contains many personal details about the applicant.

DISCLOSURE OF FINANCIAL CONDITION (SECTION 22)

Section 22 of Article III of the rules states that a bona fide customer for whom a member holds cash or securities has the right to inspect the current financial statement of the member.

NET PRICES TO PERSONS NOT IN INVESTMENT BANKING OR SECURITIES BUSINESS (SECTION 23)

Section 23 of Article III of the rules requires that transactions between members and persons not actually engaged in the securities business must be confirmed by members at a net dollar or basis price. Under no circumstances may a concession, discount, or allowance be granted.

To repeat, this important section means that *no NASD member is permitted to deal with any nonmember broker or dealer or with anyone not engaged in the investment banking or securities business except at the same prices, for the same commissions or fees, and on the same terms and conditions as are accorded to the general public by the member.*

SELLING CONCESSIONS (SECTION 24)

Section 24 of Article III of the Rules of Fair Practice states that selling concessions, discounts, or other such allowances are permitted only if they are given for services rendered in a distribution. Furthermore, they must not be allowed to anyone other than a broker or dealer actually engaged in the investment banking or securities business.

NASD MEMBER FIRM RELATIONS
WITH NONMEMBER FIRMS
(SECTION 25)

Section 25 of Article III of the rules states that all NASD members must deal with nonmember broker-dealers on the same terms as they would with members of the general public. This means that a member may not sell an over-the-counter security to a nonmember of the association at a discount from the price available to the public. This is true regardless of whether or not the nonmember firm is registered with the SEC.

A member may not pay a commission to any nonmember broker or dealer for executing a brokerage order in the over-the-counter market but may execute over the counter an order for a nonmember and charge a commission.

A member may not join with any nonmember broker or dealer in any syndicate or group contemplating the distribution to the public of any issue.

The above prohibitions do not apply to nonmember broker-dealers in foreign countries.

Section 26 of Article III of the Rules of Fair Practice was discussed in detail on page 404. This section relates to the activity of NASD members in connection with the securities of investment companies.

INVESTMENT TRUST RULE
(SECTION 26)

Section 26 of Article III of the Rules of Fair Practice discusses the activities of members in connection with securities of open-end investment companies. There are a number of restrictions of which the registered representatives should be aware. They were discussed in detail on page 404.

SUPERVISION OF
REGISTERED
REPRESENTATIVES
(SECTION 27)

Section 27 of Article III of the Rules of Fair Practice discusses the supervision of the registered representatives of NASD members. This material was discussed on pages 418–19.

TRANSACTIONS FOR PERSONNEL
OF ANOTHER MEMBER
(SECTION 28)

Section 28 of Article III of the Rules of Fair Practice requires NASD members to diligently avoid executing a transaction for a partner, officer, or employee of another member, which would be adverse to the interest of the other member. The executing member can fulfill this obligation by notifying the employer-member prior to the execution of the order.

The executing member must notify his customer's employer that he proposes to open an account for this customer and, if asked to do so, the executing member must send copies of confirmations of individual transactions or of monthly statements to his customer's firm.

VARIABLE CONTRACTS
OF AN INSURANCE
COMPANY (SECTION 29)

The following rules apply to the activities of members in connection with variable annuity contracts discussed in Chapter 6. The term variable contract means contracts providing for benefits which may vary according to the investment experience of any separate or seggregated account maintained by an insurance company.

1. No member shall sell annuity contracts with an excessive sales charge. For *multiple* payments, a sales charge shall not be considered excessive if it does not exceed 8.5% of total payments.
2. For contracts providing for *single* payments, the sales charge shall not be considered excessive if 8.5% is charged on the first $25,000 of purchase payment, 7.5% on the next $25,000, and 6.5% on amounts over $50,000.
3. Under contracts for which sales charges and other deductions from purchase payments are not stated separately in the prospectus, the total deductions for purchase payments (excluding insurance and taxes) shall be treated as sales charges and not be deemed excessive if they do not exceed the above-mentioned percentages for single payment annuities.
4. Every NASD member shall file with the Variable Contracts Department details of any changes in variable annuities sales charges.
5. A member who is a principal underwriter may not sell variable contracts through another broker-dealer unless said broker-dealer is a member and there is a sales agreement providing that the sales commission be returned to the insurance company for redemption

within seven business days after the acceptance of the contract.

6. No member shall participate in the sale of variable annuity contracts unless the insurance company makes partial or total redemption in accordance with the provisions of the contract.

MARGINS (SECTION 30)

The board of governors of the NASD sets the initial and maintenance margins required by customers of members.

1. initial margin

Any member who effects a new securities transaction in a margin account must obtain initial margin in the amount consistent with Regulation T (see page 200) of the board of governors of the Federal Reserve System. Every margin account shall have a minimum equity deposit in the account of $2,000 except that cash need not be deposited in excess of any security purchased.

Withdrawals of cash or securities in accord with Regulation T may be made provided the withdrawal does not reduce the equity in the account below $2,000.

Securities in the margin accounts are valued by the quotations of the exchanges or the NASDAQ, at current representative markets. Additional margin may be required by the association for securities in concentrated quantities.

Under Section 30 of Article III of the Rules of Fair Practice, the Federal Reserve Board establishes margins for *OTC margin stocks*, discussed in detail on page 202. OTC margin stocks are certain stocks that the board of governors of the Federal Reserve System has determined to have the degree of national interest, in depth and breadth of the market, the availability of information, and the character and permanence of the issuer to warrant their purchase on margin. The OTC margin stocks come under Regulation T of the board of governors of the Federal Reserve System as far as *initial margin* is concerned. It might be said here that margin stocks include such high-grade companies as Anheuser-Busch, American Express, and Pabst Brewing, as well as some commercial banks such as Citizens & Southern National Bank and Seattle First National Bank. However, it is unlawful for any person to represent that inclusion of a security on the list of OTC margin stocks is in any way evidence that the SEC or the Federal Reserve has passed on the merits of these issues.

2. maintenance of minimum margin

The minimum margin to be maintained in the margin account of a customer is as follows.

a.   25% of the market value of all securities "long" in the account
b. $2.50 per share, or 100% of market value, whichever is greater, of each "short" stock in the account with a market value of less than $5.00 a share
c. $5.00 per share, or 30% of the market value, whichever is greater of each stock "short" in the account with a market value of $5.00 a share or greater
d.   Minimum maintenance requirement on options, see page 200
e.   For U.S. governments or agencies with maturities of ten years or less, the minimum maintenance requirements are as follows:

Less than 1 year	0.5% of market value
1 to 2 years	1.0% of market value
2 to 3 years	1.5% of market value
3 to 4 years	2.0% of market value
4 to 5 years	2.5% of market value
5 to 10 years	3.0% of market value

SECURITIES "FAILED TO RECEIVE" AND "FAILED TO DELIVER" (SECTION 31)

No member or person associated with him may buy for his own account or as a broker for a customer a security for which there is a fail to deliver in that security of 60 days or more. For a foreign security the limit is 90 days. But for good reason exceptions might be granted on written request to the district director of the NASD.

FIDELITY BOND (SECTION 32)

Every member shall be required to carry a fidelity bond meeting the requirements of the NASD board. Members who have employees are required to join the Securities Investor Protection Corporation (SIPC), see page 196. Further, members must purchase and maintain fidelity bonds covering officers, partners, and employees against losses of securities on premises or in transit and against losses from forgery and fraudulent trading.

Members must maintain a minimum coverage of the greater of $25,000 or 120% of the firm's capital up to $600,000. Above this amount, the percentage of coverage to capital drops. For example, for a firm with $12 million or more, the minimum coverage would be $5 million.

THE CODE OF PROCEDURE FOR HANDLING TRADE PRACTICE COMPLAINTS

In the past the most frequent causes of complaints against member firms have been violations of NASD rules, in this order:

1. The basic ethical conduct rule (Section 1 of Article III)
2. Rule requiring members to deal fairly with customers when marking up securities (Section 4)
3. Rule prohibiting fradulent, manipulative, or deceptive activities (Section 18)
4. Rule prohibiting the misuse of customers' funds and securities (Section 19)
5. Rule relating to the keeping of books and records (Section 21)
6. Rules requiring certain disclosures on confirmations to customers (Section 12)
7. Rule relating to the supervision of employees (Section 27)
8. Rule relating to the propriety of recommendations for the purchase or sale of securities to or for customers (Section 2)

The amount of formal enforcement work has increased materially in recent years due to the rapid NASD membership growth. The fact that public interest in securities has widened has further contributed to the NASD enforcement task.

In addition to any improper practices of NASD member firms that may be uncovered by the association's examination program, the association learns of infractions of its rules and regulations in other ways. For example, the SEC as a matter of policy refers to the NASD any violations of the association's rules disclosed by *its* inspection program that do not indicate fraudulent activities sufficient to warrant revocation proceedings by the commission. In addition, complaints against member firms or their registered representatives received from various other sources by the NASD help it determine which member firms are violating the association's standards. Charges of violations of one or more of the Rules of Fair Practice of the association form the basis for these complaints.

When some evidence exists that an association rule violation may have taken place, the district business conduct committee may authorize an examination of members' books and records to determine whether a complaint should be filed. The committee also may require members to submit reports in writing on any matter involved in any investigation. Failures or refusal to suppy such requested information is considered sufficient cause for suspending or canceling the membership of such members.

Who May File Complaints

Complaints for violation of the association's rules may be filed with district committees by

1. any member of the public
2. any member of the NASD
3. district committees or the board of governors of the NASD

No member of the board of governors or any district business conduct committee is permitted to participate in the determination of any complaint affecting his personal interest or the interests of any person in whom he is directly or indirectly interested. If such interest is involved, the member must disqualify himself, or must be disqualified by the chairman of the board or committee.

Code of Procedure for Handling Trade Practice Complaints

A code of procedure has been adopted by the NASD to govern the handling of complaints received by the association. The procedure indicated in this code is followed regardless of the source of the complaint.

When a complaint is filed, on a form supplied by the board of governors, it must specify in reasonable detail the nature of the charges being made and the rule or rules allegedly violated by the member firm or its registered representatives.

NASD member firms and registered representatives are entitled to receive notice of the specific charge against them whenever a complaint is filed. Notification of any such charges are sent to the member as soon as possible after they are received by the district business conduct committee.

Written Answer Required

Within ten business days after the accused member firm (respondent) is notified of the charges, the accused must file a written answer to these charges with the appropriate district business conduct committee. If the respondent fails to answer within the prescribed ten business days, a second notice of the charges is sent, which must be answered within five business days. If the respondent fails to answer this second notice of charges, the committee may consider the allegations of the complaint as admitted by the respondent.

Right of Hearing

Any member firm or registered representative charged with a violation of the association's rules is entitled to a hearing before the appropriate district business conduct committee. At this hearing, resondents and complainants are entitled to be heard both by counsel and in person.

District business conduct committees may authorize examination of members' books and records for the purpose of any hearing or any complaint.

Communications to the district business conduct committees with respect to complaints against members are not privileged communications and may be considered in acting on complaints.

When all the evidence has been presented and the record completed, a decision is rendered by the proper district committee. If it is found that the member firm has, in fact, violated the association's rules, one or more penalties may be imposed.

A record must be kept of all hearings. Any determination reached in connection with a complaint must be by written decision and must set forth the specific findings of the committee.

These specific findings must include

1. any improper act or practice that the member has committed
2. the specific rule of the association that the member is deemed to have violated by the act or practice, or omission to act
3. whether or not the acts or practices of the member are deemed to constitute conduct inconsistent with just and equitable principles of trade
4. the penalty imposed

If the committee finds that no violation has occurred, the allegations are dismissed.

Penalties

Penalties that may be imposed on NASD member firms or their registered representatives or principals for violation of the rules are prescribed by the board of governors.

The penalties imposed may be one or more of the following

1. expulsion of the member firm from the NASD or revocation of the registration of any person associated with the member
2. suspension of the firm's membership or suspension, for a definite period, of the registration of a person associated with the member
3. censure of the member or any person associated with a member
4. imposition of a fine not in excess of $1,000 upon any member or person associated with a member
5. barring an NASD member firm or any person associated with that firm from associating with any other NASD member

When a member firm is found to be ineligible for continuation in NASD membership, provision is made in the law for an appeal to the SEC.

The expelled firm may file a petition seeking review by the Securities and Exchange Commission of the decision to expel it by the board of governors. Filing this petition results in an automatic stay of the expulsion order of the board of governors. The expulsion order is stayed until the SEC studies the facts and rules on the member firm petition.

A notice of this stay is sent to the main office and all registered branch offices of NASD members.

REVIEW BY THE BOARD

If the district business conduct committee shall take any action, such action shall be reviewed by the board of the NASD within 45 days. But the person aggrieved may file within 15 days after the date of his or her notice of the action of the district business conduct committee.

In the review before the board of governors the parties again may appear and be heard by counsel and in person. After reviewing all of the admissible evidence, the board renders a written decision.

As a result of its review the board can

1. concur in the decision
2. increase the penalty
3. reduce the penalty
4. modify the decision
5. cancel the action taken
6. remand the case to the appropriate business conduct committee with instructions for further proceedings

The final decision by the board of governors concerning a disciplinary case may be appealed to the Securities and Exchange Commission. The SEC may concur in the decision or modify it, but it may not increase the penalty assessed.

Any action taken by the SEC concerning these cases may be appealed to the federal courts, up to the U.S. Supreme Court.

A penalty imposed by the NASD does not become effective until after the expiration of all periods of appeal or review.

Notification of Expulsion or Suspension

When a member is suspended or expelled from the association or becomes ineligible for further association membership because of expulsion or suspension from a national securities exchange, notice must be sent forthwith to all members of the association.

Uniform Practice Code

A discussion of deliveries, transactions in securities, and units of delivery appeared in Chapter 11.

REVIEW QUESTIONS

1. Describe the background, functions, and objectives of the NASD.
2. Describe the administration, the board of governors, and the committees of the NASD.
3. Who may be a member of the NASD?
4. Who may *not* become a member of the NASD?
5. Discuss the procedure involved in becoming a member of the NASD and in registering with SEC.
6. What are the Rules of Fair Practice of NASD?
7. Discuss the *Code of Procedures* for handling trade practice complaints. Who may complain? What are most frequent complaints? What are the obligations and rights of the accused?
8. What are five possible penalties imposed on an NASD member for violation of rules?
9. What are the filing requirements for all advertisements, sales literature, market letters, and so forth?
10. What is the single most important rule to follow in making a recommendation to a customer?
11. What does churning customers' accounts mean? Illustrate.
12. List four instances of fraudulent conduct by a securities dealer.
13. What disclosures are required by a member acting as an agent?
14. Discuss the requirements a registered representative must keep in mind in handling a discretionary account.
15. What is an OTC margin stock?

TRUE AND FALSE QUESTIONS

		True	False
1.	The NASD is:		
	a. a registered national securities association	___	___
	b. created pursuant to the provisions of a federal law to adopt, administer, and enforce rules of fair practice in connection with over-the-counter securities transactions	___	___
	c. designed to set rules to promote just and equitable principles of trade	___	___
	d. supervised by the SEC.	___	___

2. The NASD: *True*   *False*
   a. requires its members to maintain high standards of commercial honor   _____ _____
   b. is the only association registered under the Maloney Act   _____ _____
   c. requires all over-the-counter dealers to be members of the NASD.   _____ _____

3. The NASD rules stress: *True*   *False*
   a. ethical as well as legal standards   _____ _____
   b. the legality as well as the illegality of a particular transaction   _____ _____
   c. that membership is a prerequisite to profitable participation in almost all underwriting and most of the over-the-counter trading.   _____ _____

4. The functions and objectives of the NASD include: *True*   *False*
   a. promotion of self-discipline among members and investigation of grievances   _____ _____
   b. adoption and administration of rules of fair practice and the promotion of just and equitable principles of trade   _____ _____
   c. provisions of a medium through which members may consult and cooperate with governmental agencies in the solution of problems affecting investors and the public   _____ _____
   d. assurance to all members of the NASD of a fair profit on all transactions.   _____ _____

5. Geographically the NASD is divided into: *True*   *False*
   a. ten divisions   _____ _____
   b. thirteen division   _____ _____
   c. sixteen divisions.   _____ _____

6. The board of governors of the NASD has the power: *True*   *False*
   a. to adopt or change the bylaws or Rules of Fair Practice without approval of the members   _____ _____
   b. to prescribe maximum penalties for violating the provisions of the by-laws or rules and regulations of the corporation, or for neglecting or refusing to comply with orders, directions, and decisions of the board of governors or any duly authorized committee   _____ _____

		True	False
c.	to call meetings of the board but not more than twelve times a year.		

7. NASD membership is open: *True*   *False*
   a. to any responsible person, partnership, or corporation engaged in the commercial banking, underwriting, or brokerage business
   b. to all properly qualified brokers and dealers whose regular course of business consists in actually transacting any aspect of the investment banking or securities business in the United States.

8. No person may become an NASD member: *True*   *False*
   a. who has been expelled from a registered securities exchange
   b. whose broker-dealer registration with the SEC has been revoked or denied
   c. who has been the cause of a suspension, expulsion, or revocation or whose registration as a registered representative has been revoked by the association or a registered national securities exchange
   d. who has been fined for speeding or any serious traffic violation.

9. All broker-dealers operating in interstate commerce are required:
       True   *False*
   a. to file with the national stock exchange in their area
   b. to file with the SEC the form known as BP.

10. Complaints for violation of the association's rules may be filed with the district committees by: *True*   *False*
    a. any member of the public
    b. any member of the NASD
    c. the district committees or the board of governors of the NASD.

11. Advertising practices of the NASD member firms: *True*   *False*
    a. are regulated under Section 1 of Article III of the Rules of Fair Practice
    b. encourage proper use of sales literature and market letters
    c. allow firms to promise appreciation of a stock if the past earnings of the company

	True	*False*
show an improving trend	_____	_____
d. forbid any exaggerated, unwarranted, or		
misleading statements in all advertising,		
sales literature, and market letters.	_____	_____

12. Each NASD member must file each advertisement for review with the executive office of the NASD in Washington, D.C.: *True* *False*

	True	*False*
a. one day after initial use	_____	_____
b. five days after initial use	_____	_____
c. ten days after initial use.	_____	_____

13. Recommendations to customers concerning the purchase of securities should be based on: *True* *False*

	True	*False*
a. the need to support the market in the stock	_____	_____
b. the fact that the broker-dealer can make a large spread on the trade	_____	_____
c. reasonable grounds that such recommendations are suitable for the customer and in his best interest	_____	_____
d. ample information being available concerning the security.	_____	_____

14. Breakpoint sales are: *True* *False*

	True	*False*
a. sales of a common stock just before it is about to decline or break in price	_____	_____
b. sales of stock by a firm from their own account that must be made to keep solvent and avoid going broke	_____	_____
c. the sale of open-end investment company shares by a dealer in dollar amounts just below the point at which the sales charge is reduced on quantity transactions.	_____	_____

15. Churning a customer's account: *True* *False*

	True	*False*
a. is good for the customer as it keeps him interested in the market	_____	_____
b. is an improper practice of encouraging investors to make frequent purchases and sales of securities without adequate jurisdiction	_____	_____
c. is of advantage to the customer only when he is advised to trade investment company shares	_____	_____
d. is a good way to make the commissions of the firm grow.	_____	_____

16. Charges for services performed by a broker, such as the collection of money, the transfer of securities, the appraisal of securities, and the safekeeping of securities: *True* *False*
    a. may be as large as the broker-dealer thinks the customer is willing to pay _____ _____
    b. should not exceed 1/2 of 1% of the value of the securities held _____ _____
    c. must be reasonable and not unfairly discriminatory among customers. _____ _____

17. A member acting as a broker-dealer: *True* *False*
    a. is not required to advise his customer if he is acting as a dealer or broker _____ _____
    b. is required to advise only the NASD if he is acting as broker or dealer _____ _____
    c. is required to notify his customer in writing at or before the completion of the transaction whether he is acting as the customer's broker, as a dealer for his own account, as a broker for some other person, or as a broker for the customer and also for some other person. _____ _____

18. A discretionary account: *True* *False*
    a. is the personal trading account of the registered representative _____ _____
    b. is the account in which the customer in writing gives the broker-dealer discretion (either complete or within limits) to buy and sell securities for him _____ _____
    c. is the trading account of the firm. _____ _____

19. Hypothecation of customers' securities: *True* *False*
    a. is the practice of pledging customers' securities as collateral by brokers and dealers to obtain loans _____ _____
    b. may be done only with the customer's written consent _____ _____
    c. may be done without the customer's consent if the firm guarantees the return to the customer of the securities. _____ _____

Appendix

IMPORTANT PROVISIONS AND RULES OF SECURITIES ACT OF 1933

1. Called Truth in Securities Act—to prevent fraud.
2. Does not approve, recommend, or guarantee accuracy of figures of securities.
3. All offerings over $1,500,000 must file *registration statement* with SEC unless exempt.
4. Statement contains type of business, purpose of issue, balance sheets, income accounts, suits, spread, price, officers and directors, underwriters, large stockholders, and counsel.
5. No sale before effective date, usually 20 days, exceptions.
6. SEC stop order, when untrue statement.
7. SEC deficiency letters, when data inadequate.
8. Prospectus: Summary of important facts of registration statement, must be given on all offerings, or sale of security.
9. Red herring: Preliminary prospectus without price amendment, not an offer to sell.
10. *Penalties:* Criminal—five years and/or $5,000; civil—difference between price paid and sold, must be brought in three years.
11. *Liable:* All signers of registration statement, directors, underwriter, controlling pensions (person with influence on management). A misstatement or withholding a material fact.
12. No secret profits: Profits made by promoter not disclosed to corporation.
13. Administered by Federal Trade Commission until the 1934 Securities Exchange Act.

IMPORTANT PROVISIONS AND RULES OF SECURITIES EXCHANGE ACT OF 1934

1. Registration and regulation of national securities exchanges, listed securities, all brokers and dealers (Section 156).
2. To control trading practices, proxies, dealings by insiders.
3. To prevent manipulation of markets.
4. 1964 amendment: All over-the-counter securities institutions with 500 or more stockholders and $1,000,000 of assets must file registration statements (all other provisions of the act apply to these companies as to proxies, etc.).
5. Insiders: Directors, officers, and owners of 10% or more must report initial holdings and monthly changes thereafter to SEC.
6. Proxies must be approved by SEC—truthful, with complete and clear information.
7. No misleading appearance of active trading, no pool, no fictitious transactions by matching orders or wash sales. No spreading rumors (Section 15C 1).
8. No short selling by officers or directors in own stock.
9. All stock must be marketed long or short. Short sales must be executed at a higher price than the last sale (plus tick) or at a price the same as the last sale that is higher than the proceeding price (zero-plus tick).
10. Formation of NASD under Maloney Act Amendment 1938—Section 15A.
11. Formation of the SEC—five members appointed by president.
12. Exchanges and broker-dealers must keep records and make reports to and be examined by SEC (Section 17a-5).
13. No action of SEC or Federal Reserve to be construed as approving merits of issue (Section 26).
14. Board of governors of the Federal Reserve System to set the margin requirements of brokers' loans to customers buying on margin under Regulation T and for banks making collateral loans under Regulation U.

IMPORTANT PROVISIONS AND RULES OF INVESTMENT COMPANY ACT OF 1940

1. To provide registration, full disclosure, and regulation of investment companies to prevent speculative abuses.
2. Not more than 60% of board may be officers, employees of

investment company, its advisors, bankers, or underwriters (except no load).

3. May not buy security if any one of its employees or its adviser own 1/2% of securities, or combined, 5%.

4. Investment policy must be in prospectus; prospectus updated every 14 months. An investment policy cannot be changed without majority vote.

5. Management contracts—two years with approval by shareholders. Renewed annually; may be canceled by directors or stockholders on 60 days' notice.

6. Redemption required in seven days at net asset value.

7. SEC regulates proxies.

8. Capital adequacy:
   a. Minimum net worth $100,000 to start fund
   b. Open-end—common only, may borrow from bank—300% coverage
   c. Closed-end may issue debt 300% coverage; preferred, 200%

9. Investors must receive complete financial reports at least semiannually (SEC quarterly reports).

10. To register as diversified investment company, must have at least 75% of assets invested in securities with not more than 5% of assets in securities of one issuer or more than 10% of vote. (Thus one segment of the fund must amount to 75% of total assets; must be diversified. The other 25% need not be diversified and may indeed be invested in securities of a *single issuer*. This statement is subject to modification depending on a state that might have a more strict regulation. California sets a maximum of 10% in any one security.)

11. Prospectus given on every offering on sale of shares of investment company (management, securities, advisor, custodian, performance, etc.).

12. Maximum load on contractual plans, 9% of offering price; on contractual plans may charge up to 50% of first year's payments (see 1970 amendment).

13. Margin purchases unlawful unless in accord with rules of SEC.

14. Short sales restricted.

15. Transaction between dealers and customers require public offering price be maintained as defined in prospectus.

16. All sales in compliance with Securities Act of 1933 and Securities Exchange Act of 1934 as well as blue-sky state laws; SEC regulates proxies.

17. Securities cash must be kept by bank or broker, member of national securities exchange.

18. Must not claim any federal agency is involved in management of funds.

IMPORTANT PROVISIONS OF THE INVESTMENT ADVISERS ACT OF 1940

1. Requires all persons engaged in the business of advising others in regard to securities to register with the SEC.
2. Covers all individuals or organizations who for compensation engage in the business of advising others:
   a. All services, investment counsels, and investment advisory service of brokerage firms that charge a fee.
   b. Exempts newspapers and magazines and brokers who give advice incidentally or gratuitously, banks, and government security houses, attorneys, accountants, engineers, and teachers.
3. Unless exempt must *register* with SEC giving
   a. Education and affiliations for ten years
   b. Reports of any changes
   c. Control over accounts
4. Investment counsel confined to registered investment advisors.
5. SEC power limited to investigations and may enjoin.
6. *May not give advice on basis of capital gains.*

IMPORTANT PROVISIONS OF THE TRUST INDENTURE ACT OF 1939

1. Administered by the SEC.
2. All trust indentures on bonds sold must conform to this act.
3. Trustees must have certain qualifications, which are
   a. One or more must be a corporation
   b. Corporation must have capital funds of $150,000
   c. Any conflict of interest, the trustee must remove the conflict or notify security holders of their rights
4. Duties of trustee defined:
   a. Must submit annual reports to bondholders
   b. Must notify bondholders in the event of default within 90 days
   c. In the event of a default, must act as a "prudent man"
   d. Authenticate the bonds
   e. Check performance of covenants: interest, taxes, sinking funds, collateral
   f. Protect the interest of bondholder
   (Note: The trustee in no way guarantees the payment of interest or principal of the bonds, but can be sued for negligence.)
5. Duties of corporation defined:

a.   Furnish trustees with evidence of recording indenture
b.   Furnish trustee with list of bondholders and keep it up to date

IMPORTANT PROVISIONS OF THE INVESTMENT COMPANY AMENDMENTS ACT OF 1970

1.   The management fee must be fair. Damages may be assessed if federal court finds the defendant violated his fiduciary duty.
2.   Sales commission or load shall not exceed 9% of total payments. For front-end load funds the act provides (a) load must be spread so that no more than 20% may be deducted in any one year or an average of 16% a year during a four-year period, or (b) a 50% front-end load certificate may be sold provided plan sponsors agree to refund 85% of gross payments plus the value of the account provided notice given sponsor with 18 months.
3.   Regardless of the plan followed for front-end loads, the investor is entitled to a full refund of the value of his account if he cancels his plan within 45 days of the mailing by the custodian of notice of charges and cancellation rights.
4.   The NASD is to promulgate rules for sales loads.
     a.   These are due August 14, 1972 (see page 463)
     b.   After this date the SEC may alter or supplement the rules.
5.   Performance fee on advisory contracts permitted under certain circumstances. These may be based on the percentage change in net asset value of the investment company as measured against an appropriate security price index.
6.   Insurance company separate account permitted as subject to state supervision.
7.   Fund holding companies regulated. Maximum of 10% of value of assets in securities of other investment companies subject to the following exceptions: (a) A maximum of 3% of stock of any investment company may be owned. (b) The sales load of the holding company may not exceed 1 1/2%. (c) Restrictions on redemptions of 1% in less than 30 days.
8.   The enforcement authority of the SEC over persons affiliated with investment companies was expanded.

IMPORTANT PROVISIONS OF THE SECURITIES REFORM ACT OF 1975

1.   The SEC is empowered to develop and establish a National Market System that would increase the availability of market quotations and the execution of security transactions.

2. The SEC is authorized to appoint and consult a National Market Advisory Board of 15 members from geographic areas.
3. The National Market Advisory Board is charged with the duties of (a) recommending to the SEC action to implement the National Market System and (b) studying the establishment of a National Market Regulatory Board to administer the National Market System.
4. Possible prohibition of the third market.
5. Comprehensive regulation is extended to all municipal broker-dealers and bank-dealers.
   a. All nonregistered municipal dealers must register with the SEC.
   b. The Municipal Securities Rule Making Board was formed. This board formulates rules and regulations for the municipal securities industry subject to SEC oversight.
6. The SEC requires the disclosure of the transactions and holdings of large institutional investors.

NET CAPITAL RULE

The following is a summary of the most important points of the net capital rule:

1. No broker or dealer engaging in the general securities business shall permit his indebtedness to all other persons to exceed 1,500% of his net capital. This is a ratio of 15 to 1. For example, with $100,000 of net capital, a broker-dealer's indebtedness could amount to $1,500,000. Furthermore, no broker-dealer shall permit his net capital to be less than 4% of his aggregate debt.
2. No broker-dealer *commencing business* shall permit his aggregate indebtedness to all other persons to exceed 800% of his net capital for 12 months after commencing business. Also at all times a broker-dealer must maintain net capital of not less than $25,000.
3. A broker-dealer who does not carry customers' accounts shall have net capital of not less than $5,000. These broker-dealers usually trade for their own account, participate in best efforts deals, and clear with another broker.
4. Broker-dealers engaged solely in the sale of redeemable shares of investment companies and certain other share accounts must have at least $2,500 of net capital.
5. There is an alternate net capital rule under which a broker-dealer must at all times maintain net capital of at least $100,000 ($25,000 in the case of a broker-dealer trading solely in municipals).

Aggregate Indebtness

The term *aggregate indebtedness* means the total liability of the broker-dealer in connection with any transaction whatsoever. However, there are certain exclusions from the total indebtedness of the firm. The most important of these are as follows

1. Credit balances of general partners
2. Deferred tax liabilities
3. Liabilities that are effectively subordinated to claims of creditors
4. Fixed liabilities that are adequately secured by assets acquired for use in the ordinary course of business
5. Amounts payable against securities failed to receive which securities are carried long by dealer and which have not been sold
6. Amounts payable against securities loaned which securities are carried long by the broker-dealer and which have not been sold

Net Capital

The term "net capital" is deemed to mean the net worth adjusted by the following

1. Adding unrealized profits (or deducting losses) in the accounts of the broker-dealer.
2. All long and short positions in listed options should be marked to their market value, as well as all long and short positions in other securities and in commodities.
3. Deducting fixed assets and assets that cannot readily be converted into cash; also should be deducted from assets are goodwill, organization expenses, furniture, exchange membership, prepaid rent, insurance, and other expenses.
4. Giving all securities held by the firm as assets a "haircut." This means writing them down to provide for a possible decline in price.
   a. U.S. government and agency securities: 0% for one year, 1–3% for five years or more
   b. Municipals: 1% for one year, 2–5% for five years or more
   c. Municipal bond and liquid asset funds: 5% of the market value of the greater of the long or short position
   d. Non convertible debt securities: 1% for one year or less, up to 7% for five years or more, bonds must be in four highest ratings
   e. Preferred stock: 20% of the market value of the greater of the long or short position
   f. All other securities including common stocks and convertible securities: 30% of market value of the greater of the long or short position
   g. Additional writedowns are made for securities with limited markets as well as for undue concentration in any type of securities that might be hard to move: Deductions of as much

as 100% of the carrying value are made on securities where there is no ready market.

Limitation on Withdrawal of Equity Capital

No equity capital of a broker-dealer in the form of contribution of the partners, retained earnings, or other capital accounts may be withdrawn if, after giving effect to such withdrawals (under satisfactory subordination agreements that are scheduled to occur within six months following such withdrawals), the aggregate indebtedness would exceed 1,000% of its net capital, or its net capital would fail to equal 120% of the minimum dollar amount required thereby or it would be less than 7% of aggregate debit items. Further, satisfactory subordination agreements must not exceed 70% of the debt-to-equity ratio.

SALES CHARGES (LOAD) ON OPEN-END INVESTMENT COMPANIES

No NASD member shall offer shares of any open-end investment company, if the public offering price includes an excessive sales charge. Sales charges shall be deemed excessive if they do not conform to the following provisions:

(1) The maximum sales charge on any transactions shall not exceed 8.5% of the offering price.

(2) (a) Dividend reinvestment shall be made available at net asset value per share to any person who requests such reinvestment at least ten (10) days prior to the record date, subject to the right to limit the availability of the dividend reinvestment to holders of a stated minimum value of not greater than $1,200, and provided that a reasonable service charge may be applied against each reinvestment of dividends.

(b) If dividend reinvestment is not made available on terms at least as favorable as those specified in subsection (2)(a), the maximum sales charge on any transaction shall not exceed 7.25% of the offering price.

(3) (a) Rights of Accumulation (cumulative quantity discounts) shall be made available to any person for a period of not less than ten (10) years from date of first purchase in accordance with one of the alternate quantity discount schedules provided in subsection (4)(a) as in effect the date the right is exercised.

(b) If Rights of Accumulation are not made available on terms at least as favorable as those specified in subsection (3)(a), the maximum sales charge on any transaction shall not exceed:

1. 8% of the offering price if the provisions of subsection (2)(a) are met; or

2.   6.75% of offering price if the provisions of subsection (2)(*a*) are
     not met.

(4) (*a*) Quantity discounts shall be made available on single purchases by any person in accordance with one of the following two alternatives:

1.   A maximum sales charge of 7.75% on purchases on $10,000 or
     more and a maximum sales charge of 6.25% on purchase of
     $25,000 or more.
2.   A maximum sales charge of 7.50% on purchases of $15,000 or
     more and a maximum sales charge of 6.25% on purchases of
     $25,000 or more.

(*b*) If quantity discounts are not made available on terms at least as
favorable as those specified in subsection (4)(*a*), the maximum sales charge
on any transaction shall not exceed:

1.   7.75% of the offering price if the provisions of subsections (2)(*a*)
     and (3)(*a*) are met.
2.   7.25% of offering price if the provisions of subsection (3)(*a*) are
     met but the provisions of subsection (3)(*a*) are not met.
3.   6.50% of offering price if the provisions of subsection (3)(*a*) are
     met but the provisions of subsection (2)(*a*) are not met.
4.   6.25% of offering price if the provisions of subsections (2)(*a*) *and*
     (3)(*a*) are not met.

(5) Every member who is an underwriter of shares of an open-end
investment company or of a single payment investment plan issued by a
unit investment trust shall file with the Investment Companies Department
of the NASD, prior to implementation, the details of any changes or
proposed changes in the sales charges on any such securities, if the changes
would increase the effective sales charges.

TRUE ANSWERS TO MULTIPLE CHOICE QUESTIONS

These questions are designed to test the student's knowledge of the
various chapters but are not intended to resemble the questions on the
NASD qualifying examinations.

1.   Equities: Common and Preferred

1. e	5. c	9. b	13. b and c
2. a and c	6. c	10. b	14. b
3. b and c	7. a	11. a	15. b
4. a	8. b	12. b and c	16. c

2. Bonds

1. b	5. b	9. b	13. g
2. a	6. c	10. b	14. a and b
3. b	7. d	11. b and c	
4. c	8. b	12. b	

3. U.S. Treasury and Agency Securities

1. b	4. d	7. a, b and d
2. b	5. d	8. a, c and d
3. e	6. a and b	9. b, c and d

4. Municipal Securities

1. c	4. a	7. a, b and c
2. c	5. a, b and c	8. c
3. d	6. d	

5. Investment Companies

1. b	7. a	13. a, c and d	19. a, b, c and d
2. b and c	8. b and c	14. a, b and d	20. a and c
3. a and c	9. a	15. b	21. a
4. b and d	10. b and c	16. d	
5. a and b	11. a, b and c	17. b	
6. b	12. a, b and d	18. a and b	

6. Individual Retirement Plans

1. b and c	5. a and b	9. b, c and d
2. a, b, c and d	6. a, b, c and d	10. a, b and c
3. b and d	7. a and c	
4. a, b and c	8. b and d	

7. Direct Participation Programs

1. b and c	5. a and d	9. b and c
2. a, b and c	6. a, b and d	10. a and b
3. c	7. a and b	
4. b and c	8. a	

8. New Issue Market

1. a	4. b	7. a and c
2. b	5. a and b	
3. b	6. b and c	

9. The Over-the-Counter Market

1. f	3. b, c and e	5. c	7. d
2. a and c	4. a, b and c	6. b	8. a, b and c

10. The Organized Securities Exchanges

1. a and c	5. a, c and d	9. b
2. b and c	6. b	10. c
3. e	7. c	11. b
4. b and c	8. c	12. b and c

11. Stock and Bond Transactions
     1. b and c   4. b   7. b
     2. a   5. e   8. b and c
     3. b and c   6. b

12. Options
     1. a   5. b and c   9. a, b and c   13. b
     2. a and c   6. b   10. c   14. b, c, d, e and f
     3. b and d   7. b and c   11. a, c and d   15. b, c, d and e
     4. b and c   8. c and d   12. a and b

13. Clients' Accounts
     1. d   4. a, b and c   7. a, b and c
     2. a   5. a, b and d   8. c and d
     3. a and b   6. a, b and c   9. b

14. Economics
     1. a and b   4. a, b, c and d 7. b and d
     2. a and b   5. a, b and c   8. b and d
     3. c and d   6. a

15. Technical Analysis of the Stock Market
     1. c   4. b   7. b and c
     2. c   5. a, b and c
     3. a and c   6. a

16. Industry Analysis
     1. b   4. a and c
     2. a and b   5. b and c
     3. c and d

17. Security Analysis I—Balance Sheet
     1. c and f   6. a   11. a   16. c
     2. d   7. a   12. b   17. b
     3. b   8. b   13. b
     4. b   9. a, b and c   14. a
     5. c   10. a   15. b and c

18. Security Analysis Income Account
     1. c   6. d   11. c
     2. b   7. b   12. b
     3. a and c   8. b, c and d   13. c
     4. a, b and c   9. c
     5. d   10. a

19. Investment Risks and Portfolio Policies
     1. a   5. c   9. a and d
     2. b, c and d   6. a and c   10. c
     3. a, c and d   7. b and c
     4. c and d   8. a, b and c

20. Taxes

1. c	5. a	9. a and c
2. c	6. d	10. d
3. c	7. b	
4. b and c	8. a, b and c	

21. Federal and State Securities' Regulations

1. a, b and e	5. a and c	9. b
2. d	6. f	10. a
3. a, b and d	7. c	11. c
4. a	8. b, c and d	

22. Investment Company Regulation

1. d	6. d	11. b and c
2. b and c	7. c	12. b and c
3. b	8. a	13. a
4. a and b	9. d	14. b
5. a and b	10. c	

23. National Association of Securities Dealers, Inc.

1. a, b, c and d	6. b	11. a, b and d	16. c
2. a and b	7. b	12. b	17. c
3. a, b and c	8. a, b and c	13. c and d	18. b
4. a, b and c	9. b	14. c	19. a and b
5. b	10. a, b and c	15. b	

Index

Index

N

Q